COLONIAL LAND LEGACIES in the PORTUGUESE-SPEAKING WORLD

Global Indigenous Issues Series

SERIES EDITOR: Roberta Rice, Professor,
Department of Political Science, University of Calgary
ISSN 2561-3057 (PRINT) ISSN 2561-3065 (ONLINE)

The Global Indigenous Issues series explores Indigenous peoples' cultural, political, social, economic and environmental struggles in para-colonial and post-colonial societies. The series includes original research on local, regional, national, and transnational experiences.

No. 1 · **Flowers in the Wall: Truth and Reconciliation in Timor-Leste, Indonesia, and Melanesia**
Edited by David Webster

No. 2 · **Indigenous Territorial Autonomy and Self-Government in the Diverse Americas**
Edited by Miguel González, Ritsuko Funaki, Araceli Burguete Cal y Mayor, José Marimán, and Pablo Ortiz-T

No. 3 · **Protest and Partnership: Case Studies of Indigenous Peoples, Consultation and Engagement, and Resource Development in Canada**
Edited by Jennifer Winter and Brendan Boyd

No. 4 · **Doing Democracy Differently: Indigenous Rights and Representation in Canada and Latin America**
Roberta Rice

No. 5 · **Colonial Land Legacies in the Portuguese-Speaking World**
Edited by Susanna Barnes and Laura S. Meitzner Yoder

 UNIVERSITY OF CALGARY Press

COLONIAL LAND LEGACIES in the PORTUGUESE-SPEAKING WORLD

EDITED BY
Susanna Barnes and
Laura S. Meitzner Yoder

Global Indigenous Issues Series
ISSN 2561-3057 (Print) ISSN 2561-3065 (Online)

© 2025 Susanna Barnes and Laura S. Meitzner Yoder

University of Calgary Press
2500 University Drive NW
Calgary, Alberta
Canada T2N 1N4
press.ucalgary.ca

All rights reserved.

This book is available in an Open Access digital format published under a CC-BY-NCND 4.0 Creative Commons license. The publisher should be contacted for any commercial use which falls outside the terms of that license.

LIBRARY AND ARCHIVES CANADA CATALOGUING IN PUBLICATION

Title: Colonial land legacies in the Portuguese-speaking world / edited by Susanna Barnes and Laura S. Meitzner Yoder.
Names: Barnes, Susanna, editor. | Meitzner Yoder, Laura Suzanne, editor.
Series: Global indigenous issues series ; no. 5.
Description: Series statement: Global Indigenous issues ; no. 5 | Includes bibliographical references and index.
Identifiers: Canadiana (print) 20250193221 | Canadiana (ebook) 20250193272 | ISBN 9781773856339 (softcover) | ISBN 9781773856322 (hardcover) | ISBN 9781773856346 (EPUB) | ISBN 9781773856353 (PDF) | ISBN 9781773856360 (open access PDF)
Subjects: LCSH: Land tenure—Portuguese-speaking countries. | LCSH: Land use—Portuguese-speaking countries. | LCSH: Indigenous peoples—Land tenure—Portuguese-speaking countries. | LCSH: Indigenous peoples—Portuguese-speaking countries—Government relations. | LCSH: Settler colonialism—Portuguese-speaking countries.
Classification: LCC GN449.3 .C65 2025 | DDC 333.2—dc23

The University of Calgary Press acknowledges the support of the Government of Alberta through the Alberta Media Fund for our publications. We acknowledge the financial support of the Government of Canada. We acknowledge the financial support of the Canada Council for the Arts for our publishing program.

This book draws on research supported by the Social Sciences and Humanities Research Council.

The manufacturer's authorized representative in the EU for product safety is Mare Nostrum Group B.V., Mauritskade 21D, 1091 GC Amsterdam, The Netherlands. Email: gpsr@mare-nostrum.co.uk

Copyediting by Ryan Perks
Cover image: Colourbox image 3377747; Image comparing settlement patterns from the late 1950s and the 1980s in Malanje, Angola. Sources: Missão Geografica de Angola, ca. 1965, and IGCA, ca. 1989.
Cover design, page design, and typesetting by Melina Cusano

Contents

Maps, Tables, Figures, and Images	VII
Acknowledgements	IX
Preface Laura S. Meitzner Yoder and Susanna Barnes	XI
Foreword: Colonial Land Legacies: Questions and Insights from Southeast Asia Tania Murray Li	XV
Introduction: Colonial Portuguese Land Legacies in Comparative Perspective Susanna Barnes and Laura S. Meitzner Yoder	1

Part I—Administrative Practices and Governance Strategies   21

1. The Roots of Inequality: *Sesmaria* Land Grants in Colonial Brazil   23
   Carmen Alveal

2. From Squatters to Smallholders? Configurations of African Land Access in Central and Southern Colonial Mozambique, 1910s–1940s   41
   Bárbara Direito

3. "Everyday" Displacements in Colonial Angola: Changing Political Geographies of Infrastructure, Gender, and Quotidian Village Concentration   63
   Aharon deGrassi

4. *Baldios*, Communal Land, and the Portuguese Colonial Legacy in Timor-Leste   87
   Bernardo Almeida

Part II—Indigenous-Settler Entanglements   105

5   Dutch Colonialism and Portuguese Land Legacies in Flores   107
     Hans Hägerdal

6   Land Access in a Slave Society: The Case of Maranhão Province, Northern Brazil   127
     Matthias Röhrig Assunção

7   The Impact of Portuguese Development Thought and Practice on Land Relations in the Late Portuguese Colonial Period   151
     Susanna Barnes

8   The Remaking of Territories and Political Institutions: Community Land Delimitation in Northern Mozambique   171
     Elisio Jossias

Part III—Economic Imperatives and Global Articulations   193

9   The Trajectory of the Plantation System in Mozambique: The Case of Madal in Micaúne   195
     José Laimone Adalima

10   Land Governance as a Source of Legal Opportunities in Struggles Around Large-Scale Land Acquisitions in Mozambique   219
     Laura Gerken

11   Colonial Concessions: The Antinomies of Land Policy in Portuguese Timor   241
     Douglas Kammen and Laura S. Meitzner Yoder

Afterword: The Amphibious Colonial Empire   261
     Ricardo Roque

About the Contributors   281
Index   285

Maps, Tables, Figures, and Images

Maps

2.1.	Map of Mozambique, 1929	43
2.2.	Map of native reserves, hunting reserves, and national colonization reserves, 1944	49
3.6.	Map of village geo-location contemporary data and main roads in Angola	80
5.1.	Flores in the late colonial period.	123
6.1.	Eastern Maranhão—parishes and the importance of small ownership	132
6.2.	Population of Maranhão, by micro-region (1838)	137
7.1.	Map of Maliana	158
8.1.	Administrative post of Cóbuè	173
8.2.	Community delimited lands, representing the territories of *régulos*	177
9.1.	Map of the *prazos* in the Zambezi Delta	198
9.2.	Map of Prazo Mahindo	202
10.1.	ProSavana research area in northern and central Mozambique	231

Tables

3.1.	Differential pay rates for traditional authorities based on village size were included in 1923 legislation	73
6.1.	Number of declarations, properties, and landowners in nine parishes of eastern Maranhão, 1854–7	133
6.2.	Gender of landowners and forms of property in nine Maranhão parishes, 1854–7	133
6.3.	Property size in nine parishes of Maranhão, 1854–7	136
6.4.	Property size in nine parishes of Maranhão, 1854–7 (with extrapolated depth)	136
10.1.	Comparison of Wanbao and ProSavana	226
11.1.	Recipients of major land concessions in 1900	253

Figures

3.1.	Quotidian village concentration and relocation in western Malanje	65
3.2.	Growth in reported kilometres of roads in Angola, 1911–33	71
3.3.	Erasure of villages on Malanje colonial land registry map, ca. 1960s	76
3.4.	Erasure of colonial villages, Figueira plantation, ca. 1970	77
3.5.	Former house locations (red dots for 1950s), overlaid on 1980s map (villages as black rectangles)	78
5.1.	Main mytho-historical elements of the emergence of Larantuka and Sikka	122
6.1.	Properties according to size in Itapecuru parishes, 1854–7	135
6.2.	Properties according to size in Parnaiba parishes, 1854–7	135

Images

5.1	The last raja of Sikka, Thomas da Silva, with his consort Dua Eba Sadipung	121

Acknowledgements

This book is the product of a collective effort, and we are deeply grateful to the many individuals who contributed to its development. It began with a symposium, held online from 24 to 27 May 2021, and supported by the Social Sciences and Humanities Research Council of Canada, which brought together scholars studying colonial land legacies in the Portuguese-speaking world. We are deeply grateful to all who participated and shared their insights.

We would like to extend our sincere thanks to Tania Murray Li, whose keynote address at the symposium provided a crucial intellectual foundation for this volume. Her willingness to contribute a foreword to this book has further enriched its scope and depth. Ricardo Roque's provocative closing remarks at the symposium challenged us to think more critically about the themes of land, colonialism, and continuity, and we are grateful for his afterword, which provides an incisive reflection on the contributions in this volume.

The discussions at the symposium were sharpened by the engaged participation of our readers, including Susana Matos Viegas (Instituto de Ciências Sociais–University of Lisbon), Matthew Mitchell (University of Saskatchewan), and David Webster (Bishop's University). Their thoughtful feedback helped shape the papers that have now become chapters in this book. We also wish to acknowledge the invaluable support of Jessica Jack and Michelle Gowan, graduate students at the University of Saskatchewan, who helped organize and run the symposium. Additionally, Michelle Gowan's work in recording the *Lusophone Land Legacies* podcasts played an important role in extending our conversations beyond the symposium itself.

Our sincere thanks go to Rui Pinto for his map-making skills, which have greatly enhanced the visual clarity of this volume. We are also grateful to Max Pospisil, graduate student at the University of Saskatchewan, whose careful attention to detail in converting notes and footnotes of draft chapters ensured the clarity and coherence of this volume. Brian Scrivener and the editorial team at University of Calgary Press embraced this project with enthusiasm, and we deeply appreciate their commitment to its publication. We also extend our gratitude to our external reviewers, for their insightful comments, which helped refine this edited volume. Our thanks also to Ryan Perks, who provided meticulous copyediting, helping to refine and polish the final text, and to Laura Atkinson for her invaluable administrative support.

A book like this is, above all, shaped by its contributors, and we extend our deepest gratitude to all the authors who participated in the symposium and contributed their work to this edited volume. Their scholarship, dedication, and collegiality have made this book possible.

Finally, we would like to express our appreciation to friends and colleagues who generously read draft papers and provided nuanced feedback, and to our families for their patience and support.

This book is a testament to the power of collaboration, and we are fortunate to have had such a dedicated and thoughtful group of scholars, colleagues, and friends contribute to its realization.

Preface

Laura S. Meitzner Yoder and Susanna Barnes

This project emerged from persistent questions and quandaries facing a group of scholar-practitioners conducting ethnographic, historical, and legal research on emerging land issues in newly independent Timor-Leste.[1] In our fieldwork, we observed first-hand the profound ongoing impacts of Portuguese (until 1975) and Indonesian (1975–99) land policies and practices on the fledgling nation's legal systems, public debates over Indigenous practices and customary land, civil service functionality, tenure security, and land access for vulnerable or marginalized groups.[2] Ongoing influence also came in the form of international land policy experts who carried, promoted, and implemented particular models of land administration worldwide. As a result, the new nation inherited a hodgepodge of legal and political phenomena, ranging from imported laws to multiple successive cadastral programs conducted with support of USAID, AusAID, and a Portuguese company.[3] To make sense of what we saw in Timor-Leste, we felt a critical practical need, paralleling a notable scholarly gap, to better understand colonial land policy processes in the dimensions necessary to enable and promote just land relations after modern-day governance transitions.[4]

The effects of land policy mobility across both time and space were clearly evident in Timor-Leste, but we wanted to track the actual mechanisms of this influence. We realized that to illuminate this fundamental aspect, we needed to examine the trajectories and outcomes of land policy formation across other former Portuguese colonies—with their diverse times and circumstances of independence, governance priorities, economic models, and cultural contexts. Formerly, as now, we can trace the mobility of ideas and practices regarding land through regions and systems, so we sought to hold the Portuguese contexts in tandem with perspectives from other post-colonial contexts and their own layered land histories.[5] In this, Tania Murray Li's extensive work on Indonesia and across Southeast Asia was particularly influential for us.

These questions were the impetus for the interdisciplinary international symposium Lusophone Land Legacies in Comparative Perspective—hosted by the University of Saskatchewan and held online in May 2021—that lay the groundwork for this volume. The symposium gathered scholars from, and of, Canada, Brazil, Portugal, Mozambique, Angola, Singapore, Timor-Leste, the Netherlands, Sweden, and the United States of America, to consider how colonial-era land practices continue to shape land classification, policies, administration, and legislation in independent nations. Contributors to this volume include participants in the international symposium, in which we intentionally sought to bridge various boundaries: temporal and geographic in our topics, but also linguistic and disciplinary in our peer-review interactions. The symposium paired established and early-career scholars from different regions as co-readers and mutual commentators on the submitted papers, allowing for the diverse contexts and disciplinary experiences of each participant to inform the questions and discussion. We sought to include a diversity of methodological and analytical approaches of the many disciplines that examine land policy formation and implementation, from law, anthropology, history, geography, and environmental studies. This is also evident in chapter authors' diverse backgrounds—including nine scholars for whom English is not their primary language. Reviewers noted that this collaboration has produced one of the few publications in English with this range of cases on Lusophone colonialism, making this scholarly work accessible to Anglophone readers.

It is our hope that readers of this volume take inspiration from our orienting questions and glean new insights for and from their own contexts through the cases presented here. We learned a great deal from close engagement with each other's cases. Most symposium participants specialized closely in one or two of the Lusophone regions, and we found in this rare interaction across continents many productive discoveries of both familiarity and difference in the administrative processes, economic practices, and socio-political creativity of both local populations and implementing bureaucrats with regard to land policy. Lively debates challenged and enriched our own understandings of concepts and practices we thought we understood, such as *baldios*, registration, and land grants or concessions. And for readers who are new to the world of Lusophone imperial formations, we welcome you to compare and contrast the cases presented in the following chapters with the colonial and modern situations you know best. May this book give you newly expanded perspectives on the importance of land policy formation in today's world.

NOTES TO PREFACE

The editors would like to thank Jessica Jack and Michelle Gowan for their assistance before, during, and after the international symposium from which chapters for this volume are drawn. We also thank Jessica Jack, Alex Smith, and especially Max Pospisil for their assistance in preparing the manuscript for publication. The editors would also like to thank and acknowledge additional colleagues with strong interest in this topic who represented their work on Macau, Goa, São Tomé e Príncipe, as well as additional scholars of Brazil and Timor-Leste whose life circumstances did not allow them to fully participate in the symposium or the production of this volume.

1. Hans Hägerdal, *Lords of the Land, Lords of the Sea: Conflict and Adaptation in Early Colonial Timor, 1600–1800* (Brill, 2012); Bernardo Almeida, *Land Tenure Legislation in Timor-Leste* (Asia Foundation, April 2016), https://landportal.org/library/resources/land-tenure-legislation-timor-lestebernardo-almeida2016/land-tenure-legislation; Bernardo Almeida, "Expropriation or Plunder? Property Rights and Infrastructure Development in Oecusse," in *The Promise of Prosperity: Visions of the Future in Timor-Leste*, ed. Judith Bovensiepen (ANU Press, 2018), 99–118; Susana Barnes, "Origins, Precedence and Social Order in the Domain of Ina Ama Beli Darlari," in *Land and Life in Timor-Leste: Ethnographic Essays*, ed. Andrew McWilliam and Elizabeth Traube (ANU E-Press, 2011), 23–46; Meabh Cryan, "'Empty Land'? The Politics of Land in Timor-Leste," in *A New Era? Timor-Lest after the UN*, ed. Sue Ingram, Lia Kent, and Andrew McWilliam (ANU Press, 2015), 141–54; Daniel Fitzpatrick, Andrew McWilliam, and Susana Barnes, *Property and Social Resilience in Times of Conflict: Land, Custom and Law in East Timor* (Ashgate, 2012); Laura S. Meitzner Yoder, "Political Ecologies of Wood and Wax: Sandalwood and Beeswax as Symbols and Shapers of Customary Authority in the Oecusse Enclave, Timor," *Journal of Political Ecology* 18, no. 1 (2011): 11–24.

2. Centre of Studies for Peace and Development, *Women's Access to Land and Property Rights in the Plural Justice System of Timor-Leste* (Centre of Studies for Peace and Development, 2014); Simon P. J. Batterbury et al., "Land Access and Livelihoods in Post-Conflict Timor-Leste: No Magic Bullets," *International Journal of the Commons* 9, no. 2 (2015): 1–29; Meabh Cryan, *Whose Land Law? Analysis of the Timor-Leste Transitional Land Law* (Asia Foundation, 2016).

3. Bernardo Almeida, "The Main Characteristics of the Timorese Legal System—a Practical Guide," *Verfassung und Recht in Übersee* 50, no. 2 (2017): 175–87; Rede ba Rai, *Land Registration and Land Justice in Timor-Leste: Culture, Power and Justice* (Haburas Foundation, 2013).

4. Daniel Fitzpatrick and Susana Barnes, "Rules of Possession Revisited: Property and the Problem of Social Order," *Law & Social Inquiry* 39, no. 1 (2014): 127–51; Sandra F. Joireman and Laura S. Meitzner Yoder, "A Long Time Gone: Post-Conflict Rural Property Restitution under Customary Law," *Development and Change* 47, no. 3 (2016): 563–85; R. Gerard Ward and Elizabeth Kingdon, "Land Tenure in the Pacific Islands," in *Land, Custom and Practice in the South Pacific*, ed. R. Gerard Ward and Elizabeth Kingdon (Cambridge University Press, 1995), 36–64.

5. James Holston, "The Misrule of Law: Land and Usurpation in Brazil," *Comparative Studies in Society and History* 33, no. 4 (1991): 695–725; Malyn Newitt, "Formal and Informal Empire in the History of Portuguese Expansion," *Portuguese Studies* 17, no. 1 (2001): 1–21; Bridget O'Laughlin, "Class and the Customary: The Ambiguous Legacy of the *Indigenato* in Mozambique," *African Affairs* 99, no. 394 (2000): 5–42; Philip J. Havik and Malyn Newitt, eds., *Creole Societies in the Portuguese Colonial Empire* (Cambridge Scholars Publishing, 2015); Harry G. West and Gregory W. Myers, "A Piece of Land in a Land of Peace? State Farm Divestiture in Mozambique," *Journal of Modern African Studies* 34, no. 1 (1996): 27–51; C. Young, *The African Colonial State in Comparative Perspective* (Yale University Press, 1994); José Vicente Serrão, Bárbara Direito, Susana Münch Miranda, and Eugénia Rodrigues, eds., *Property Rights, Land and Territory in the European Overseas Empires* (CEHC-IUL, 2014).

Foreword

Colonial Land Legacies: Questions and Insights from Southeast Asia

Tania Murray Li

The following text was presented as the opening keynote to the symposium Lusophone Land Legacies in Comparative Perspective, *hosted online in May 2021 by the University of Saskatchewan, which formed the basis for this volume. It serves as an orienting reflection on the underlying importance and problems of enduring colonial impacts on land relations. With a focus on another colonial context, it demonstrates the commonalities still faced by post-colonial nations worldwide.*

The aim of this volume is to track how far classifications, rationalizations, infrastructures, and laws that were forged to govern land relations in the Portuguese colonial period persist today, albeit perhaps refashioned or repurposed. My contribution, first presented as the symposium keynote, takes up this question from the perspective of Southeast Asia, especially Indonesia.

Land relations are a key domain for the exercise of what Foucault called a "governmental rationality" that seeks to arrange relations between "men and things" to achieve diverse ends.[1] Colonial authorities had to balance multiple objectives, and contemporary authorities must do the same. In relation to any regime, past or present, it is useful to consider three sets of questions.

First, to *what ends* do authorities attempt to govern land relations? Do the ends include increasing production to raise revenues or taxes? Order, pacification, and the administration of populations? The demonstration of territorial control vis-à-vis internal opponents or external competitors? The generation of profits for shareholders? Native improvement? The attraction of settlers or the reward of allies?

Second, through *what means* is land government exercised? Is there direct control over territory or indirect rule through local elites or native chiefs? Are natives addressed as individuals or as members of communities? Are they fixed to the land or detached to form a "free" proletariat? Are they targets of productive investment or treated as irritants to be swept aside?

Third, *what is the rationale* under which land government proceeds? What narrative or authoritative body of knowledge links problems identified to solutions proposed? How is a given rationale defended from counternarratives and critiques? Under what conditions does it morph and realign?

These are questions to be examined through empirical research in different contexts, and they form the subject matter of many of the chapters in this collection. Here I want to stand back from the details of the terrain of inquiry to ask several key questions: Why are colonial land legacies important? What is potentially problematic about their persistence? Why should we be concerned about what Ann Stoler calls "imperial debris" or the "rot that remains" from colonial rule?[2] Why, precisely, is it rotten?

The argument I will make here, specifically in relation to Indonesia, is that racialism—the construction of racial or race-like divides and their arrangement in a hierarchy—was intrinsic to colonial land relations. It provided the rationale for the occupation of territory, rule over subject populations, and the extraction of profit for the metropole. The rot that remains is the persistence of racialism in the contemporary period in a format that is only lightly revised. It is embedded in land law, in development policy, and in everyday ways of thinking and acting. Although it passes almost without notice, it is the enabling condition for the widespread misery, dispossession, and disenfranchisement that persist in Indonesia today.

Imperial Debris

What is the imperial debris of which Ann Stoler speaks? In the sphere of land relations, the nature of this debris has been well examined by Brenna Bhandar in her book *The Colonial Lives of Property*.[3] Her argument, in brief, is that racial (or race-like) divisions are constitutive of colonial and contemporary land regimes in which the association between a kind of person, the kind of land use they practice, and the quality of their property rights is circular. In contemporary Indonesia the chain of reasoning goes like this: The national land agency grants concessions to plantation corporations on the grounds that they can utilize the land efficiently; implicitly, customary landholders cannot use land efficiently; hence their customary land rights do not qualify as full property rights; their low productivity and incomplete property rights confirm that they are people of low value; as people of low value they cannot be expected to use land efficiently, and they can legitimately be displaced by corporations.[4]

Contemporary land government sustains the reasoning behind the 1870 Land Law of the Dutch East Indies. The 1870 Land Law claimed that all land was the domain of the Dutch Crown, except for tiny areas that were recognized as individual private property. It gave nominal recognition to customary land rights, which it declared to be communal and inalienable. But it did not map or gazette communal land and offered customary landholders individually or collectively very little protection. The main purpose of the 1870 Land Law was to free up land to allocate for plantation, timber, and mining concessions. This law is *still basically in place*. Its racialized premise was retained on independence in the clause of Indonesia's 1945 constitution that gives the state the right to control and allocate land in the national interest. It is the unspoken premise of the 1960 Land Law, which has not been replaced. The 1960 Land Law was a compromise among nationalist, communist, and Islamist forces and the army, brokered by Indonesia's first president, Sukarno. The 1960 law promised a land-to-the-tiller-style land reform that was not implemented; it included clauses about the rights of customary communities but no process to map or protect them; and it continued the colonial practice of issuing corporate land concessions for mining and plantations.

The colonial land legacy has led to a situation in which around 40 per cent of Indonesia's farmland is covered by corporate land concessions. Corporations—the kinds of "person" trusted to use the land efficiently—have secure land rights. Meanwhile the customary land rights of most rural people in Indonesia are weak and inferior rights because the people who use this land, and the ways in which they use it, are deemed to be inferior. There have been challenges: Some colonial officials and scholars challenged the 1870 Land Law at the time, appalled by the losses that corporate land concessions imposed on native farmers. They demanded that land be set aside for the native population; but they did not challenge the racial contours of land law or its dispossessory effects. Similarly, contemporary advocates seeking to strengthen the legal rights of Indonesia's customary communities contest their dispossession from the land and forests on which they depend, but the entire logic that constitutes these people, their land uses, and their land rights as inferior is not subject to a thoroughgoing post-colonial critique. This is imperial debris—a racial logic that is so deeply entrenched in the law and in the national psyche that it is barely noted.

Delving into the colonial history, how did the three elements of Bhandar's satanic circle combine? How did a (deficient) kind of person become linked to a (deficient) kind of production, worthy of a weak and inferior kind of right to land? How did this form of governing, reasoning, and acting come to be? And how does it shape contemporary configurations?

Dividing Practices[5]

A classic technique for governing populations in the late colonial period (ca. 1870–1940) was to divide them into distinct types and govern them according to these types. In much of colonial Africa, where colonial rule was indirect, a distinction was made between natives who were fit to become citizens (urban, educated) and rural people who should be treated as subjects of customary chiefs who administered communal territories on their behalf, and who governed both people and land under so-called customary laws.

In much of Southeast Asia, the axis of difference was spatially organized in terms of elevation. Peasants, especially rice producers in the fertile valleys and lowlands, were deemed fit to hold land individually. People living in the uplands (called "hill tribes" in Thailand, non-Christian tribes in the Philippines, and Montagnards in the French colonies) were to be firmly attached to communal land and governed as collectivities. This particular imperial debris resonates strongly and perhaps positively in the Philippines, where the Spanish-era category of "non-Christian tribes" morphed into the contemporary, globally circulating category of "Indigenous peoples," a group that were legally enfranchised in 1997 with IPRA, the Indigenous Peoples' Rights Act. In Thailand, hill tribes are still treated as "others" with an emphasis on their ethnocultural identity as "non-Thai"; many still do not have Thai citizenship and are vulnerable to eviction. In the former French colonies (Vietnam, Laos, and Cambodia), highlanders or Montagnards are still treated as distinct and deficient, and subject to policies such as forced resettlement and loss of access to their forestland.

The colonial history in Indonesia is rather different. During a brief British interregnum from 1812 to 1816, Sir Thomas Stamford Raffles inadvertently laid the groundwork for a legal trajectory that was diametrically opposed to the one he advocated. He brought with him a concept popular among British colonial officials in India who regarded Asian villages as timeless little republics. On this basis he determined that villages would be a convenient vehicle for tax collection until such time as individual land titles could be granted. When the Dutch resumed control, they decided that villages could be used as vehicles for tax collection (and forced production) permanently. This approach was in keeping with a racialized axiom that asserted the natural collectivism of Asian people, assuming them to be the opposite of Europeans in every way. To maintain this divide the colonial authority had to disallow contradictory evidence. In 1833, for example, a regent toured one region of Java to collect and subsequently burn the lontar leaves on which natives had recorded their individual land titles; thus was the racial difference of the purportedly communalist native created and confirmed.

In contrast to other colonial powers in Southeast Asia, the Dutch did not divide the native population into peasants versus tribes on the basis of elevation. All people who were not Dutch (or mixed Indonesian Dutch) were equally native from the perspective of law, including land law. Hence neither lowland rice farmers nor highlanders were issued with individual land titles. To this day only about 20 per cent of agricultural land parcels held by Indonesian farmers have been individually titled. Nor have communal titles been issued, with the consequence that almost all rural Indonesians are chronically vulnerable to state-authorized dispossession. People who can be robbed of their land are not enfranchised citizens; they are still in a colonial situation. The colour of the ruling group may have changed, but the scorn of today's political and economic elites for rural people and the capacity of the elite to grab their land with impunity remain intact.

Evaluating Productivity[6]

Raffles was impressed by the diligence and productivity of Javanese rice farmers. He expected them to prosper and develop in ways that were similar to yeoman farmers in Britain—that is, through their hard work and their capacity to "truck, barter, and trade." In contrast, Dutch officials applied a racial lens that held natives to be lazy and inept; hence they had to be compelled to produce a surplus beyond their subsistence needs. Based on this evaluation, the Dutch installed a system of forced cultivation of the export crops of sugar and coffee (1830–70) to raise revenue to run the colonial state and to furnish profits for Dutch corporations. After this system ran its course, the 1870 Land Law enabled the regime to issue large land concessions to foreign investors, and the plantation era began. Both these systems—coerced production among smallholders, and the displacement of smallholders by corporate plantations—hinge on the same racialized evaluation memorably caricatured by historian Syed Husain Alatas as the "myth of the lazy native," which asserts that "natives" are incapable of developing their land or producing a surplus on their own.[7]

The same assessment—that natives are inefficient and/or unwilling producers of global market crops—still justifies the expansion of corporate plantations in Indonesia today. It is especially virulent outside areas of intensive rice production where shifting cultivation and extensive agro-forest systems still prevail. These systems are taken to confirm that "lazy natives" run their farms in a disorderly manner. Purveyors of this racialized stereotype overlook the fact that extensive farming systems are very efficient in relation to labour, which is often the scarce resource. Even in relation to the production of global market crops, there is no evidence to support the claim of native deficiency. Farmers in Java and Sumatra eagerly adopted the production of coffee early in the eighteenth century as soon as seedlings became available and a global market opened up. They lost interest when the Dutch imposed a monopoly on the coffee trade and set prices so low that farmers tore up their coffee groves in disgust. From then on, coffee production had to be coerced. It was a similar story with other crops: Managers of large tea and tobacco plantations demanded that native production be suppressed as they were afraid of being outcompeted; and in the case of rubber smallholders, they did actually outcompete plantations and drove many into bankruptcy.

The promotion of corporate agriculture at the expense of smallholders is a story that is being repeated today with the current boom crop, oil palm, as industry lobbies insist that the proper way to grow this crop is on huge, professionally managed monocropped plantations. To make this argument, they characterize smallholders as inefficient, overlooking the high levels of productivity that smallholders achieve when they have access to high-quality seedlings and the necessary infrastructure. The ongoing displacement of Indonesian villagers and the issue of massive land concessions to oil palm corporations is imperial debris. Recognizing that Indonesian villagers are competent producers would remove the alibi for corporate expansion; meanwhile, plantation corporations are under no obligation to prove that they are efficient producers—the myth seems to suffice. State subsidies accorded to plantation corporations are enormous: virtually free land, low-cost labour, favourable access to credit, and bailouts when bankruptcy looms. The investment in ordinary farms and farmers is miniscule in comparison. Indonesia's land relations are still organized for extraction at the people's expense.

Toward a Comparative Analysis[8]

Looking around the Southeast Asian region for comparative cases, diverse trajectories and outcomes stand out. There are echoes of racialized practices and rationalities through Southeast Asia, but the picture is not uniform. Indeed, the region provides a panorama in which differences among British, Dutch, French, and Portuguese colonial powers, their land policies and their legacies, can be examined. Throughout, the most pervasive colonial rot that remains is the dismissal of highlanders, especially shifting cultivators, as forest destroyers and primitives. In relation to lowland populations, the pattern is more varied.

There were plantations in French Indochina in the colonial period, but the period of revolution and independence signalled a more complete rupture with colonial land law than occurred in Indonesia. In Vietnam, the rights and entitlements of lowland citizens are quite robust. There are few new plantation concessions, the productive capacity of farmers is trusted and supported, and farmers have reasonably secure land tenure (though ownership remains with the state). In Thailand, which was not subject to direct colonial rule, there are very few plantations and oil palm is grown by smallholders who receive good state support. To a significant extent, Thai peasants in lowland areas are enfranchised citizens who are capable of making their demands stick.[9] Land titling is well advanced. In Malaysia, colonial-era plantations have morphed and expanded, together with lazy-native rationales.[10] Yet the popular push-back is not intense because Malaysia has undergone an "agrarian transition": A great many citizens, including young people, have found their way to the cities and to urban jobs, and consequently are less interested in becoming farmers or holding on to customary land. So there is imperial debris, but it is less damaging than elsewhere in the region where agriculture-based livelihoods remain crucial to huge segments of the population. Indonesian migrant workers do most of the work on Malaysia's plantations.

In Indonesia since the colonial period corporations have been granted land concessions, while customary landholders are legally vulnerable and, in practice, the people and their claims are regularly swept out of the way. The rot that remains is stubborn indeed. Similar practices are observed in Cambodia, Laos, and the Philippines, where the people are similarly disenfranchised, both legally, through their weak land rights, and vis-à-vis rapacious regimes that displace customary landholders at will. There are massive new plantations in these countries where old and new rural elites grab land and rule coercively. Yet, as I noted earlier, the Philippines is also the site of the Indigenous Peoples' Rights Act, a progressive law that came out of a hard-fought advocacy campaign; and in Laos and Cambodia, colonial land law was interrupted by communist rule, which has its own legacies, some of which provide modest protections. Across the region, similar outcomes may mask the extent to which legal underpinnings and discursive rationalizations diverge.

The comparative framework I have laid out suggests ways to track different land regimes historically and offers three sets of questions that can be used to examine their key features. Further research could usefully explore how certain colonial regimes influenced others as officials looked over their shoulders to see what their peers were doing and evaluated different approaches. Colonial land legacies present a rich and multi-faceted domain of inquiry.

NOTES TO FOREWORD

1. Graham Burchell, Colin Gordon, and Peter Miller, "Governmentality," in *The Foucault Effect: Studies in Governmentality* (University of Chicago Press, 1991).
2. Ann Stoler, "Imperial Debris: Reflections on Ruins and Ruination," *Cultural Anthropology* 23, no. 2 (2008): 191–219; Ann Stoler, *Duress: Imperial Durabilities in Our Times* (Duke University Press, 2016). See also the discussion in Tania Murray Li and Pujo Semedi, *Plantation Life: Corporate Occupation in Indonesia's Oil Palm Zone* (Duke University Press, 2021).
3. Brenna Bhandar, *Colonial Lives of Property: Law, Land, and Racial Regimes of Ownership* (Duke University Press, 2018).
4. Here I draw directly on Li and Semedi, *Plantation Life*.
5. For a fuller development of the argument in this section and sources, see Tania Murray Li, "Indigeneity, Capitalism, and the Management of Dispossession," *Current Anthropology* 51, no. 3 (2010): 385–414.
6. This section draws on Li and Semedi, *Plantation Life*, and Tania Murray Li, "The Price of Un/freedom: Indonesia's Colonial and Contemporary Plantation Labor Regimes," *Comparative Studies in Society and History* 59, no. 2 (2017): 245–76. See these publications for a complete list of sources. See also Jan Breman, *Mobilizing Labour for the Global Coffee Market: Profits from an Unfree Work Regime in Colonial Java* (Amsterdam University Press, 2015).
7. Hussein Alatas, *The Myth of the Lazy Native: A Study of the Image of the Malays, Filipinos and Javanese from the 16th to the 20th Century and Its Function in the Ideology of Colonial Capitalism* (F. Cass, 1977).
8. For a summary and comparative analysis of past and present land policies in Southeast Asia, see Philip Hirsch, Derek Hall, and Tania Murray Li, *Powers of Exclusion: Land Dilemmas in Southeast Asia* (University of Hawai'i Press, 2011).
9. Andrew Walker, *Thailand's Political Peasants: Power in the modern rural economy* (University of Wisconsin Press, 2012).
10. Rob A. Cramb, "Re-inventing Dualism: Policy Narratives and Modes of Oil Palm Expansion in Sarawak, Malaysia," *Journal of Development Studies* 47, no. 2 (2011): 274–93.

Introduction

Colonial Portuguese Land Legacies in Comparative Perspective

Susanna Barnes and Laura S. Meitzner Yoder

How were colonial land interventions implemented and transformed across time, geographies, and local contexts, and through what means did they leave their traces up to the present day? Where and how are historical connections drawn among groups of people, their land uses, and differential land access or control evident? This volume draws on case studies of land relations primarily in five former Portuguese colonies—Brazil, Angola, Mozambique, Flores, and Portuguese Timor—to address the enduring effects of colonial land policies and their legacies in post-colonial contexts worldwide.[1] Drawing on ethnographic, historical, and legal methods and analyses we highlight the legacies of colonialism and their ongoing influence on contemporary issues of pressing concern such as access to land, bureaucracies of resource control and social exclusion, and land policy mobility.[2]

Locating Portuguese Land Policy Priorities and Principles across Time and Space

Research on the persistent effects of colonial land governance in the Portuguese-speaking world requires us to consider how knowledge about people, places, and things produces laws and policies governing land resources in specific contexts,[3] and also to trace how these laws and policies then "travel," resurfacing later and elsewhere. In tracing these so-called colonial legacies we are mindful to "avoid the assumption that they [colonial histories] should appear in the same locations and with the similitude of easily identifiable forms."[4] The chapters in this volume push us to consider the notion of Portuguese *colonialisms*, acknowledging the differential experiences of people across time and space; together they emphasize the (dis)continuities and afterlives of colonial land governance principles and practices in the present. Contemporary land and property regimes are deeply entangled in and with the colonial project. Taken-for-granted meanings and socio-legal conventions that underpin present-day land and property regimes are indeed the "imperial debris" or "the rot that remains," as discussed in Tania Murray Li's contribution to this volume—that is, colonial remnants embedded in everyday practices.[5]

What sets Portugal's imperial history apart from that of other European powers is its exceptional duration, spanning from the Conquest of Ceuta in 1415 to the transfer of Portuguese sovereignty over Macau to China in 1999. Throughout the long course of the imperial enterprise, Portuguese colonizers sought to acquire, dominate, and rule over people, places, and things, including land, from Asia to the Americas. Nevertheless, the process of empire building varied across both time and space and was as dependent on political circumstances and economic priorities back in Portugal as it was on the local realities, societies, and institutions encountered on the ground worldwide.

Typically characterized as comprising three distinct phases, the first Portuguese Empire was short-lived but had a significant impact on Portuguese identity and the country's perception of its global position.[6] From 1415 to 1580, the sphere of Portuguese interest was predominantly Asia, with a focus on the establishment of a powerful trading network in the Indian Ocean. Key ports such as Goa, Malacca, and Macau were crucial hubs in this expansive trade network, facilitating the trade in spices and other lucrative commodities. The second Portuguese Empire, from 1580 to 1822, centred on the development of sugar plantations and, later, gold and diamond mines in Brazil, which was integrated as a vital part of the empire. The political and social organization of Portugal and its overseas territories during this period took the form of a feudal and monarchical system deeply rooted in traditional hierarchical structures, privileges, and economic practices. Despite the economic potential, the rigid social hierarchy and reliance on slave labour created systemic inefficiencies and social tensions.

The third and final Portuguese Empire marked a significant transformation from the *ancien régime* to liberalism. Spanning Brazil's independence in 1822 to independence in most Portuguese regions of Africa and Asia by 1975, this phase saw the gradual dismantling of feudal relations and the consolidation of control over colonial territories, particularly in Africa. This period included efforts to modernize the economy and to integrate colonial possessions more directly into the global capitalist system. Despite the formal end of the slave trade in the Portuguese Empire in 1869, colonial economies remained heavily reliant on forced labour and extractive practices. The colonies, particularly Angola,

Mozambique, and Guinea-Bissau, became primary sources of wealth for the Portuguese state. However, the economic benefits were unevenly distributed, and the persistence of colonial exploitation and resistance movements eventually led to the decolonization process, accelerated by the 1974 Carnation Revolution in Lisbon.[7]

In Portugal, and as the Portuguese Empire expanded, the meaning and value of land changed as feudal land relations gave way to commercialism, agrarian capitalism, and market capitalism.[8] As noted by Roque in the afterword to this volume,[9] these changing values and meanings were reflected in changing language. For example, while the Portuguese word for land, *terra*, was once understood to refer almost exclusively to "coastal land," and thus juxtaposed to "hinterland," by the early twentieth century the emphasis was on *terra* as "the soil that produces." The meaning and value of land thus transformed from a feature of the landscape to a productive asset. These changing meanings also reflected a change in the way Portugal regarded its overseas possessions. While the emphasis in the fifteenth and sixteenth centuries was on capturing ports and trading routes to advance commerce and trade in Asia, by the late seventeenth and early eighteenth centuries the focus was on plantations and mines in Brazil and central Africa. By the turn of the twentieth century, this shifted again toward consolidating territorial control and exploiting natural resources, particularly in Angola and Mozambique, while integrating these colonies into the global capitalist economy through infrastructure development and forced labour systems.[10] In a mutually constitutive process, changes in the meaning and value of land brought about changes in the way the colonial authorities from Portugal, as elsewhere, sought to govern land relations.

In the sixteenth and seventeenth centuries, the *sesmaria* system in Brazil and Angola and its *prazo* counterpart in Portuguese possessions in Asia (India and Goa) and Mozambique were initially premised on existing feudal land relations in Portugal.[11] *Sesmarias* were a Crown grant that can be broadly described as a conditional right to control land in return for cultivating it. However, while in Portugal the *sesmaria* system was established in order to stimulate cultivation, in Brazil it was used to regularize colonial settlement.[12] The appropriation of land and people was strongly supported by notions of the right to conquest and the expansion of Christianity enshrined in the so-called Doctrine of Discovery.[13] Similarly, *prazos* were large land grants given by the Portuguese Crown to settlers, typically of Portuguese or mixed Portuguese and African descent, designed to encourage settlement and development in the region while consolidating Portuguese control.[14] Land grants or leases, often linked to a suite of other privileges, were given to Portuguese settlers and traders in exchange for goods or services to the Crown—a reward for allegiance given or expected. Similar in principle and purpose, *sesmarias* and *prazos* were aimed at assuring control over territory and access to resources in the name of the Crown. However, in the process of implementing these systems of land grants in different territories, agents of the Crown (and later, of the state) had to contend with existing and developing land uses and relations. In many cases the process involved violent replacement of the social practices of Indigenous populations; in others, colonial agents were forced to coexist and compromise, not only with powerful Indigenous authorities,[15] but also with other settlers and even enslaved labourers[16]—thus creating new *colonial* forms[17] that reflected the entangled and enmeshed nature of relations between colonizer and colonised.[18]

In Angola, *sesmarias* gave way to vassalage treaties aimed not at occupation of territory but expropriation of people and finally straightforward land expropriation in the nineteenth century.[19] It was enslaved African labour enabling the exploitation of resources and the development of agriculture in Brazil that bolstered the Portuguese economy in the seventeenth and early eighteenth centuries. The official abolition of slavery in 1869 and the general decline in the slave trade thereafter coincided with a rise in demand for raw materials such as cotton, ivory, and wax. With the loss of Brazil in 1822, the appropriation of land and labour thus became an issue of central concern to the colonial authorities in what is now Angola and Mozambique.[20] Agriculture and the development of cash crops drove land appropriation and redistribution, and both were justified as essential to the civilizing mission of colonialism. Indeed, land ownership and agricultural production were markers of an individual's "civilized status."[21] Indigenous people could aspire to own land as long as they cultivated it. But failure to successfully demonstrate continuous agricultural use of land left people's rights to land vulnerable. For example, in Angola, the Portuguese authorities refused to recognize the seasonal and migratory nature of local agricultural practices or the fluidity of the political boundaries recognized by local rulers, or *sobetas* as they were known.[22] By failing to conform to colonial standards of land ownership and use, local rulers and their populations found themselves dispossessed of their land and dependent on others for protection and resources.

Liberal reforms in the nineteenth century, influenced by Enlightenment ideas and revolutions across Europe, sought to dismantle the entrenched feudal system in Portugal and its overseas possessions. Under the *ancien* régime, much of the land was held by the nobility and the church as Crown land grants, such as *prazos* and *sesmarias*, embedded within a complex hierarchy of obligations and rights. The shift to liberalism brought about a transition to private property, where land could be owned outright by individuals. This was a significant change that laid the groundwork for a capitalist economy.

A central mechanism of land dispossession became the land concession, a land use form that has endured and become associated with widespread deforestation and plantation agriculture worldwide.[23] From the mid- to late nineteenth century the concept of *concessão* (pl. *concessões*) was used to describe formal grants of land given by the colonial government to individuals, companies, or organizations to exploit for agricultural, mining, or other productive economic activities. In Portuguese Timor, the move toward concessions emerged over time and resulted from changes starting in the 1860s, first emulating an extractive economic system that governors had deemed a Dutch success in Java, then borrowing legal innovations to bolster state claims to land, making state-owned lands alienable and giving colonial governors the authority to make concessions at the turn of the twentieth century.[24] In 1900, land was seized and privatized, granted as concessions for plantations to Lisbon-based men with plantation holdings elsewhere in the Portuguese Empire, alongside well-connected men in Timor, setting the stage for control of land by external individuals and entities. The imposition of liberal land policies in Timor, as elsewhere, often clashed with local land tenure systems, leading to resistance and social upheaval.[25] Thus, while liberalism modernized property relations and integrated colonial economies into the global capitalist system, it also introduced new challenges and conflicts, reshaping the socio-economic fabric of the Portuguese Empire.

Access to land, economic exploitation, and maintenance of sovereignty were top priorities for Portugal at the turn of the twentieth century.[26] Yet, following the Berlin Conference of 1884, and more specifically article 6 of the General Act of 1885, the Portuguese were also under pressure to demonstrate their commitment to bringing "the blessings of civilization," ensuring the "protection of the native populations" and "the improvement of the conditions of their moral and material well-being," and more generally reaffirming their aim to "abolish slavery, and especially the slave trade," in these territories.[27] Portuguese land policy at the time reflected an inherent contradiction between the promotion of capitalist processes and the demonstration of concern for the "improvement" of "native peoples." Based on paternalistic and racialist arguments, clearer legal distinctions were established between "native" and "non-native," "uncivilized" and "civilized," and different policies and laws were developed in relation to each.[28]

Direito has argued that the 1901 Carta de Lei (Legal Charter) that was promulgated for seven Portuguese overseas possessions indicates the position of Portuguese legal scholars of the time.[29] Underpinning the Carta de Lei was, firstly, a nominal respect for native land holdings. While this was presented as an ethical obligation in line with Portugal's purported "civilizing mission," it was also used as a means of assuaging the growing critique of and even overt resistance to colonial power.[30] For example, articles 2–6, dealing with "native property" (*Da propriedade dos indígenas*), recognized Indigenous property rights to land that they habitually cultivated, as well as to residential areas. What constituted "native land," however, was ultimately defined by the colonial power and did not take into consideration Indigenous social, economic, spiritual, or political connections to land.[31] Rights to "native property" were predicated on economic exploitation. Land that was not usefully and continuously cultivated was therefore considered "vacant" and available for exploitation.[32] Accordingly, the Carta de Lei outlined ambitious and detailed procedures of land classification, valuation, and demarcation in administering state land concessions. Under these procedures, eligibility for land concessions was limited to the following entities: Portuguese citizens with the ability to make contracts, naturalized foreigners or qualified residents, Portuguese companies, administrative corporations, and Catholic missions.

Secondly, the prevalence of what colonial authorities determined to be "communal" land use arrangements was seen as a sign of "primitive" land tenure systems. Within a broad evolutionary framework, collective rights and use of land were considered "inferior" to individual "property" rights. Indigenous populations could aspire to, but were often deemed "not ready" for, individualization, and therefore required "protection" from non-natives acting in bad faith.[33] Special rules regarding land were applied to colonized peoples and settlers. In Angola and Mozambique, natives and non-natives were not permitted to compete freely for the same lands. Indigenous populations were offered "protection" on "reserves" or *aldeamentos* (settlements) apart from "white" settlers, or settlers from other parts of the Portuguese Empire such as the Azores and Goa, and commercial enterprises. Often more fertile and productive parcels of land were granted to non-natives.[34] In Portuguese Timor, the Carta de Lei guaranteed property transmission through succession according to non-specified local custom but required prior state administrative authorization for native land transfers to non-native people.[35] Later in the 1910s a distinctive *alvará indígena*, or native title, was created to provide native Timorese with the opportunity, "individually and optionally, [to] formalize their right to land by registering them, and obtaining a formal land use right (*aforamento*)."[36] Almeida has written how the preamble to the regulation establishing this new form of title exemplifies a "paternalist view of them [Timorese] as prodigal and incapable to navigate 'modern' formal land tenure systems, and therefore the need for state protection."[37]

And thirdly, for Portuguese colonial administrators to successfully implement the preceding points, local populations, customs, and land relations had to be studied and codified. Here, the example of the Dutch East Indies but also British colonies in Africa had a strong influence on the Portuguese. Codification was a political act, often fixing boundaries and identities that were previously flexible and dynamic. Codification became a useful tool to reward allies and punish enemies. For example, in Portuguese Timor, the Carta da Lei established that all land not held by Portuguese title was deemed to belong to the state. A map of Portuguese Timor was produced dividing land held by loyal *liurai* (local kings) and land "without a master." The latter was vested in the Portuguese state and therefore could be the subject of land title.[38] Similarly, in Mozambique the process of granting titles and recognizing the authority of local chiefs lends legitimacy to contemporary claims to jurisdiction over people and land.[39]

Central to the ideas or principles outlined above was a racial concept of the human, which determined who could own land and under what conditions.[40] The 1901 Carta da Lei established *indígena* (natives) in a separate legal and economic category regarding land, giving some recognition to customary practice while mandating state regulation of their land transactions. The distinction between *indígena* and *não-indígena* (non-natives), first developed in the African context, became a fundamental feature of an imperial model in which Indigeneity implied a priori "uncivilized" status.[41] In the 1930s, with the advent of the Salazar regime, these distinctions became institutionalized by law; however, reflective of the social evolutionary thinking of the time, Indigenous subjects could strive to transcend their *indígena* status through the civilizing mission of the colonial state assisted by the Catholic Church.[42] In Portuguese Timor, defining who was indeed Indigenous, or native Timorese, and who was not proved problematic, with officials noting that some people were claiming "native" legal status to sell land to other native Timorese while refusing it in order to avoid paying the head tax.[43]

After World War II, as a new global order emerged and anti-colonial movements gained momentum, the Portuguese government faced mounting pressure to decolonize and recognize subject peoples' right to self-determination. The "Estado Novo" (New State) government led by António de Oliveira Salazar (1933–74) responded to these pressures by implementing various reforms aimed at retaining Portuguese control over colonial territories and resources. This included altering the official title of colonies to "overseas provinces" (*províncias ultramarinas*), outlawing forced labour, and granting Portuguese citizenship to Indigenous individuals. These adjustments were also evident in land-related laws that afforded additional protection to customary land rights and eased the process of obtaining formal recognition for these rights through administrative procedures that allowed oral presentations. Despite these changes, the process still required a significant amount of time and knowledge about the importance of formalizing land rights. In some cases, payments were also necessary. Consequently, this limited the number of individuals and communities that were able to formalize their rights. In addition, legal protections were often limited to housing and cultivation, and did not extend to other significant aspects of customary tenure such as grazing, hunting, foresting, sacred areas, and areas reserved for future use. Ultimately, the main focus of the formal land tenure policy in the late colonial period was similar to previous legislation—the concession of land for economic exploitation.[44]

It is evident that the land policies and classifications enacted on the ground in various arenas of the Portuguese Empire bore imprints of the socio-economic models borrowed from other colonial powers, as well as legal principles circulating within the European colonial ideologies of the time. The allocation of land through *sesmarias*, *prazos*, and concessions laid the foundation for enduring inequities in landholding through the dispossession of Indigenous peoples. As discussed in the following chapters, these colonial land governance structures created patterns of land ownership and use that privileged colonial elites and marginalized local populations. As these colonies transitioned to independence or subsequent regimes of control, the legacy of these land policies persisted, contributing to ongoing land disputes and socio-economic inequality. The remnants of the *sesmaria* and *prazo* systems can still be seen today in the persistence of corporate institutional forms, the concentration of land ownership among an elite, and the struggles for land rights by Indigenous and rural communities. Understanding the historical context of these policies is essential for addressing the contemporary challenges they have created and for promoting more equitable and sustainable land governance practices in these former Portuguese colonies.

Orienting Reflections and the Thematic Organization of the Chapters

In Tania Murray Li's orienting charge to the chapter authors, reproduced in the foreword to this volume, she noted the close link Brenna Bhandar drew between what Li described as "a kind of person, a kind of land use, and the quality of their property rights."[45] As detailed in the cases presented here, people's identities—as political elites, Indigenous, enslaved, and freed labourers, traders, cultivators, customary authorities, settlers—had profound impacts on their land relations. This was true not only in their influence on official processes, but also in how we see multiple actors disregard, subvert, manipulate, and transgress the land governance mechanisms set in place. The types of people, range of land uses, and property rights (or land access and ownership) evolved through the period examined here. We see the advent of new legal persons in the form of corporations and state enterprises, new landforms, including monoculture plantations, and the marked development of legal regimes. For this reason, it is helpful to have a set of anchoring questions that we can use to understand land governance in different contexts across time and space. Tania Murray Li provided us with three in her contribution to this volume:

> First, to *what ends* do authorities attempt to govern land relations? Do the ends include increasing production to raise revenues or taxes? Order, pacification, and the administration of populations? The demonstration of territorial control vis-à-vis internal opponents or external competitors? The generation of profits for shareholders? Native improvement? The attraction of settlers or the reward of allies?
>
> Second, through *what means* is land government exercised? Is there direct control over territory or indirect rule through local elites or native chiefs? Are natives addressed as individuals or as members of communities? Are they fixed to the land or detached to form a "free" proletariat? Are they targets of productive investment or treated as irritants to be swept aside?
>
> Third, *what is the rationale* under which land government proceeds? What narrative or authoritative body of knowledge links problems identified to solutions proposed? How is a given rationale defended from counternarratives and critiques? Under what conditions does it morph and realign?

These questions inform the three thematic sections of this volume, "Administrative Practices and Governance Strategies," "Indigenous-Settler Entanglements," and "Economic Imperatives and Global Articulations." While we highlight these thematic sections to facilitate comparative analysis, readers will see many common threads and recurrent topics, characters, and regulations running throughout the chapters. By examining these interconnected themes, this volume offers a comprehensive understanding of the multi-faceted issues surrounding land governance and Indigenous-settler relations. Chapter authors used a range of methods appropriate to their topics and disciplines: archival analysis, ethnographic field research, oral histories, descriptions of transnational networks, historical map analysis, in-depth case studies, and historical overviews.

Our first thematic section focuses on *administrative practices and governance strategies*, which were intricately linked to the broader objectives of maintaining colonial authority and facilitating economic exploitation. Land administration practices included establishing bureaucratic systems and institutions to systematically manage land distribution, enforce colonial regulations, and monitor compliance with legal frameworks, such as the *sesmaria* grant system in Brazil (Alveal). Governance strategies involved large-scale infrastructure development projects and population management programs, including constructing roads to enhance mobility and control (deGrassi), establishing reserves to segregate and manage Indigenous populations (Direito), and implementing villagization programs to reorganize and concentrate communities for easier oversight and economic exploitation (Direito and deGrassi). Together, these administrative practices and policy mechanisms served to define who could access land, for what purposes, and under what conditions. Supported by colonial language and prevailing ideologies (Almeida), they were crucial in conceptualizing, regulating, and controlling land while at the same time remaining open to interpretation, manipulation, transgression, and subversion.

Through a detailed case study of the Guedes-Brito family, Carmen Alveal brings to life the complexity of the *sesmaria* system in Brazil. *Sesmarias*—Crown land grants established in fourteenth-century Portugal to incentivize the repopulation of plaque-ravaged agricultural areas—were introduced to Brazil to ensure defence and cultivation of the vast territory to which the Portuguese laid claim. However, inconsistent Crown policy regarding management of *sesmaria* land grants in Brazil, involving multiple actors and levels of government, coupled with an entitled social elite seeking to consolidate their rights over land, led to conflict and complexity. Alveal's study reveals how powerful elites took advantage of slow, convoluted bureaucracies and incomplete legal processes to gain and retain control over vast areas, manipulating the *sesmaria* system for territorial control and sovereignty. The *fidalgos* (members of the noble class) often did not feel the need to cultivate the land themselves, but used their power to evict renters and squatters, consolidating their holdings and reinforcing their socio-economic status. The *sesmaria* system became a tool not just for land management, but for maintaining and reinforcing the social hierarchies that favoured European descendants and marginalized Indigenous and mixed-race populations. This chapter underscores the ongoing effects of these colonial processes, how they were open to manipulation by self-interested parties, and the enduring legacy of colonial land policies and their role in shaping contemporary social and economic inequalities in Brazil.

Barbara Direito's chapter delves into the practical implementation of colonial strategies in Mozambique, focusing on the legal status of Africans living on both European land concessions and vacant lands that were granted legal recognition. This shift marked a departure from previous policies that had severely restricted Africans' property rights and treated them as squatters. The resulting resettlement schemes involved parcelling and distributing plots to African smallholders in an effort to increase agricultural yields. Resettlement was justified by the need for higher productivity, responding to the demands for agricultural commodities and the decline in settler farming exacerbated by the Great Depression; to this end, separate plots within native reserves were allocated to individual smallholders, a move intended to boost effectiveness through technical intervention. This approach combined incentives with coercion, promoting rural differentiation while also being constrained by European farmers' fears of African competition. Despite the ostensible aim of improving African living standards, these instruments were underpinned by paternalism and coercion. The colonial authorities' strategies were designed to serve non-Indigenous interests and mitigate the economic crisis facing settler farmers. The intervention in African agricultural production thus reflected a broader tension between ideological aspirations and the pragmatic need to control and exploit African labour.

Turning to dispossession caused by infrastructure development projects and population management strategies, Aharon deGrassi examines the pervasive and often overlooked colonial practice of quotidian village concentration along newly constructed roads in Angola. This policy, significantly implemented in the early twentieth century, was designed to facilitate administrative control, resource extraction, and labour mobilization. The forced relocation, which predominantly burdened women with increased labour and limited access to essential resources like water, had profound impacts on the daily lives and socio-economic structures of rural populations. deGrassi argues that these everyday displacements, driven by colonial policies, continue to shape contemporary Angolan society and governance. By drawing on ethnographic fieldwork, colonial reports, and archival maps, he highlights the dynamic and interactive relationship between state power and spatial organization, challenging traditional theories of state power as static. The legacy of these colonial practices is evident in ongoing rural-urban inequalities and reinforces the need for re-theorizing the geographical and gendered impacts of state policies.

One element of the considerable "imperial debris" that stems from the Portuguese colonization of Timor-Leste is legal language, including the language concepts that classify, describe, and regulate land rights and the use of land. The chapter by Bernardo Almeida focuses on one specific example of such imperial flotsam that travelled and reappeared far in space and time from its original uses or intent, the Portuguese word *baldio* (pl. *baldios*). In Portugal, the word has had multiple contradictory meanings across centuries, and the regulation of *baldios* has been one of the central ideological disputes concerning land rights in the country for centuries. Nowadays, in legal language the word is used to refer to legally protected, communally owned and used land, but in popular speech it is also used to refer to land that is abandoned, unused, unfarmed, or underused. Portugal implemented its formal land tenure system in its colonies as a way of affirming sovereignty over these territories and exploiting their natural resources; *baldios* are problematic because they do neither. This chapter discusses the possible causes and effects of the term's sudden, unprecedented appearance in a near-final 2017 draft of the first comprehensive national land law of independent Timor-Leste, bearing critically important implications for state land claims and protection of communal land rights. The incident illustrates the social boundaries of knowledge, the administrative limitations of borrowing undefined foreign legal terms that refer to land uses in dramatically different landscapes and agricultural contexts, and how the political biases of non-agrarian governing elites can render local practices invisible, deeming them unproductive relative to potential control by the state.

Our second thematic section delves into the complex and often contentious dynamics of *Indigenous-settler entanglements* across diverse colonial and post-colonial contexts. These chapters explore how colonial powers inherited and transformed land governance systems from previous regimes, integrating local land authorities and creating hybrid land practices (Hägerdal, Röhrig Assunção, Barnes, and Jossias). Across vastly different contexts colonial administrators grappled with existing systems and politico-religious institutions, facing challenges in establishing their presence (Hägerdal, Jossias, and Barnes). Socio-economic inequalities were exacerbated by colonial policies that favoured certain groups, leading to long-lasting land disputes and reconfigurations of land ownership (Röhrig Assunção and Barnes). Despite these challenges, Indigenous communities persisted in their efforts to reclaim authority over appropriated lands and maintain their cultural practices (Jossias), while newly freed populations were able to assert their new-found autonomy (Röhrig Assunção). In the case of post-Independence Brazil, the evolving mechanisms of land claims and possession highlight the strategic navigation of legal and administrative requirements during transitional periods (Röhrig Assunção). Colonial development interventions often disrupted Indigenous land practices, redefining property relations and deepening socio-economic divides (Barnes). Contemporary community-based approaches to land governance, intended to formalize customary land rights, often overlook the colonial distribution of power and authority, leading to conflicts over territorial control (Jossias). Together, these sub-themes reveal how power dynamics and socio-economic goals shaped land policies and practices, determining land access, purposes, and conditions and their implications for contemporary land governance and Indigenous-settler relations.

Hans Hägerdal grapples with the Portuguese land legacies on Flores as inherited by Dutch colonial powers and already bearing the significant influence of various Indigenous polities—a relatively peaceful intercolonial land transfer from the Portuguese to the Dutch in exchange for land on Timor. Between the sixteenth and nineteenth centuries, when Portuguese control focused on trade rather than landholding, colonial hybridities entwined Luso and local categories of land authorities. This chapter discusses how the Dutch perceived these inherited elements of land governance and practices—including Dutch resentment toward plantations managed by Catholic clergy, frustration with the limitations on territorial control of "civilized" Luso-Catholic local rulers, and disappointment that the Dutch administrative presence was slow to surpass that of Catholic missionary stations. Dutch administrators viewed the inroads made by earlier Portuguese Christian institutions as beneficial for their own colonial penetration and access to land, as well as amenable to ongoing colonial interventions.

Focusing on the Maranhão Province of northern Brazil in the nineteenth century, Matthias Röhrig Assunção examines land registers to understand how various actors claimed land by possession. Ownership of land and the control over coerced labour were central to Portuguese colonization, as subsistence agriculture and communal ownership or possession competed with cotton and rice plantations relying primarily on enslaved labour and other forms of agrarian enterprises. The *sesmaria* royal land grants had created a class of powerful landowners who held vast swaths of land through Brazilian independence in 1822 to the abolition of the transatlantic slave trade in 1850. Many Indigenous groups and formerly enslaved people (*quilombos*) acquired land during this time, often in collective holdings around the unoccupied edges of plantations and agrarian frontiers, creating new classes of landholding and blurring the boundary between ownership and possession. Landowners employed strategic variability in registration details during the 1850s, often subverting or sidestepping administrative requirements to maintain control over their holdings. Drawing on archival research and fieldwork, including the examination of land registers, Röhrig Assunção reveals the evolution of land uses by various groups and highlight the complex interplay of ownership and labor within Maranhão's agrarian landscape. This dynamic period saw the re-codification of land use and ownership within the post-/neo-colonial framework of Brazil, and the continued existence of a peasantry that developed in the interstices of the plantation economy.

The chapter by Susanna Barnes examines how Portuguese development strategies during the Estado Novo period reshaped land access and use in Timor-Leste. The colonial shift toward modernization and economic development introduced policies that favoured lowland irrigated rice farming over traditional upland shifting cultivation, leading to significant reconfigurations of land ownership in the long term. These policies often privileged local elites and those with ties to the colonial administration, exacerbating inequalities and creating long-lasting land disputes. By detailing the specific case of rice development on the Nunura plain of Maliana sub-district, the chapter illustrates how colonial land interventions disrupted Indigenous land practices, redefined property relations, and entrenched socio-economic divides between Indigenous communities and settler authorities. This analysis underscores the enduring impact of colonial land policies on contemporary Indigenous-settler relations, highlighting the deep-rooted challenges involved in resolving land claims and achieving equitable land governance in post-colonial contexts.

Looking specifically at the enduring effects of colonial interventions on contemporary land policy, Elissio Jossias discusses the implementation of "community land delimitation" processes in Mozambique between 1997 and 2006. Community land delimitation was conceived as the better way to mobilize communities for protecting communal natural resources, including land, and to promote local development. Jossias explores how the land delimitation process led to moments of competition over territorial hierarchies between local chiefs. This ethnographic account from Cóbuè region shows how an emphasis on community approaches to land governance and territorial organization can create the potential for conflict and disputes between chiefs in the process of claiming control over political territories. In such a situation, the land delimitation process did not only represent the formalization of customary land or communal property rights, as stipulated in the 1997 land law. Rather, this process was incorporated in a historical contestation of hierarchies and statutes among traditional chiefs and the corresponding territories.

Our third and final thematic section focuses on the *economic imperatives and global articulations* that transformed land policy from the late nineteenth century. Portugal needed its overseas possessions to provide income for the state, so establishing land policies and mechanisms that yielded income was an increasingly urgent priority. To accomplish this, Portuguese and sought models and forged alliances with a range of external entities that could produce commodities for profitable export: borrowing peasant taxation models from neighbouring colonizers (Kammen and Meitzner Yoder) and leasing vast territories to other European corporations (Adalima, Gerken). Transnational political and corporate actors have had outsized economic, political, and legal influence in land use for over a century, and tracing their involvements through time demonstrates the gradual and multi-step processes of introducing administrative and policy elements that accompany an evolving economic strategy. Alongside new land laws that transformed land rights for citizens, independent states continued foreign investments in plantations by continuing land concessions, prompting Adalima to query how modern World Bank processes represent continuity with the mechanisms of the colonial state.

Studying the French-owned Madal copra plantation in northern Mozambique, José Laimone Adalima demonstrates continuity from colonial land governance to modern agribusiness, highlighting land policy contradictions and the role of the political elite in developing plantations. With the failure of Portuguese private investment, Portugal leased two-thirds of Mozambique to the corporate entities of other European powers, which were henceforth given broad mandates to exploit and manage their territories. This chapter traces the development of the company through political changes resulting from Mozambique's 1975 independence through to the 2000s, by which time Madal was the largest private landholder in the nation. Adalima notes that plantations met the desired criteria of effective occupation and economic development through resource and labour exploitation, creating an enduring ecological and economic model that dispossesses local people to produce monoculture plantations.

Laura Gerken brings a modern perspective to large-scale land acquisition in Mozambique, focusing on the period since 2000, when international organizations began to give more attention to land and tenure security. This chapter traces the development of land laws that assign legal recognition based on continuous land use and focuses on popular resistance to two large-scale agricultural projects for irrigated rice and maize and soy production in Mozambique. In both cases, transnational activists' rejection of plantation projects yielded either a reduction in the size of a given project, or caused it to be paused altogether, prompting consideration of legal instruments as tools of resistance to large-scale mechanisms of land acquisition for export agriculture.

Transforming land ownership and land use were the intent of concessions, the focus of the chapter by Douglas Kammen and Laura Meitzner Yoder. Late-colonial land policy is best understood as a series of overlapping, borrowed, and phased transitions that faded and rose in succession. Focusing on Portuguese Timor, the authors show that the early practice of minimal interference in native land authority gave way to legal dispossession of Indigenous land in tandem with gradual development of a land market; these elements often came from outside of Timor, emulating older Dutch legal and commodity production innovations or arising in response to broader international economic opportunities and norms. State plantation land concessions in the 1860s gave rise to the confiscation of Indigenous land for large-scale private concessions to prominent business leaders in Lisbon, their political allies in Timor, and others for oil and mineral prospecting, as well as for agricultural plantations. An important legacy of colonial land policy in Timor-Leste is the continued coexistence of competing land regimes.

Conclusion

Returning to Tania Murray Li's contribution to this volume, she asserts that colonial land legacies are important and that their persistence is potentially problematic because they still reflect the racial divides and hierarchies from their colonial inception. She laments "the persistence of racialism in the contemporary period in a format that is only lightly revised. It is embedded in land law, in development policy, and in everyday ways of thinking and acting," and thus can go unnoticed and unchallenged. In the words of Ann Stoler, this is part of the "imperial debris" or the "rot that remains" from colonial rule.[46] It contributes to the continuing vulnerability of rural and marginalized people, whose land claims remain precarious, limited, inequitable, and chronically subject to dispossession by more powerful actors, including the state. Li asks, "How did a (deficient) kind of person become linked to a (deficient) kind of production, worthy of a weak and inferior kind of right to land? How did this form of governing, reasoning, and acting come to be? And how does it shape contemporary configurations?"

The chapters in this volume address these questions from multiple angles as they examine the policies, interactions, and influences of a range of cases with close attention to the administrative, socio-political, and legal mechanisms of imperial formations and land legacies in diverse contexts. What they demonstrate is that the imperial debris is neither stable nor uniform; there are many forms of mutual influence. In their encounters with colonial policies, the actors involved—at various places on the power continuum—also shape the nature of the debris, making their own contributions to the composition of vestiges preserved, discarded, and repurposed. These chapters show there is scope for agency even within the constraints of governance and powerful forces' impetus toward controlling land for certain kinds of uses that benefit elites, the state, international entities, and corporations. Laws are not only enacted simply in their formal implementation, but also in their selective disregard and evasion as various parties seek to ignore, manipulate, or superimpose pre-existing norms and practices (Alveal, Direito, Röhrig Assunção, Kammen and Meitzner Yoder, Almeida, deGrassi). Because governance is often subverted, these cases help us see in their analyses of practices and interactions how determinative power relationships persist and change over time. Multiple actors show us gradations of resistance.

Applying Tania Murray Li's three questions to such diverse circumstances can serve to open our imaginations about how land relations could be different. Once we come to readily see and name the strategic confluence of low social status, denigrated land uses, and precarious land rights, they need not remain bound together as an inevitability. We can also pose these questions to high-status entities whose uses are praised by the powerful and whose land rights are upheld and strongly protected by states (even when they rely on coerced labour). For example, when corporate concessions are not productive, what happens to their land rights? Historically, we have seen that in such instances, powerful actors may escape or ignore the expectation of productivity (Alveal), redirect blame for unsatisfactory production (Direito), or inventively switch tactics without losing land claims (Adalima) to suit their own agendas and priorities. By examining these different contexts in parallel, we came to recognize similarities that reflect the common origins of the administrative apparatus, including legal structures dictated from the metropole. These shared origins influenced how land governance systems were established and evolved in various colonies. Yet, in these chapters, we also see different trajectories in land policy, customs, and practice in Portugal, Brazil, Angola, Mozambique, Flores, and Timor-Leste. Even starting from a common administrative root, these regions developed unique adaptations and responses to local conditions and pressures. This divergence illustrates the dynamic nature of land governance, showing how local actors and contexts shape the implementation and impact of colonial and post-colonial land policies. By comparing these varied experiences, we gain a deeper understanding of the complex interplay between global influences and local realities in the realm of land relations.

NOTES TO INTRODUCTION

1. While we focus on key territories such as Brazil, Angola, Mozambique, Flores, and Portuguese Timor, it is important to acknowledge the limitations of this focus. The exclusion of regions such as Goa and São Tomé, despite their significant roles in the development of the Portuguese plantation system in the nineteenth century, does not diminish their importance. This approach is not intended to offer a comprehensive coverage of all former Portuguese colonial spaces, but rather to highlight specific examples that illuminate broader patterns and consequences.
2. Jan Michiel Otto, "Rule of Law Promotion, Land Tenure and Poverty Alleviation: Questioning the Assumptions of Hernando de Soto," *Hague Journal on the Rule of Law* 1, no. 1 (2009): 173–94; Toon Van Meijl and Franz von Benda-Beckham, *Property Rights and Economic Development: Land and Natural Resources in Southeast Asia and Oceania* (Routledge, 2012); Daniel Fitzpatrick, "'Best Practice' Options for the Legal Recognition of Customary Tenure," *Development and Change* 36, no. 3 (2005): 449–75.
3. See Li, this volume.
4. Ann Stoler, *Duress: Imperial Durabilities in Our Times* (Duke University Press, 2016), 32.
5. Stoler, *Duress*. See also Li, this volume.
6. See Roque in this volume on seafaring imaginaries. On the stages of the Portuguese Empire, see W. G. Clarence-Smith, *The Third Portuguese Empire, 1825–1975: A Study in Economic Imperialism* (Manchester University Press, 1985).
7. Clarence-Smith, *The Third Portuguese Empire*, chap. 1.
8. See also Brenna Bhandar, *Colonial Lives of Property: Law, Land, and Racial Regimes of Ownership* (Duke University Press, 2018), 8.
9. Roque, this volume.
10. Vicente Serrão, Bárbara Direito, Susana Münch Miranda, and Eugénia Rodrigues, eds., *Property Rights, Land and Territory in the European Overseas Empires* (CEHC-IUL, 2014, 2014).
11. While *sesmarias* and *prazos* were present in both Angola and Mozambique, they were unequally represented there.
12. Márcia Motta, "The Sesmarias in Brazil: Colonial Land Policies in the Late Eighteenth Century," *e-Journal of Portuguese History*, no. 2 (Winter 2005): 2.
13. Papal "Bulls of Discovery" (Doctrine of Discovery): *Romanus Pontifex* (1455), issued by Pope Nicholas V, and *Inter caetera* (1493), pronounced by Pope Alexander VI. The 1455 bull explicitly authorized King Alfonso of Portugal to conquer and subjugate the territories and people of Africa and beyond.
14. Mariana Pinho Candido, "Conquest, Occupation, Colonialism and Exclusion: Land Disputes in Angola," in Serrão et al., *Property Rights*, 223–35. See also Adalima this volume.
15. For example in Goa, see Luis Frederico Dias Atunes, "A persistência dos sistemas tradicionais de propriedade fundiária em Damão e Baçaim (século XVI)," in Serrão et al., *Property Rights*, 155–68; Hägerdal, this volume.
16. See Alveal, Röhrig Assunção, both this volume.
17. Or mutations, see Roque, this volume.
18. Serrão et al., *Property Rights*, 10; Ricardo Roque, "Mimesis and Colonialism: Emerging Perspectives on a Shared History," *History Compass* 13, no. 4 (2015): 201–11.
19. Mariana Pinho Candido, *Fronteiras da escravidão: Escravatura, comércio e identidade em Benguela, 1780–1850* (Universidade de Katyavala Bwila/Ondjiri Editores, 2018), 224. See also Pinho Candido, "Conquest, Occupation, Colonialism and Exclusion."
20. Serrão et al., *Property Rights*.
21. See António de Saldanha da Gama, *Memória sobre as colónias de Portugal: Situadas na costa occidental d'África* (Casimir, 1839), 30–2, in Pinho Candido, *Fronteiras*, 227.
22. Pinho Candido, *Fronteiras*, 228.
23. Tania Murray Li and Pujo Semedi, *Plantation Life: Corporate Occupation in Indonesia's Oil Palm Zone* (Duke University Press, 2021).
24. Kammen and Meitzner Yoder, this volume.
25. René Pélissier, *Timor en guerre: Le crocodile et les Portugais, 1847–1913* (Orgeval, 1996).
26. Bárbara Direito, "African Access to Land in Early 20th Century Portuguese Colonial Thought," in Serrão et al., *Property Rights*, 255–66.

27. Miguel Bandeira Jerónimo and António Costa Pinto, "A Modernizing Empire? Politics, Culture, and Economy in Portuguese Late Colonialism," in *The Ends of European Colonial Empires: Cases and Comparisons*, ed. Miguel Bandeira Jerónimo and António Costa Pinto (Palgrave Macmillan, 2015),11.
28. Clarence-Smith, *The Third Portuguese Empire*, 139.
29. Direito, "African Access to Land." See also Laura S Meitzner Yoder, "Genealogy of Colonial Land Registration and State Land in Portuguese Timor," *European Legacy* 25, no. 5 (2020): 519–34; Bernardo Ribeiro de Almeida, *A Sociolegal Analysis of Formal Land Tenure Systems: Learning from the Political, Legal and Institutional Struggles of Timor-Leste* (Routledge, 2022).
30. Almeida, *A Sociolegal Analysis*.
31. Direito, "African Access to Land," 261. See also Almeida, *A Sociolegal Analysis*.
32. Meitzner Yoder, "Genealogy," 524; Almeida, this volume.
33. See Meitzner Yoder, "Genealogy"; Almeida, *A Sociolegal Analysis*; Li, this volume.
34. See Direito, this volume.
35. Meitzner Yoder, "Genealogy," 524.
36. Almeida, *A Sociolegal Analysis*, 61.
37. Almeida, 61.
38. Daniel Fitzpatrick, Andrew McWilliam, and Susana Barnes, *Property and Social Resilience in Times of Conflict: Land, Custom and Law in East Timor* (Routledge, 2016), 216. Later, in 1910, the governor of Timor issued a decree enabling him to make grants of up to 2,500 hectares of "unoccupied" land; to establish native tenure the occupier had to have built up or cultivated at least half the area.
39. Jossias, this volume.
40. See also Bhandar, *Colonial Lives*.
41. Douglas Kammen, "Progress and Propaganda in Timor-Leste: Visions of the Future in Comparative Historical Perspective," in *The Promise of Prosperity: Visions of the Future in Timor-Leste*, ed. Judith Bovensiepen (ANU Press, 2018), 29–42.
42. Susana Barnes, "Customary Renewal and the Pursuit of Power and Prosperity in Post-Occupation East Timor: A Case Study from Babulo, Uato-Lari" (PhD diss., Monash University, 2017).
43. Meitzner Yoder, "Genealogy."
44. Almeida, *A Sociolegal Analysis*, 62.
45. Bhandar, *Colonial lives of Property*.
46. Ann Stoler, "Imperial Debris: Reflections on Ruins and Ruination," *Cultural Anthropology* 23, no. 2 (2008): 191–219; Stoler, *Duress*.

PART I
Administrative Practices and Governance Strategies

1

The Roots of Inequality: *Sesmaria* Land Grants in Colonial Brazil

Carmen Alveal

The inequalities and injustice that pervade land ownership and occupation in Brazil are notorious. While much of the population (in both urban and rural areas) lives in precarious conditions with no official title to the land on which they live, a very small minority owns vast estates and the wealth and influence that go with them.[1] This inequality permeates every aspect of social, political, and cultural life in the country. Numerous studies have emphasized the importance of examining colonial land legacies to better understand their impact on present-day realities. Tania Murray Li, Ann Stoler, and Brenna Bhandar have, from different perspectives, considered how the race and social class of the individuals involved in agrarian conflicts influenced property rights and judicial decisions.[2] These factors have had, and continue to have, a very significant role in land rights in Brazil, particularly given the close social ties between the Brazilian judiciary and landowning classes and corporations.

The origin and development of land inequality in Brazil is closely related to the system of *sesmaria* land grants, which the Portuguese colonizers introduced into the country in the mid-sixteenth century.[3] The Portuguese jurist Marcello Caetano states that the social reality of the Portuguese colonization of Brazil led to distortion of the key principles underlying the original concept *sesmaria*, and Delmiro dos Santos has described the way in which the application of the *sesmaria* regime in the colony led to the creation of a dominant group of landowners (landlords) who controlled immense swaths of land.[4] *Sesmarias* can be broadly described as a conditional right to occupy land in return for cultivating it. They were introduced in Portugal in 1375, as a response to the social and economic ravages of the plague. Rural areas had suffered drastic depopulation. Crops withered in the fields and there was a persistent threat of food shortages in the towns and cities. In order to re-establish agricultural production, the Portuguese Crown issued *sesmarias* granting those who cultivated land lifelong rights to remain on it.[5]

With the expansion of Portuguese control over overseas territories in the sixteenth century, the Crown applied the system of *sesmarias* to the use and occupation of newly settled land. However, the attempt to impose the Portuguese model of *sesmaria* onto a vastly different territorial and social reality proved, in the long run, to be unworkable. Marcia Motta, in her work *Right to Land in Brazil*, describes in detail many of the serious problems that ensued in Portuguese America.[6]

Essentially, while *sesmarias* in Portugal were focused on the need to ensure agricultural production, in Portuguese America there were other pressing concerns. The territory was vast and sparsely populated by Indigenous people. Rival European powers were seeking to expand their possessions on the continent and there was an ever-present threat of invasion by other Europeans. The Indigenous populations in some areas were hostile to the Portuguese presence and engaged in armed conflict. The Crown's overriding aim was to ensure that its vast territory was occupied and secured against incursion. To that end, many of the *sesmaria* grants conferred in Brazil, particularly during the early years of colonization, were over very large areas of land that, in practice, were impossible for grantees to cultivate. Many of these grants were made to Portuguese nobles or others who had connections with the Crown or who had played key roles in the conquest and colonization of territory. Cultivation was not the primary objective of these individuals. The large land grants conferred social status and influence and considerable political power, akin to that of the seigneurial class in *ancien régime* Europe.[7]

The Portuguese Crown needed to ensure that it had allies in the colony who would defend its interests. That, to a very large extent, meant drawing on a relatively small group of people—namely, the *fidalgos*, Portuguese nobles, loyal to the Crown, who had access to the necessary social, political, and military means with which to exercise control in the colony.[8] *Fidalgos* were appointed to key posts, such as *capitão-mor* (administrative and military governance), *ouvidor* (administration of justice), and *provedor* (administration and collection of taxes and other revenue).

Many *fidalgos* were granted *sesmarias* over vast areas of land as a reward for their services (or to ensure their continued loyalty). As the land area of the colony increased following further incursions into the hinterland and successful military campaigns against Indigenous populations, this practice of granting *sesmarias* as a *mercê* (benefit) was widened to include land grants as a reward conferred on soldiers and other Crown agents in recognition for their service.[9]

The granting of *sesmarias* as a *mercê* had important consequences. In its original form in Portugal, the *sesmaria* was a conditional land grant—the main condition being that the grantee was to cultivate the land in order to ensure an adequate supply of agricultural produce to population centres. The *fidalgos* in Portuguese America, however, did not, in the main, consider themselves bound by this requirement. They were "nobles," born to rule over others and to reap the benefits of social position and prestige. For these individuals, the purpose of an extensive *sesmaria* grant in the colony was to enable them to exercise their role as seigneurs (major landowners), as their forefathers had done in Portugal, with others cultivating the land for their benefit and subject to their control.[10] Those who received land grants in reward for services rendered (e.g., army officers) were also inclined to this world view. They did not see themselves as the holders of a conditional grant. In their minds, they had the status of owners above the law, although in legal terms that clearly was not the case.

For a while, the system appeared to be working in some areas. The territory was vast and there was no shortage of fertile land. New settlers arriving in the colony, from Portugal and elsewhere in the empire, simply set up home in areas that were unoccupied, without the need to obtain any formal instrument or without knowledge of how to request a formal land title, and began to cultivate the land, mainly for their own subsistence. In many cases, they settled on land that had already been granted in *sesmaria* to another party. They were commonly referred to as *posseiros* (squatters) or *lavradores* (peasant-farmers). Over time, their number increased significantly. Other forms of land occupation emerged. For example, it was common practice for slave owners to give slaves (and former slaves) an area of land to cultivate for subsistence.[11] This coexistence of various forms of occupation and use of land became an established custom that was widely recognized in the colony, but was never reflected in legislation or the formal rules governing *sesmarias*.

The *fidalgos* and other major landowners, considering themselves to be landlords (*senhores da terra*) believed that the *posseiros*, *lavradores*, and other dwellers on "their" land were under a social and moral duty to pay rent (*rendas*) and yield, just as in the *ancien régime*. Charging *rendas* and yield was technically illegal under the applicable *sesmaria* legislation, but it was a widespread practice and was, in the main, tolerated, at least when the seigneurs were not excessive in their demands.[12] Jurist Paulo Grossi has stated that ownership of land is, above else, a matter of "mentality."[13] The powerful *senhores da terra* who held vast *sesmaria* land grants were in fact the holders of conditional land titles, but their mental construct was such that they had special ownership rights over land and people.[14]

As the number of new arrivals to the colony continued to increase, so did the demand for land. That led to considerable conflict over land rights. When, in the eighteenth century, there was a shift away from cattle rearing and agricultural production toward large-scale sugar production and the mining of precious minerals, the *senhores da terra* sought to interfere directly in the established customary rights of dwellers who had no formal instrument. They used their wealth and influence to evict *posseiros* and *lavradores* and usurped the rights of the holders of small-scale *sesmarias*. Research into the historical records, particularly petitions filed to the Overseas Council (Conselho Ultramarino) in Lisbon and other correspondence exchanged between holders of *sesmaria* grants and the central authorities in Portugal, has revealed the extent of the bitter conflict that ensued between powerful *senhores da terra* and less influential *sesmeiros*.[15] Some *sesmeiros* fought long and hard for recognition of their rights, occasionally with the support of local municipal authorities. Ultimately, however, the more socially and economically powerful landholders prevailed, and tens of thousands of *sesmeiros*, *posseiros*, and *lavradores* (the precise number is impossible to calculate) were unlawfully deprived of their land rights. The Crown was initially slow to intervene and when, from the 1750s onward, it made more serious attempts to tackle the gross violations being perpetrated in the colony, its efforts had limited success.[16]

In fact, the system of *sesmarias*, highly bureaucratic as it was, was weighted against less privileged members of colonial society. Settlers who wished to secure a definitive grant of a *sesmaria* were under a duty to cultivate the land following the provisional grant. These provisional grants were often very vaguely worded, and the precise area of the land unclear. The *sesmeiros* were required to arrange for formal measurement and demarcation (a complex and time-consuming process they had to pay for themselves) and then submit a petition to the king in Lisbon in order to receive formal and definitive land title.[17]

The way in which the system was administered also made life difficult for many *sesmeiros*. The Portuguese Crown sought to maintain ultimate control over colonial territories by establishing administrative bodies that had overlapping jurisdiction.[18] This meant that much of the work done by these bodies involved overseeing each other. In the case of *sesmarias*, captains-major (*capitão-mor*), revenue officials (*provedores*), legal ombudsmen (*ouvidores*), and local councils (*concelhos* or *camaras municipais*) were all involved in the administration of grants of *sesmaria* and frequently clashed over the question which measures were to be implemented, and how. Captains-major (governors) tended to be more concerned with security issues above all else and more inclined than other authorities to defend and even encourage occupation of land by undocumented *posseiros* and *lavradores*, because occupation of the land was a means of deterring invasions by foreign powers and Indigenous groups. The Crown, later, was more resistant to grants of *sesmarias* over large areas of land when the scale of the grants risked conflict with existing settlers.[19] Captains-major tended to be more aligned with local interests, which often clashed with centralized Crown policies.[20] *Provedores*, on the other hand, were usually focused on raising revenue for the Crown, even when that meant undermining established (but undocumented) land rights or demanding a high level of payments from *sesmeiros*. *Ouvidores* jealously guarded their prerogatives of demarcating *sesmaria* land, in legal lawsuits (and charging the respective fees), but they had several other legal duties, over and above their function of dealing with *sesmaria* disputes and demarcations, and in practice they were unable to effectively meet the demand for land measurement. The demarcation process was unwieldy and involved travelling to remote areas and then walking around vast areas of land. Demarcation disputes were common and *ouvidores* quite often found themselves embroiled in bitter conflicts, with threats of violence or intimidation. Despite the substantial fees they were entitled to charge, it was not uncommon for *ouvidores* to avoid exercising their duties far away from urban centres.[21]

Given these limitations on the exercise of the functions of the centralized colonial authorities, much of the work of administering *sesmarias* in rural areas was left to local town councils, known as *câmaras municipais* or *concelhos*. Members of the council sat as judges (known as *juizes ordinários* and without a formal law degree), dealing with local issues, including land disputes. Frequently, the geographical location of the councils and the consequent difficulties in communicating with the rest of the empire led to their developing distinct styles of governing and administering justice, which was sometimes out of step with official Crown policy. In larger towns, many of the councils were controlled by groups of local landholders, who used their position to expand their own power and influence.[22] In smaller towns and more remote areas, councils were often less homogenous in terms of their composition, with several illiterate members, as well as those from less privileged backgrounds, holding judicial office as *juizes ordinários*.[23] However, these smaller councils generally had less political leverage and were less able to effectively resist interference by colonial authorities or major landowners (*senhores de terras*).

The disparate nature of the councils meant that there was often a significant variation in their application of the rules on *sesmarias* and other land-related legislation. The *juizes ordinários* frequently relied on local customs when interpreting the statutory provisions, applying a case-by-case approach that was typical of the *ancien régime*.[24] In Portuguese America, custom-based rules were particularly important, given that it was not easy to apply Portuguese legal codes to a very different local reality, and also because there was still a huge influence of the *ius commune*.[25] These customs and the *ius commune* included acceptance of the simultaneous existence of various forms of conditional property rights (both documented and otherwise) over the same area of land. From early colonial times the notion of the property rights over land (*propriedade senhorial*) held by major landowners (the *senhores da terra*), often extending over vast areas, coexisted with the notion of conditional property rights, including *sesmarias* and the informal rights of *posseiros, lavradores*, former slaves, and Indigenous inhabitants.[26] On the other hand, there was, as we saw earlier, widespread social acceptance of the right of the *senhores da terra* to demand payment *(rendas)* from *posseiros, lavradores*, and others, even though the practice was prohibited by the applicable rules.

Throughout much of the colonial period, the courts upheld and sought to protect the custom-based rights of undocumented *posseiros* and *lavradores* to remain on the land. However, the advent of mineral and gold prospecting, particularly in the eighteenth century, led to an increased demand by the *senhores de terra* for unrestricted access to land. This in turn led to a surge in conflicts over land rights, including frequent allegations by smaller *sesmeiros* that their rights were being usurped by the *senhores de terra*. The local councils were, in the main, unable to curb illegal conduct by powerful *senhores da terra*. The individuals in question succeeded in consolidating their power either through violence or through influence trafficking with higher courts and the general government. Archived case records of local litigation and petitions submitted to the authorities in Lisbon reveal the extent to which small-scale *sesmeiros* and peasant-farmers (*lavradores*) were subjected to the greater power and influence of the *senhores de terras*. As a result, many "undocumented" inhabitants, including *sesmeiros* who had not been able to obtain royal confirmation of their definitive grant, were expelled from land their families had cultivated for generations.[27]

The divergent nature of the local councils was a source of concern for colonial authorities, and in the seventeenth century, in a drive to increase control over the territory, the Crown appointed circuit judges (*juizes de fora*) to sit in the principal towns and cities for three-year periods.[28] While their duties were initially limited to Crown revenue matters, these judges soon extended their jurisdiction to cover all types of lawsuits, including land issues. According to the Brazilian researcher Maria Fernanda Bicalho, historians have generally viewed these judges as agents of the Crown who were frequently at odds with municipal authorities, but it can also be argued that they played a valuable role in standardizing (and thus rendering more effective) the sometimes confusing legal and administrative parameters issued from Portugal.[29]

The Crown also established an appellate court—the Tribunal de Relação, the highest-instance court in colonial Brazil, sitting in Salvador (from 1609 onward) and, much later (beginning in 1750), in Rio de Janeiro. Appeals were permitted to the Overseas Council—or Conselho Ultramarino—in Lisbon and to the Portuguese Supreme Court (Casa da Suplicação) and the Royal High Court (Desembargo do Paço).[30] Many individuals bypassed the first-instance courts and submitted their case directly either to the Tribunal da Relação or one of the appellate courts in Lisbon, or even directly to the king.

There was considerable rivalry between the courts (particularly between the *juizes ordinários*, the *juizes de fora*, and the Court of Appeal (Tribunal da Relação), and frequent disputes as to jurisdiction. In practice, it was difficult for most *sesmeiros* to file proceedings before any court other than the local council (*câmara municipal*), and there are few recorded instances of ordinary *sesmeiros* successfully challenging powerful landowners before the higher courts.

The lack of effective recourse to justice meant that some individuals took the law into their own hands, while many others were simply deprived of their rights because they had no means of enforcing them.

Case Study: The Guedes de Brito Family

One of the main aims of historical research into *sesmarias* is to examine how the legal rules worked (or failed to work) in real life. That involves detailed investigation of the original legislation, the deeds of *sesmaria*, the records of cases filed before the courts, petitions submitted to central authorities in Lisbon, correspondence exchanged between administrative authorities in Brazil and the Portuguese Crown and Overseas Council, as well as first-hand accounts by contemporaries of events in the colony. One of the most striking histories pieced together by researchers, using the sources referred to above, is that of the Guedes de Brito family, a history that is in many ways emblematic of the failings and injustices of the *sesmaria* system in Brazil.

A manuscript stored at the National Library of Rio de Janeiro traces back through time a bitter land dispute that had persisted for decades in colonial Brazil. The document is a petition sent by the municipal council of Jacobina (Bahia Captaincy) in the late 1770s to Queen Dona Maria I (1777–1816).[31]

In its petition, the council described the harassment and violence perpetrated against local *sesmeiros* by the agents of an individual known as Dona Francisca Joana Josefa da Câmara Coutinho, the widow of Manoel de Saldanha da Gama.[32]

It was discovered from the records that in fact *sesmeiros* and other local inhabitants had been the victims of a concerted campaign of harassment that had started over fifty years earlier, perpetrated by the first wife of Manoel de Saldanha da Gama, Dona Joana da Silva Guedes deBrito. Further analysis of the document revealed that the problems had in fact begun with the actions of Joana's grandfather, Antônio Guedes deBrito.

Antônio Guedes de Brito (ca. 1627–94) was a notorious Indian-hunter who was given the title by the colonial authorities to the land he seized. He was granted several *sesmarias* that were registered in the Books of the Treasury in Salvador, but they were never formally confirmed in Portugal.

In fact, he obtained his first *sesmaria* in 1652, as a reward for military services, after he had "pacified most of the savage people" and had "spent a lot of money" doing so. On the basis that "there were pasture lands between the Tayaihu and Caguaohe hills that had never been populated," and since Antônio Guedes and his father "possessed wealth and many cattle," the colonial treasurer (*provedor-mor*) granted them an area of eight leagues each (approximately 1,118 square kilometres) "as it is merited, on the grounds of their financial capacity and the benefit to the common good."[33]

Antônio Guedes, together with his father, obtained a second *sesmaria* in 1655.[34] The historian Luiz Alberto Moniz Bandeira states that the Guedes de Brito family filed their applications for *sesmaria* land on the basis of a need to graze cattle (i.e., that they were going to use the land for agricultural purposes), whereas in truth their real interest was to obtain access to areas where there was a potential for mining.[35] In the light of the assets that the Guedes de Brito declared in their application, the colonial treasurer decided that they had sufficient means to adequately cultivate the land, and again he had no hesitation in granting the application.

Antonio Guedes de Brito continued to wage war against Indigenous people and to hunt fugitive slaves who fled to *quilombos*.[36] This increased his prestige with the colonial authorities. He is also reported to have fought against Dutch forces in northeastern Brazil and to have led several expeditions into the hinterland to expand colonial territory.[37] He commanded what was, in effect, a private army, paying the wages of the troops from his personal resources.

The area of land held by Guedes de Brito in *sesmaria* was enormous, even by the standards of the time. The Filipinas Ordinances (Ordenações Filipinas) of 1603 did not place any limit on the scale of grants, merely stating that the area of land granted should be commensurate with the *sesmeiro*'s capacity to cultivate it. It was perfectly consistent with colonial policy at that time to grant Antonio

Guedes de Brito, a wealthy soldier who owned livestock and had a solid record of enslaving or expelling Indigenous people, all the land he requested.

In 1663, Antonio Guedes de Brito applied for a third *sesmaria*, this time jointly with Bernardo Vieira Ravasco, a former military officer who, interestingly, had been the secretary of state who registered Brito's two earlier *sesmarias* in the treasury records in Salvador. Brito and Ravasco justified their application on the grounds that the land they sought, in the hinterland, could be used for cattle rearing and crops and that they were prepared to cultivate it at their own expense. This, they argued, would be of great benefit to the royal treasury and the common good (the same grounds Brito had used for his previous applications). The application was successful, and they were granted a *sesmaria* over land extending from the source of the River Itapicuru up to the São Francisco River, and "also as many leagues as there are from the source of the Tapicurú to that of the Paraguassú" (a distance of approximately 250 kilometres).[38]

None of the three *sesmarias* granted to Antônio Guedes de Brito were confirmed by the king in Portugal, which means that they were not completely legally valid, and could therefore be foreclosed by the Crown. This, however, did not prevent Antônio Guedes de Brito from becoming one of the largest landowners (*senhores de terra*) in the colony. In addition to amassing vast areas of land, he was awarded a series of military honours, including the titles of sergeant major (*sargento-mor*) and field marshal (*mestre de campo*).[39] In January 1671, he inherited title to a notary public's office—a highly strategic position in the colonial administration. Later, in 1679 he became a knight of the realm (*fidalgo cavaleiro da casa real*) by royal appointment, definitively establishing himself as a member of the colonial nobility.[40]

Antônio Guedes da Silva married Guiomar Ximenes de Aragão in 1677, but they produced no heirs. He did, however, father a daughter, out of wedlock, by an Indigenous woman named Serafina de Sousa Dormundo. He appointed the child, Isabel Maria Guedes da Silva, his official heir. Following Antonio's sudden death in around 1692 (the exact date is unknown) Isabel inherited her father's fortune.

Isabel Maria Guedes da Silva grew up and married Colonel Antonio da Silva Pimentel, who also owned a considerable amount of land (including *sesmarias* that were not confirmed by the Crown in Portugal).[41] They did not produce male heirs, and their vast wealth passed to their daughter, Joana da Silva Guedes de Brito.

Both Isabel Maria and her daughter Joana (Antonio Guedes de Brito's granddaughter) suffered considerable discrimination and ridicule because of their Indigenous ancestry.[42] They nevertheless succeeded in protecting and increasing their fortune and, over time, they were able to secure a certain degree of social status. In 1717, Joana da Silva Guedes de Brito married a *fidalgo*, Dom João de Mascarenhas (the son of Count Coculim), who, unusually for the time, agreed to move from Portugal to take up residence with his wife in the Portuguese colony. The marriage was widely considered to be a strategic alliance. Joana Guedes da Silva possessed vast wealth and Dom João de Mascarenhas was of "noble blood." The match was not, however, a happy one. Dom João de Mascarenhas was contemptuous of his wife's racial background. He also began to misappropriate property and money. Eventually, Joana and her mother joined forces and denounced him to the king. Dom João de Mascarenhas was arrested and returned to Lisbon in disgrace.

Joana da Silva Guedes de Brito married again, aged forty. Her second husband was another Portuguese *fidalgo*, Manoel de Saldanha da Gama, twenty-one years her junior. He was the son of Dom João Saldanha da Gama, the fifth Count of Ponte and viceroy of the Indies. Following Joana and Manoel's marriage, the assets of the Guedes de Brito family were renamed the estate of the House of Ponte (Casa de Ponte) and the Guedes de Brito *sesmarias*, despite not having been confirmed by the king, were merged into the joint estate.

Joana died, childless, in 1762, leaving her husband as sole heir. The widowed Manoel de Saldanha da Gama returned to Portugal in 1776, where he married Francisca Joana Josefa da Câmara Coutinho and fathered four children,[43] who inherited the estate, including the former assets of Joana Guedes de Brito.[44]

The wealth of the Guedes de Brito family was based on extensive *sesmaria* holdings. These holdings were never given the required assent by the Crown (in fact there is no record that the family ever applied to Lisbon for confirmation of their grants). In other words, the family did not comply with the requirements of *sesmaria* legislation.[45] In legal terms, their *sesmarias* lapsed approximately five years after the date of the initial provisional grant and thus could (should) have been foreclosed by Crown authorities. However, having succeeded, by strategic marriage and political alliances, to acquire the status of "nobles," the family was able not only to retain and increase its wealth, but to exploit and disrupt the legitimate rights of other land users.

Throughout the eighteenth century the Guedes de Brito family and its successors engaged in legal battles and in unofficial, illegal manoeuvres (including threats and violence) to expel local residents from their lands or to otherwise exploit them. The family, which lived in Salvador and later in Portugal (following Manoel de Saldanha daGama's return to Lisbon), relied on a network of agents (lawyers, bailiffs, and henchmen) who acted on their orders.

The Historical Overseas Archives (Arquivo Histórico Ultramarino) in Lisbon contain several representations, petitions, and reports submitted to the Crown by colonial authorities in Brazil reporting abuses perpetrated by the Guedes family against the inhabitants of the land that fell within their *sesmarias*. The records of the National Library of Rio de Janeiro (Biblioteca Nacional do Rio de Janeiro) also contain a similar representation to the king submitted by the Jacobina municipal council.

The conflict in the Jacobina region came to a head during the eighteenth-century gold rush. Mines had been discovered in Jacobina and Rio de Contas and the area offered the potential for great wealth.[46] This led to disputes over the control of the best sites (*datas*). Smallholders (*posseiros, lavradores*, or small-scale *sesmeiros*) who discovered gold or other precious minerals on the land they cultivated were targeted by powerful individuals and groups, who used official and unofficial means (including violence) to evict them.[47] Joana da Silva Guedes de Brito and Manoel de Saldanha da Gama began to extort payment of rent on "their" land in an attempt to persuade the occupants to move away. When that failed, they likely resorted to forced evictions.

The residents of Jacobina filed suit before the municipal council, arguing that they had been the first settlers to make productive use of the land and that they were already paying heavy duties to the Crown in the form of tithes and duty on foodstuffs, slaves, and religious sacraments. Now the Guedes de Brito family was demanding further payments.[48]

They asked the first-instance judge to examine the "fantastical" land deeds held by the Guedes de Brito family. The petitioners were fully aware that the *sesmaria* instruments were not valid in the eyes of the law because the grant had not been confirmed by the Crown and that the areas in question were much larger than the half-league of land stipulated in the current legislation. In a subsequent submission to the king they wrote that "the Respondent [Joana Guedes de Brito] holds no valid title whatsoever, but is merely an intruder."[49]

In fact, even before the case was heard at first instance, Dona Joana Guedes de Brito filed suit before the Court of Appeal (Tribunal da Relação) in Salvador, where she lived, requesting eviction orders against dwellers on land in the Jacobina region and asserting her legal rights as the holder of a *sesmaria*. The court in Salvador ruled in her favour, on the basis that the defendants were in default (i.e., they had not travelled 365 kilometres to attend a hearing, about which they had probably not been notified).[50] Following her victory, Joana Guedes de Brito's agents, together with armed soldiers from Salvador, went to the home of some of those who opposed her and caused "significant destruction."[51]

Appalled by these events, a member of the Jacobina municipal council, João Dias Rego, appealed on behalf of the inhabitants of the town of Santo Antonio de Jacobina to the Supreme Court (Casa da Suplicação) in Lisbon and directly to the king himself.[52] In accordance with standard practice, his petition was submitted first to the Council for Overseas Affairs (Conselho Ultramarino) before being forwarded to the king.

In their representation to the king, the residents of Jacobina stated that Joana Guedes de Brito had secured a favourable court order by manipulation (*industriozamente*)[53] and that her agents had then perpetrated acts of violence in the area, "unlawfully evicting dwellers from their farms, then selling or leasing the land to whom they saw fit, committing the greatest barbarities, for which losses we beg redress from Your Majesty."[54]

The Council for Overseas Affairs (Conselho Ultramarino) consulted the Portuguese secretary of state, Diogo de Mendonça Corte Real, in Lisbon. He voiced suspicions as to the decision taken by the Court of Appeal in Salvador, Brazil, and stated that Joana Guedes de Brito was seeking "to charge rent [*rendas*], on the basis of alleged and supposed *sesmarias*, over lands that contain gold mines, which belong to your Majesty."[55] The Council asked the ombudsman-general (*ouvidor-geral*) of Bahia, José dos Santos Varjão, to hear the parties, investigate the *sesmarias* of Joana Guedes de Brito, and report back.

Having considered the report then sent to him, the king, Dom João V, in 1737 ordered the Court of Appeal (Tribunal da Relação) in Bahia to take all the necessary measures to "put an end to the violence perpetrated by Donna Joana da Silva Guedes de Brito." The king further directed that the order granted by the Court of Appeal (the Tribunal da Relação in Salvador) in favour of Joana Guedes de Brito be stayed and that Joana Guedes de Brito submit all *sesmarias* for inspection by the "highest authority." Astonishingly, the supreme justice of the Court of Appeal simply refused to submit to the king's order, almost certainly at the instigation of Joana Guedes de Brito, and it was effectively ignored.[56]

The final outcome of the appeal of the residents of Jacobina to the Supreme Court (Casa da Suplicação) is still unknown as it has not been possible to access all of the case records at the National Archives of the Torre do Tombo in Portugal.

What is known is that almost forty years later, the situation was largely unchanged, and the descendants of the Guedes de Brito family were still perpetrating abuses in the Jacobina area. The municipal council, in 1770, again petitioned the king. The Guedes de Brito/House of Ponte were accused of extorting unlawful payments from smallholders and other residents and of harassment and threats. The council again stated that the House of Ponte had failed to comply with the legal requirement of cultivating *sesmaria* land within the statutory period of five years, and that their entitlement to title had therefore lapsed. According to the petitioners the Guedes de Brito family was farming only a few small areas on the banks of the São Francisco River, yet at the same time was using its influence in the area to impose a series of obligations on residents, such as the payment of duties on certain products or rent on lands they (the House of Pontes) were (unlawfully) leasing out.[57]

The argument of failure to cultivate the lands raised a key legal issue.[58] According to the applicable ordinance—tome 4, title 43, paragraph 16—if *sesmaria* land was not cultivated within the stipulated period, it was to be transferred to another *sesmeiro* or to the persons who effectively cultivated it. The residents argued that as the Guedes de Brito family had neither demarcated their land nor adequately cultivated it, they had forfeited their right to the *sesmarias*. In such circumstances, those who were actually occupying and farming the land had legitimate entitlement to acquire title, which was also presented in *ius commune* tradition.

Conclusion

The various arguments as to the facts and the law raised in this litigation were symbolic of the social forces at play, and of the construction of discursive practices and mechanisms of power.[59] The Guedes de Brito/House of Ponte regarded themselves as *senhores da terra* exercising land ownership rights (*senhorio*), so that their titles to the land, unlike an unconfirmed *sesmaria*, were not subject to any requirement for cultivation.

While there was provision for status of *senhor da terra* in the legislation applicable to colonial Brazil, and the law distinguished such individuals from ordinary *sesmeiros*, both the Manuelina and Filipinas Ordinances made it very clear that any disputes as to *sesmarias* involving *senhores de terra* were to be resolved by the courts. In that sense, the *senhores da terra*, despite their privileged social status, were officially subject to the same treatment as "common" *sesmeiros* and had no authority to take the law into their own hands. Furthermore, the use of "agents" (*procuradores*) to manage and administer land was prohibited by the legislation, although this rule was often ignored in colonial Brazil.

The Guedes da Silva/House of Ponte believed themselves to be legitimately and morally entitled to own huge swaths of land, and to demand rent (*renda*) from those who farmed it (i.e., they considered themselves to have ownership rights over land and rights to charge rent). The residents of Jacobina, on the other hand, believed themselves, on the basis of *ius commune* and the *sesmaria* system, to have an undeniable right to the land they cultivated and from which they contributed to the royal coffers.[60] It was the local settlers, they argued, that had been responsible for the development of the region, and for securing the land against hostile incursions. They also argued that as mining lands were subject to the jurisdiction of the Crown, only the king was entitled to exercise the relevant prerogatives.[61]

At the time of the submission of this representation to Dona Maria I, the lawsuit filed by João Dias Rego before the Supreme Court (Tribunal de Suplicação) forty years earlier had still not been decided. The order issued by the king had been ignored, as described above, and the successor to the Guedes de Brito/Casa de Ponte estate, Dona Francisca da Câmara Coutinho, was continuing to exploit and harass local residents. The residents argued before the queen that, pending a final order on the Supreme Court case, no one was entitled to "innovate" in terms of making demands of the residents based on recent mining legislation, nor could anyone be deprived of their legitimate possession of land they cultivated even if the *senhores da terra* were *fidalgos*.[62]

The residents expressed a fear that the records of the long-standing case before the Supreme Court might somehow be lost, thereby benefitting their opponents.[63] Their concern was that the records might be deliberately removed by someone with a vested interest, or indeed that they might already have been lost in the major earthquake that devastated Lisbon in 1755.

The final outcome of the representation sent to Dona Maria is not known. Given the fifty-year history leading up to it, however, it seems unlikely that the response (if any) led to a timely and just solution. This dispute exemplifies the way in which the occupation and use of land was viewed by different agents in colonial society. The *sesmaria* was a conditional property right governed by a complex, highly bureaucratic administrative and legal system. The distribution of lands by *sesmaria* was a privilege that was highly sought after by influential individuals who aspired to be being *senhores de terras* in the Portuguese Empire.

NOTES TO CHAPTER 1

1. Less than 1 per cent of agricultural landowners own over 45 per cent of rural land. Large land estates (i.e., those of over 1,000 hectares in area) receive over 43 per cent of government agricultural credits but produce only 40 per cent of the country's agricultural yield, 70 per cent of which is produced by smaller landholdings. "Menos de 1% das propriedades agrícolas é dona de quase metade da área rural brasileira," Oxfam Brasil, 27 August 2019, https://www.oxfam.org.br/publicacao/menos-de-1-das-propriedades-agricolas-e-dona-de-quase-metade-da-area-rural-brasileira/.
2. Tania Murray Li, *Land's End: Capitalist Relations on an Indigenous Frontier* (Duke University Press, 2014); Ann Stoler, ed., *Imperial Debris: On Ruins and Ruination* (Duke University Press, 2013); Brenna Bhandar, *Colonial Lives of Property: Law, Land, and Racial Regimes of Ownership* (Duke University Press, 2018).
3. José da Costa Porto, *Estudo sobre o sistema sesmaria* (Imprensa Universitária, 1965); Ruy Cirne Lima, *Pequena História territorial do Brasil: Sesmarias e terras devolutas* (Sulinas, 1954). *Sesmarias* existed only in the Atlantic Portuguese Empire. In Mozambique the term used was *prazos*, as explained by José Adelina in this volume.
4. Marcello Caetano, "As sesmarias no direito luso-brasileiro," *Revista do Instituto Histórico e Geográfico Brasileiro*, no. 348 (1985): 19–34; Delmiro dos Santos, *Direito Agrário: Sesmarias, terras devolutas, registro paroquial e legislação agrária* (CEJUP, 1986).
5. Virginia Rau, *Sesmarias medievais Portuguesas* (Estampa, 1946).
6. Marcia Maria Menendes Motta, *Right to Land in Brazil: The Gestation of the Conflict 1795–1824* (Universidade Federal Fluminense, 2014).
7. Alberto Passos Guimarães, *Quatro séculos de latifúndio* (Paz e terra, 1988); Erivaldo Fagundes Neves, *Estrutura fundiária e dinâmica mercantil: Alto sertão da Bahia, séculos XVIII e XIX* (EDUFBA/UEFS, 2005); Luiz Alberto Moniz Bandeira, *O feudo: A Casa da Torre de Garcia d'Ávila: Da conquista dos sertões à independência do Brasil* (Civilização Brasileira, 2000); Margarida Sobral Neto, *Terra e conflito: Região de Coimbra 1700–1834* (Palimage Editores, 1997); Porto, *Estudo*.
8. Rodrigo Ricúpero, *A formação da elite colonial* (Alameda, 2009); João Fragoso, "A nobreza da República: Notas sobre a formação da elite senhorial do Rio de Janeiro (séculos XVI e XVII)," *Topoí* 1, no. 1 (2000): 45–123.
9. Fragoso, "A nobreza"; Carmen Alveal, "Converting Land into Property in the Portuguese Atlantic World, 16th–18th Century" (PhD diss., Johns Hopkins University, 2007).
10. Célia Nonata da Silva, *Territórios de mando: Banditismo em Minas Gerais, século XVIII* (Crisálida, 2007); Carmen Alveal, "De senhorio colonial a território de mando: Os acossamentos de Antônio Vieira de Melo no Sertão do Ararobá (Pernambuco, século XVIII)," *Revista Brasileira de História*, no. 35 (2016): 41–64.
11. Ciro Cardoso, *Escravo ou camponês? O protocampesinato negro nas Américas* (Brasiliense, 1987); Jacob Gorender, *O escravismo colonial* (Editora Ática, 1985). See also Rohrig, this volume.
12. Bandeira, *O feudo*.
13. Paolo Grossi, *História da propriedade e outros ensaios* (Renovar, 2006), 30.
14. Carmen Alveal, "A eficácia da ordem régia de 1697 na zona de pecuária das Capitanias do Norte," in *O domínio de outrem: Posse e propriedade na Era Moderna (Portugal e Brasil)*, ed. Márcia Motta and Monica Piccolo (Editora UEMA, 2017), 69–90; Carmen Alveal, "As vexações e opressões dos senhores coloniais e a constituição da carta régia de 1753 no brasil colonial: A tradição da posse e o justo título," *Outros Tempos* 14, no. 23 (2017): 158–74.
15. In this chapter, we refer to the holders of *sesmaria* grants as *sesmeiros*. Originally, in Portugal, the term *sesmeiro* referred to the official who was responsible for the grant and administration of *sesmarias*.
16. Porto, *Estudo*.
17. Porto.
18. José Mattoso, *História de Portugal* (Editorial Estampa, 1994); António Manuel Hespanha, *Ás vésperas do Leviathan*: Instituições e Poder Político—Portugal, *Século XVII* (Livraria Almedina, 1994).
19. Only in 1697 was the maximum size of a *sesmaria* finally established at 3 leagues by 1 league. Porto, *Estudo*; Lima, *Pequena*; Nelson Nozoe, "A aplicação da legislação sesmarial em território brasileiro," *Estudios Historicos* 6, no. 12 (2014): 1–26; Alveal, "A eficácia."
20. Porto, *Estudo*; Lima, *Pequena*; Nozoe, "A aplicação"; Alveal, "A eficácia."
21. Patrícia de Oliveira Dias, "O demarcador de terras: Atuação do desembargador Cristóvão Soares Reimão no processo de demarcação de sesmarias na ribeira do Jaguaribe (Capitania do Ceará—Brasil) (1700–1710)," *Revista de História da UEG* 5, no. 2 (2016): 86–109; Alveal, "Converting."

22 Maria Fernanda Batista Bicalho, "As Câmaras Utramarinas e o Governo do Império," in *Antigo Regime nos Trópicos: a Dinâmica Imperial Portuguesa, Séculos XVI–XVIII*, ed. João Fragoso, Maria de Fátima Gôuvea, and Maria Fernanda Bicalho (Civilização Brasileira, 2001), 189–221; Pedro Puntoni, "Bernardo Vieira Ravasco, Secretário do Estado do Brasil: Podere Elites na Bahia do Século XVII," in *Modos de Governar: Idéias e Práticas Políticas no Império Português, Séculos XVI ao XIX*, ed. Maria Fernanda Bicalho and Vera Lúcia do Amaral Ferlini (São Paulo: Alameda, 2005), 157–78.

23 E.g., Santo Antonio de Jacobina and Nossa Senhora do Livramento das Minas do Rio de Contas, in the captaincy of Bahia, and the town of Moucha (now called Oeiras), in the captaincy of Piauí. Alveal, "Converting."

24 Arno Wheling and Maria José Wheling, *Direito e Justiça no Brasil Colonial: O Tribunal da Relação do Rio de Janeiro (1751–1808)* (Renovar, 2004).

25 Antonio Manuel Hespanha, *Como os juristas viam o mundo (1550–1750): Direitos, estados, coisas, contratos, ações e crimes* (Livraria Almedina, 1994).

26 Carmen Alveal, "Land, Politics, and Society in Late Colonial Brazil: A Native American Perspective," in *International Seminar on the History of the Atlantic World, 1500–1800*, ed. Bernard Baylin (Harvard University, 2004), 1–31; Maria Regina Celestino de Almeida, *Metamorfoses Indígenas: Identidade e Cultura nas Aldeias Coloniais do Rio de Janeiro* (Arquivo Nacional, 2001).

27 See the authoritative work of the legal historian Laura Beck Varela, who studied the transition in Brazil from the system of *sesmarias*, with its emphasis on conditional ownership of land, to modern laws of property (as expressed in the Napoleonic Code and other civil codes), which make far greater provision for absolute property rights based on formal, registered title. Laura Beck Varela, *Das sesmarias à propriedade moderna: Um estudo de história do direito brasileiro* (Renovar, 2005).

28 *Juízes de fora* sat both as first-instance judges and as appellate judges, hearing appeals from the *juízes ordinários*, who were first-instance local judges, members of the municipal councils, who tried local issues.

29 Bicalho, "As Câmaras."

30 The Royal High Court, or "Court of the Royal Palace" (Desembargo do Paço), became a higher appellate court in its own right in 1521, when it was granted autonomy from the Supreme Court (Casa de Suplicação). Ana Maria do Rosário S. Rodrigues, *Desembargo do Paço* (Instituto dos Arquivos Nacionais/Torre do Tombo, 2000), 13–27. Unfortunately, the archives of civil lawsuits before the Casa da Suplicação are not yet available for public inspection, unlike the records of criminal proceedings.

31 The petition was signed by the following representatives of the council: the judge José Moreira Maia São Payo and council members Manuel Pimenta, Vasconcelos, João Mariano Xavier, and Pedro José Gonçalvez Vitoria. "Representação da Câmara de Jacobina a S. M. pedindo obstasse a continuação dos vexames que faziam os procuradores de D. Francisca da Camara, viúva de Manoel Saldanha aos moradores ali, e historiando a origem da sesmaria da dita senhora," 3 February 1775, 425, Manuscript Section, II-33, 27, 8, National Library of Rio de Janeiro. Hereinafter referred to as "Representation."

32 Representation, 425.

33 "Carta de sesmaria a Antonio Brito Correa e Antonio Guedes de Brito," in *Documentos Históricos* 18 (1928), 346–8.

34 "Carta de sesmaria a Antonio Brito Correa e Antonio Guedes de Brito," in *Documentos Históricos* 18 (1928), 339–41.

35 Bandeira, *O feudo*, 161.

36 A *quilombo* is a settlement founded by people of African origin.

37 André João Antonil, *Cultura e Opulência no Brasil* (Edições Melhoramentos, 1976), 233–5, 211.

38 "Carta de sesmaria a Antonio Guedes de Brito," in *Documentos Históricos* 21 (1928), 185–7.

39 Neves, *Estrutura*.

40 The term "colonial nobility" in this context refers to the group of people, born in the colony or émigrés from Portugal or another part of the Portuguese Empire who settled in Brazil, cultivated and developed lands, and were actively involved in local political and administrative circles. For further analysis of the term, see Fragoso, "A nobreza."

41 Bandeira, *O feudo*, 174.

42 For a biography of Isabel Maria Guedes da Silva and her daughter Joana da Silva Guedes da Silva, see Maria Aparecida Schumaher, *Dicionário Mulheres do Brasil: De 1500 até a Atualidade* (Jorge Zahar Editor, 2000), 283–4, 291–2.

43 Including the sixth Count of Ponte, João de Saldanha da Gama Melo Torres Guedes de Brito, who inherited the family fortune and came to Brazil in 1808 together with the Portuguese royal family. He was governor and captain-general of Bahia until his death one year later.
44 Pedro Calmon, *História da Casa da Torre: Uma dinastia de pioneiros* (Livraria José Olympo Editora, 1958), 85.
45 Some scholars argue that Antônio Guedes de Brito legally altered his assets (estate) into a primogeniture (*morgado*), which was then inherited by Isabela Guedes de Brito. See Bandeira, *O fuedo*, 161; Calmon, "História," 83. If that is in fact the case, it could be argued that some provisions of the *sesmaria* legislation no longer applied to the estate (e.g., the requirement to cultivate the land).
46 No specific date is given for the discovery of gold in Jacobina. Boxer fixed the discovery of gold in the Rio das Mortes and Rio Doce regions between 1693 and1695. Charles Boxer, *A Idade de Ouro do Brasil* (Nova Fronteira, 2000), 62.
47 Boxer, *A Idade*, 74.
48 "Consulta do Conselho Ultramarino ao rei D. João V sobre o pedido de João Dias e como procurador dos moradores e roceiros do continente das Minas da vila de Santo António da Jacobina," Papéis Avulsos, Bahia, Arquivo Historico Ultramarino, 17 March 1736, Box 65, Doc. 47.
49 Consulta, "A suplicada não é dona de título algum, mas somente intrusa."
50 Seigneurs (*senhores de terra*) who were also *fidalgos* were legally entitled to file suit directly before the Court of Appeal bypassing the first-instance court. *Ordenações Filipinas*, book 2, title 25.
51 Consulta.
52 Consulta.
53 Representation, 428.
54 Representation.
55 Consulta, Diogo de Mendonca Corte Real was appointed secretary of state for the navy and overseas affairs in 1750, as a substitute for António Guedes Pereira.
56 Representation, 428.
57 Representation, 425.
58 Representation, 426.
59 Pierre Bourdieu, "A força do direito: Elementos para uma sociologia do campo jurídico," in *O Poder Simbólico* (Difel, 1989), 209–54.
60 The representation also confirms that the region had been cultivated by "the people," some of whom participated in the mining of gold, with others spread throughout the countryside, establishing smallholdings and farms for their subsistence and constructing mills. Representation, 426.
61 *Ordenações Filipinas*, book 2, titles 27 and 43.
62 Representation, 429.
63 Representation, 430.

2

From Squatters to Smallholders? Configurations of African Land Access in Central and Southern Colonial Mozambique, 1910s–1940s

Bárbara Direito

Introduction

In 1906, Machoana, an *indígena* (native) African woman, was granted a temporary individual land title, for which she paid 5,000 reis, regarding a tract of land she had been occupying for five years. In the same year, Gimo made a similar request regarding a vacant tract, and was also granted a land title, for which he paid 30,000 reis.[1] These are just two examples of the several land concessions to African *indígenas* that can be found at the Arquivo Histórico Ultramarino in Lisbon, which holds most of the documentation regarding Portugal's former colonies. The narrow notion of "native property" applicable at the time meant that, in theory, Africans could obtain individual rights to land after twenty years of continuous use of such land.[2] A few years later, once the 1909 Mozambique Land Law came into effect and purportedly increased the protection awarded to Africans while at the same time stimulating concessions to settlers, the wording was discreetly changed. The new provisions spoke merely of "concessions to natives," of "occupancy" rights in vacant land, and of "native" reserves. The two worlds of "civilized populations"—mostly of European origin, subject to "modern" legislation and the principles of individual property—and of "natives"—African populations, subject to African customary law and principles of communal property—were to be almost totally separated, with few exceptions.

These subtle changes in land legislation reflected one aspect of the "native" policy that was beginning to take shape as the Portuguese gradually took effective control of Mozambique in the first years of the twentieth century. And much like in other colonial contexts, in Africa and other continents, the Portuguese were "constructing racialized difference" through these laws.[3]

But the provisions of the land laws, the ideals that inspired the land policies put in place by officials, and the actual reality on the ground were different.[4] And these three dimensions were in themselves influenced by international, national, and local dynamics that need to be taken into consideration, as well as by different agents, often with opposing interests and powers. Bearing in mind these different nuances and layers, the present chapter will discuss the changing configurations of African land access in Mozambique between the 1910s and the 1940s. It will do so in the context of the tension between divergent goals, new and old: maintaining a steady supply of African labour to public and private projects; maintaining "native" tax revenue; addressing the decline of European settler farming in the 1920s, worsened by the Great Depression; and responding to the demand for agricultural commodities through an agrarian intervention in African production. The latter goal, discussed in Mozambique as much as in Portugal and in international fora during this period, involved the expansion of cash crops, the promotion of "rational" agricultural practices, and technical assistance for Africans, but also population displacement and resettlement. Unlike previous policies that excluded the majority of Africans from land tenure and viewed them mostly as squatters, the plans inspired by this goal proposed a new perspective on African land access and use.

This transformation was justified by the need to increase yields and by a narrative concerning the improvement of living standards for Africans, but it was also based on a degree of paternalism and coercion, laying the ground for post-1945 calls for African "rural development."

Drawing on an array of sources consulted in different archives and libraries in Portugal and Mozambique, the chapter will discuss the outcomes of the tensions between these different goals in southern and central Mozambique by focusing on three specific configurations: The legalization of Africans living on alienated and vacant land; the separation of plots for individual smallholders inside native reserves; and *colonatos*, or model settlements, involving the parcelling and distribution of plots to African smallholders on vacant land.[5] This will allow us to understand the complexity of rural life in colonial Mozambique, to observe the conditions of changing agrarian relations, and to view land as a disputed resource. By looking at the evolution of these instruments in two distinct regions of Mozambique, one governed by a chartered company and the other under direct

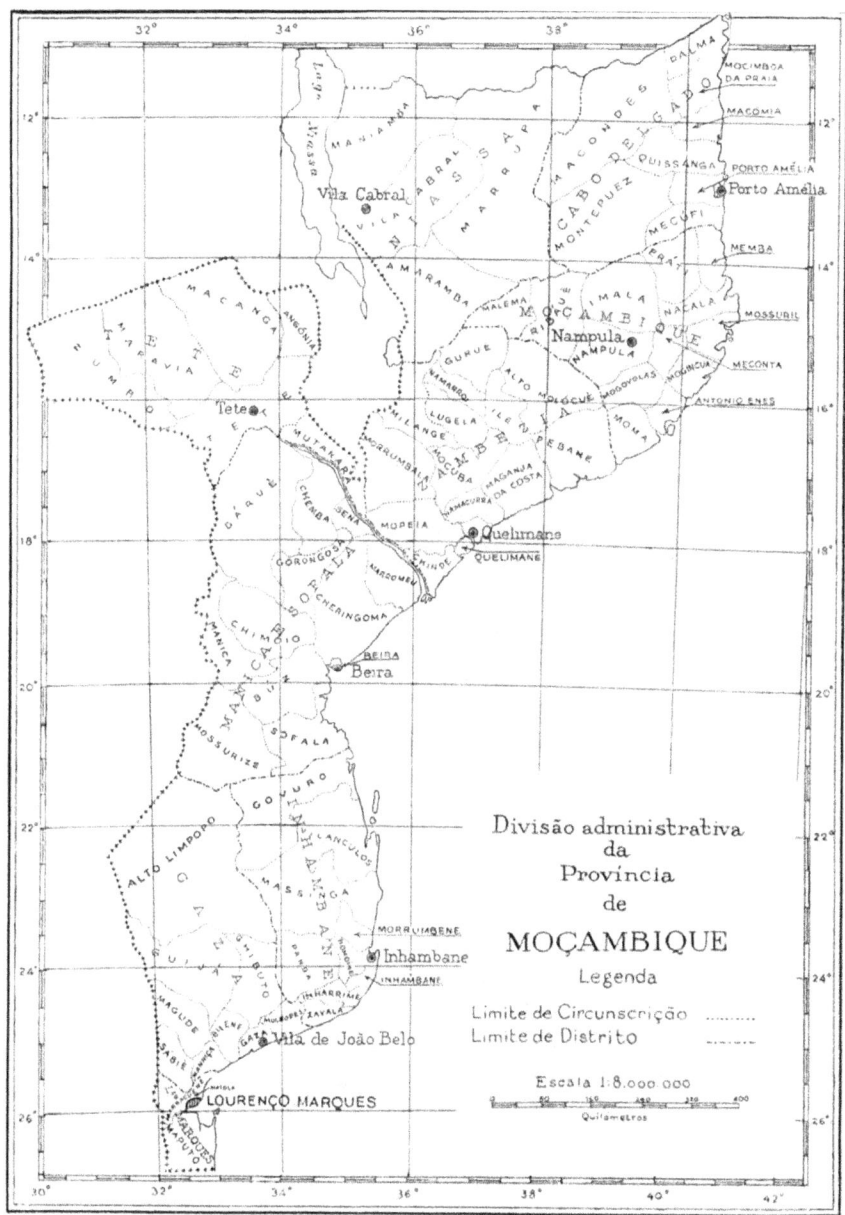

Map 2.1. Map of Mozambique, 1929

Source: *Boletim Geral das Colónias*, no. 50 (1929): 5.

Portuguese rule, the chapter furthermore seeks to highlight the importance of context by showing how similar circumstances on the ground could lead to different configurations in terms of African access to land. Finally, I also want to discuss how African populations dealt with encroachment upon their land and with mounting disputes with settlers, but also with attempts to transform their farming practices, while trying to maintain their own autonomy.

Land Tenure in Early Twentieth-Century Colonial Mozambique: Principles and Practice

The dominant perspective in Portuguese colonial thought in the late nineteenth and early twentieth centuries, inscribed in the period's land laws, dictated the limited access of Africans to land in the name of the economic development of colonial territories, the fight against land speculation, and the safeguarding of Portuguese sovereignty in Africa. More specifically, this meant that the presence of African populations, cultivated lands, and livestock did not constitute an impediment to land concessions. It also meant that the new landholders would have the prerogative to decide the fate of these African occupants, or "squatters." These principles applied equally to the regions of Manica and Sofala, in central Mozambique, under the rule of a chartered company—the Mozambique Company—between 1892 and 1942, and to the south of Mozambique, a region under direct Portuguese rule (see map 2.1).[6]

The main colonial thinkers and officials of the time argued that this dual system was justified because of the backwardness of African populations and their traditional farming system, based on the periodic search for better agricultural land. They also believed that Africans' lack of understanding of the concept of individual property could jeopardize the colonial state's control over land allocation for agriculture and European settlement plans.[7] Africans were thus to make way for settlers while maintaining their own traditions. This perspective was a clear corollary of the dominant view about African populations as intellectually and morally inferior, and it became a convenient ally of the system of forced labour, the crux of Portuguese colonial policies in Mozambique.[8]

But as important scholarship has shown regarding other territories in southern Africa, the reality of agrarian life was much more complex than colonial officials anticipated in Lisbon, in Lourenço Marques, or in the boardroom of the Mozambique Company. Indeed, the economic and social impact of these laws in the lives of African populations differed from region to region, according to elements such as settler presence, the dimension of land concessions, labour demand, economic interests, the availability of transport infrastructure, population density, and ecological conditions. Some regions would not experience significant dispossession until the 1950s, when Portugal invested in earnest in white settlement in Mozambique. In other areas, as will be shown below, increasing competition over land between Africans and the new landowners, and between their different agricultural practices, interests, and expectations, can be documented as early as the 1900s.

In response to these tensions over land and fearing the loss of a pool of readily available rural labourers and decreasing tax revenue, colonial thinkers and officials, in both Portugal and in Mozambique, called for further "protection" measures, or rights of occupancy, to be extended to African populations. Colonial officials were slowly realizing the difficulty of reaching the delicate balance between promoting economic expansion and maintaining a steady labour force. The "native reserve" (*reserva indígena*), ubiquitous in southern and southeastern Africa in this period, was one of the instruments used by colonial governments to address these concerns, but also to alleviate mounting rural disputes and to encourage Africans to settle.[9] Though with specific histories and consequences in South Africa, Southern Rhodesia (today's Zimbabwe), or Mozambique, to name only three of the territories where this policy was put in place, reserves were generally aimed at dividing space between settler and African populations, at the symbolic and economic levels. This not only strongly affected the latter's lives under colonial rule but would in some cases have lasting consequences in post-independence African states. Why colonial officials resorted to reserves and how they justified their existence, as well as the day-to-day reality inside the reserves and their role in the economic and social lives of African populations, varied even within territories and across time, depending on different factors.[10]

In the case of Mozambique, Inhambane, a province located in the southern part of the territory, constitutes a particularly interesting case for the study of the land question in this period, as well as the practical consequences of native reserves and other instruments of rural ordering of space, populations, and economic activities. Specific local ecological conditions—namely, the fact that the region's soils are predominantly sandy and lacking in water and that rainfall is irregular, making it prone to periodic hunger and drought—strongly shaped the type of occupation and uses of the land in Inhambane. Understandably, the majority of the population and the economic activities of the province were concentrated in the fertile lands along the Indian Ocean coast.[11] The majority of the population in the province (339,501 in 1917) lived on subsistence farming and occasionally sold coconuts, cashews, and mafurra (*Trichilia emetica*) in markets. Cultivators mostly grew foodstuffs like maize, manioc, sweet potato, banana trees, and coconut trees, among other crops. Cashew and madura trees grew naturally across the region.[12] Migrant labour would play a key role in the history of the province: Thousands of men would eventually join migrant labour flows to Natal's sugar plantations and the Rand's mines across the border, a movement that Portuguese and South African authorities later turned into a profitable business through bilateral agreements.[13]

From the 1860s, Inhambane's coastal areas attracted a number of settlers and companies interested in growing sugar cane, a crop that seemed exceptionally suited to local ecological conditions. But instead of growing it for actual sugar production and perhaps turning Inhambane into a smaller Natal, they quickly realized that better profits could be obtained from the *sope* business. *Sope* was the local name for the alcoholic spirit made from sugar cane that was extremely popular among African populations.[14] Unable to resist the gradual land alienation occurring in the region, many Africans were forced by landowners to grow sugar for *sope* instead of traditional foodstuffs. By the early twentieth century, Inhambane's coastal areas had become a point of contention between different authorities in Mozambique and the metropole, but also the site of growing tensions between settlers and African farmers, to which the latter sometimes responded by moving to avoid forced sugar cultivation.

Dismayed by the concentration on sugar cane in a region they believed could become a centre of agricultural production and fearing that African farmers would leave Inhambane without a labour force and stop paying their taxes, local officials proposed the creation of native reserves in the region, a possibility that was already included in the 1909 Land Law. Reserves, the governor of Inhambane argued, could be used to allow African farmers to grow foodstuffs, to ensure a stable labour force, or to keep European and African areas separated.[15] As a result of official pressure, the first reserve in the region, covering the entire district of Zavala, with 102,575 inhabitants and the highest population density in the province, would be created in 1911, with several others being created in the following years.[16]

The districts of Manica and Chimoio, located in central Mozambique near the border with Southern Rhodesia, witnessed similar developments during the same period. These districts were part of the provinces of Manica and Sofala, an area of approximately 135,000 square kilometres placed under the rule of the Mozambique Company between 1892 and 1942. Formed mostly with foreign capital, this chartered company had a corporate structure with headquarters in Lisbon and an administrative structure in Manica and Sofala centred in Beira, its capital. Like other chartered companies, it had obligations vis-à-vis its shareholders and vis-à-vis the Portuguese state, but in many ways, it did not act much differently from other colonial powers with territories under their direct administration.[17]

When it came to the land question, company officials were faced with the same dilemmas as officials in Mozambique under direct Portuguese rule. As they were interested in attracting white settlers and companies to Manica and Sofala, regions like Manica were a priority. Located in the west of the territory and bordering Southern Rhodesia, the district of Manica, with 10,050 square kilometres and a budding gold mining industry, took on a central role in the company's initial years, concentrating an important part of the African labour demand, for mines, infrastructure construction, and agriculture.[18] Shona-speaking peoples in the region had historically engaged in agriculture in the region's fertile lands, their preferred foodstuffs being millet, sorghum, and maize, but were also involved in gold mining in mountainous areas.[19] Understandably, this centrality of Manica was reflected in the geography of land concessions. Indeed, the company's land policy in the first years of the twentieth century reflected the aspiration to develop the western area of the territory, as the best lands—namely, in the districts of Manica and Chimoio—were swiftly set aside for settlers, many of them interested in growing maize for export and to supply the region's mines. Manica and Chimoio would quickly become centres of maize production, largely as a result of the company's supply of forced labour to settler farmers, but also due to a generous land concession policy and other forms of support.[20] As small and medium-sized land grants increased in strategic areas near the railway line connecting central Mozambique to Southern Rhodesia, so did the conflicts between white settlers and African farmers, who were responsible for significant agricultural production in the region.[21]

To avoid conflicts with settlers, damages to their gardens, or simply to avoid forced labour, in the early 1910s many African farmers escaped to other areas, while others were evicted by landowners without any compensation. Similar to what happened in the coastal areas of Inhambane, as a reaction to the situation in Manica and Chimoio, in 1913 a number of company officials proposed the demarcation of native reserves in these districts to "protect" African crops, but also to ensure a labour supply and maintain tax revenues.[22] The first reserves in Manica and Chimoio would, however, only be created in 1916.[23]

The districts of Zavala, in Inhambane, and Manica and Chimoio, in the Mozambique Company's territory, thus had a great deal in common at the beginning of the twentieth century: Both regions' best lands had attracted settlers, in one case interested in growing sugar cane, in the other maize; landowners depended on African labour for their production; conflicts had arisen between settler and African farmers, and situations of abuse had been reported; and authorities had come to perceive these tensions as a result of the confluence of the labour, land, tax, and agriculture questions, to which native reserves had been advanced as a solution. These cases were also similar on another level. According to available sources, even though reserves were created on paper in specific areas of Inhambane and Manica and Chimoio, they did not have their intended results. In Manica and Chimoio, few farmers moved to the reserves and authorities did not force them to do so. In both Inhambane and Manica and Chimoio, some reserves originally included land concessions that were not vacated, while parts of others were eventually granted to or illegally occupied by settlers, thus revealing the porous boundaries of property divisions in these regions, the volatility of official policies, and the ineffectiveness of the government of Mozambique and of the company. African populations, in turn, were not always informed about reserves or were understandably dubious about their merits, especially when they included lands with poor soils or when they were situated in peripheral areas, far from markets, roads, or their workplaces, as was the case in Manica. Farmers would furthermore continue to periodically move to better agricultural lands near riverbanks, especially in times of drought, showing that officials had also been unable to curb one of the African farming practices to which they most objected.[24]

Reserves were therefore not the panacea some officials had naively hoped they would be, nor did they contribute to a neat and stable separation between Africans and settlers or to conflict-free rural areas. They were furthermore not consensual in Mozambique's colonial society. In the 1920s, official land policies in Inhambane faced opposition, particularly from groups of European farmers, who feared reserves would bar them from accessing the best land they felt they were entitled to, jeopardise the supply of a steady labour force, and ultimately allow African farmers to become their competitors.[25] Reserves nevertheless continued to be created on paper, and by 1942, as map 2.2 shows, thousands of hectares had been set aside.

In central Mozambique under company rule, until the 1940s several reserves would also be created, in the province of Manica but especially in the Zambezi Valley (province of Sofala), which was increasingly attracting the interest of companies determined to expand sisal, sugar, and cotton plantations. Reserves were furthermore created in areas where African rice, cotton, coconut, or fruit tree production was particularly strong, activities that the company wanted to stimulate.[26] Ultimately, the company's native reserve geography followed a specific logic: In areas of strong European settlement, like the districts of Manica and Chimoio, reserves were mostly created in areas with poor soils and located far from markets and roads; in the Zambezi Valley and in existing sites of African production, reserves were normally larger in size and located in areas with a higher African population density. In the first case, reserves solved the

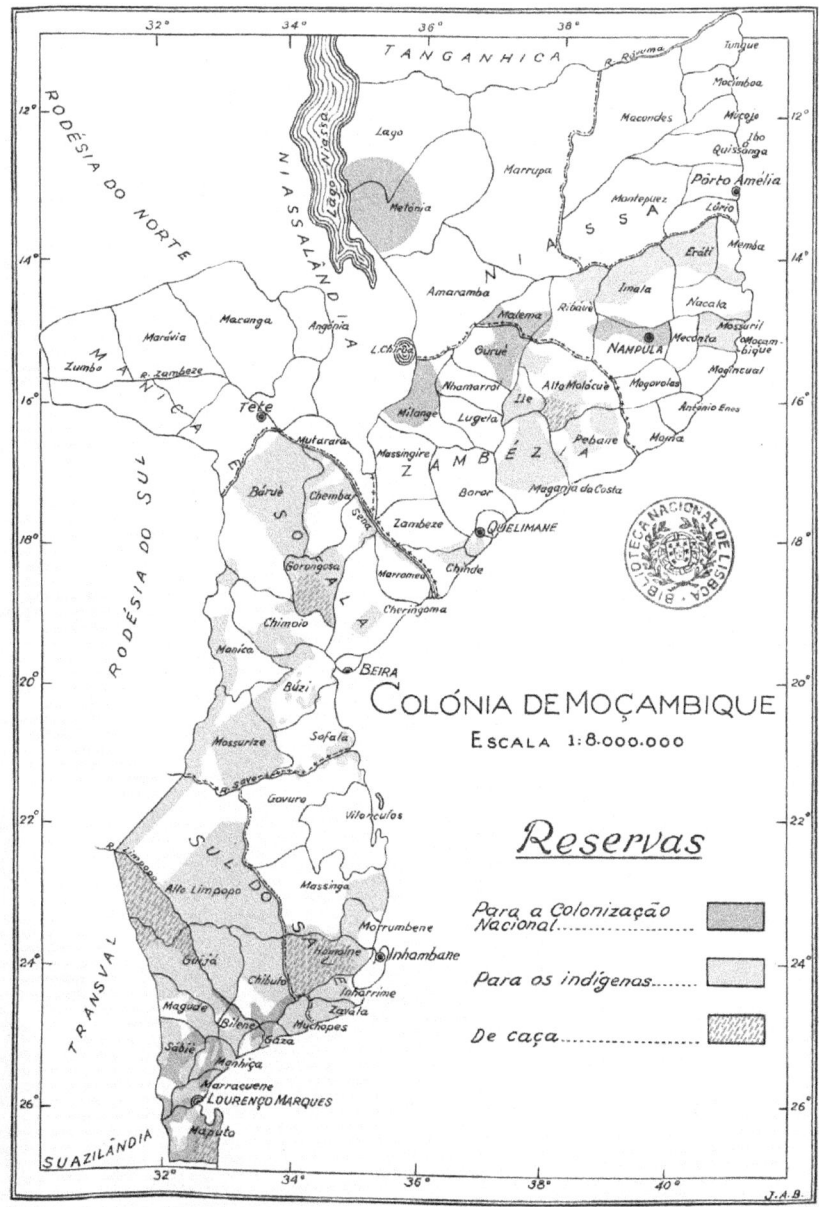

Map 2.2. Map of native reserves, hunting reserves, and national colonization reserves, 1944

Source: Colónia de Moçambique, *Relatório do chefe dos serviços de agricultura 1940–1944, partes II e III* (Imprensa Nacional, 1944), 296.

competition for the best lands in favour of settlers, barring African farmers from competing with settler agriculture, while in the second case reserves were spaces of inclusion of African farmers in the capitalist system, under company and large concessionary surveillance, and were also thought of as an incentive to African agriculture.[27]

The Legalization of Africans Living Inside Alienated and Vacant Land

Though advanced as a solution to the problems that some officials perceived in rural areas, the native reserves created since the 1910s in Mozambique were not the only instrument of ordering of space available to administrations. Indeed, while new reserves were put in place in the 1920s, authorities also turned their attention to what was happening inside alienated and vacant land.

In the company's territory, in the early 1900s officials had not legislated specifically on the possibility of African individual property because they argued Africans could avail themselves of the general law. Some Africans had in fact already received land titles in Sofala, and authorities would just need to protect their rights in case landholders decided to evict them from their concessions.[28] And even when tensions between Africans and European settlers emerged in the districts of Manica and Chimoio in the early 1910s, as European farmers often encroached on African gardens, forced African farmers to work, or evicted them altogether, not all officials were convinced that native reserves were the right solution, arguing that the territory had a "labour problem," not a land one. Convinced of the need to support European agriculture in Manica and Chimoio by ensuring a stable and readily available labour force, some officials argued that the company needed to encourage Africans to remain on alienated land, even though European farmers might feel this was against their interests.[29]

A few years later, the situation of African farmers in alienated land had worsened, as a report from Chimoio shows, with African chiefs complaining of several abuses in European farms. Though difficult to quantify, the situation was so worrying that during the *banjas* that were held between local colonial officials and African chiefs, the district administrator had advised populations to move to native reserves.[30] When in the early 1920s the territory was faced with what European farmers and many officials called a "labour crisis" and therefore could not afford to lose more labour force, authorities felt it was finally time to act. In the new 1924 Land Law, the company was unequivocal about the need to compensate African farmers when the landowners occupied their gardens and it laid out a procedure with official intervention to move African farmers to areas with sufficient acreage inside alienated land.[31] These measures, officials hoped, would be sufficient to end the abuse in alienated lands.

In parallel, the 1920s witnessed the steady decline of European production in Manica and Chimoio. For the president of the company's board of directors, writing in a 1923 report, the farmers were the ones to blame for this outcome, as they had followed poor economic strategies, especially by concentrating almost exclusively on maize, a crop whose price was volatile in international markets.[32] For the director of the recently created Native Affairs Division, António Serpa, the solution for the decline of European agriculture and for what he saw as the "problem of the productivity" of the region was two-pronged: investing in African agriculture, a strategy he had been defending for a few years, as well as in companies, rather than in small and medium individual European settlers. Investing in African agriculture and companies, Serpa claimed, was cheaper and more effective than continuing to support settler farms—namely, in Manica and Chimoio—since European settlers required considerable company financial support, and African farmers tended to move from areas of European settlement to avoid encroachment on their lands.[33] To encourage Africans to produce more, access to individual property would be essential, Serpa argued. Without it Africans would neither settle permanently nor fully dedicate themselves to agriculture.[34] Since, in the context of international criticism against Portuguese labour policies, the company felt it was important to show it was acting to improve labour practices in its territory, these changes were explicitly envisaged not only as a way of boosting the economy, but also as a way of promoting the well-being of African populations and "civilizational progress."[35]

One of the ways of increasing African productivity discussed in this period was improving the conditions for African farmers living inside alienated land, a concern that was not exclusive to the Mozambique Company. Indeed, in Mozambique under direct Portuguese rule, Africans could since the 1918 Land Law receive occupation titles when living in vacant land under specific circumstances.[36] The 1918 bill also entrusted the Native Affairs and Survey Departments with overseeing compensation and eviction procedures in alienated land, on which African "squatters" had to be consulted before a decision was to be taken. Local administrators were, moreover, urged to defend "natives" against any "attacks" on their occupancy rights.[37] But when Africans were indeed evicted, they would only be given lands with similar conditions inside reserves, or alternatively they could occupy new vacant lands and eventually request an occupancy title. Other tailor-made solutions could also be reached, as in the dispute that opposed a Portuguese owner and African tenants in Maxixe, Inhambane. The latter had traditionally benefited from a number of trees in the area that later had been included in a land concession. When the owner tried to bar tenants from picking cashew from the trees to profit from the increasing price of copra and cashew nuts, African tenants complained to authorities. An agreement was eventually reached between the owner and the African farmers, with the latter agreeing to pay two cans of cashew nuts annually in order to remain on the property.[38]

As conflicts in alienated land continued, in 1927 a commission was nominated by the government of Mozambique to draft the rules on the amount of land to be demarcated for squatters inside concessions. Two categories of land were defined, and two corresponding areas for squatters generally recommended: "poor" soils, where tracts for Africans should be of five hectares per hut, and "rich" soils, where two hectares per hut would be sufficient.[39] To further contribute to the "protection" of African squatters and prevent abuses, in the late 1930s additional legislation was enacted. By demanding that tenancy be made official in a contract approved by local authorities, where squatters agreed to pay landlords in cash, wage work, or in kind, they were in effect transformed into tenant labourers or sharecroppers.[40]

In the Mozambique Company's territory, the Great Depression had brought new opportunities for African farmers, who had been growing their crops on vacant or alienated land newly abandoned by impoverished European landowners. To stimulate this emerging sector, company authorities decided to officially designate the most dynamic ones as "African farmers," a suggestion previously made in Portuguese and international fora by experts and colonial officers.[41] This formal recognition, benefiting, for instance, farmers who were growing maize in the district of Manica—once the stronghold of European agriculture—using imported implements and even animal traction, was made through incentives such as an exemption of forced labour to those who had yields of up to thirty bags of maize.[42] Officials nevertheless acknowledged that these measures had to be limited to avoid competition with settlers, since the company wanted to continue to encourage European agriculture.[43]

Research about the regions of Manica and Sofala where Africans benefited from this formal recognition as "African farmers" shows that it contributed to social differentiation and an improvement of living conditions, but also that this differentiation confirmed pre-existing hierarchies present in local societies. Furthermore, it shows that these farmers where not completely shielded from disputes with European settlers, who feared their competition in the agricultural sector.[44]

The Separation of Plots for Individual Smallholders inside Native Reserves

As discussed above, even though reserves were originally created to "protect" African farmers and their livelihoods, the reality on the ground was often very different. Sources from mid-1920s Inhambane show how easily areas inside reserves that were actually being used by African farmers were alienated to settlers, or how Africans were forced by settlers to pay to stay and use land that had supposedly been set aside for them freely.[45] This situation was probably a result of factors such as authorities' unwillingness to intervene more strongly in the agrarian relations that were forming in rural areas, in spite of the injustice to African farmers; the continuing will to alienate land to settlers; the lack of a cadastral survey and of clear demarcations between alienated land and reserves; and the limited presence of officials in the districts.

But unlike in the districts of Manica and Chimoio under company rule, where most Africans refused to move to reserves because of their poor quality and location, and therefore probably did not perceive reserves as a way of improving their situation, in Inhambane there is some indication that farmers actually valued local reserves. In fact, Africans were actually the ones proposing the demarcation of individual tracts of land inside reserves: In 1926, for instance, a group of local African chiefs presented a written plea to authorities regarding what they viewed as "the land shortage problem" in the province and asked for individual plots to be assigned to them inside reserves.[46] This proposal was rejected in early 1927.

The reason put forth by Augusto Cabral, the director of the Native Affairs Department and a fervent supporter of the reserves, for rejecting their plea was that setting aside plots inside the reserves would violate the principle that underpinned their very creation. He also feared it would lead to the same "dangers" for the rest of Africans living in them identified inside European estates: differentiation and the establishment of servile relations.[47] For Cabral, the author of ethnographies of Inhambane and of Mozambique more generally, reserves should ideally be areas where populations would live according to local custom, where Africans would enjoy the land communally, and not individually, as Europeans did.[48] Interestingly, even though Augusto Cabral took this decision in 1925, he apparently was not familiar with the new land law applicable to the territory under the rule of the Mozambique Company, and specifically with its provisions on titling inside the reserves.[49]

How did the company come to approve these provisions? Sources show how this outcome was informed by the practice of land concessions in Manica and

Sofala and the "problems" that officials perceived. Following a surge in requests for individual land titles under the 1924 Land Law by African farmers, the Cadastral Department had been faced with their inability to afford demarcation fees. To avoid these costs while at the same time satisfying the requests made by these farmers, authorities decided to allow land titling for Africans inside reserves, where in their view demarcation was not necessary.[50] According to the provisions in the 1924 Land Law, these farmers could eventually become actual owners of the plots after twenty years of permanent occupation. Furthermore, similarly to the rules that applied outside reserves, a plot inside a reserve would be considered vacant and therefore susceptible of being titled if it had not been cultivated or if its occupiers had been absent for twenty-four months consecutively.[51]

The first individual plots inside reserves would be titled in 1931 in Sofala, after authorities confirmed that the farmers making the requests had already been tilling the land for a considerable period of time.[52] By 1932, as requests for similar titles increased and several doubts arose, the company's administrative advisory board issued an opinion on the size of the plots to be set aside inside reserves. It recommended one hectare of land per farmer and additionally half a hectare per child over fourteen or per wife for polygamous farmers, up to a total maximum of fifteen hectares.[53]

In the same year, in the meantime, José Ferreira Bossa, the acting governor of Manica and Sofala, issued his "Instructions for the Development of Native Agriculture." The 1932 legislation based on these instructions aimed at stimulating African agriculture through the organization of "native property" was partly a response to the shortcomings of the 1924 Land Law when it came to defining plots inside native reserves.[54] While continuing to encourage Africans to settle in reserves through individual property titles, without which Bossa felt Africans would be limited to their "ancestral practices" and nomadism, it adopted measures aimed at "modernizing" and "rationalizing" agricultural and economic practices, in line with international debates on this topic and plans put in place elsewhere in southern Africa.[55] But since this plan had to be compatible with the "labour crisis" and the "rhythm of the national interest," unsurprisingly not all reserves would be included so as to avoid creating direct competition to European agriculture, then facing a steady decline.[56] The districts of Manica and Chimoio, as well as other centres of "European colonization," would be excluded from this plan. The technical support given to Africans inside the reserves would also be more limited than in European areas, with seeds and implements being lent, rather than freely distributed. And the trade-off for the fact that farmers would have the ability to grow the crop of their choice was the stronger presence of extension services in the company's reserves, and therefore of vigilance on their activities, as well as the limits to the areas they could have under cultivation and the fact that a correctional sentence would be the consequence of the abandonment of the plots distributed.

The Nhangau *Colonato* and the Parcelling and Distribution of Land to African Smallholders on Vacant Land

A third type of configuration advanced in this period to stimulate African agriculture was the *colonato*, or model settlement. Available evidence shows that between the 1920s and the early 1940s only one settlement of this type was created in Mozambique, in the Mozambique Company's territory. In the 1950s and '60s, however, as settlement and villagization schemes gained popularity across colonial Africa as social engineering tools, becoming part and parcel of late colonialism's "development" apparatus (see deGrassi's chapter in this volume), Mozambique would also come to know several comparable settlements created for different purposes.[57]

Perhaps influenced by a similar idea suggested by a former governor, or by the discussions on African agriculture taking place across Africa and in European metropoles, Abel de Sousa Moutinho, the district administrator of Beira in the early 1930s, was the Portuguese official behind the *colonato* created in the Mozambique Company's territory.[58] In December 1933 he sent a draft project on *aldeias indígenas*, or native villages, to the governor of the territory, hoping they would be created in different parts of Manica and Sofala. But even before that, in June 1932, he had decided to visit the prospective site of the first model settlement near Beira, the capital of the territory, alongside the director of the Department of Agriculture, Lereno Antunes Barradas. Since much of the land in the vicinity had already been alienated, he chose the forest of Nhangau, an area with several hamlets of a sizeable density where African farmers mostly cultivated rice.[59]

Having finally received government ascent for this unique project, construction work started in the area shortly thereafter. In early October 1935, the first group of Africans started settling in the areas allocated to them inside the Nhangau settlement. With 80 hectares, 51 houses built according to a style of "transition to the European civilization," and 174 inhabitants chosen by the local chief, Moutinho hoped Nhangau would help promote a "segregation of interests," whereby African production would be stimulated but without competing with European agriculture.[60] The model settlement would also work as a "centre of civilizational dissemination."[61] The aims of the *colonato* of Nhangau were thus productive, in that Moutinho hoped to transform African farming systems, as much as social and political ones. But like the reserves or the tracts of land set aside in alienated land analyzed in this chapter, the settlement was not meant to jeopardize the settler sector.

Because of the nature of this specific model settlement—under which each family would receive a plot of land that would have to be cultivated for a specified number of hours each day, while the children would take care of the livestock, with company officials and experts providing technical supervision and assistance—this configuration of African land access had a clear paternalist dimension. But it also had a coercive dimension that was not present in the other instruments of rural ordering analyzed in this chapter.[62] Nhangau was clearly planned as a social engineering tool, where African farmers would be taught "modern" farming techniques and grow the crops authorities directed them to.

Given that populations in the region had been known to escape their fiscal and labour duties when necessary, while also taking advantage of opportunities to improve their livelihoods by remaining on alienated land, it would be difficult to anticipate what the outcome of an experiment like Nhangau could be. By 1940, in a paper analyzing the first years of the model settlement, Moutinho thought that it had been a success. Those that argued Africans should be left to their traditions had been proven wrong, he added.[63] He also believed that as many as twenty-two families were ready for their "emancipation" and could become individual landholders of plots of at least four hectares. After three years they would receive a temporary title, and after seventeen they would become full landowners.[64] The use of the word "emancipation" is particularly interesting in this case: From what would those families be emancipating themselves? African "traditions"? On the conditions they were experiencing inside the model settlement, Moutinho made no mention, choosing to simply celebrate the socio-economic differentiation that seemed to be taking place in Nhangau.

Despite his optimism, Moutinho's pet project would come to an end shortly thereafter. With the termination of the Mozambique Company's charter, in 1942 the territory of Manica and Sofala came under direct Portuguese rule, and a number of the new officials working in the region considered Nhangau a failure.[65] In 1949, what was left of the settlement was turned into an asylum for beggars living on the streets of Beira. A prison, where many Africans would be incarcerated over the years, would later be built in its vicinity. As an investigation carried out in the region has shown, the Nhangau settlement had been built by correctional workers, and the families chosen to live in it had remained there against their will.[66] This coercive dimension probably helps to explain the failure of Nhangau. In other model settlement schemes in colonial Africa, native smallholders managed to negotiate with officials and experts and even influence the agricultural practices being promoted.[67] The evidence thus far shows that this was not the case at Nhangau. But another partial explanation for the failure of Nhangau, which needs to be further explored, could lie in the opposition of the company's own director of the Native Affairs Department to the settlement, as he explicitly opposed the social model proposed by Moutinho.[68]

In spite of this short-lived experience, the idea of villagization and agricultural schemes for African smallholders would continue to gain ground in the following years, attracting officials with ambitious economic plans and motivated experts from different areas.[69] And the perception in official circles in Portugal was actually relatively favourable to Nhangau, which would be discussed in coming projects in the 1940s aimed at promoting the "social and economic organization of native populations" as an example of the move toward fixed agriculture.[70]

Final Notes

During the period analyzed in this chapter, officials in both Mozambique under direct Portuguese rule and in the Mozambique Company's territory seemed to be constantly trying to adjust to the agrarian reality that they had helped create in Mozambican colonial society through a system that institutionalized "racialized difference" in terms of access to land and dispossessed Africans. The tensions between the divergent goals discussed in the chapter's introduction were always present, with different agents with unequal power, from governors to district officers, to European farmers, to African chiefs, defending varied interests and placing an emphasis on the land question or on the labour one. Land and labour were, however, inextricably linked.

The configurations of African land access discussed here were the result of multiple negotiations, did not receive unanimous support, and were not particularly "successful," not even by colonial administrators' standards, perhaps because the contradictions between a steady supply of African labour to European farms and the creation of a class of African yeoman farmers in areas of competition for land could not be solved; because the clash between different farming practices in alienated land, a site of unequal power relations, was inevitable; or because African farmers resisted becoming tenant labourers, sharecroppers, reserve dwellers, or model settlement residents in unfair conditions and fought to maintain their autonomy. There was also a great deal of experimentalism and paternalism, certainly in the case of Nhangau, where the use of coercive methods is still engrained in the memories of the populations in the region today.

If the 1920s signalled an increasing concern on the part of the state and the company with the regulation of agrarian relations inside and across boundaries, which as we saw were porous, the crisis caused by the Great Depression and the further decline of the settler economy would lead authorities to turn even more to the question of African production in the 1940s, a context in which arguments in favour of African access to individual property, with different goals, gained ground. The labour question would nevertheless always be present, as would that of the competition between African and European farmers. The "nomadic habits" of Africans were also increasingly seen as a "problem" for some, or a "backward tradition" for others, incompatible with a territory that had built a network of boundaries and acceptable behaviours. In this context, local land custom and "traditional" agricultural practices were increasingly seen as obstacles to economic growth.[71] And even though native reserves would still be considered necessary in the 1930s and '40s, officials aimed to make them more effective through technical intervention, while other solutions outside reserves were also proposed, combining incentives and coercion.[72]

NOTES TO CHAPTER 2

Research for this chapter was supported by the Fundação para a Ciência e a Tecnologia, IP, through a CEEC contract (CEECIND/01948/2017), as well as by the Centro Interuniversitário de História das Ciências e da Tecnologia (UIDB/00286/2020, https://doi.org/10.54499/UIDB/00286/2020, and UIDP/00286/2020, https://doi.org/10.54499/UIDP/00286/2020).

1. Arquivo Histórico Ultramarino, *Concessão de terrenos: Moçambique: catálogo*. Introdução de Maria Luísa Abrantes (ME, IICT, 1989), AHU.Arquivo Histórico Ultramarino-SEMU-S/N°-1D-SEMU-DGU-PT 1905 1906 Concessão de terrenos-Proc° 645-681 MOÇ.
2. Carta de lei of 9 May 1901 and the Regulamento geral provisório para a execução da carta de lei de 9 de Maio de 1901 sobre concessões de terrenos no ultramar, of 2 September 1901, in *Colecção da legislação novíssima do ultramar—1901*, vol. 29 (Companhia Typographica, 1902).
3. Tania Murray Li, *The Will to Improve: Governmentality, Development, and the Practice of Politics* (Duke University Press, 2007), 48. For a recent reflection on the construction of "racial regimes of ownership" in Canada, Australia, and Israel and Palestine with a strong comparative approach, see Brenna Bandhar, *The Colonial Lives of Property: Law, Land, and Racial Regimes of Ownership* (Duke University Press, 2018).
4. When highlighting this distinction, Malyn Newitt spoke of a "trinity" of "native" policies. Malyn Newitt, *Portugal in Africa: The Last Hundred Years* (C. Hurst and Co., 1981), 100.
5. By choosing to focus on these three particular configurations in this specific period I am necessarily leaving out other configurations that could also be particularly telling—from the scheme for African smallholders put in place by Swiss Protestant missionaries in the 1910s, to the so-called cotton concentrations of the late 1940s, to cotton co-operatives in the late 1950s. For a discussion of the farming scheme put in place by Swiss missionaries in southern Mozambique in the 1910s, see Heidi Gengenbach, "'I'll Bury You in the Border!': Women's Land Struggles in Post-War Facazisse (Magude District), Mozambique," *Journal of Southern African Studies* 24, no. 1 (1998): 19–22. On the "cotton concentrations," see Tiago Saraiva, *Fascist Pigs: Technoscientific Organisms and the History of Fascism* (MIT Press, 2016), 179–80. On co-operatives, see Allen F. Isaacman, "The Mozambique Cotton Cooperative: The Creation of a Grassroots Alternative to Forced Commodity Production," *African Studies Review* 25, nos. 2–3 (1982): 5–25.
6. The land law applicable to the regions under direct Portuguese rule in this period was the Carta de lei of 9 May 1901 and the Regulamento geral provisório para a execução da carta de lei de 9 de Maio de 1901 sobre concessões de terrenos no ultramar, of 2 September 1901, in *Colecção da legislação novíssima do ultramar—1901*, vol. 29 (Companhia Typographica, 1902). The first land law approved for the region of Manica and Sofala under company rule was the Regulamento para a concessão de terrenos por aforamento no território da Companhia de Moçambique, e sobre a ocupação provisória dos mesmos, of 2 July 1892, in *Boletim da Companhia de Moçambique* (hereafter *BCM*) no. 2 (30 July 1892). It is important to note that the company's land law was prepared by the company but approved by the Portuguese government.

7   For a broader discussion of these developments, see Bárbara Direito, "The Land Question in Early Twentieth-Century Portuguese Legal Colonial Thought," *Portuguese Journal of Social Science* 16, no. 2 (2017): 181–93; Bárbara Direito, "Land and Colonialism in Mozambique—Policies and Practice in Inhambane, c.1900–c.1940," *Journal of Southern African Studies* 39, no. 2 (2013): 353–69; and Bárbara Direito, "African Access to Land in Early Twentieth Century Portuguese Colonial Thought," in *Property Rights, Land and Territory in the European Overseas Empires*, ed. José Vicente Serrão, Bárbara Direito, Eugénia Rodrigues, and Susana Münch Miranda (CEHC-IUL, 2014), 255–63.

8   On forced labour and Portuguese labour policies in Africa, see Miguel Bandeira Jerónimo, *The "Civilising Mission" of Portuguese Colonialism, 1870–1930* (Palgrave Macmillan, 2015). On labour policies in Manica and Sofala, see Eric Allina, *Slavery by Any Other Name: African Life under Company Rule in Colonial Mozambique* (University of Virginia Press, 2012).

9   The 1909 Land Law was the first in Mozambique under direct Portuguese rule to allow for the possibility of native reserves. Regímen provisório para a concessão de terrenos do estado na província de Moçambique, de 9 de Julho de 1909, in *Colecção da legislação novíssima do ultramar—1909*, vol. 37 (Companhia Typographica, 1910).

10 On native reserves in southern Africa and their consequences, see Colin Bundy, *The Rise and Fall of the South African Peasantry* (David Philip, Currey, 1988); Robin Palmer, *Land and Racial Domination in Rhodesia* (Heinemann, 1977); Christopher Youé, "Black Squatters on White Farms: Segregation and Agrarian Change in Kenya, South Africa, and Rhodesia, 1902–1963," *International History Review* 24, no. 3 (2002): 558–602; Jeffrey Butler, Robert I. Rotberg, and John Adams, *The Black Homelands of South Africa: The Political and Economic Development of Bophuthatswana and KwaZulu* (University of California Press, 1977). On native reserves in Angola, see Vicente Ferreira, *A situação de Angola: Circular-consulta enviada às associações comerciais, industriais e agrícolas da província de Angola* (Imprensa Nacional, 1927), and also *Angola: Relatório da repartição dos serviços de cadastro e colonização* (Agência Geral das Colónias. Divisão de Publicações e Biblioteca, 1933). According to the latter report (pp. 12–13), between 1912 and 1932, 154,556 hectares in Angola were declared native reserves.

11 Mouzinho de Albuquerque, *Moçambique, 1896–1898*, vol. 2 (Agência Geral das Colónias, 1934), 36; Carlos A. dos Santos, *Relatório do govêrno do distrito de Inhambane nos anos de 1931, 1932, 1933 e 1934* (Agência Geral das Colónias, 1937), 14–15.

12 In his ethnographic report on Inhambane, Cabral distinguished the crops preferred by the different peoples of the region in different areas and was very critical of the slash-and-burn farming method used. Augusto Cabral, *Raças, usos e costumes dos indígenas do districto de Inhambane* (Imprensa Nacional, 1910), 102–4. On demographic aspects of Inhambane, see José B. C. Araújo, *Relatório acerca da administração do distrito de Inhambane, 1917* (Imprensa da Universidade, 1920).

13 Centro de Estudos Africanos, *O mineiro moçambicano: Um estudo sobre a exportação de mão de obra em Inhambane* (Centro de Estudos Africanos—Universidade Eduardo Mondlane, 1998); Patrick Harries, *Work, Culture, and Identity: Migrant Laborers in Mozambique and South Africa, c. 1860–1910* (Heinemann, 1994).

14 Local African populations in Inhambane distilled, for instance, maize, cashew, and manioc to produce local spirits, but also produced fermented spirits. For a detailed description of the techniques they used, see Cabral, *Usos e costumes dos indígenas do districto*, 94–8. See also Eduardo Medeiros, *Bebidas moçambicanas de fabrico caseiro* (Arquivo Histórico de Moçambique, 1988).

15 José Cabral, *Relatório do governador, 1911–1912—Distrito de Inhambane* (Imprensa Nacional, 1912), 47–8.

16 According to official sources, Zavala had a density of 63.9 inhabitants per square kilometre. Araújo, *Relatório*, 110. Not all, however, were in favour of reserves. For a strong critique of reserves, see Augusto Baptista, "Concessão de terrenos. VI. Propriedade e Reservas Indígenas," *O Africano*, December 12, 1913. For more on the case of Inhambane, see Direito, "Land and Colonialism."

17 The origins and powers of the Mozambique Company are discussed in Bárbara Direito, *Terra e colonialismo em Moçambique—a região de Manica e Sofala sob a Companhia de Moçambique, 1892–1942* (Imprensa de Ciências Sociais, 2020), 47–67.

18 Eric Allina-Pisano, "Negotiating Colonialism: Africans, the State, and the Market in Manica District, Mozambique, 1895–c.1935" (PhD diss., Yale University, 2002), 61–2.

19 Allina-Pisano, "Negotiating Colonialism," 32–5.

20 The company provided different forms of support to European farmers—namely, financial, through credit and loans, but also technical, distributing advice, and seeds. See Direito, *Terra e colonialismo*, chap. 5.

21 Respostas aos quesitos sobre os três centros de produção à data existentes no Território, anexo à carta n.º 222 do governador interino para o administrador delegado, 17-2-1910, pp. 3–16, Arquivo Nacional da Torre do Tombo (hereafter "ANTT")-Fundo da Companhia de Moçambique (hereafter "FCM"),

n.º de ordem 2166, n.º 380-AH11. For an early effort at collecting local custom in Manica by one of its administrators, see Cezar Augusto Cardotte, "Usos e costumes indígenas da circunscrição de Manica," *Revista de Manica e Sofala* 47 (1907): 128–42. Another company administrator proposed the codification of African custom more broadly in Manica and Sofala in 1909. As many other similar exercises, it was very sparse when it came to the land question. Manoel Monteiro Lopes, "Subsídios para um código de usos e costumes indígenas no território," *BCM*, no. 16 (16 August 1909): 117–24.

22 Ofício do chefe da circunscrição de Chimoio para o governador, 21-5-1913, Arquivo Histórico de Moçambique (hereafter "AHM")-FCM, Administração de Lisboa, processo "Concessões de terrenos," caixa 140, pasta 7. Carta do governador para o administrador delegado, 21-5-1913, attached to carta da administração da Companhia de Moçambique de Lisboa para os comités de Paris e de Londres, 24-12-1914, p. 7, AHM-FCM, Administração de Lisboa, processo "Concessões de terrenos," caixa 141, pasta 11.

23 Ordem n.º 3648, 15 February 1916, BCM n.º 4, 15 February 1916. Ordem n.º 3659, 13 March 1916, BCM n.º 6, 16 March 1916.

24 Cópia de quesitos e conclusões da conferência sobre o problema indígena de 15 a 23 de Dezembro de 1925, pp. 10–11, attached to carta n.º 323 do governador para o administrador delegado, 26-12-1925, ANTT-FCM, n.º de ordem 2193, RA40. Nota da direcção dos negócios indígenas n.º 64/749, 29-7-1929, AHM-FCM, Negócios Indígenas, processos, caixa 24, pasta "P.149, cx 25, Terrenos B) Reservas Indígenas." See also Cabral, *Usos e costumes dos indígenas do distrito*, 52–3; Soares Zilhão, "Reservas indígenas," *Jornal União*, 20 January 1934.

25 José Cardoso, "Associação do fomento agrícola da província de Moçambique," *Boletim da Agência Geral das Colónias* 54 (1929): 161.

26 For the case of rice production in the district of Beira, see Ofício n.º 43 do chefe da circunscrição da Beira para o director da agrimensura, 23-2-1921, AHM-FCM, Secretaria Geral, processo n.º 2744, caixa 675. On reserves in Sofala, see Cópia de quesitos e conclusões da conferência sobre o problema indígena de 15 a 23 de Dezembro de 1925, pp. 9–10, attached to carta n.º 323 do governador para o administrador delegado, 26-12-1925, ANTT-FCM, n.º de ordem 2193, RA40; and also Luís de Sá Pereira, *Relatório da visita do especialista de algodão à Chemba em novembro de 1925* (Imprensa da Companhia de Moçambique, 1926).

27 For a development of this argument, see Direito, *Terra e colonialismo*, 249.

28 Relatório sobre o projecto do regulamento de concessões de terreno nos territórios de Manica e Sofala, de 17-4-1907, p. 31, attached to carta do governador para o administrador delegado, 1-8-1907, AHM-FCM, Administração de Lisboa, processo "Concessões de terrenos," caixa 140, pasta 3.

29 Carta do governador para o administrador delegado (contendo notas de vários chefes de circunscrição e directores de serviços), 21-5-1913, attached to carta da administração da Companhia de Moçambique de Lisboa para os comités de Paris e de Londres, 24-12-1914, pp. 11–14, AHM-FCM, Administração de Lisboa, processo "Concessões de terrenos," caixa 141, pasta 11.

30 Ofício do chefe da circunscrição de Chimoio para o governador, 15-11-1917, and acta da banja, AHM-FCM, Secretaria Geral, processo n.º 2744, caixa 675. Available sources do not allow us to quantify the exact number of Africans living in alienated land in Manica and Sofala. Youé provides estimates for South Africa (over 1 million), Southern Rhodesia (400,000), and Kenya (100,000) during World War I. See Youé, "Black Squatters," 558.

31 See articles 8–10 of the 1924 Land Law, Ordem n.º 4669, 12 August 1924, *BCM*, no. 16 (16 August 1924).

32 Relatório do presidente do conselho de administração Ruy Ulrich, 11-1923, pp. 70–1, ANTT-FCM, n.º de ordem 2193, RA2.

33 Allina-Pisano, "Negotiating Colonialism," 326–7; Cópia da nota do director dos negócios indígenas, anexo n.º 11 à acta da sessão n.º 17 da JCA, 19-12-1929, pp. 2–3, AHM-FCM, Secretaria Geral, Processos, Processo n.º 506—JCA, caixa 138, pasta "1929."

34 Relatório sobre assistência social ao indígena, de 1929, pp. 13–14, AHM-FCM, Negócios Indígenas, Processos, caixa 18, processo "112/25."

35 Relatório sobre assistência social ao indígena, de 1929, pp. 13–14, AHM-FCM, Negócios Indígenas, Processos, caixa 18, processo "112/25." On the origins and reactions to the criticism against Portuguese labour policies in the 1920s, see Jerónimo, *The "Civilizing Mission."*

36 Regulamento para a concessão de terrenos do estado na província de Moçambique, Decreto n.º 3983, of 16 March 1918, Diário do Governo, I ͣ série, n.º 62, 27 March 1918.

37 See articles 156–64 on African rights to land outside reserves.

38 Areosa Pena, "Distrito de Inhambane fim do milando dos terrenos?," *Tempo* 88 (1972): 32–40.

39 Circular n.º 893 A/9/B do director de Agrimensura, 6-5-1927, p. 2, attached to nota do director de agrimensura para o director dos negócios indígenas, 14-10-1927, AHM-Fundo da Direcção dos Serviços de Negócios Indígenas (hereafter "FDSNI"), caixa 1275, pasta "1926–1927."

40 Portaria provincial n.º 3286, de 19 de Janeiro de 1938, BOM n.º 3, I série, de 19 de Janeiro de 1938; portaria n.º 3796, de 23 de Agosto de 1939, BOM, n.º 34, I série, de 23 de Agosto de 1939.

41 At the Institut Colonial International's sessions, the link between the increase in African production and individual land tenure, and the idea of creating special conditions for African progressive farmers, was discussed since the 1920s. Daniel Zolla, "Les méthodes à appliquer pour faire produire aux colonies les matières premières à utiliser dans la mère-patrie," in *Compte-Rendu de la Session Tenue à Paris les 17, 18 et 19 mai 1921*, ed. Institut Colonial International (Institut Colonial International, 1921), 564–7; E. De Wildeman, "Enquête sur l'extension intensive et rationnelle des cultures indigènes dans les colonies tropicales," in *Compte-rendu de la session tenue à Bruxelles les 24, 25, 26 juin 1929*, ed. Institut Colonial International (Établissements Généraux d'Imprimerie, 1929). Similar ideas were supported in Portugal in the 1930s but were met with opposition from officials and experts concerned with the labour question. See José Penha Garcia, "Assistência económica aos indígenas," in *III Congresso colonial nacional de 8 a 15 de Maio de 1930, Actas das sessões e teses*, ed. Sociedade de Geografia de Lisboa (SGL, Tip. and Pap. Carmona, 1934); and *Conclusões, notas e bases propostas nas teses, comunicações e memórias apresentadas ao primeiro congresso de agricultura colonial* (Imp. Moderna, 1934).

42 Joel Maurício das Neves, "Economy, Society and Labour Migration in Central Mozambique, 1930–c.1965: A Case Study of Manica Province" (PhD diss., SOAS, London University, 1998), 135; Allina, *Slavery by Any*, 163–5; Allina-Pisano, "Negotiating Colonialism," 334–5. According to Anderson and Throup, the measures to improve "African agriculture" put in place in Kenya during the Depression were aimed at ensuring families earned enough to pay their taxes. Without this revenue, they argued, the very survival of the colonial state was at risk. David Anderson and David Throup, "Africans and Agricultural Production in Colonial Kenya: The Myth of the War as a Watershed," *Journal of African History* 26, no. 4 (1985): 327–45.

43 Acta n.º 5 da sessão da CAI de 6-6-1934, AHM-FCM, Negócios Indígenas, Processos, caixa 6, pasta "P.32-Cx2.a, Assistência social B-Actas da Comissão de Assistência ao Indígena." Unlike Manica, in the 1930s Chimoio continued to be the stronghold of European farmers, and officials felt there was no room to stimulate African agriculture. Neves, "Economy, Society," 145.

44 Neves, "Economy, Society," 136; Allina, *Slavery y Any*, 175.

45 "Reservas indígenas," *O Brado Africano*, 7 March 1925; "Reservas indígenas," *O Brado Africano*, 11 June 1927.

46 Ofício n.º 1470 da direcção de agrimensura para o director dos negócios Indígenas, de 25 de Agosto de 1926, AHM-FDSNI, caixa 1275, pasta 1926–1927.

47 Ofício n.º 427/49 do director dos negócios indígenas para o director de agrimensura, de 22 de Fevereiro de 1927, AHM-FDSNI, caixa 1275, pasta 1926–1927.

48 Augusto Cabral, *Racas, usos e costumes dos indígenas do districto*; António Augusto Cabral, *Raças, usos e costumes dos indígenas da província de Moçambique* (Imprensa Nacional, 1925).

49 See articles 5 and 6 of Ordem n.º 4669, of 12 August 1924, BCM n.º 16, 16 August 1924.

50 Relatório do presidente do conselho de administração Ruy Ulrich, 11–1923, p. 42, ANTT-FCM, n.º de ordem 2193, RA2.

51 Article 7 of Ordem n.º 4669, of 12 August 1924, BCM n.º 16, 16 August 1924.

52 Acta da 3.ª sessão da JCA, 20-3-1931, p. 2, AHM-FCM, Secretaria Geral, processo n.º 506, caixa 139. Attachment to acta da 9ª sessão da JCA, 3-9-1931, AHM-FCM, Secretaria Geral, processo n.º 506, caixa 139. Relatório da direcção de agrimensura relativo ao ano de 1931, p. 6, AHM-FCM, Relatórios, Agrimensura, caixa 23.

53 Acta da 11.ª sessão da junta consultiva de administração, 11-11-1932, p. 2, AHM-FCM, Secretaria Geral, processo n.º 506, caixa 138.

54 Ordem n.º 6501, of 30 September 1932, BCM n.º 19, 1 October 1932.

55 José Ferreira Bossa, "O Regime de concessão de terras aos indígenas nas colónias de África," *Boletim Geral das Colónias*, no. 117 (1935): 3–27. The 1932 legislation mentioned the survey on the "extension of native agriculture" carried out by the Institut Colonial International in 1929 as an influence to its principles and wording. Ordem n.º 6501, 30 September 1932, BCM n.º 19, 1 October 1932. The Master Farmer Scheme, implemented in neighbouring Southern Rhodesia, aimed to solve the problems of overcrowding and overstocking on reserves. On this scheme and its consequences for progressive African farmers, see Eira Kramer, "The Early Years: Extension Services in Peasant Agriculture in Colonial Zimbabwe, 1925–1929," *Zambezia* 24, no. 2(1997): 159–79; and Terence Ranger, *Peasant Consciousness and Guerrilla War in Zimbabwe: A Comparative Study* (James Currey, 1985).

56 Preamble, Ordem n.º 6501, of 30 September 1932, BCM n.º 19, 1 October 1932.

57 On other *colonatos* and *aldeamentos* created in late-colonial Mozambique, see César de Castro Coelho, *Aspectos da política de povoamento em Moçambique* (ISCSPU, 1965); and Neves, "Economy, Society."

The possibility of draining wetlands and parcelling lands for European and African farmers had been discussed in the context of the 1920s surveys of the Limpopo Valley, in southern Mozambique, but work would only start in the 1950s. On the Inhamissa scheme, created exclusively for African farmers, see José Firmino de Sousa Monteiro and Viriato Faria da Fonseca, "Breve notícia sobre o resgate e parcelamento do machongo de Inhamissa," *Moçambique: Documentário Trimestral*, no. 71 (1952): 6-36; and also J. L. Torres, "Some Settlement Schemes in the Gaza District of Southern Mozambique," *South African Journal of Economics* 35 (1967): 244-55. For a discussion of similar schemes put in place in the context of the liberation war in Mozambique, see João Paulo Borges Coelho, "Protected Villages and Communal Villages in the Mozambican Province of Tete (1968-1982): A History of State Resettlement Policies, Development and War" (PhD diss., Bradford University, 1993). For the case of Angola, see F. Boaventura, "Os colonatos indígenas em Angola," *Agros*, nos. 1-2 (1951): 44-50; Samuël Coghe, "Reordering Colonial Society: Model Villages and Social Planning in Rural Angola, 1920-45," *Journal of Contemporary History* 52, no. 1 (2017): 16-44; and Bernardo Pinto da Cruz, "The Penal Origins of Colonial Model Villages: From Aborted Concentration Camps to Forced Resettlement in Angola (1930-1969)," *Journal of Imperial and Commonwealth History* 47, no. 2 (2019): 343-71.

58 Massano de Amorim, governor of Manica and Sofala in the early 1920s, had suggested the creation of farms to stimulate African agriculture in his agricultural development plan. His idea was rejected due to the fear that these farms would require labourers needed in European farms. See his Bases para a organização dos serviços e trabalhos agrícolas e para o desenvolvimento e fomento da agricultura nos territórios da Companhia de Moçambique, 13-8-1923, pp. 1-2, ANTT-FCM, n.º de ordem 2199, n.º 11-RG11.

59 Abel de Sousa Moutinho, "Colonização indígena," *Boletim da Sociedade de Estudos de Moçambique* 15 (1934): 75-95; Abel de Sousa Moutinho, "Colonização indígena. A povoação-granja modelo do Nhangau," *Boletim da Sociedade de Estudos de Moçambique* 42 (1940): 47-68.

60 Moutinho, "Colonização indígena," 1940, 47-9; and "Colonização indígena," 1934, 76. Several photographs documenting the construction of the settlement and the first agricultural works at Nhangau can be consulted online at the Arquivo Nacional da Torre do Tombo's website (accessed 10 November 2021): https://digitarq.arquivos.pt/details?id=3678321 and https://digitarq.arquivos.pt/details?id=3678345. Although the photographs were taken at Nhangau, located near Beira, in Sofala, they are wrongly catalogued as having been taken in the district of Chimoio, in Manica.

61 Moutinho, "Colonização Indígena," 1940, 67.

62 Moutinho, 53-4.

63 Moutinho, 53.

64 Moutinho, 60.

65 Zachary Kagan-Guthrie, "Labor, Mobility and Coercion in Central Mozambique, 1942-1961" (PhD diss., Princeton University, 2014), 213.

66 Zack Kagan-Guthrie, "The Chili Pepper and the Banana Tree—Methods and Narratives in the Colonial History of Central Mozambique," unpublished paper presented at the Colonialism and Imperialism Workshop, Princeton University, December 2011, 7-8. I thank the author for his permission to cite this unpublished paper.

67 Monica M. van Beusekom, "Disjunctures in Theory and Practice: Making Sense of Change in Agricultural Development at the Office du Niger, 1920-60," *Journal of African History* 41, no. 1 (2000): 79-99.

68 Parecer n.º 22/II relativo ao projecto de decreto intitulado organização social e económica das populações indígenas, Diário das sessões da Assembleia Nacional, Câmara Corporativa, 3º suplemento ao n.º 104, de 16 de Abril de 1941, 10.

69 On agricultural policies and the role of experts, see Joseph M. Hodge, *The Triumph of the Expert: Agrarian Doctrines of Development and the Legacies of British Colonialism* (Ohio University Press, 2007).

70 Francisco J. V. Machado, "Projecto de organização social e económica das populações indígenas," *Boletim Geral das Colónias*, no. 178 (1940): 163-80. Parecer n.º 22/II relativo ao projecto de decreto intitulado organização social e económica das populações indígenas, Diário das sessões da Assembleia Nacional, Câmara Corporativa, 3º suplemento ao n.º 104, de 16 de Abril de 1941, 10.

71 Sara Berry, "Debating the Land Question in Africa," *Comparative Studies in Society and History* 44, no. 4 (2002): 646-7.

72 Agricultural policies promoting cash crops in post-World War II Mozambique would resort to similar combinations of incentives and coercion, but also technical assistance. See Otto Roesch, "Migrant Labour and Forced Rice Production in Southern Mozambique: The Colonial Peasantry of the Lower Limpopo Valley," *Journal of Southern African Studies* 17, no. 2 (1991): 239-70; M. Anne Pitcher, "From Coercion to Incentives: The Portuguese Colonial Cotton Regime in Angola and Mozambique, 1964-1974," in *Cotton, Colonialism and Social History in Sub-Saharan Africa*, ed. Allen Isaacman and Richard Roberts (Heinemann, James Currey, 1995), 119-43.

3

"Everyday" Displacements in Colonial Angola: Changing Political Geographies of Infrastructure, Gender, and Quotidian Village Concentration

Aharon deGrassi

Introduction

In 2012, Mama OMA, an elderly woman from a cassava-farming village near where I conducted fieldwork in western Malanje, shared a story with me. She recounted how, during the colonial period, she and her fellow villagers had been forced to carry heavy stones to build the nearby road.[1] Raising her hands above her head to mimic the burdensome weight, she let out a small, exasperated laugh of relief that the dreadful practice was long over. Later research revealed that her forced labour in road construction in western Malanje Province was part of a larger, Angola-wide program of manual dirt road building combined with village concentration (see figure 3.1 below).

Another day, a *soba* (chief) explained to me that their small village had been relocated along a built road. Previously, it was situated a short distance away, down the sloping hill, closer to the Carianza stream (see figure 3.1 below). I had inquired about his village's location after carefully examining detailed older maps of the area, which seemed to show the village in a different place. I had also discussed with other researchers the existence of villages with similar names on these maps, and which were now in different locations. As these pieces of a broader story about long-standing quotidian road construction and village relocation began to coalesce, I recalled earlier visits to different areas with agricultural extension officers who pointed out the remnants of various villages, with low lines of crumbling rounded earthen adobe blocks used for walls still sometimes visible in the grass, often accompanied by palm or mango trees in the vicinity.

The concept of quotidian village concentration refers to the everyday, routine practice of relocating rural communities to specific areas, often along newly constructed roads, to facilitate administrative control, resource extraction, and labour mobilization. Today, the persistent memories and narratives surrounding quotidian village concentration continue to influence contemporary governmental discourse. For example, shortly after taking office, the governor of Malanje Province, who is also a prominent national political figure and a long-standing member of the Movimento Popular de Libertação de Angola (MPLA), urged villagers to "join together in the same communities to avoid dispersion," arguing that dispersion "makes it difficult for the government to deliver public services." He further encouraged traditional authorities in scattered villages to "consolidate with other traditional authorities to achieve a greater concentration of population."[2]

The central argument of this chapter is that quotidian processes of village concentration along roads expanded significantly in the early twentieth century throughout Angola, affecting a significant proportion or even a majority of the rural population. Colonial administrative policies and practices played a crucial role in shaping these processes, often forcing rural communities into concentrated villages along infrastructure routes to facilitate control and resource extraction. Quotidian processes of village concentration were pervasive and deeply affected the daily lives of the rural population under colonial rule, and their legacy continues to influence rural life in the post-independence era.

Traditional theories of state power often assume a static political geography, where state power is exerted over fixed locations. However, the dynamic processes of village concentration and road construction in Angola illustrate a more fluid and interactive relationship between state power and spatial organization. This chapter contends that colonial authorities, through policies like village concentration and road construction, actively reshaped the geography to enhance control and resource extraction.

There is also an important relationship between gender and geographies of state power in villagization processes. The forced relocation of villages along roads increased the burden of labour on women. Women had to travel longer

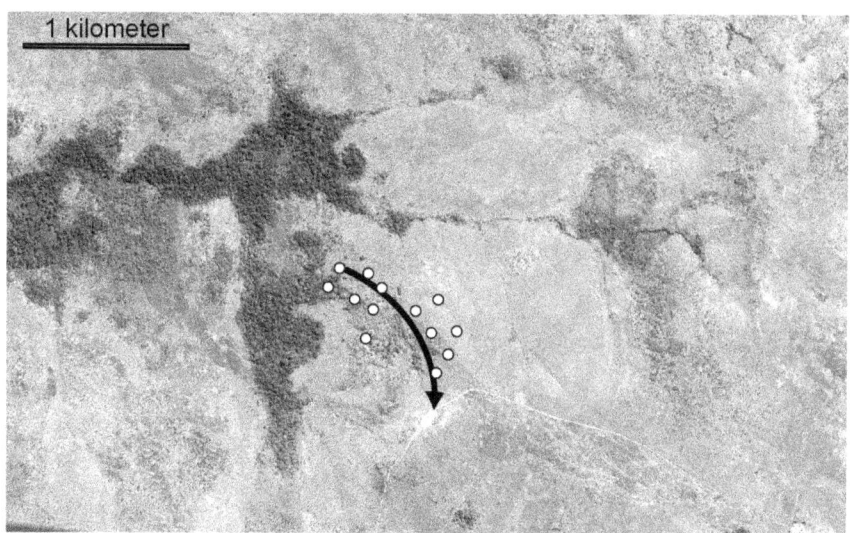

Figure 3.1. Quotidian village concentration and relocation in western Malanje
Sources: Missão Geográfica de Angola, ca. 1959, Carta de Angola; Google Earth.

distances to access water sources and agricultural fields, as villages were often moved away from streams to ridges. Forced labour for road construction also disproportionately affected women and children. Colonial policies often conscripted women and children for the arduous labour of breaking rocks into gravel for road construction. This form of forced labour was effectively a form of taxation that reinforced patriarchal control while exploiting women's labour.

This chapter focuses on everyday practices of roadside village concentration as one component of what I have detailed elsewhere as a long-term, cumulative, recursive expansionary dynamic that was "constituted by the sextuplet of military conquest, indirect rule through 'traditional' authorities, regularized labour recruitment, extensive road building, concentration of villages, and transport and commercial regulation."[3] The extent and continuing significance of this practice have been severely underappreciated.[4] Because processes of displacement were local and happened in the course of normal governance, they often occurred without being documented in detail, which makes it quite difficult to study and to appreciate their extent. I therefore make my argument by drawing on a mix of six sorts of evidence: ethnographic fieldwork, laws, colonial administrative reports, maps, miscellaneous literature, and land registry archives.[5]

Limited Large Modernist Schemes vs. Extensive Everyday Displacement

The large, grand modernist schemes involving camps, strategic hamlets, and planned villages have been sharply analyzed by James Scott and others.[6] Yet critical scholars' emphases on the follies of utopian modernist projects risk turning those failures themselves into distracting spectacles that can blind us to much more widespread dynamics affecting the day-to-day lives of the popular majority of people. Bender's classic book on Angola states that by the early 1970s nearly a fifth of Angola's population was in strategic hamlets (roughly 1 million people out of 5.6 million, including Portuguese).[7] This striking exercise in social engineering rightly garnered international attention and criticism, particularly given the similarities with other related processes in Algeria, Vietnam, and so on. However, aside from the fact that in Angola the vast majority of these settlements appear to have been in the East and North, very little reliable precise information is available about them.[8] Moreover, the important question of what happened with the rest of the 4 million people not in the border war zones has largely been ignored.

The broader importance of quotidian villagization far exceeded both modernist agricultural and settlement schemes as well as health-driven colonial "model villages." Colonial villagization for health reasons—foremost among them being reduction of sleeping sickness (trypanosomiasis) transmitted by tsetse flies (*Glossina*) that prefer moist vegetation—has been widely recognized over past decades.[9] Coghe's recent work on villagization in colonial Angola rightly points to colonialists' emphasis on villagization for health reasons, the broader *inter*colonial networks shaping such approaches to health, and the patchy way such health-related model villagization occurred in practice.[10] It is crucial to recognize, however, that early patterns of villagization actually preceded the later health-related projects. This early villagization was more widespread, driven by concerns with administration, taxation, labour, and road building.[11] The villages were often located next to new roads, which were built through forced labour. Placing villages along these roads facilitated the forced mobilization of villagers for labour on additional road projects, creating an expansionary dynamic.[12]

Overemphasizing large-scale modernist schemes also risks overshadowing women's conditions and resources, and the consequent relevance of concentration along ridgetop roads that displaced them from stream-side villages with better access to water. Space, water, and gender are key elements in processing the starchy roots of cassava (the primary staple food of the region): "In some circumstances, a minor change in the sequence of the different processing steps can lead to up to a hundred-fold increase levels of cyanogenic compounds in the final food product."[13] Access to water is really important because soaking is a complex process involving a range of micro-organisms and biochemical processes. People vary the duration of soaking (number of days) according to different types of cassava, water sources and conditions, ambient temperature, availability of sunshine, climate conditions, end uses, and so on.

The responsibilities of women in ensuring safe food production extend beyond the often-cited example of cassava cyanide being an issue only during exceptional wartime food emergencies. The effects of cyanide poisoning can be far more extensive than the most visible indication of acute poisoning, known as konzo. Konzo is an acute irreversible condition that can present in varying stages, from weakness (including trembling, muscle cramping, numbness, aching, and blurred vision) to reliance on a cane, dependence on crutches, and total immobilization. Beyond this acute visible condition, repeated exposure to lower levels of cyanide can produce a range of significant but less immediate and less visible effects, which can emerge progressively. There may also be cognitive effects that have not yet been thoroughly studied. These conditions are reported not just in war-displaced areas of Congo, but by journalists in contemporary Angola as well as in day-to-day conversations in the field.[14]

Increased exposure to cassava cyanide due to the distance from water sources for soaking is compounded by a lack of access to fish, whose proteins help break down cyanide in the body. Village concentration also makes it more time-consuming to collect a varied diet of products (mushrooms, herbs, insects, etc.) that counteract cyanide.[15] Additionally, concentrating villages increases reliance on bitter, cyanide-rich cassava varieties to deter theft. Planting cassava in drier areas further increases the roots' cyanide content, as the plants produce more cyanide to protect against predators made hungrier by drought-induced scarcities.[16]

There are important spatial constraints related to accessing water, where gendered divisions of labour mean that women often engage in extra work to access water for domestic uses and, most significantly, for cassava processing. For many villages, access to water has been made more difficult and time-consuming by the concentration of villages along roads and away from streams, as well as the fragmentation of the landscape into plantations spanning streams. Some villages do have boreholes for water for cooking, washing, drinking, and bathing. However, spending more time carrying water to fermentation barrels, or cassava to soaking pits, means less time for other productive activities. Even in those villages with transport access, the fragmented and concentrated agrarian and transport structures combine with gendered divisions of labour to constrain the amount of cassava that can be produced for market.

Evolution of Road Construction and Village Concentration in Angola

The concentration of villages along often newly built roads occurred in Angola particularly from the 1910s onward. In this section I trace chronologically the development of roads and village concentration, drawing on laws, archives, and various reports, supported by a few examples mostly from Malanje. My conceptual argument is that contemporary patterns of settlement and forms of state administration are the *products of spatial dialectical relations* between state and society. Roads and concentrated villages did not emerge all at once everywhere and remain unchanged, but rather emerged and changed dynamically over time through interactions. Hence it is useful to outline some basic chronological periods in which these dialectical relations occurred: pre-1900s, conquest, early administration, pre–World War II, post–World War II, and post-1961.

Centuries before the 1900s, the Jesuits introduced some of the earliest concepts and practices of concentrated villages, particularly in Brazil and Latin America. These settlements, known as reductions (or *reduções*), were established for Indigenous people and sometimes referred to as missions.[17] The specific lines of influence of these earlier experiences of twentieth-century resettlement remain to be studied, as well as their relation to roadworks from the sixteenth century onward.[18]

For a long time, before the renewed conquest efforts of the late nineteenth century, paths were essential trade routes and received active attention and maintenance. Roads were emphasized amid renewed efforts at military conquest, particularly by General João de Almeida, who reportedly compiled some of the first detailed road maps in 1906, perhaps drawing on the work of the cartographer Diniz.[19] Such routes were key to the logistics of military supply chains that relied not simply on porters, but also on wheeled transport and cavalry, but were not yet motorized. By the early 1900s, as occupation was solidified in various forms in various parts of Angola, there was a gradual and uneven shift away from emphasizing roads for military personnel and equipment to conquer and occupy, and toward roads for automobiles for trade and administration.[20]

During this period of conquest, many people were forced out of their villages near roads when these villages were destroyed, often burned by soldiers, functionaries (Portuguese or Angolan), or staff of traditional authorities. While some people whose homes were burned fled further away from roads and military or administrative posts, some people also relocated to the new administrative villages alongside roads. Early colonial reports of conquest in Malanje and elsewhere explicitly mention burning numerous villages and encountering others abandoned.²¹ In eastern Malanje, for example, Portuguese Army Lieutenant Ultra Machado's column burned dozens of villages during its sixteen-day campaign in 1911 to conquer Kassanje, a significant centre for trade in commodities and enslaved people in West Central Africa for centuries.²² After violent military conquest campaigns, certain *sobas* (chiefs) were obliged to move their villages nearer to the administrative posts.²³ It was also explicitly prohibited for anyone under the authority of chiefs newly subordinated to the Portuguese to move away from roads.²⁴

By the 1910s there was a broader shift in colonial directives away from prizing only glorified monarchism and military conquest, and toward liberal rational administration. This was driven partly by the downfall of the Portuguese monarchy in 1910 and the rise a new republican Portuguese government. In Angola, the monarchist Governor Roçadas was replaced by the republican Coelho, who instituted administrative measures on roads and settlements. The transition from occupation to administration in Angola occurred at the same time as a global rise of automobiles. By 1902 Angola already had one of its first cars, imported from Hamburg by a private company.²⁵ And by 1911 the government had issued an official itinerary of Angola's road network.²⁶

In 1911 and 1912, incentives in the form of reduced hut taxes were established for people living closer to municipal capitals, regional roads, and military posts.²⁷ In Coelho's lengthy 1911 local government regulations, he drew significantly from experiences in Mozambique, particularly a 1908 law, emphasizing the importance of extending administrative control and taxation without prompting a wholesale exodus. In the case of Mozambique, the threat was particularly salient given the option of migrating to the mines in South Africa.²⁸ In early 1912, additional measures were instituted to encourage settlement along regional roads by exempting residents from hut taxes, particularly for areas that were seen to have been depopulated by commercial trade that used people for porterage to the detriment of settled agricultural production.²⁹

The large-scale shift to motorized roads for administration really came under Angola's modernizing Governor Norton de Matos, who also emphasized village concentration along roads.³⁰ De Matos arrived in Angola in May 1912, and quickly prohibited new settlements in areas with tsetse flies that transmitted sleeping sickness, mandated the removal of existing settlements from these areas, and required a five-hundred-metre radius of cleared vegetation around any settlements that could not be relocated. Additionally, he banned the construction of new roads through tsetse fly zones.³¹ Within only a couple months of arriving in Angola, de Matos was guided by Lieutenant Ultra Machado, mentioned above, on a car tour of the colony in the dry season of July 1912. They passed through

Kassanje on their way to the Lundas roughly a year after Machado's dry-season conquest of Kassanje. This formative trip led de Matos to swiftly emphasize a massive road-building campaign, with specific legislation, that included providing cars for governors of districts after they had built three hundred kilometres of road, with an additional car for each thousand-kilometre stretch built.[32]

After returning from this car tour of Angola, De Matos asserted that

> the existence of roads that permit rapid transit is one of the principal means of rapid and effective administrative occupation of the territories of Angola. . . . These roads and automobiles will permit the rapid circulation of functionaries, indispensable for a good execution and financing of all the public services, and making possible the integrated administrative occupation of the Province. . . . [As] always the use of force becomes indispensable, in a region so vast and still with nuclei of insubmission. . . . The construction of "automobile roads" would become one of the best ways of avoiding any attempt at revolt, and, in the case of alterations in order, it would be easy to repress these with the rapid deployment of armed forces permitted by the roads and trucks.[33]

During de Matos's tenure, road building in Angola increased significantly (see figure 3.2), as did collection of direct hut and head taxes.[34]

De Matos's major reform came on 17 April 1913, updating the detailed administrative regulations outlined in the August 1911 law, again with explicit measures on roadworks and village concentration.[35] The 1913 law required *circunscrição* (circuit or county) administrators to hold "*sobas* responsible for clearing roads and conserving their alignment" and to "direct the opening of roads, making their plans [*traçado*] and teaching the indigenous." *Chefes de posto*, in charge of *circunscrições*, were required to "oversee the conservation of roads," and *sobas* were obliged to "gather the indigenous of their lands necessary to clean and open roads and to rebuild their settlements. . . . Clearing service of the roads will be done two times, at least, each year, once at the end of dry season and once immediately after the rainy season."[36]

A further update in September 1914 again required that Indigenous people live in villages composed of no fewer than sixty houses, situated in sites without *Glossina* flies, or at least away from water courses, lakes, and dense vegetation.[37] De Matos had also unsuccessfully tried to push through legislation giving *regedors* (also called *soba grandes*, or sector chiefs) a financial incentive for village

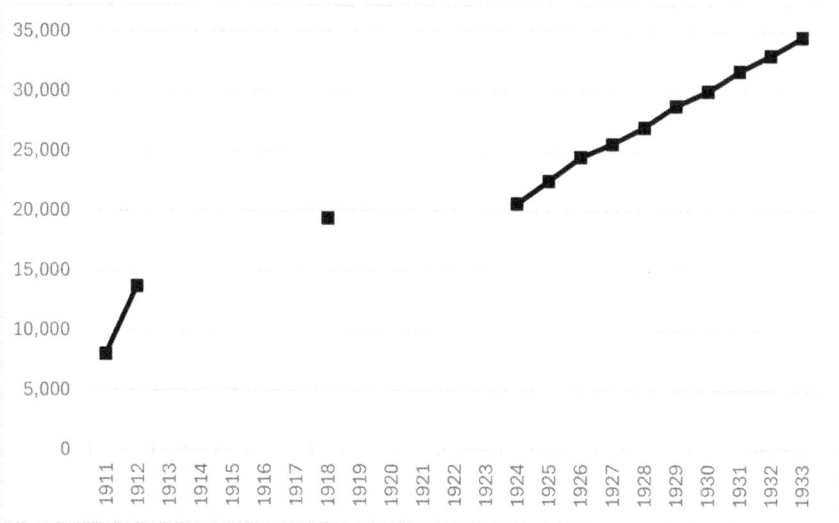

Figure 3.2. Growth in reported kilometres of roads in Angola, 1911–33

Source: Aaron de Grassi, "Provisional Reconstructions: Geo-Histories of Infrastructure and Agrarian Configuration in Malanje, Angola" (PhD diss., University of California, Berkeley, 2015).

concentration, raising their stipend by five escudos for every 25 houses, up to 150 houses (though this was only later instituted in 1923).[38]

It appears that de Matos may have been influenced by the secretary of Indigenous affairs, João Ferreira Diniz, whom he had appointed upon arriving in Angola. Charged with censusing Angolans in order to calculate and enforce taxes and labour recruitment, Diniz faced the problem of people fleeing both the census and attempts at enforcement. And so, he proposed some overly ambitious regulations that put forward a maximum period of five years for the concentration of all villages, after which all other houses would be demolished. Diniz later published this proposal in which local administrative commissions would choose the locations for villages, based on five criteria: (1) access to water, (2) existing nuclei, (3) resources, (4) road access to administrative capitals, and (5) other administrative conveniences.[39]

Apparently only parts of this proposal were included in later legislation and practice; the balance or trade-off between the criteria is also unclear. Villages would be segregated by "tribes," have at least fifty houses, in clusters no smaller than ten, with no more than 150 metres between clusters of houses. Each house would be required to have five square meters per inhabitant and could only be built after getting a licence from the administration and following rules about hygiene. Licences would help fund a yearly prize for the best house in terms of "aesthetics and hygiene." The respective traditional authority would be responsible for enforcing rules, and liable to a fine of between one and twenty escudos (also payable in labour) if villagers did not meet the rules. Local administrators would then be able to more easily enforce collection of hut taxes, which, if unpaid, would skyrocket (doubling the first year unpaid, tripling the second, etc.).

While the fate of Diniz's proposal remains unclear, it does illustrate some of the contemporary thinking: namely, that access to water was subordinated to administrative control via roads. This is because when Machado himself was briefly governor general in 1915 he ordered the further restructuring of Angola's geography by decreeing that all new roads (and hence concentrations of villages) be relocated on ridgetops to minimize river crossings (and hence away from former path routes and water access).[40] The location of new roads along ridgetops was part of a broader interrelated standardization, mechanization, and industrialization of transport. That standardization included drainage and other details for the roads, which were to be 6 metres wide with drainage ditches on each side measuring 0.6 metres wide and 0.2 metres deep, with a maximum curve of a radius of 10 metres, maximum incline of 12 per cent, and other specifications. Road building included clearing vegetation and levelling the surface, as well as building bridges. But it also involved breaking rocks into gravel, or macadam, an arduous labour-intensive activity occurring at hundreds of gravel pits and quarries across the colony.

In 1920, officials shifted policy to head taxes and emphasized administrative control, prompting people to flee. In response, officials implemented a mix of spatial measures that combined reduced pressure with tighter control. So, again in 1921 there was a re-emphasis on living in concentrated settlements or facing stiff fines.[41] Head taxes were restricted to men only in 1923, prompting them to seek out cash wage work, or being compelled to work, in off-farm mines, plantations, and towns, leaving administrators to force women and children to build local roads.

Table 3.1. Differential pay rates for traditional authorities based on village size were included in 1923 legislation.[42]

Class of Indigenous Chief	Number of houses	Monthly pay (escudos)
1	10-25	20
2	25-50	25
3	50-75	30
4	75-100	35
5	100-150	45
6	>150	60

This is the sort of *dialectical* sequence that is crucial but not sufficiently appreciated in most analyses: As the military and police ability to enforce taxation increased, so there were more exactions made on villages for labour and tax; people responded in the 1920s by fleeing; and the government *in turn responded* by emphasizing villagization.[43]

Resettlement provisions were included in the updated 1931 individual tax regulations, and the major 1933 Overseas Administrative Reform Law also further institutionalized requirements for administrators to concentrate villages.[44] The 1931 law states that in order to "facilitate tax census operations" the administrators should "oblige, in the shortest term possible, all the indigenous to group their houses in locations chosen" based on terms set by a health delegate as well as with the "concentration of indigenous populations" where there were already people, grouped by tribe, *sobados*, and families subordinate to the same chief, and "should not, by rule, establish settlements with less than 10 houses."[45]

After Salazar's New State dictatorship had begun to entrench itself, the 1933 Overseas Administrative Reform Law reiterated the responsibility of administrators to "Direct the opening of roads and correction of plans/sketches [*traçados*]; [and] oblige the indigenous to link their villages with paths," with lower *chefes de postos* similarly tasked.[46] This 1933 law likewise emphasized roadside villagization, charging administrators with "ensuring the cleanliness and linearity of indigenous villages, seeking to relocate them closer to the roads, situating them in locales that are salubrious and where they can find the best plots for the usual crops, wherever possible in accord with health/sanitary authorities."[47]

This process was reported for numerous villages in northern coffee areas since the early 1930s, as later described by one first-hand witness in 1957:

During 1932 and 1933, for reasons which the Portuguese colonial administration has kept secret, all our villages were moved. We were forced to construct other villages along automobile roads. Certain villages whose inhabitants were not able to move themselves in the time allowed by the administration were burned.[48]

Another example comes from a 1934 report by the local administrator of Kalandula (Duque de Bragança) in Malanje, which states that villages there were already being concentrated. It noted that the Overseas Administrative Reform had set forth native villagization. And stated that bringing "the indigenous together with the roads, making it easier to regulate [*fiscalisção*] their livelihoods, the censusing for native tax, and the easy and careful conservation of roads, given that we have in that way the indigenous readily at hand, for repairs, making it unnecessary for sepoys to over mountains and valleys, looking for people for the works and committing all sorts of vexations and violences." It stated (fairly unrealistically) that all village relocations should be completed within three or four years. It depicted village concentration in similar terms as Diniz and de Matos, whose laws the report cites.[49]

This example from Kalandula was occurring throughout Malanje Province (and quite likely Angola), exemplified by a circa 1933 instruction on "Villagization of the Indigenous," which was issued by the governor of Malanje Province himself, Vasco Lopes Alves, and sent to the local administrators.[50] The governor's six-page, eleven-article instruction outlined several key directives: Villages should comprise people of the same race; fields should be demarcated and cleared; houses should be constructed from local materials; irrigation projects should be studied and implemented by the Indigenous population; large land concessions near Indigenous villages should be avoided, as well as the presence of trading stores and European residences within these villages. Additionally, each village was to have a school and be regularly visited by health and agricultural extension agents. Each village would also have a *regedor* (sector chief) who would act as the intermediary between the inhabitants and the authorities. In November 1935, Malanje Provincial Governor Alves also ordered the administrator of Malanje Municipality to compose a report on villagization within sixty days.[51] He mentioned that the governor general of Angola had recommended the building of Indigenous villagizations to facilitate services. The report was to count the numbers of Indigenous who are not in villages above fifty houses, count the number of villages with fifty to one hundred houses to group these people, determine where the new villagizations would be located, and calculate the cost of construction and links with roads. Likewise, the governor of Luanda Province noted in 1935 that "all *circunscrições* are working on the construction of villages aimed at concentrating the natives" in new villages "close to the roads."[52]

Indicative of a broader renewed Portuguese attention to colonization, and thus villagization, a Colonization Congress was held in 1934, with recommendations promoting villagization.[53] The next year a questionnaire addressing villagization was circulated by the colonial minister at the 1935 Imperial Economy Conference.[54] Two years later, at the second conference of colonial governors in 1937, Melo Vieira presented a session on "Conditions of Fixation of Fixing Indigenous to the Land."[55]

Concerns had been raised, however, since the 1930s about implications of villagization for access to water and land, being voiced again in the 1950s.[56] A new, more extensive fourteen-article draft decree was written up and submitted in June 1939 by Colonial Minister José Vieira Machado, proposing that governors be responsible for gradually grouping villages into twenty or more families, with villages grouped by "race" and organized for various social and economic development purposes. This was followed by a report around 1940 on villagization by the former high commissioner of Angola, Vicente Ferreira. However, in 1941 ministers voted against the draft decree.[57] Given the contradiction between villagization and labour recruitment, and the thorny question of rights for villagized people "in an intermediary state between Portuguese citizenship and the *indigenato*," the issue was discussed and debated for several years at the highest levels, including in the Colonial Council around 1948.[58] In practice, such high-level uncertainty meant on-the-ground discretion for local administrators to continue.[59]

The Erasure of Former Settlements

The processes of road building and village concentration and relocation along roads continued in the periods after World War II and after the 1961 outbreak of the liberation war and increase in counter-insurgency measures.[60] Some evidence of this was found in the Malanje land registry archives, which survived the war (the city of Malanje was not captured by UNITA, the União Nacional para a Independência Total de Angola), and which I spent some time studying. The map in figure 3.3 below reveals traces of villages (denoted by clusters of dots representing houses) that were displaced and then were "removed" from the map by marking over them with a dark pen, some of which has worn away over time, once again revealing the villages (see left corner).

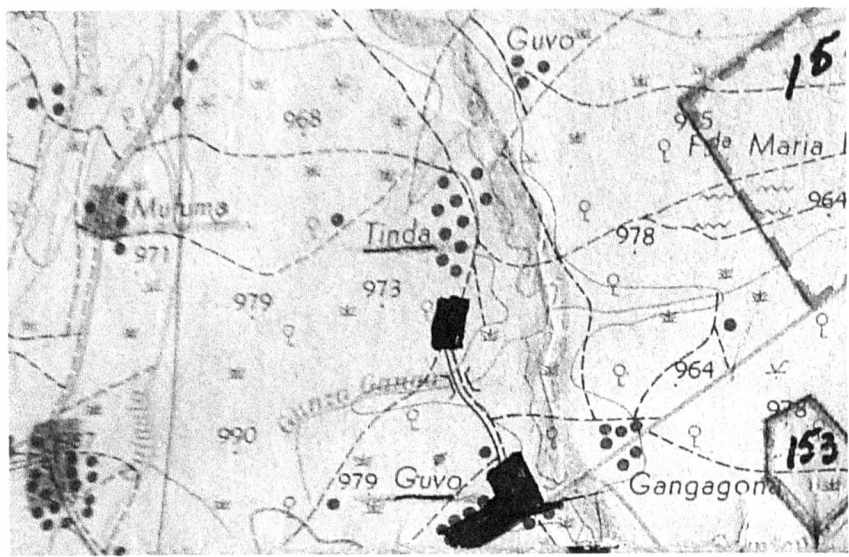

Figure 3.3. Erasure of villages on Malanje colonial land registry map, ca. 1960s

Another example in the Malanje land archives is from near Cacuso in the early 1970s, where José de Matos Figueira filed a land claim of one thousand hectares. The map of his plantation claim shows various villages crossed off and blacked out (figure 3.4 below). And yet, Figueira stated in his description of the area that there were no other rights holders.[61] This was despite the fact that there were still farms (including some coffee plants) in the area. Figueira noted in a 1970 letter that a former claim on the land had been abandoned about ten years prior, leaving only ruins of the adobe houses and some burnt mango and orange trees. In sum, the landscape was being constructed through new plantation claims in which past ruins of villages were being erased, while it still bore marks of habitation and use (coffee and farms), as well as abandonment during the political tumult since 1961.

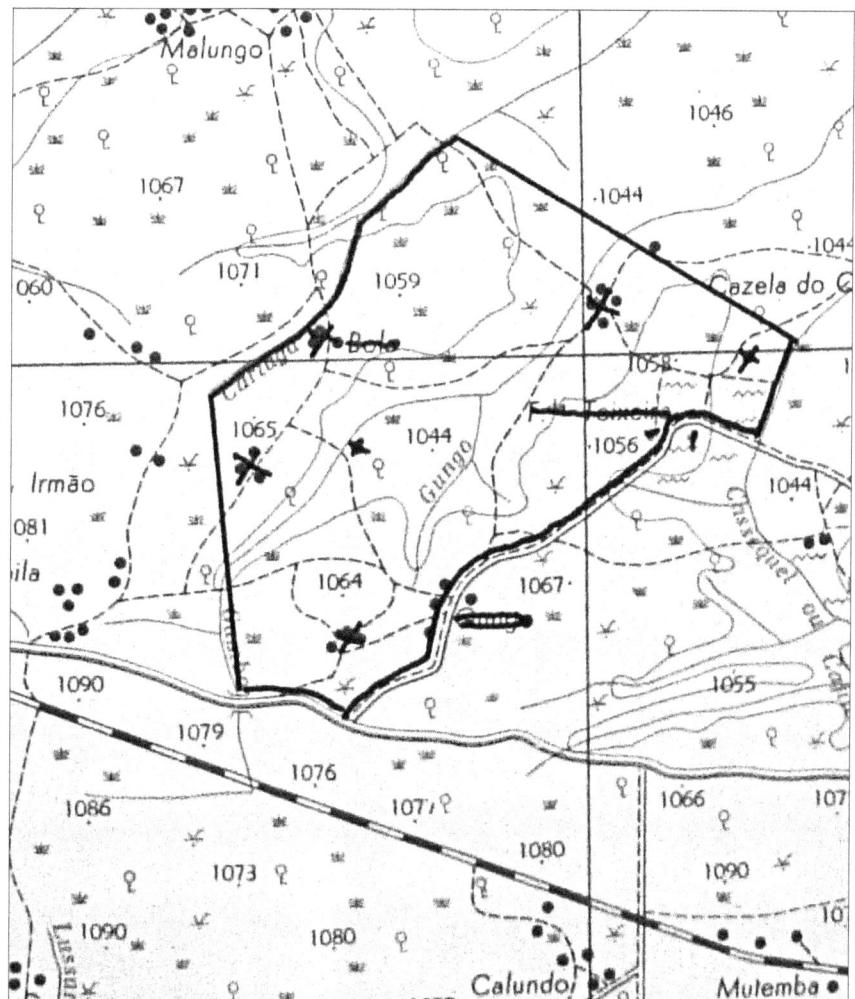

Figure 3.4. Erasure of colonial villages, Figueira plantation, ca. 1970
Source: IGCA Malanje Archive.

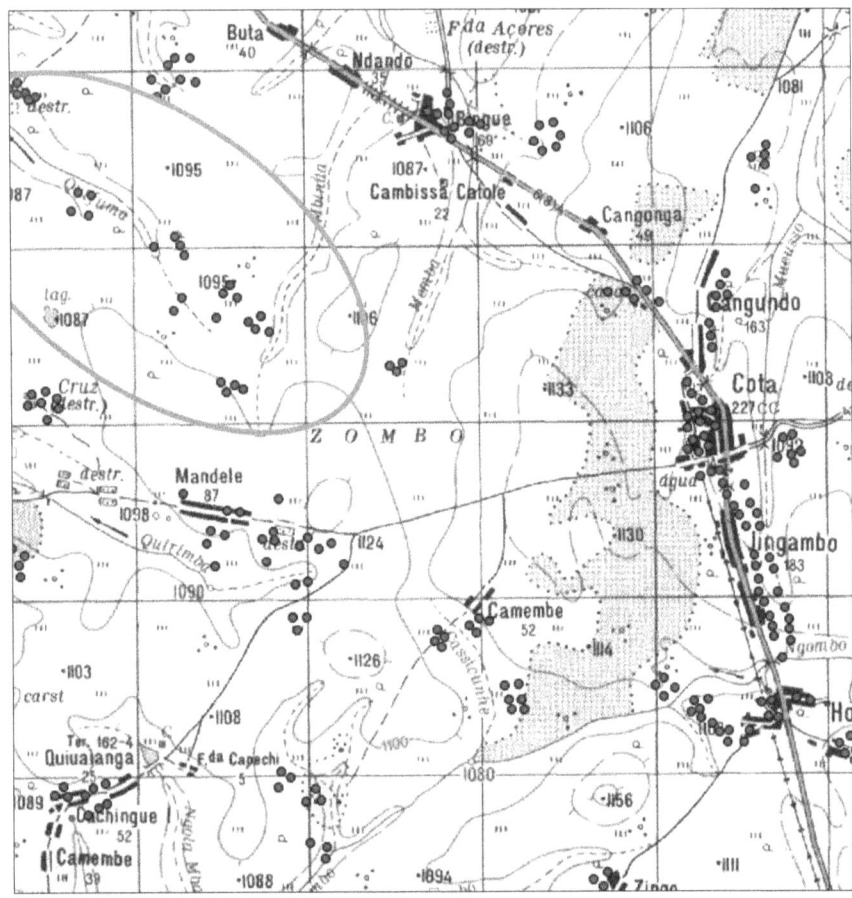

Figure 3.5. Former house locations (dots for 1950s), overlaid on 1980s map (villages as black rectangles)

Sources: Missão Geografica de Angola, ca. 1965, and IGCA, ca. 1989.

Looking at figure 3.5, settlement changes are also visible by overlaying the locations of houses from the older 1959 map (indicated by dots) on the more recent map from around 1980. The contrast clearly shows that in the past dispersed houses were often along streams, but subsequently became more concentrated and located along roads.

For example, above the village of Mandele, the 1959 map shows numerous houses along the Quifuma stream (area of oval). This area had been claimed by a

Portuguese settler in Kota named Alípio Machado as part of a hundred-hectare plantation that he applied to formalize in 1969. The local use of the stream and the existence of the houses along it were administratively written off, with remarks that only a small field was in use, but the rest had never been cultivated nor used for cattle by Indigenous inhabitants. The subsequent 1979–80 map shows only the ruins of *some* of the neighbouring villages, with no indication of other villages nor the settlements near the Quifuma stream that Machado enclosed. After 1980, it is likely that further concentration in larger villages and along roads may have occurred as war increased (in this specific area starting around 1983, periodically until 2002).

A broader picture about the relative extent of such changes emerges if one examines the "annotated" old maps that show villages being covered up (literally black-boxed) or crossed out, as well as the overlay of the older and newer map series. For Malanje Province alone the number of smaller settlements and villages that have disappeared is on the order of *a thousand*.

The likelihood is that, Angola-wide, the number is multiple times this, though of course the processes varied, particularly for more dispersed, arid, and pastoral areas (and Malanje did have a relatively high proportion of white colonial settlers). An extremely rough approximation is illustrated in the map I have composed from available GIS data (shown in map 3.1 below), which overlays digital databases of the geographic coordinates of contemporary (ca. 1980s) villages with main roads. The patterns of villages along roads is unmistakable and striking, particularly for the northern half of the country, where the liberation war was intense due to Angolan forces mobilizing across the border in the Democratic Republic of the Congo. In central Angola, the correlation is less clear visually, partly because the settlement density is greater and many non-primary roads are not shown, while in arid and sparsely populated southern Angola, locations near rivers and streams is common.

Comparing old and subsequent maps is often a fraught exercise. However, there are unmistakable instances where villages marked on early 1900s maps either do not appear at all on detailed 1950s maps or appear in distinctly different locations, typically along new straight roads. This was a quotidian process involving a few dozen people or households in each instance. It was often liminal, not requiring careful reporting, with a lack of means or incentive to record it accurately. A challenge is that only those villages that explorers saw or heard about during their travels are shown on early maps. Their routes relied on existing paths between villages, meaning they travelled where there were people and paths, making their routes self-selecting rather than arbitrary. The resolution of these maps is often low. Sometimes locations mentioned in texts do not appear

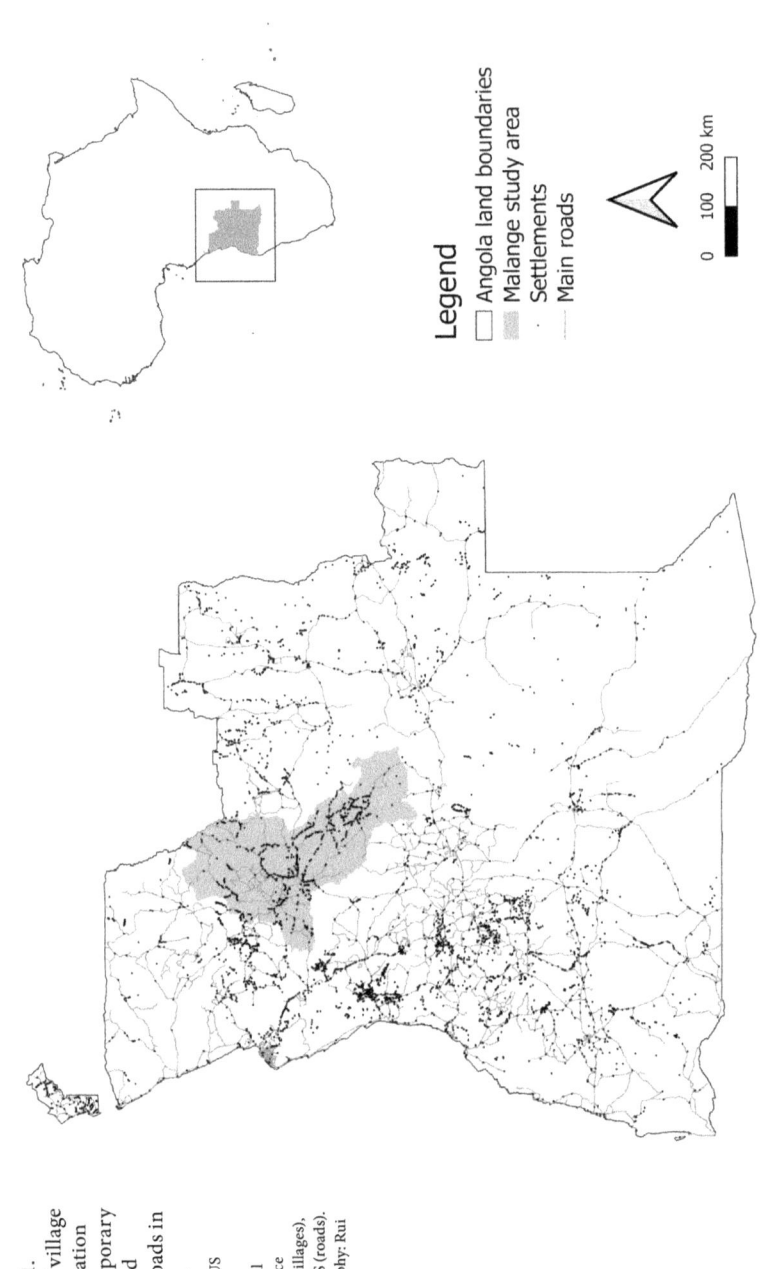

Map 3.1. Map of village geo-location contemporary data and main roads in Angola

Sources: US National Geospatial Intelligence Agency (villages), DIVA-GIS (roads). Cartography: Rui Pinto.

on maps, and vice versa. Nonetheless, many villages depicted on these maps still exist today. Further detailed research is needed to understand the extent to which people in post-colonial and postwar Angola have been able or inclined to move to or return to locations formerly occupied decades ago (anywhere from ten to ninety years prior). Elsewhere, I have emphasized understanding key questions of land legacies in terms of dynamic "cumulative combinations."[62]

Conclusions and Implications

There is broader suggestive evidence from numerous studies mentioning village grouping and roadside concentration in dozens of African countries. Detailed maps of village settlement patterns across various regions further support the prevalence of this roadside concentration policy.[63] Similar experiences in Mozambique, both pre– and post–World War II, and in Guinea Bissau's post-1960 wartime experiences, also point to this trend. While various authors mention colonial village concentration along roads, the broader patterns and extent have not yet been thoroughly studied. Understanding the specificities of Lusophone networks and experiences in relation to broader inter-imperial connections remains an ongoing challenge.[64]

These findings have practical implications, firstly for contemporary postwar road reconstruction programs that are reinforcing these historic patterns. Approximately $20 billion has reportedly been spent on rebuilding over twelve thousand kilometres of roads from early 2008 to 2017, though the data require further scrutiny.[65] Despite promises that such roads would facilitate the sale of goods from the countryside and spur agricultural production and rural livelihoods, there remain significant urban-rural inequalities in poverty levels.[66] More recently, such patterns are further entrenched by using satellite imagery processed with machine learning and artificial intelligence, now influencing development research, policy, and projects.[67]

Secondly, these findings help recast theories of state power by challenging the assumption of fixed geography. For example, Soares de Oliveira's assumption of Angola's "enduring limitations of geography" and Portugal's relative "weakness" in early colonial Angola is problematic.[68] In contrast, Boone rightly moves past the binary of total "state presence" or complete absence, recognizing that "levels and quality of stateness vary . . . across functional domains of state action . . . and across social groups."[69]

Thirdly, gender is crucial to all these dynamics, yet insufficiently addressed in the literature.[70] Much of the increasingly rich literature on women, land, and the Portuguese Empire has focused primarily on *tenure* rather than situating land in its *integrated* geographic contexts.[71] Gender-blind assumptions about colonial Portuguese spatial weakness suggest that when faced with taxes individuals (whose gender goes unspecified) could simply flee, but this ignores the importance of access to water, and particularly gendered differences in domestic responsibilities.[72] "Exiting" was not available equally to men and women, and could place a disproportionate burden on women. Exiting to mountainous or forested areas difficult for state agents likewise could entail heightened challenges for women's access to water. Analysts who invoke "exit" have hitherto largely assumed a unitary household or village as an actor, and hence left as an unexamined "black box" exactly *who* decided *who* should exit, on which bases, and through which decision-making procedures.[73]

Furthermore, forced labour for road construction was very often disproportionately done by women and children, and effectively constituted a form of taxation. Village concentration along roads could thus both rely upon and reinforce patriarchy. While men may have faced pressure from state taxes to exit, conversely, they also may have had incentives to collaborate with the colonial state in order to reinforce their advantages and control over women. These countervailing incentives affected different men differently. Indirect rule as a form involving violence and governmentality also relied on reinforcing and reconfiguring patriarchy, even as it also involved *some* less significant restrictions on patriarchal rule and was also subject to new forms of women's resistances and claims.

This chapter has focused on extensive quotidian roadside village concentration as one component of a long-term, cumulative, recursive expansionary dynamic. This dynamic was constituted by military conquest, indirect rule through "traditional" authorities, regularized labour recruitment, extensive road building, concentration of villages, and transport and commercial regulation. Recognizing this more broadly as a common colonial practice also prompts re-theorizing of geographies of the state, and, consequently, the political possibilities and strategies for substantively changing these impoverishing historic infrastructures and displacements.

NOTES TO CHAPTER 3

Research for this chapter was supported by a post-doctoral fellowship at the Yale Program in Agrarian Studies, and I am grateful for comments on an earlier version, "Cassava Capitalism? Gendered Land, Space, and States in Rural Angola's Pasts and Futures," presented as part of the panel "Land Access and Property Rights in Angola, Mozambique, and Brazil," at the 61st Annual Meeting of the African Studies Association, Atlanta, 30 November 2018.

1. "OMA" designated her involvement (presumably as the village representative) with the Organização das Mulheres de Angola (Organization of Angolan Women), which is affiliated with the MPLA, but held broader significance during the one-party period.

2. ANGOP, "Governador exorta populações a viver em comunidades," 23 February 2013; ANGOP, "Governador exorta população a produzir mais para reduzir importações," 18 September 2014; ANGOP, "População exortada a unir-se para facilitar acções da administração municipal," 22 August 2014.

3. Aaron deGrassi "Provisional Reconstructions: Geo-Histories of Infrastructure and Agrarian Configuration in Malanje, Angola" (PhD diss., University of California, Berkeley, 2015).

4. Much scholarship has been preoccupied with modernist spectacles and often unrealized land grabbing, thereby compounding the analytical marginalization faced by a much larger majority of smallholder peasants in Africa. Older literature on settlement geography, despite its limitations, has gone out of fashion, while newer GIS-based literature often lacks sufficient critical analysis. Cf. Marilyn Silberfein, ed., *Rural Settlement Structure and African Development* (Westview, 1988); Martha Wilfhart, *Precolonial Legacies in Postcolonial Politics* (University of California Press, 2022).

5. Partly inspired by James Fairhead and Melissa Leach, *Misreading the African Landscape* (Cambridge University Press, 1996).

6. James Scott, *Seeing Like a State: How Certain Schemes to Improve the Human Condition Have Failed* (Yale University Press, 1998); Scott, *The Art of Not Being Governed* (Yale University Press, 2009).

7. Gerald Bender, *Angola Under the Portuguese* (University of California Press, 1978). Bender's figures are cited by W. S. van der Waals, *Portugal's War in Angola, 1961–1974* (Ashanti, 1993), and John Cann, *Counterinsurgency in Africa* (Greenwood Press, 1997). Cann cites van der Waals (*Portugal's War*, 120), in turn citing Bender (*Angola Under the Portuguese*, 164–5, 200–1, 227, 232).

8. Bender does not provide a source for the one million number; it appears to be pieced together from scattered references, and, in particular, a smuggled trove of confidential documents from a classified high-level 1968 symposium on experiences with and approaches to counter-subversion in Angola. See Caroline Reuver-Cohen and William Jerman, eds., *Angola: Secret Government Documents on Counter-Subversion* (IDOC, 1974), 29, which gives a figure of 887,923 in camps by 1968–9, paraphrasing page 3 of report IV-e. Similarly, there are problems with the figures given in the more recent history by the Portuguese Army, which notes that by 1971, in the Eastern Military Zone of Angola, 960,054 people had been resettled into 1,936 villages. EME, *Resenha histórico-militar das campanhas de África*, vol. VI, tomo I—Angola, livro 2 (Estado-Maior do Exército, 2006), 482. But again, this is without citing any precise source. EME (*Resenha histórico-militar*) also gives a table of *some* eastern camp figures, but only about 194,000. But census figures from 1970 for the eastern provinces add up to only 628,000 people. So presumably this figure also includes the roughly 300,000 people in the North estimated to also be in camps. Major strategic settlement had started in the North in the coffee lands after the 1961 rebellion. Cann, *Counterinsurgency*, 155, notes that by 1964, 150 *aldeamentos* had been built in the North, with total capacity of around 300,000 people, citing van der Waals, *Portugal's War*, 120. Bender also mentions resettlement around Bie.

9. Particularly after Kjekus's path-breaking study of Tanzania. See Helge Kjekshus, *Ecology Control and Economic Development in East African History* (Heinemann Educational Books, 1977). See also Maryinez Lyons, *The Colonial Disease* (Cambridge University Press, 1992); and on Angola P. Janssens, "La Trypanosomiase en Angola a l'aube du 20e Siècle," *Bulletin des Séances* 42, no. 3 (1996): 537–69.

10. Samuël Coghe, "Reordering Colonial Society: Model Villages and Social Planning in Rural Angola, 1920–45," *Journal of Contemporary History* 52, no. 1 (2017): 16–44; Samuël Coghe, *Population Politics in the Tropics: Demography, Health, and Transimperialism in Colonial Angola* (Cambridge University Press, 2022).

11. See also Maria da Conceição Neto, "In Town and Out of Town: A Social History of Huambo (Angola), 1902–1961" (PhD diss., School of Oriental and African Studies, 2012).

12. Although Coghe briefly notes taxation and administration, he does not examine these aspects in detail and completely overlooks road construction. My emphasis also differs from the dynamics of colonial discourses that promoted villagization as a means to stabilize "itinerant" agriculture. See Coghe, "Reordering," 27, 36, 38.

13   Daniel Okitundu, Dieudonné Mumba, and Desiré Tshala-Katumbay, "Konzo: Neurology of a Permanent and Non-Progressive Motor Neuron Disorder Associated with Food (Cassava) Toxicity," in *Neglected Tropical Diseases and Conditions of the Nervous System*, ed. Marina Bentivoglio et al. (Springer, 2014), 328.
14   E.g. ANGOP, "Defendida necessidade de se continuar estudos sobre as razões da paraparezia," 8 December 2011; ANGOP, "Paraparezia espática possível doença que afecta Caungula," 12 October 2010; ANGOP, "Cuanza Norte: Criança morre por alegado consumo de mandioca amarga," 16 August 2016; ANGOP, "Síndrome febril preocupa comunidade na Lunda Norte," Lusa, 27 May 2016. Cf. Amy Maxmen, "Poverty Plus a Poisonous Plant Blamed for Paralysis in Rural Africa," *NPR*, 23 February 2017, https://www.npr.org/sections/thesalt/2017/02/23/515819034/poverty-plus-a-poisonous-plant-blamed-for-paralysis-in-rural-africa.
15   Paulin Mutwale Kapepula et al., "Traditional Foods as Putative Sources of Antioxidants with Health Benefits in Konzoi," in *Antioxidants in Foods and Its Applications*, edited by Emad Shalaby and Ghada Azzam (InTechOpen, 2018), 117–36.
16   Jane Guyer, *An African Niche Economy* (International African Institute, 1997).
17   Teófilo Duarte, "A concentração populacional indígena e os Jesuítas," *O Mundo Português* 9, no. 102 (1942): 249–59; no. 103: 305–14; nos. 104–5: 343–57; no. 106: 407–15. See also Beatrix Heintze, "Angola Under Portuguese Rule," in *Africae Monumenta*, ed. Ana Paula Tavares and Catarina Madeira Santos (IICT, 2002).
18   Aharon de Grassi, "Changing Paths and Histories: Mapping Pre-Colonial Connections in Africa," *Radical History Review*, no. 131 (May 2018): 169–75; Beatrix Heintze and Achim von Oppen, eds., *Angola on the Move* (Lembeck, 2008).
19   Whereas Couceiro had complained about lack of road maintenance in the Dembos, the building of the Ambriz–Quinzonve road was important. Tavares, *Africae monumenta*, 39; Henrique de Paiva Couceiro, *Dois Anos de Governo* (Edições Gama, 1907), 65.
20   For an example of the military purposes, see *December 1907 Instrucções para o encarregado da abertura d'uma arreteira entre Senze Itombe e os comandos dos Dembos e Lombige*, in d'Almeida, João. *Operações Militares Nos Dembos Em 1907* (Typographia Universal, 1909).
21   E.g., José Martins dos Santos, Diligência ao Hollo e Ginga: Relatório, No. 2/2/15/4. Arquivo Histórico Militar (Lisbon, 1909).
22   Fernando de Ultra Machado, *No Distrito da Lunda: A Ocupação de Cassanje* (Imprensa Nacional, 1913).
23   Machado, *No Distrito*, 139.
24   Standard allegiance form Model A in Machado, *No Distrito*, 140.
25   Sentença 1 January 1902, *Boletim Oficial* [hereafter *BO*] 5.
26   Portaria 520-A, *BO* 18.
27   1911 Regulamento das circumscripções civis da provincia de Angola, Art. 110, 1 August signed by Gov. Coelho. See also Portarias 377, *BO* 13, 28 March (Governor Macedo), and Portaria 378 of 1912 (*BO* 13).
28   Angola's 1911 Regulamento drew on Portaria 671-A, 12 Setembro 1908, Regulamento das Circumscrições Civis dos Distritos de Lourenço Marques e Inhambane, signed by Gov. Freire de Andrade. See also Freire de Andrade's *Relatórios sobre Moçambique*. I'm indebted to insights from Barbara Direito, "Políticas colonais de terras em Moçambique" (PhD diss., University of Lisbon, 2013). See also Barbara Direito, *Terra e colonialismo em Moçambique* (Imprensa de Ciências Sociais, 2020).
29   Portarias 377 and 378, *BO* 13, 1912.
30   De Matos's background is relevant here. His attention to spatial engineering was shaped by his background as a military engineer influenced by British practice in India while he was called there to Portuguese Goa to put down a tax revolt and to manage an agricultural land survey to revamp tax collection. De Matos diverged from the militarism of Gomes da Costa. See José Norton, *Norton de Matos: Biografia* (Bertrand, 2002). See also Norton de Matos, *A Província de Angola* (Edição de Maranus, 1926), Norton, *Norton de Matos*; Norton de Matos, *Memórias e Trabalhos da Minha Vida* (Editora Marítimo Colonial, 1944).
31   Portaria 627, *BO* 20, 17 May 1912. See also Portaria 998, *BO* 31, 1 August 1912, and Jill Dias's work on the subject.
32   Portaria 520-A, *BO* 18.
33   Quoted in de Matos, *A Província de Angola*, author's translation.
34   Aaron de Grassi, "Provisional Reconstructions: Geo-Histories of Infrastructure and Agrarian Configuration in Malanje, Angola" (PhD diss., University of California, Berkeley, 2015).

35 The 1911 reforms focused on decentralizing administrative powers to make local governance more efficient. The territory of Angola was reorganized into a system of districts, municipalities (*concelhos*), and counties (*circunscrições*). This reorganization aimed to improve the administrative oversight and control over different regions. 1913, Portaria 375, Regulamento das Circunscrições Administrativas da Província de Angola, Art. 15 §15, Art. 37 §7.

36 Respectively, Art. 26 §5 and §22, Art. 58 §3, Art. 78.

37 Decreto 1224, *BO* 45 of 1914.

38 De Matos, *A Província de Angola*.

39 *Populações Indígenas de Angola* (Coimbra University, 1918), 747–9.

40 "Instruções provisórias a seguir no estudo e construção de estradas carreteiras," §A.4, approved by Portaria Provincial 1064-A, 17 November 1915.

41 Portaria 137, 16 December 1921, *BO* 51, reproduced in de Matos, *A Província de Angola*, 267–8).

42 Decreto 237, Art. 48, *BO*, 16 February 1923. By Norton de Matos.

43 The 1926 census cited by Diniz needs further research.

44 This was also shaped by thinking by the 1930s on land restructuring in Portugal, particularly around *emparcelamento* and internal colonization. See Alfonso Álvarez and Fernando Baptista, *Terra e Tecnologia* (Celta Editora, 2005).

45 Diploma Legislativo 237 Art. 16.

46 Art. 53 §4 on administrators, and Art. 70 §3 on *chefes de posto*.

47 See Decreto Lei 23229, of 15 November 1933, especially Art. 50 §11.

48 The quotation is from a 1957 document to the UN, reproduced in Ronald Chilcote *Emerging Nationalism in Portuguese Africa* (Hoover Institution Press, 1972), 47. See Jeffrey Paige, *Agrarian Revolution* (Free Press, 1975), 242–3, for the coffee areas.

49 Othello Fonseca, *Provincia de Malanje, Circunscrição Administrativa do Duque de Bragança* (1935), 161.

50 In Fonseca, 162–7. Cf. Vasco Alves, *Relatório Anual do Governador da Província de Malange* (1935), 55. See "Instruction #10."

51 See Despacho 23-G, Ordem de Malange, n10, 1935, pp. 4–5.

52 Quoted in Coghe, "Reordering," 34; after pp. 19, 40–2 of J. G. de Lencastre, "Relatório do Governador da Província de Luanda, 1934–1935,"Arquivo Histórico Ultramarino, Lisbon, MU, ISAU 2246. Also, 1936 legislation mandated that administrative state farm depots supply trees for the new roads and concentrated villages, and failures to pay taxes could be made up with labour in constructing new villages, and new roads. See Regulamento das Granjas Administrativas, Diploma Legislativa 823, *BO* 22 Suplemento, 2 June 1936, art. 12, sec.1.c, and Portaria 1874, art. 13, *BO* 47, of 30 November 1936.

53 See, e.g., J. Bossa, "O Regime de Concessão de Terras aos Indígenas nas Colónias de África," *Boletim Geral do Ultramar* [hereafter *BGU*] 11, no. 117 (1935): 3–27. See also *Conclusões das Teses Apresentadas ao Primeiro Congresso de Colonização* (Imprensa Moderna, 1934).

54 *BGU* 11, no. 127 (1935): 117–19.

55 *BGU* 13, no. 139 (1937): 46.

56 J. Bebiano, *Angola: Alguns Problemas* (Imprensa Nacional, 1938), 52; Mesquitela Lima, "A Concentração Populacional Indígena," *Mensário Administrativa*, nos. 135–6 (1958): 21–5; "A Concentração Populacional Indígena: Subsídios Para um Estudo de Geografia Humana," *Actividades de Angola* 1 (1959): 51–6.

57 The proposed decree was entitled "Social and Economic Organization of Indigenous Populations." For extensive details, views, votes, and discussion on the proposed regulation, see *BGU* 17, no. 191 (1941): 7–119.

58 H. Cabrita, "Será Vantajoso Realizar o Aldeamento Indígena,' *BGU* 23, no. 268 (1947): 72. See the text of the proposed decree "Social and Economic Organization of Indigenous Populations" in J. Machado, "Colonização Portuguesa em África," *Boletim Geral das Colónias* 16, no. 178 (1940): 7–370. See Sampaio e Melo, "Organização Social e Económico das Populações Indígenas," *BGU* 17, no. 191 (1941): 7–9.

59 While Coghe rightly notes that the lofty "model village" projects were "only incompletely and unevenly realized," my argument also differs qualitatively in going beyond such relatively few "model villages" that have garnered disproportionate academic attention. Instead, I emphasize that quotidian village concentration was widespread and dialectical. Here, detailed geographic analysis is crucial to assessing overall state power and its limits, in contrast to the anecdotal and metaphorical approach of Fredrick Cooper's influential notion of a "gatekeeper state"—the difference has important implications for both theory and contemporary political stakes. See Aharon de Grassi, "Beyond Gatekeeper Spatial Metaphors of the State in Africa," *Third World Thematics* 3, no. 3 (2018): 398–418.

60 See also Bernardo Pinto da Cruz and Diogo Curto, "The Good and the Bad Concentration: *Regedorias* in Angola," *Portuguese Studies Review* 25, no. 1 (2017): 205–31. By 1944, there were 4,216 vehicles (562 belonging to the state), quickly increasing by 1948 to 7,482 (958 state). *Anuário Estatístico 1944–1947* (Imprensa Nacional, 1948), 373; *Anuário Estatístico 1948* (Imprensa Nacional, 1950), 287.

61 Each land claim was required to file a description of the area, bordering parcels, planned crops, and other claims.

62 Aharon de Grassi and Jesse Salah Ovadia, "Trajectories of Large-Scale Land Acquisition Dynamics in Angola: Diversity, Histories, and Implications for the Political Economy of Development in Africa," *Land Use Policy* 67 (2017): 115–25.

63 For example, studies mention such processes for Burkina Faso, Cameroon, the Central African Republic, Chad, the Democratic Republic of the Congo, Cote d'Ivoire, Gabon, Ghana, Guinea, Kenya, Lesotho, Mali, Mozambique, Nigeria, South Africa, Rwanda, Sierra Leone, Tanzania, Zambia, and Zimbabwe. See Pourtier's striking maps of village concentration in Gabon (contrasting prior to 1944 and after 1970), partly inspired my early digging into these issues in Angola. Roland Pourtier, *Le Gabon*, vol. 2 (Harmattan, 1989). See also, for example, Franklyn Kaloko, "African Rural Settlement Patterns," *Ekistics* 50, no. 303 (1983): 459–62; Catherine Boone, *Political Topographies of the African State* (Cambridge University Press, 2003), 182; Jan Vansina, *Being Colonized: The Kuba Experience in Rural Congo, 1880–1960* (University of Wisconsin Press, 2010), 227, 236.

64 For example, Coghe, *Population Politics*; Alexander Keese, *Living with Ambiguity* (Franz Steiner, 2007); Keese, *Ethnicity and the Colonial State* (Brill, 2015).

65 Mustapha Benmaamar, Fatima Arroyo, and Nelson Eduardo, *Angola Road Sector Public Expenditure Review* (World Bank, 2020); *Rede Angola*, "Cada quilómetro de estrada custou USD 2,1 milhões," *Rede Angola*, 16 March 2016, http://m.redeangola.info/cada-quilometro-de-estrada-custou-usd-21-milhoes/.

66 Cf. Inge Tvedten, Gilson Lázaro, and Eyolf Jul-Larsen, *Comparing Urban and Rural Poverty in Angola* (Chr. Michelsen Institute, 2018).

67 "Mapping the World to Help Aid Workers, with Weakly, Semi-Supervised Learning," *Meta AI*, 9 April 2019, https://ai.facebook.com/blog/mapping-the-world-to-help-aid-workers-with-weakly-semi-supervised-learning/; Devin Coldewey, "Facebook's AI Team Maps the Whole Population of Africa," *TechCrunch*, 9 April 9 2019, https://techcrunch.com/2019/04/09/facebooks-ai-team-maps-out-where-everyone-in-africa-lives/; Benmaamar, Arroyo, and Eduardo, *Angola Road*; Ruha Benjamin, *Race After Technology* (Polity, 2019).

68 Ricardo Soares de Oliveira, "Post-War State-Making in the Angolan Periphery," *Politique africaine* 130 (2013): 165–87.

69 Boone's analysis also tends to take geography as given, rather than seeing it as actively produced. Herbst is more glaring in this error, contending that African rulers encountered a "political geography they were forced to take as a given," assuming Portugal had only "preposterous pretenses" and "the most limited abilities to project power." Even Boone's nuanced work, which seeks to explain the unevenness of state power, still takes "geographically uneven distributions of population" as fixed variables, rather than phenomena that need explaining. See Catherine Boone, "Territorial Politics and the Reach of the State: Unevenness by Design," *Revista de Ciencia Política* 32, no. 3 (2012): 637, and Jeffrey Herbst, *States and Power in Africa* (Princeton University Press, 2000), 12, 76.

70 See deGrassi "Provisional Reconstructions."

71 Mariana Candido and Eugénia Rodrigues, "African Women's Access and Rights to Property in the Portuguese Empire," *African Economic History* 43 (2015): 1–18; Mariana Candido, *Wealth, Land, and Property* (Cambridge University Press, 2022).

72 Jane Guyer, "Book Review: The African Frontier," *Human Ecology* 18, no. 1 (1990): 143–6.

73 Kathleen A. Staudt, "Uncaptured or Unmotivated? Women and the Food Crisis in Africa," *Rural Sociology* 52, no. 1 (1987): 37–55; Goran Hyden and Pauline Peters, "Debate on the 'Economy of Affection': Is It a Useful Tool for Gender Analysis?," in *Structural Adjustment and African Women Farmers*, ed. Christina H. Gladwin (University of Florida Press, 1991), 303–35.

4

Baldios, Communal Land, and the Portuguese Colonial Legacy in Timor-Leste

Bernardo Almeida

Introduction

This chapter explores, from a socio-legal perspective, the Portuguese colonial land legacy in legal language and political thought in Timor-Leste through the concept of *baldio*. To do so, the chapter establishes a parallel between the uses of the word *baldio* in both Portugal and Timor-Leste and discusses the ideological views that surround the various uses of this multi-dimensional concept, with definitions ranging from communal to abandoned land. In other words, I consider whether the ideology of a colonial administration is passed on through legal language, whether legal language is passed on through ideology, or something else or in between. To this end, the chapter reflects on two interconnected questions: First, to what extent does (legal) language work as "imperial debris" and promote the perpetuation of colonial legacies regarding land-related policies?[1] Second, to what extent can a look at the national land-related laws and policies of colonial powers provide a complementary view of colonial practices related to the exploitation of resources, and therefore a better understanding of those colonial legacies?

Like other colonial powers, one of the main aims of the Portuguese colonial project was the exploitation of natural resources, in which state laws and institutions played a central role. Laws that racialized recognition and protection of some land rights, allowed for forced displacement and land occupation, and prioritized commercial exploitation of the land over local uses and practices were central in this objective. However, such objectives were not limited to the colonized territories; with all due differences, at the domestic level the colonizing state also attempted, often to the detriment of local populations, to intensify the commercial exploitation of land. The creation of a Commission for Internal Colonization, highlighted below, established by the central government to "civilize" and better exploit rural areas, is an example of that.

The issues surrounding the *baldios*, both in Portugal and its colonies, provides an interesting field for exploring the above-mentioned questions and the overlaps between colonial and national land laws and policies during the colonial period. The word has had multiple contradictory meanings across space and time, and the realities those meanings represent have been at the centre of ideological disputes about land rights for centuries. Nowadays, in legal language the word is used to refer to legally protected, communally owned and used land, but in current usage the word can also refer to abandoned, unused, unfarmed, or underused land.[2] The idea of a sub-optimal use of the land—usually by the poor rural communities that depend on that land for sustaining their way of life—has long been an excuse in Portugal for many attempts to take land from rural communities, and has been a source of many grievances. This ideological focus on an economic exploitation of the land, with limited regard for other uses and users, was also a key characteristic of Portugal's colonial land policies throughout its colonies, including Timor-Leste. But while the designation *baldio* was used to capture land in earlier colonial legislation, it disappeared from more recent Portuguese colonial laws. In Timor-Leste, in the years following independence in 2002 the word *baldio* appeared every now and then in debates about land rights but was not used in law. However, its sudden inclusion in Timor-Leste's 2017 Land Law, with a very unclear meaning, raises questions about its application in practice, and the ideological agenda behind its inclusion. Given the various waves of contestation that communal land has been through in Portugal, one must ask if such inclusion of this Portuguese concept in Timorese legislation is an inconsequential imperial debris or an ideological colonial inheritance, capable of causing another "aftershock of the empire."[3]

The next section describes the origins and meanings of the word *baldio* and briefly discusses regulations and disputes over the *baldios* in Portugal, with a special focus on the Commission for Internal Colonization. The following section then discusses the word *baldio* in the context of the Portuguese overseas colonies, followed by the inclusion of the concept in modern Timorese legislation. The final section concludes with several reflections on the topic.

Baldios in Portugal

For the average lawyer used to working on issues related to rural land in Portugal, the concept of *baldio*—now understood there as communally owned and used land—does not raise much complexity. However, the definition of this word, as well as the legal protection that it nowadays represents, has a complex history.

The etymological origin of the word *baldio* is disputed among Portuguese authors. Some claim that it derives from the Arabic *balda* or *batil*, meaning useless, empty, or without value, but also *baladi*, loosely meaning native or indigenous.[4] Others argue that it might have a Roman origin, and link it with the Latin word *evalidus*, meaning unfarmed and unprotected land.[5] It is also argued that the word *baldio* might be connected with the Germanic word *bald*, which referred to land without trees, used communally by a community.[6]

Beyond its etymological origin, the meaning of the word *baldio* in Portugal has varied over time and therefore must be understood in its historical context. Depending on the century and the region, the word was at times used, in legal as well as non-legal documents, interchangeably with the words *maninhos* and *bens do conselho*, while other times clear distinctions between these different concepts were established.[7] The confusion regarding the different definitions is particularly complex because sometimes it refers to the legal status of the land, while at other times to the use given to it.[8] Even nowadays the meaning of the word *baldio* in Portugal varies depending on the context. Legally speaking, it is used to refer to land that belongs to and is collectively managed by a local community, as currently regulated by Portuguese Law 75/2017. But the same word is also commonly used in everyday, vernacular speech to refer to other, very different realities, such as land without a known owner, uncultivated land, or land without buildings or a clear use.[9] Importantly, the realities that these different definitions cover—communal land, uncultivated land, and unused land—have been regulated in many different legal formats throughout the centuries, but have also been a source of many political and legal disputes. Although far from complete, the rest of this section gives an overview of the most important historical moments of the *baldios* in Portugal.

Although communal property existed in Portugal since time immemorial, it was during the sixteenth and seventeenth centuries that Portuguese legislation started to, in a more consistent and generalized way, recognize a right to communal property, and its importance to local populations.[10] However, the recognition of these rights remained limited, and conditional to the land necessary for the subsistence of local communities.[11] Moreover, during the eighteenth and nineteenth centuries, physiocracy emerged as a dominant economic theory in

Portuguese policy-making.[12] This theory highlighted the role of nature and agriculture as the starting point in the production of wealth, and as crucial even for industrial development.[13] Such an economistic view of the role of land, combined with steep population growth and a deficit of cereal grains, drove demand for available arable land and individualization of land rights.[14] From this perspective, the idea of collective land represented by the *baldios* was seen as an archaic way of using the land, and became a target of legal reforms.[15] However, the legislative initiatives aimed at dismantling and privatizing the *baldios*, and even the hostile occupation of these lands by state authorities and powerful individuals, were received with strong protests from local populations, with these struggles increasing social cohesion among some communities.[16] The protests against the individualization of *baldios* led to a new recognition of communal property in 1822, preventing its disappearance from Portugal's legal framework.[17] However, more subdued attempts at privatizing the *baldios* continued.[18]

Those *baldios* that had escaped the efforts at privatization conducted during the eighteenth, nineteenth, and early twentieth centuries again came under threat between the 1930s and the 1960s, at the height of Salazar's dictatorship, marked by its authoritarianism and economic interventionism.[19] This time the state aimed to nationalize the *baldios* and to implement large-scale afforestation that excluded the users of *baldios* from accessing them and from earning any profit from the state's exploitation of these areas.[20] Decree-Law 27207 from 1936 and subsequent legislation created a Commission for Internal Colonization (Junta de Colonização Interna), and started a systematic identification of *baldios* for subsequent state-led afforestation, mostly with pine trees, and later some distribution of individual plots.[21]

A parenthesis is necessary here to elaborate further on the Commission for Internal Colonization. As described by Silva, the "colonization" of Portuguese territory had been debated by politicians, state officials, and academics as a crucial step for the modernization of agrarian structures and the country's economy.[22] However, it was only during the Salazar dictatorship that the government took stronger measures in this direction. Internal colonization was defined as a "set of measures that aim to achieve ... the most complete use of land and to settle there, in the most rational way, the greatest number of families."[23] While resettling the population was part of the concept, the central focus was on maximizing land productivity.[24] A significant emphasis on a more scientific approach to agriculture and forestry characterized this colonization movement.[25] Moreover, mirroring the practices in overseas colonies, this process aimed to instill order and to "civilize" rural Portugal, viewed by the central state as unproductive and backward.[26] This commission became the bureaucratic and scientific epicentre of the political process of social engineering.

It was under this political and administrative scenario that the nationalization of the *baldios* was conducted. Some of the main arguments used to justify such a measure included addressing issues such as erosion, as well as a more profitable exploitation of rural areas, but the main beneficiaries of such policies were the cellulose, paper, and chemical fertilizer industries.[27] This policy disregarded the roles of the *baldios* for the rural populations, and had an especially negative impact on those who lived off of small-scale agriculture and relied on *baldios* to complement their livelihoods, in activities such as grazing and the collection of firewood.[28] The expectation of an easy intervention in the issue of the *baldios* by the Commission for Internal Colonization, under the assumption that it would not cause major disruptions in society, illustrates well the state's lack of knowledge about—or, alternatively, its lack of respect for—the importance of these lands for rural populations.[29] Moreover, the bureaucratic, formalistic, and modernistic view of land rights held by state officials responsible for implementing this process was at odds with the much more informal and customary-based practices of the rural populations.[30] For instance, the fact that many land parcels were never registered or were not correctly updated in the Property Registry resulted in accusations of illegal expropriation by the state.[31]

As such, the policy was met with strong opposition.[32] While some local populations managed to force the state to share some of the profits of the forest or to maintain some communal areas,[33] this policy considerably affected the way of life and the livelihoods of many, and caused higher social and economic inequality in these areas.[34] This policy also contributed in part to a rural exodus during this period, with a considerable part of the rural population moving to urban areas within Portugal or migrating abroad.[35] The impact suffered by rural populations due to the nationalization of *baldios* and the resulting protests is probably best represented in the 1958 book *When Wolves Howl* (*Quando os lobos uivam*), by the Portuguese writer Aquilino Ribeiro, based on a reality that the author himself had experienced. Through a fictionalized story, he describes how the rural populations—already those most ignored by the central government—with very limited access to public infrastructure and social services, were deprived of these lands essential to their livelihoods. The book was so controversial that Ribeiro was sued by the state.[36]

During the 1960s the project of internal colonization started to lose strength inside the government, with the last law on the topic approved in 1962.[37] However, it was with the Carnation Revolution of 1974, which ended forty-eight years of dictatorship, that the nationalization of *baldios* was stopped and reversed.

Decree-Laws 39/76, 40/76, and subsequent legislation established the process for returning to the local communities the *baldios* that had previously been nationalized for forestry purposes and regulated the procedures for their administration by local commissions of residents in the area.[38]

Nowadays, and after the various attempts to eradicate the *baldios*, they are no longer a common reality throughout the country, and exist only in the northern and central regions of Portugal.[39] Under current legislation (Law 75/2017), the *baldios* are property of, and managed by, a community, through a locally elected commission of residents (*compartes*). With some exceptions, the *baldios* cannot be sold, appropriated, acquired through adverse possession (i.e., long-term possession), nor seized, and even the scope for their expropriation is limited.[40] However, and despite the legal recognition and protection given since 1976 to the *baldios*, the topic remains a source of political contestation. For instance, a regime that allows a stronger financialization of the *baldios* has been pushed by some, but opposed by others that see this as another way of, yet again, taking benefits away from local populations and exacerbating local inequalities.[41] The several legal changes made since 1976 illustrate well how the *baldios* and the idea they represent—land owned and managed by a local community—remain a contested topic in Portuguese society.[42] Finally, there is now a National Association of Baldios (BALADI—Federação Nacional dos Baldios), which brings together the representatives of the different *baldios* and works as a platform for discussion and collaboration among the different communities that own *baldios* in Portugal.

This section illustrates how the legal protection of communal land in Portugal—the *baldios*—has varied over time and, despite various attempts to privatize and nationalize them, communal lands persist there. The "productivity of the land," in one way or another, was always the core argument for attacks on the *baldios*, often with little consideration for the users of the land and its role in their livelihoods. Moreover, this section shows that the word *baldio* is politically loaded, its meaning has changed throughout history, and it still has various contradictory meanings which, as the next section shows, can cause problems.

Baldios in the Portuguese Overseas Colonies

As happened in Portugal, the use of the word *baldios* in Portuguese colonies varied significantly and was intrinsically connected with ideological views on land rights and exploitation of land. Like other colonial powers, Portugal implemented its formal land tenure system in its colonies as a way of affirming sovereignty over the territory and exploiting its natural resources.[43] One issue common to all colonial powers was the need to deal with the land rights of the local populations, who used and claimed large tracts of land the colonial powers wanted for their economic exploitation. Conceiving of land as "empty" or being "unproductively used" allowed colonial powers to justify land tenure systems that gave limited recognition to local populations' land rights.[44] This also happened in Portuguese colonies; while throughout the years Portuguese law recognized some land rights of local populations, this recognition was always limited in scope (predominantly land use rights and not ownership) and area (mostly residential areas and cultivated land), and was marked by complex administrative processes that only a few ever followed.[45] The much more diverse uses of land by local people, and the complexity of rights and obligations of the local land administration systems, were seen as primitive by the colonial administration and not represented in these laws.[46] Conversely, all land to which local populations were deemed to have no rights was considered state land, and therefore legally available to be distributed by the state to others through concessions, primarily for economic exploitation.[47] In sum, the Portuguese colonial land tenure system was geared toward attracting investment for economic exploitation of land,[48] not to protecting local populations' rights and ways of life.

As described above, the variable use of the word *baldio*, alongside the push to nationalize and privatize communal land, marked the lives of rural populations in Portugal. Similar trends can also be found in the legislation that regulated land in the Portuguese colonies. For instance, the law of 21 of August 1856 regulated the sale of state-owned *baldios* in the Portuguese colonies, establishing that the *baldios* that *belong to the state* and are not used collectively by the local population of a *concelho* (an administrative area) could be sold by the state.[49] The law did not define *baldios*, leaving its interpretation open.[50] Other laws also raised similar confusion regarding the legal concept of *baldio*, and the push for the nationalization and privatization of communal land. The Carta de Lei (Law) of 1901 that regulated the awarding of land rights in the colonies, without using the word *baldio*, classified the common-use areas around the villages of local populations as state land, although it established that these areas could not be given to private parties.[51] Also without referring to *baldios*, this law established that the state could award rights over *uncultivated* and *unexplored* land to private parties.[52] From these provisions only, and considering the possible definitions of *baldios*, one would think that the word had been abandoned. However, the same law, on a section specific to Cape Verde, explicitly mentioned the awarding of land rights over *baldios*,[53] although it is not clear why the word was used specifically regarding Cape Verde.

The Portuguese colonial land-related legislation approved specifically for Portuguese Timor did not use the word *baldio*.[54] Even legislation where the issue of state versus communal land was central did not make any mention of *baldios*;

it was notably absent from key legislation for the region, including the Decreto (Decree) of 5 December 1910, which regulated the awarding of land rights in the province of Timor,[55] Portaria (Ordinance) No. 193 of 27 July 1914, which approved what became known as the *alvará indígena* (native title),[56] and Diploma Legislativo (Legislative Decree) No. 865 of 25 September 1971, which further regulated the Regulation on the Occupation and Concession of Land at the Province of Timor.[57] The Decreto from 1910 makes reference to "free and uncultivated land" (*terrenos livres e incultos*)[58] and, as happened with other colonial legislation, the Diploma Legislativo from 1971 uses the expression "vacant land" (*terrenos vagos*) to refer to land on which there is no other formal land right,[59] but never *baldio*.[60]

However, this does not mean that the *baldio* concept was not used in practice by the Portuguese colonial authorities in Portuguese Timor. For instance, in the same edition of the *Official Gazette* where the native title legislation from 1914 was published, the term *baldio* is used in a public announcement of the awarding of a land right. This announcement mentions that the land to be granted borders a *baldio*. It does not define *baldio*, leaving unclear the meaning ascribed to the term, but my experience with Portuguese land registry suggests that it was referring to land with neither a visible use nor a clear owner.

In conclusion, the Portuguese law for the colonies (and later, for overseas provinces) used the word *baldio* to refer to land that was seen as "underused" or "unproductive" by the colonial authorities, although the expression was never clearly defined. However, while in Portugal the word's use in a legal context was increasingly associated with communal land, in the colonial legislation the word was progressively abandoned, replaced by expressions such as "vacant land" (*terrenos vagos*), often to affirm the rights of the state over these lands. In the colonial legislation specifically drafted to regulate land rights in Portuguese Timor, I cannot find a single use of *baldio*, although the word is used in other legal documents.

Baldios in Independent Timor-Leste

With the Indonesian occupation of Timor-Leste in 1975, the word *baldio* disappeared from the Timorese legal lexicon and, even after full independence in 2002, remained absent from Timorese legislation until the approval of the Land Law in 2017.[61] This law was first drafted in 2009 with the intention of establishing mechanisms that could address the various layers of land disputes from the past and clarify who has which land rights. One especially important feature of this law is the legal recognition of individual and communal customary land rights that, despite their prevalence throughout the country, received very limited legal recognition from both the Portuguese and Indonesian administrations. From

2009, the draft law went through various discussions and iterations, finally being approved by Parliament and promulgated by the president in 2017. Throughout the various drafts of the law—in whose legal drafting I also participated—the word *baldio* was never used, but during the final debates by Parliament's Commission A, it was suddenly introduced into the law.[62] The possible reasons for this sudden appearance are debated below.

The way in which the word *baldio* is used in the law leaves much room for interpretation and can be a source of confusion. Article 9.4 establishes that "land without a known owner, and the *baldios*, are state land." The law does not define *baldio* and, depending on the interpretation applied, the word's consequences can have effects ranging from the inconsequential to an open door to attack the land rights of individuals and communities. I will use the various definitions of *baldio* analyzed above to show how at least three different interpretations are possible. First, if *baldio* is used to refer to *land with an unknown owner*, its use is inconsequential, but a clear example of poor legislative drafting.[63] Using this definition, the article would read, "the land without owner and the land without owner is state land," which repeats the same idea twice. A second definition of *baldio* defies the internal logic of the law. As debated above, from a Portuguese legal point of view a *baldio* is land that belongs to and is collectively used by a community. If such interpretation is followed, the article would read, "the land without owner, and the land that belongs to and is collectively used by a community, is state land."[64] However, one of the key features of this law is precisely establishing the collective ownership of land by communities; such an interpretation would completely contradict chapter 6 of the law, and leave those applying it with a question: Who, then, owns the land that is communally used? The state or the communities? A third interpretation is achieved if we define *baldio* as *uncultivated land* or *land without buildings* or *land without a clear use*. In this case article 9.4 would mean that "the land without owner, uncultivated, without buildings, or without a clear use is state land." However, such an interpretation would make this article clearly unconstitutional. Landowners—individuals and communities—have no legal obligation to cultivate, build on, or give a visible use to their land, and for all kinds of reasons their land can remain uncultivated or unused. While ownership is not an absolute right, and the use of land by landowners can be conditioned by public interests, such conditioning needs to serve a clear interest and be part of a legally regulated process.[65] The possibility that the state might consider itself the owner of land just because land is, at a certain moment, uncultivated or not used clearly violates the right to private property established in article 54 of the Timor-Leste constitution.[66] As further argued below, especially when considering the voracity of the Timorese state's claims to land ownership, such an interpretation would open a (new and) very dangerous Pandora's box for arbitrary state-led dispossessions.

The former Timorese President Taur Matan Ruak, aware of the problems regarding the interpretation of the word *baldio* introduced by Parliament in article 9.4 of the Land Law, requested in 2017 that the Court of Appeal conduct a preventive review of the constitutionality of this and a few other articles.[67] However, the reply given by the court showed little understanding of the problem raised by the use of this word, and revealed some of the fragilities of the Timorese justice system in providing adequate legal reasoning to address the gaps and contradictions of the system, to promote legal certainty, and to work as a buffer against unjust legislation.[68] In five lines, and without much legal reasoning, the court replied that it saw no problem with the inclusion of the word *baldio*, and defined it as "land without owner, characterized by lack of maintenance, high bush, and trash." Coincidently or not, this definition is the same as that used in the Portuguese Wikipedia entry for the word *baldio*.[69] This court decision is a double-edged sword in the protection of communal land rights. On the one hand, by defining a *baldio* as "land without owner," the court takes a more benign interpretation of *baldio* in the context of article 9.4, saying twice that land without an owner belongs to the state. On the other hand, the court's definition introduces new criteria in the definition of *baldio*: the *lack of maintenance, high bush, and trash*. The problem is that, in the Timorese context, a selective and biased interpretation of the law by politicians and state officials in favour of the state, to the detriment of individuals and communities, is a very common practice.[70] For those familiar with the current Timorese land administration, it is not difficult to imagine a situation where, through a quick look at a piece of land, a state official declares that it "lacks maintenance," and therefore belongs to the state, leaving landowners with the uphill battle of proving that the official's approach does not comply with the law. Moreover, these new elements can also be used to push for a more limited definition of communal land. In summary, introducing the word *baldios* in the Land Law created a possible problem of interpretation in the application of the law, and the Court of Appeal did not definitively solve the issue.

But this case raises another question: Why was the word *baldio* introduced in the Land Law? Was this last-minute change a legal mistake introduced by a member of Parliament with experience in Portuguese administration, or a result of poor legal advice from one of the many *go-betweens*—Portuguese-speaking legal experts participating in the development of the Timorese legal system?[71] Or is it, rather, a colonial land legacy, identified in other newly independent post-colonial countries, in which the state retains colonial land frameworks that centralize the state's rights over the land and becomes a "property monster"?[72]

In my opinion, both factors played a role in the introduction of the word *baldio* in the Land Law. On the one hand, the weak procedural devices of the Timorese law-making process easily allow for changes in legal drafts without much consideration for their impact on the logic and implementation of the law, which happens often.[73] Moreover, even for lawyers trained in Portugal, the history and legal framework of the *baldios* described above is mostly unknown, unless they come from Portugal's northern interior, where the *baldios* still exist. Considering these circumstances, it is easy to imagine this change in the Timorese law being rushed in the approval process, without enough time or technical assistance to fully assess the consequences of introducing the word *baldios* in the draft.

On the other hand, the introduction of *baldios* in the Land Law also appears to be a colonial legacy. While the specific colonial-era legislation for Timor-Leste did not use the word *baldio*, it was for a while used in general colonial legislation for Portuguese colonies to classify land as "empty" and "unproductive." Also, the word was used by the Portuguese colonial administration in Timor-Leste in other legal documents, such as public announcements, to describe land that was perceived as having neither a visible use nor a clear owner. Moreover, the different meanings of *baldio*, and the conceptions of land they represent, were part of tense political debates in Portugal and its colonies throughout most of the twentieth century. Also in Timor-Leste, throughout the Portuguese administration, the communal claims to land were mostly reduced to land that was being farmed, and the objective of a more intense and scientific exploitation of "unproductive" land was constant.[74] The resurgence of this concept with colonial origins in the Timorese legislation, inserted in the law in such a way that it can be understood as further enabling large state claims, seems to represent a legacy of a particular way of seeing land. As seen in the case of the Portuguese administration, politicians and state officials tend to render invisible the local norms, practices, economies, and connections to land, thereby making land "empty" and "unproductive" in their eyes. They also tend to support strong state control of land, justified by a need to make the use of land "more productive."[75] As in the Portuguese internal colonization described above, in Timor-Leste we observe a strong determination on the part of the central state to extract more economic profit from rural areas without a careful understanding of, and respect for, the way of life of those residing there, or the impact that state interventions can have in their lives.[76]

Conclusion

This chapter discusses the Portuguese colonial land legacy in legal language and political thought in Timor-Leste through the concept of *baldio*. Nowadays the word has a clear legal meaning in Portugal: land that belongs to and is managed independently by communities and is used mostly for rural activities such as grazing and collection of firewood. But in Portugal today the word is also used colloquially to refer to abandoned, unused, unfarmed, or underused land. The reason for such contradictory meanings can be understood once one considers that communal land has been seen by many in Portugal as not being exploited to its highest economic potential. This idea of unproductive use of land has been invoked throughout the history of Portugal and in its colonies to justify several attacks on communal land rights: in the colonies, mostly by restricting legal recognition of land rights over cultivated land; and in Portugal through the nationalization of *baldios*, implemented by the Commission for Internal Colonization.

In independent Timor-Leste, after centuries of struggle under colonial policies, the same law that in 2017 finally gave strong legal recognition to communal land rights risks undermining this recognition with the last-minute introduction of the word *baldio* in the law without a clear definition. In other words, a legal concept inherited from colonial times, used with an outdated and unclear meaning, risks disrupting the first Timorese legal protection of communal land rights, central to the lives and livelihoods of most Timorese.

One commonality between the struggles around communal land in Portugal and in Timor-Leste is politicians' desire to offer limited recognition of communal land rights. If, in the eyes of central governments, land is deemed unproductively used, unused, and without ownership, they argue that it should belong to the state. This way, it can be reallocated for productive use, with the profits from such use benefiting the nation. While this may seem logical, such a simple argument resonates with the paradigm of a "natural evolutionary process" from (underproductive) communal to (productive) individualized land rights that persists since colonial times, which has a clear bias against some uses and users of land and has been disproven in practice.[77] In both Portugal and Timor-Leste, decisions about land located far away from decision makers were made at best with little knowledge of, and at worst with blunt disrespect for, the roles and social functions that land has for (often poor rural) communities, and even the economic value that these types of land produce at the local level.[78] As argued by Brouwer, the nationalization of *baldios* in Portugal diverted "the revenues of the 'communal good' from the community to the 'public good' as perceived by the national authorities in Lisbon."[79] Moreover, as the case of the above-mentioned

Commission for Internal Colonization well exemplifies, politicians and state officials tend to have a certain fascination for "technical and scientific solutions" to what they perceive to be the problems of rural areas, and in which communal land rights can be understood by those at a distance to be an obstacle to progress.

As argued by Berasain,[80] communal land rights do not necessarily ensure that community members benefit from the land in an equal or equitable way, and this kind of romanticized view of such systems is misguided. However, as demonstrated by Ostrom,[81] it is similarly naive to think that inequalities at the local level can be easily addressed by state systems, especially when state systems are physically, socially, and ideologically distant from those who depend on communal rights. This was clear in the case of the intervention of the Commission for Internal Colonization in the *baldios* in Portugal. Commanded by the physically and culturally distant central government, and with little respect for the lifestyles and livelihoods in the rural areas, the intervention became a source of many grievances and more misery for the local populations.

The sudden appearance of the world *baldios* in the Timorese legislation, especially insofar as it was inserted without clarity of meaning, raises concerns about opening a new door to similar processes in independent Timor-Leste. For now, the law gives room to several interpretations, and the use of the word *baldios* might be only a legal mistake to ignore. However, if a more harmful interpretation of the word *baldio* in the Timorese legislation were to prevail, this imperial debris could cause another "aftershock of the empire."

NOTES TO CHAPTER 4

The author would like to express his gratitude to António Bica, Laura Yoder, Laura Ogden, Ingrid Samset and Bárbara Direito for their support and knowledge in the drafting of this chapter.

1. On "imperial debris," see Ann Stoler, "Imperial Debris: Reflections on Ruins and Ruination," *Cultural Anthropology* 23, no. 2 (2008): 191–219.
2. In English, *baldio* is often translated as "wasteland" or "commons," but these concepts can be misleading when debating the specificities of *baldios*. Roland Brouwer, "Planting Power: The Afforestation of the Commons and State Formation in Portugal" (PhD diss., University of Wageningen, 1995), 7. Therefore I do not use these terms in this chapter. However, this chapter relies heavily on literature on the commons.
3. Stoler, "Imperial," 2008.
4. João Antunes Barroca, "Os baldios portugueses—Breve comentário à Lei nº 75/2017, de 17 de Agosto" (master's thesis, University of Coimbra, 2018), 12; Brouwer, "Planting Power," 7; Teresa Rebelo da Silva, "Baldios," in *e-Dicionário da terra e do território no Império Português* (CEHC-IUL, 2014), https://edittip.net/2014/03/04/baldios/.
5. Teresa Rebelo da Silva, "Maninhos, *baldios* e bens do concelho no Algarve medieval," *Revista do Arquivo Municipal de Lolé* 14 (2014): 61.
6. António Bica, *Baldios—Quadro histórico; caracterização do direito sobre os baldios* (s.n., 2010), 23, cited by Diogo Filipe Pinheiro Frazão, "O Regime Jurídico dos *Baldios* e a sua importância no desenvolvimento de regiões desfavorecidas" (master's thesis, ISCTE—Instituto Universitário de Lisboa, 2013), 7.

7   Barroca, "Os baldios," 16; António Bica, Armando Carvalho, and João Carlos Gralheiro, *Breve enquadramento histórico e jurídico em áreas comunitárias* (BALADI—Federação Nacional dos Baldios, 2018); Margarida Sobral Neto, "As estruturas agrárias: A força da tradição," *Revista de História* 10 (1990): 131; Margarida Sobral Neto, "Propriedade e renda fundiária em Portugal," in *Terras Lusas: A questão qgrária em Portugal*, ed. Márcia Maria Menendes Motta (Editora da Universidade Federal Fluminense, 2007), 15; Silva, "Maninhos."

8   Brouwer, "Planting," 7; Silva, "Maninhos." *Compásco* is another word that at times surfaces in the literature to refer to communal grazing rights. See Bica et al., *Breve*, 10; Neto, "As estruturas," 16.

9   "Baldio," *Dicionário Priberam da Língua Portuguesa* (2008–21), accessed 7 January 2025, https://dicionario.priberam.org/*baldio*; "Baldio," *Infopédia: Dicionários Porto Editora* (2003–23), accessed 7 January 2025, https://www.infopedia.pt/dicionarios/lingua-portuguesa/*baldio*. The word *baldío* is used in Spanish (from Spain) to refer to unfarmed, empty, or abandoned land that belongs to the state and can be transferred to private parties, but with not reference to communal land. See "Baldío," *Diccionario de la lengua española*, accessed 7 January 2025, https://dle.rae.es/bald%C3%ADo?m=form

10 Barroca, "Os baldios," 16; Brouwer, "Planting," 4; Frazão, "O regime," 8; Rita Paiva, Ricardo Cabral, and Critiana Lopes, "*Baldios*—Historia e legislação," *Voz da Terra* 92 (2019): 12; António Cardoso, Goretti Barros, and Carlos Matias, "Communities' Resistance Towards Common Lands: A Communal Property Historically Disputed by Private Entities, Municipalities and the Government," *Journal of Agriculture and Environmental Sciences* 8, no. 2 (2019): 87.

11 Frazão, "O regime," 9.

12 Neto, "Propriedade e renda," 15.

13 Phillipe Steiner, "Physiocracy," *Encyclopedia of Political Theory* 3 (2010): 1053.

14 Barroca, "Os baldios," 17; Bica et al., *Breve*, 24, 27; Frazão, "O Regime," 10; Neto, "As estruturas," 130. Although outside the scope of this work, it is essential to highlight that the economic and political environment in Portugal during this period must be considered in conjunction with the changes occurring in its colonies.

15 Margarida Sobral Neto, *O universo da comunidade rural—Época moderna* (Terra Ocre, 2010), 314; Maria Elisa Oliveira da Silva Lopes da Silva, *Estado, território, população: As ideias, as políticas e as técnicas de colonização interna no Estado Novo* (PhD diss., Universidade de Lisboa, Iscte—Instituto Universitário de Lisboa, Universidade Católica Portuguesa, Universidade de Évora, 2020), 130; Cardoso et al., "Communities' Resistance," 88. Also note similarity to the reasoning Tania Murray Li describes in this volume for maligning smallholders' land uses elsewhere.

16 Barroca, "Os baldios," 17; Frazão, "O regime," 12; Neto, "Propriedade e renda," 14; Neto, *O universo*, 315.

17 Neto, "Propriedade e renda," 27. Art. 8 of Decree No. 177, known as the Lei dos Forais, from 10 June 1822.

18 The push for the privatization of communal land was not exclusive to Portugal. For instance, on the issue of enclosures in the United Kingdom, see E. P. Thompson, *Whigs & Hunters: The Origin of the Black Act* (Breviary Stuff Publications, 2013).

19 Bica et al., *Breve*, 26; Brouwer, "Planting," 10; Cardoso et al., "Communities' Resistance," 90.

20 Bica et al., *Breve*, 27.

21 Brouwer, "Planting," 166; Margarida Sobral Neto, "Propriedade e usos comunitários em Portugal," in *O domínio de outrem*, vol. 1, ed. Márcia Motta and Monica Piccolo (Editora UEMA, 2017), 19. It was at the time estimated that there was a total of 7.638 *baldios*, covering around 507,369 hectares. José Estevão, "A florestação dos baldios," *Análise Social* 19, nos. 77–9 (1983): 1190.

22 Silva, "Estado."

23 Abel Pereira de Andrade, "Parecer referente a dois projectos de colonização interna," *Diário das Sessões*, 10º complemento ao nº 192, 1938, 842, as cited by Silva, "Estado," 119.

24 Silva, "Estado," 123. See also Dulce Freire, "Os baldios da discordia: As comunidades locais e o Estado," in *Mundo rural: Transformação e resistência na Península Ibérica (Século XX)*, ed. D. Freire, I. Fonseca, and P. Godinho (Edições Colibri, 2004), 200.

25 Fernando Rosas, "Rafael Duque e a política agrária do Estado Novo (1934–44)," *Análise Social* 26 (1991): 778.

26 Silva, "Estado," 281. See also Freire, "Os baldios," 199.

27 Estevão, "A florestação"; Neto, "Propriedade e usos," 20; Silva, "Estado," 131.

28 Freire, "Os baldios," 193

29 Freire, "Os baldios," 193, 199; Silva, "Estado," 129.

30 Silva, "Estado," 132.

31 Freire, "Os baldios," 209.
32 Bica et al., *Breve*, 30, 32; Brouwer, "Planting," 12.
33 Brouwer, "Planting," 169; A. de Vale Estrela, "A reforma agrária portuguesa e os movimentos camponeses: Uma revisão crítica,"*Análise Social* 14, no. 54 (1978): 251.
34 Brouwer, "Planting," 175.
35 Frazão, "O Regime," 16; Neto, "Propriedade e usos," 20.
36 Freire, "Os baldios," 191; Cardoso et al., "Communities' Resistance," 91.
37 Silva, "Estado," 20.
38 Bica et al., *Breve*. Bica and colleagues detail the different ways in which the management of *baldios* has been organized throughout Portuguese history.
39 See "Perguntas Frequentes," BALADI— Federação Nacional dos Baldios, accessed 12 February 2025, https://www.baladi.pt/a-baladi/faqs/. See also Brouwer, "Planting," 11.
40 Fernanda Paula Oliveira and Dulce Lopes, "A ponderação entre o interesse comunitário e o interesse público: Equipamento público em *baldios*," *Cooperativismo e Economía Social (CES)* 39 (2017): 2017. One relevant point for the purpose of this article is the possibility of a *baldio* becoming state property if clearly not used form more than fifteen years (art. 38.2 of Law 75/2017). However, this would depend on a request from the local public administration (*freguesia*), and judicial recognition of the lack of use.
41 Barroca, "Os baldios," 43; Bica et al., *Breve*, 21, 35; Brouwer, "Planting," 231; Cardoso et al., "Communities' Resistance," 93; Pedro Manuel Hespanha, "The Role of Communal Land in the Revitalization of Rural Areas in Portugal," in *Sharing Society: The Impact of Collaborative Collective Actions in the Transformation of Contemporary Societies*, ed. Benjamín Tejerina, Cristina Miranda de Almeida, Ignacia Perugorría (Proceedings of the International Conference Sharing Society, 2019); Oliveira and Lopes, "A ponderação." For instance, while the 2014 law allowed the lease of *baldios*, the 2017 law terminated this possibility (art. 51) and limited the use of *baldios* to more traditional ends, such as grazing and collection of wood (art. 3.1). However, the law also includes production of energy in the list of possible uses, to encompass the now common situation in which the *baldios* are used for wind farms and the local communities receive a rent for this use.
42 Barroca, "Os baldios," 25; Brouwer, "Planting," 224; Frazão, "O regime," 20; Cardoso et al., "Communities' Resistance," 93.
43 José Vicente Serrão, "Property, Land and Territory in the Making of Overseas Empires," in *Property Rights, Land and Territory in European Overseas Empires*, ed. José Vicente Serrão, Bárbara Direito, Eugénia Rodrigues, and Susana Münch Miranda (CEHC-IUL, 2014), 9.
44 Tor A. Benjaminsen, Stein Holden, Christian Lund, and Espen Sjaastad, "Formalisation of Land Rights: Some Empirical Evidence from Mali, Niger and South Africa," *Land Use Policy* 26 (2008): 28; Christian Lund, *Local Politics and the Dynamics of Property in Africa* (Cambridge University Press, 2008), 13.
45 Bárbara Direito, "African Access to Land in Early 20th Century Portuguese Colonial Thought," in *Property Rights, Land and Territory in the European Overseas Empires*, ed. José Vicente Serrão, Bárbara Direito, Eugénia Rodrigues, Susana Münch Miranda (CEHC-IUL, 2014), 260.
46 Henri A. I. Dekker, *In Pursuit of Land Tenure Security: Essays on Land Reform and Land Tenure* (Pallas Publications, 2005), 163; Laura Suzanne Meitzner Yoder, *Custom, Codification, Collaboration: Integrating the Legacies of Land and Forest Authorities in Oecusse Enclave, East Timor* (PhD diss., Yale University, 2005), 300.
47 J. G. Montalvão Silva, *Mão d'obra em Timor* (A Editora, 1910), 34. On the same topic in the Dutch Indies, see Franz von Benda-Beckmann and Keebet von Benda-Beckmann, "Myths and Stereotypes About Adat Law: A Reassessment of Van Vollenhoven in the Light of Current Struggles Over Adat Law in Indonesia," *Bijdragen tot de Taal-, Land- en Volkenkunde* 167, nos. 2–3 (2011): 179.
48 Fernando Augusto de Figueiredo, *Timor—A presença portuguesa (1769 – 1945)* (Centro de Estudos Históricos da Universidade Nova de Lisboa, 2011), 205.
49 Art. 1. Published in *Diário do Governo*, no. 202, 27 August 1856. I adapted the translation of this provision for simplicity; the law does not use the expression "collective use," but instead says that the areas of *logradouro* of local communities cannot be sold.
50 At times legal documents refer to "*baldios* or uncultivated land [*incultos*] that belong to the state." See for instance Government of Portugal, *Colecção da Legislação Novíssima do Ultramar—Volume V, 1864 e 1865* (Imprensa Nacional, 1895), 4, 49. Later documents dropped the final part of the expression and only refer to "*baldios* or uncultivated land." See for instance Government of Portugal, *Colecção da legislação novíssima do Ultramar—Volume IX, 1875 e 1878* (Imprensa Nacional, 1880).
51 Arts. 7 and 8.2. Published in *Boletim Oficial de Timor*, no. 33, 17 August 1901.

52 Arts. 12.4, 12.6, and 12.7.
53 Arts. 69 to 75.
54 Besides general colonial legislation, each Portuguese colony had the power to, within certain limits, approve specific legislation for that colony. Esmeralda Simões Martinez, "Legislação portuguesa para o Ultramar," *Sankofa: Revista de História da África e Estudus da Diáspora Africana* 3, no. 5 (2010): 42–65.
55 Published in *Diário do Governo*, no. 53, 7 December 1910.
56 Published in *Boletim Oficial de Timor*, no. 31, 1 August 1914.
57 Published in *Boletim Oficial de Timor*, no. 39, 25 September 1971.
58 Art. 9.
59 Arts. 8 and 55.
60 See for instance the preamble of Decreto No. 47486 of 6 January 1967, which establishes a process through which land occupants can obtain ownership and *aforamento* rights. Published in *Diário do Governo*, no. 5, 6 January 1967; arts. 4 and 8 of *Diploma Legislativo*, no. 865, 25 September 1971 further regulates the Regulation of the Occupation and Concession of Land at the Province of Timor, published in *Boletim Oficial de Timor*, no. 39, 25 September 1971; Lei No. 6/73 of 3 August 1973, which approved the Land Law of the Overseas Provinces, *Diário do Governo*, no. 189, 3 August 1973, but never entered into force in Timor-Leste.
61 Its official name is Law 13/2017—Special Regime for the Determination of Ownership of Immovable Property (Regime Especial para a Determinação de Direitos de Propriedade sobre Bens Imóveis), but it is often simply called the Land Law.
62 Bernardo Almeida, *A Sociolegal Analysis of Formal Land Tenure Systems: Learning from the Political, Legal and Institutional Struggles of Timor-Leste* (Routledge, 2022), 130; Méabh Cryan, "Property, State Land and Lisan: Assembling the Land and the State in Post-Independence Timor-Leste" (PhD diss., Australian National University, 2019), 186.
63 I should highlight that, contrary to what often happens in practice in Timor-Leste, it can only be considered as land without an owner if the land was not claimed by individuals or communities in the land claims process established in this law. Random declarations from state officials that a piece of land does not have owner are common practice, but legally these do not suffice to classify it as such. On this topic and on legislative drafting in Timor-Leste, see Almeida, *A Sociolegal*.
64 In some countries customary communal land rights are recognized for communities, but the ownership of the land still belongs to the state. In the case of Timor-Leste is clear that communities own their communal land (art. 27.1 of the Land Law).
65 For instance, many legal frameworks allow municipalities or other legal entities to order landowners to clean their land to prevent risks of fire.
66 The details about the protection given to private property by article 54 of the constitution are beyond the scope of this chapter, but it suffices to say here that, even considering article 289.3 of the Civil Code, such a simplistic provision would clearly be unconstitutional. On the interpretation of article 54 of the constitution see Bernardo Almeida, "Expropriation or Plunder? Property Rights and Infrastructure Development in Oecusse," in *The Promise of Prosperity: Visions of the Future in Timor-Leste*, ed. Judith Bovensiepen (ANU Press, 2018), 105.
67 Process n.º 03/Constitucional/17/TR. On the preventive review of constitutionality, see Bernardo Almeida, "The Main Characteristics of the Timorese Legal System: A Practical Guide," *Verfassung und Recht in Übersee VRÜ* 50, no. 2 (2017): 184.
68 On the topic of the importance of legal interpretations, see Adriaan Bedner, "Autonomy of Law in Indonesia," *Recht der Werkelijkheid* 37, no. 3 (2016): 10–36.
69 *Wikipedia: A enciclopedia livre*, "Terreno baldio," last modified 18 May 2021, https://pt.wikipedia.org/wiki/Terreno_baldio.
70 Bernardo Almeida, *Land Tenure Legislation in Timor-Leste* (Asia Foundation, 2016); Almeida, *A Sociolegal*, chap. 7.
71 On the concept of go-betweens, see Raj, Kapil. "Go-Betweens, Travelers, and Cultural Translators," in *A Companion to the History of Science*, ed, Bernard Lightman (Wiley and Sons, 2016).
72 Franz von Benda-Beckmann, "Mysteries of Capital or Mystification of Legal Property," *Focaal: European Journal of Anthropology* 41 (2003): 189. See also Lorenzo Cotula, "'Land Grabbing' and International Investment Law: Toward a Global Reconfiguration of Property?," in *Yearbook on International Investment Law & Policy 2014–2015*, ed. Andrea K. Bjorkund (Oxford University Press, 2016), 195; Liz Alden Wily, "Communities and the State: Rethinking the Relationship for a More Progressive Agrarian Century," in *Environmental Forum* (Environmental Law Institute, July–August 2016), 70.

73 Almeida, *A Sociolegal*, chap. 5.
74 Gonçalo Pimenta de Castro, *História de Timor* (Editorial Atica, 1944).
75 Almeida, *A Sociolegal*, chap. 4; Cryan, "Property"; Daniel Fitzpatrick, Andrew McWilliam, and Susana Barnes, *Property and Social Resilience in Times of Conflict: Land, Custom and Law in East Timor* (Ashgate, 2013), 10. Such positions were common in the debates over the Land Law. For instance, Cryan reports how during the debate of the law in Parliament, the members of FRETILIN (Frente Revolucionária de Timor-Leste Independente) consistently tried to bolster the definition of state land. Cryan, "Property," 186. She also reports how, just before the change about the *baldios*, MPs had considered declaring all national parks as state land, ignoring the impacts of such a decision on the thousands of residents in these areas. Cryan, "Property," 186. As often happens in law-making processes in Timor-Leste, such a disastrous decision was avoided by a providential coffee break that allowed NGOs in the audience to lobby MPs about the impacts of such a decision.
76 For a few examples on this matter, see Almeida, "A Sociolegal."
77 David A. Atwood, "Land Registration in Africa: The Impact on Agricultural Production," *World Development* 18, no. 5 (1990): 659.
78 Atwood, "Land," 662; Christian Lund, *African Land Tenure: Questioning Basic Assumptions* (International Institute for Environment and Development, 2000), 13; Jan Michiel Otto and André Hoekema, "Legalising Land Rights, Yes but How? An Introduction," in *Fair Land Governance: How to Legalise Land Rights for Rural Development*, ed. Jan Michiel Otto and André Hoekema (Leiden University Press, 2012), 20; Liz Alden Wily, "From State to People's Law: Assessing Learning-by-Doing as a Basis of New Land Law," in Otto and Hoekema, *Fair Land Governance*, 85–110.
79 Brouwer, "Planting," 14.
80 José Miguel Lana Berasain, "From Equilibrium to Equity: The Survival of the Commons in the Ebro Basin: Navarra from the 15th to the 20th centuries," *International Journal of the Commons* 2, no. 2 (2008): 162–91.
81 Elinor Ostrom, *Governing the Commons: The Evolution of Institutions for Collective Action* (Cambridge University Press, 2015).

PART II
Indigenous-Settler Entanglements

5

Dutch Colonialism and Portuguese Land Legacies in Flores

Hans Hägerdal

Introduction

In 1859, after ten years of diplomatic activity, two European colonial powers eventually agreed on the details of a territorial partition that largely took place over the heads of the populations involved. After 250 years of uneasy colonial rivalry, ownership of the sizable islands of Timor and Flores was settled. East Flores and parts of the Solor Islands formally left the Portuguese fold for the Dutch colonial state.[1] It was a drastic step that engendered some local resentment, but the consequences for the local populations were as yet somewhat limited.[2] Globally, the late nineteenth century was the high tide of European colonial expansion. However, the metropolitan Dutch government preferred a non-interventionist policy, an *onthoudingspolitiek*, up to the years around 1900, meaning that local self-ruling polities, *zelfbesturende landschappen*, were able to mind their own business as long as they followed the Dutch lead.[3] In eastern Flores the main polities were the Catholic Sikka and Larantuka realms, headed by rajas with roots back in proto-historical times, and also with an element of Portuguese political and religious culture.[4]

This raises intriguing questions about the consequences of colonial hybridity, in the sense of the creation of new transcultural forms in a contact zone. In this chapter I study colonialism as a historical process that involved not only European but also indigenous agencies. How was Portuguese cultural impact embedded in a regional Florenese governance that sought to manage land and labour? Can we even speak of self-colonization—an acceptance of the ways of the dominant foreigner that is set in motion through the pressure of European expansion, but that allows a degree of political, economic, and cultural choice? And how was this hybridity assessed by the new colonial suzerains, the Dutch, who had a long history of rivalry with Iberian powers and harboured supposedly progressive (economically and administratively rational) ideas about land use? In fact, the East Flores case highlights the legacy of an inter-European colonial transfer that, unlike in most cases, was carried out under relatively peaceful if strained conditions.

The investigation is carried out, first, by surveying the construction of a Luso-hybrid society from the sixteenth to the nineteenth centuries, and second, by scrutinizing how Dutch colonial writers perceived the intersection between the Portuguese and indigenous past of East Flores, especially with an eye to governance over land. Here, I investigate how continuities and discontinuities—the persistence of a Luso-Florenese hybrid heritage—are reflected in the Dutch colonial records from the nineteenth century to the eve of World War II. In particular I scrutinize the *Memories van Overgave* (memorandums of succession) that officials with responsibility for a territory were asked to write for their successors.[5] As pointed out by Cees Fasseur in a massive study, colonial officials of the Netherlands underwent extensive training before being assigned to posts such as *controleur, asistent-resident*, or *resident*.[6] This is reflected in an intellectual curiosity in their reports, which often went far beyond immediate practical needs, frequently including historical and ethnographical details of great value for posterity. In fact, a personal intellectual interest does not conflict with colonial discourses: Even if certain data is of little use for colonial governance, ethnography could serve to reinforce a sense of epistemic superiority.[7]

How are we to assess these sources? As noted by Bernard Cohn, history and anthropology both have to do with the creation, formalization, and practise of knowledge that is deeply embedded in one's own historical experience. As Europe expanded, the history that it constructed for itself was also part of a quest for control over space. The non-European past had to be reconstructed by Western methods, which in turn constructed colonial sociologies.[8] To quote Ann Stoler, "If a notion of colonial ethnography starts from the premise that that archival production is itself both a process and a powerful technology of rule, then we need not only brush against the archive's received categories. We need to read for its regularities, for its logic to recall, for its densities and distributions, for its consistencies of misinformation, omission and mistake, along the archival grain."[9]

Flores Society in Portuguese Times

The evolution of the former Portuguese possessions in Flores has been studied by attentive scholars such as Robert Barnes, Stefan Dietrich, and Douglas Lewis.[10] The most detailed analysis of land and politics in Florenese history is by Dietrich, who warns against seeing the society documented in the nineteenth and twentieth centuries as "traditional"; in fact, Florenese society has had a long history of external contact with Asian and European groups. Dietrich sees disposition of land through territorial *Rechtsgemeinschaften* (communities defined by customary right) as central. Here, ancestry and mytho-chronological sequence play a large role in defining the relations between social groups. Origin stories explain the emergence of polities and villages and give vital frames of reference on an island that is often mountainous and infertile and thus characterized by material scarcity. Custodians of a territorial unit, in Malay *Tuan Tanah* (lords of the land), are descendants of the original settlers who allocate the land resources and may combine this with priestly and even political functions.[11] In the Lamaholot-speaking area of East Flores and the Solor Islands (Solor, Adonara, and Lembata), these structural principles are seen in the ritual contradiction between the Paji and Demon groups, which largely overlaps with the Islam-Catholicism division, and also with the division in Dutch- and Portuguese-affiliated areas.[12]

The commercial interest in the Timorese sandalwood resulted in the construction of Portuguese settlements in Solor from 1562 and in Larantuka after 1613, since ships loading sandalwood could easily reach the ports of Timor from these places. Whiteness and racialism were issues in Iberian society, but this in no way prevented marriages with local women and adaptation to Asian customs and uses.[13] The sandalwood trade was mostly managed by the Portuguese residing in Larantuka, who co-opted traders from Macau who would sell the fragrant wood to buyers in southern China.[14] The governors of Timor, residing in Lifau, on Timor's northern coast, after 1702, and in Dili after 1769, seldom visited Flores. From early on, Larantuka was dominated by a hybrid population of Black Portuguese, or Larantuqueiros, who were often at odds with the white Timor-based governor in the period 1702–85. There are also, however, references to a series of rajas or *sengajis* (local leaders) of Larantuka and Sikka who usually bore Portuguese Catholic names. The titles of these figures were not originally used by the indigenous populations but were imported from the outside: *raja* is Malay and ultimately Sanskrit, while *sengaji* comes from North Maluku and ultimately Java. Portuguese and early Dutch sources also often used the term king (*rei, koning*), while late colonial Dutch texts spoke of *vorst* (ruling prince) and *radja*.

According to the Jesuit and Dominican sources, a ruler of Lewonama (Larantuka) was baptized with many grandees and subjects around 1559, and during the seventeenth century several rulers with Catholic names are mentioned, starting with a certain Dom Constantino around 1625.[15] Indigenous lords may have upgraded their prerogatives, simply because the Portuguese chose to approach them as "kings" (*reis*) in the European understanding.[16] A Franciscan account from 1670 stresses the acculturation that was taking place in easternmost Flores: "In this port of Larantuka live some Portuguese and besides that a lot of indigenous Christians, to whom the clerics of the Order of our Father Saint Dominic give their service. . . . And in this Lent we preached the gospel, not only to the Portuguese but also to the natives of the land, who understood us since they know Portuguese. Because of that we had quite some work to do at this port."[17] Another text from the era also alleged that the East Florenese were "very domesticated and agreeable," in stark contrast to the "lazy" and often rebellious Timorese.[18] A lay account from 1695–6 gives an idea of the colonial geography and the possibilities, including the supposedly primitive agrarian economy in a European mercantile system:

> [After 1613], other [Portuguese] moved to the lands of Ende,[19] to the village of Larantuka on the east end of the island, near [Solor], where they already had some churches and Christianity. They crossed the river and placed a village above the place they call Praia Grande [Pantai Besar], at the foot of an eminent and famous summit, one of the largest I have seen, that the natives call Gunung Serbite.[20] It is next to the village Lewonama where the king of those lands stays, who is presently Dom Domingos Vieira. [He is] a Christian who pays obedience to the Most Serene Ruler of Portugal our Lord, together with all his vassals and landlords whom they call *atalaques* and colloquially *atacabeis* or *atacabelos*, being the name and coat of arms of their nobility, just as the *fidalgos* among us. . . .
>
> If there is more Portuguese attendance, a great conquest and expansion of grand interests can be achieved for the Portuguese Monarchy, due to the extended lands that lack culture. They are very fertile, with healthy freshness, abundant of everything necessary for a human treat, and with a grandeur that surpasses some in Europe; for agriculture requires low costs, as has been experienced, since it is just enough to plant the seedlings at the discretion of time, and [fields are] often dug with a stick that serves as a hoe.[21]

Here, one may note the perceived entwinement of Portuguese and local categories, as local lords of the land are equated with *fidalgos*. The Catholicized leaders lived a short distance from the foreign settlement and seem to have co-operated closely with the ethnically mixed Portuguese, who often had Melaka and Makassar origins. In 1679 the Dutch noted that the renowned Larantuqueiro leader António Hornay wielded power in the Timor-Flores quarters with the help of a very multi-ethnic force consisting of men armed with muskets, which were awe-inspiring since non-Christians seldom possessed them.[22] António Hornay, co-operating with the *sengaji* of Larantuka, tried to bind some far-off Lamaholot settlements to their political network by bestowing flags to the leaders.[23] Portuguese flags were very important and spiritually potent prestige objects, as shown by parallel practices in Timor, but their acceptance probably did not entail any more interference in land use than the deliverance of the kind of customary services and "gifts" sent by settlements to the rulers in the area. Rather than landowning, Larantuqueiro power was based on control over trade in Timorese sandalwood until this source of wealth was exhausted by overcutting in the eighteenth century.[24] Also, seafarers from Sikka were active in the sandalwood trade in Sumba, showing that the Catholicized elite outside of Larantuka town partook in the economic opportunities.[25]

As far as can be seen, the local rajas continued to support the Black Portuguese while keeping control over parts of Solor, Adonara, and Lembata. Missionary activities decreased greatly compared to the seventeenth century, but Catholicism persisted, at least in the core areas.[26] Nevertheless the Catholicized rajas replaced the Black Portuguese as the politically dominant force in Larantuka under very obscure circumstances. There is no evidence of any violent competition, but the leading Black Portuguese clans Hornay and da Costa seem to disappear from Larantuka in the 1760s.[27] It is only after the cession of East Flores to the Dutch colonial state in 1859 that the political system of the Larantuka polity is amply documented by missionaries and government officials.

In their pre-1859 accounts, the Dutch officials stationed on Timor held the East Florenese in somewhat higher regard than the ostensibly "barbaric" Timorese. One of the more attentive writers, Emanuel Francis (1832), identified the population with Roman Catholic so-called Black Portuguese, although this can only have applied to part of them. The literate ruler of Larantuka, Dom Lorenzo, was a bright contrast to the miserable and uncivilized rajas on Timor, and Francis noted that he had the dignities of both king and priest.[28] But he also believed that the Portuguese government should state its rights on Larantuka on Flores, and Oecussi and Noimuti on Timor, in a more clear-cut fashion. These regions kept the Portuguese flag without actually acknowledging the power of the government. Such authority should be implemented for the benefit of the "general right of the peoples."[29] We discern a political system that was more "Southeast Asian" than colonial European, where the Larantuka king was a satellite of a central Portuguese hierarchy (Dili, Lisbon) that was laden with symbolical capital but had limited administrative abilities.

Overall, little ink was spent on Flores in the Dutch surveys of the region. As a geographical report of the Timor Islands from 1850 curtly notes, "as far as [is] known, the land yields rice, jagung [maize], wild cinnamon, sandalwood, pumice stone, amber, some gold sand, buffalos, cows, pigs, goats, fowl, birds' nests and turtles."[30] Some of these products were potentially profitable, but the hearsay character of the information evoked little colonial enthusiasm, and most of Flores, apart from a toehold in Ende at the southern coast, was anyway outside their reach.[31]

Can the nineteenth-century texts, in conjunction with older sources, help us understand the legacy of three centuries of Portuguese dominance in eastern Flores and adjacent islands? There seem to have been few ambitions to impose an administrative structure on the villages, let alone to introduce a regular system of taxation. As established by Alice Kortlang, local accounts of the coming of the Portuguese are abundant but stress the consensus aspect: newcomers approached the local genealogical headmen who supervised allocation of lands, and received land on the outskirts or at the seashore of various settlements.[32] Thus, the old system of land management via membership of houses (clan segments) and marriage alliances coexisted with the trade-oriented Eurasian immigrants. At most, modern anthropology has found traces of clerical efforts to alter certain social customs, such as abolishing traditional bridewealth in favour of bride service, with partial success.[33]

However, two factors come to the fore: the presence of a Catholic community, and the emergence of a Catholicized kingdom with a partly new, sea-oriented settlement pattern.[34] While these factors tended to be downplayed in Dutch writings, this misses an important point: the system worked. While most inhabitants of the old Portuguese territories remained non-Christian until relatively modern times, the centrality of Catholicism in the power structure never seems to have been questioned, and the raja of Larantuka had, as Emanuel Francis noted, also a vital clerical position in the religious fraternity (*confraria*) of the place. The rajas were tied to the Black Portuguese elite by matrimonial alliances, socially vital in a Lamaholot (and Sikka) context,[35] and are not known to have rebelled against them.[36] Though the Sikka and Lamaholot worlds were turbulent, the predominant political position of Larantuka in East Flores, West Solor, and parts of Adonara and Lembata apparently persisted through the seventeenth century and for several hundred years thereafter. As will be discussed later, this is partly a result of their ability to co-opt local institutions and traditions, including decidedly non-Christian ones.

"Savagery" and Catholic culture in the *Memories van Overgave*

As the entirety of Flores was incorporated into the Dutch colonial state after 1859, information about the Lamaholot area (to a lesser extent Sikka) was included in the *Memories van Overgave*. The early texts were focused on political conditions in the Flores area, with limited regard for the economic resources. A *Memorie* from 1876 evokes the image of a virtual *terra incognita*, aggravated by the economical indolence of the local populations: "The highlands of Flores are still obscure, one knows almost nothing about them. In the areas of Soa, Rokka, Foa, and Potta, tin is found, possibly in large amounts, but they do not want to point it out."[37] Moreover, the local raja of Larantuka, Don Gaspar, "is in general not to be trusted." The *Memorie* relates in brief how the Raja, as the principal interlocutor for the colonial state in the area, tries to expand his influence over land beyond the Lamaholot ethnic borders by vassalization of Sikka further to the west.[38]

Beyond the self-righteous account of unco-operative and dishonest natives one may, obviously, trace tacit local resistance: Colonial tin prospecting on their land may not be in the interest of the highlanders, while the raja tries to create his own political network beyond European control. For much of the archipelago the Dutch used the policy of non-intervention (*onthoudingspolitiek*) from the 1830s to the 1890s, preferring indirect rule. This has some parallels with contemporary British colonialism.

The most obvious heritage of the Portuguese suzerainty was Catholicism, which had been suppressed in the Netherlands itself until not such a long time ago. Catholic missionary organizations were eventually able to work in the colonies.[39] Missionaries had high hopes for the raja family of Larantuka, who might co-operate with them in order to create a Catholic kingdom in East Flores. The colonial residents and *controleurs*, on the other hand, were less enchanted by the local aristocracy. In a *Memorie van Overgave* from 1878, Resident Ecoma Verstege noted a less than happy religious land legacy. The Catholic clergy, he asserted, kept coffee plantations, which were the reason for the great drought that plagued the Larantukan territory. This pitted the exasperated mountain people against the Europeans and native Christians, and violence was only averted by the arrival of the rains.[40] In the following *Memorie van Overgave* from 1880, Resident J. G. F. Riedel—otherwise known as an ethnographer of note—lists a long litany of disputes in the Timor Residency. These again include the perceived juxtaposition between unruly settlers in uphill lands and the Catholicized centre, in his reference to "the resistance of the mountain people beyond the [mountain] Ilimandiri against the Raja of Larantuka, East Flores, and their attempts to attack the central place, or rather coastal kampong, by means of headhunting, since the Raja of Larantuka, as a Christian, is no longer willing to head their pagan religious service."[41] Reflecting on all the problems in the residency, Riedel posited the development of the "neglected, still in a very primitive way handled agriculture" as a necessary remedy.

"Savagery" and heathen rites are here attributed to non-Christians, in stark contrast to the Catholic ruler, who seems to have little control over land beyond Ilimandiri, the lofty volcano behind Larantuka whose non-regal dimensions—a seaside village rather than a local capital—are accentuated. As also suggested by other texts, colonial discourse posited a doubleness in the position of the raja between a "civilized" Luso-Catholic heritage and an impotency to implement ordered governance vis-à-vis local "non-civilized" agriculturists. In fact, the preconditions of Larantuka kingship were partly misunderstood by the Dutch: The Catholic names and titles and the inclusion of the raja in a local clerical organization did not imply any European-style governance, but rather a highly segmentary power structure with parallels in many parts of eastern Indonesia and Timor-Leste.[42]

As in the rest of Indonesia, the final abandonment of the Dutch non-intervention policy, inspired by events in Aceh, led to a rapid increase of colonial control on Flores by the early twentieth century. Indigenous regimes were swiftly suppressed in Bali, South Sulawesi, Timor, and elsewhere, and Resident J. F. A. de Rooy reports in a *Memorie* from 1908 how Flores was subjected to similar subordination. By the early twentieth century, he notes, Dutch power on the island, formally divided in three *onderafdeelingen*, was in a sorry (*treurig*) state. Apart from four Catholic missionary stations and a few tiny coastal strips, there was no executive power, and the interior was entirely unknown. In 1906, however, a *controleur* was employed with the mission to enforce a more direct colonial influence, "to prepare for measures to make Flores productive for the treasury chest." It is then described how large tracts of the island were mapped, roads were projected, local populations enjoined to accept Dutch adjudication, and unwilling *kampongs* forced to yield at gunpoint. Captain Christoffel with a company of *marechausses* (military police) made a clean sweep throughout Flores, whose "savage" (*woest*) population suffered many hundreds of casualties. But new risings soon broke out, and De Rooy reflected that a more sedate colonial approach might prove more successful.[43]

However, the image of non-Christian "savagery" and recalcitrance in the face of civilized governance is not matched by any appreciation of the Luso-Catholic heritage of Larantuka. On the contrary, Resident de Rooy denounces the recently deposed and exiled Raja Don Lorenzo, who "had a usurped power, on Flores as well as the Solor Islands, and abused that; his dignity is entirely superfluous and should remain abolished."[44] This is underlined by the assertion that the Lamaholot region had been in a tranquil state since Don Lorenzo disappeared (1904). According to De Rooy, "much better results" flowed from the direct communication between the colonial authorities and the *kakang* (district heads), implying increasing colonial control over local societies and land. But not only that; the Catholic establishment that was a heritage from the Portuguese period disturbed colonial ambitions: "With one word I must point out as a warning, that the Catholic mission in Larantuka has, or at least had, an inclination to support the affairs of the exiled Catholic raja. That is the only attempt of meddling in affairs of governance which is found in the six Catholic missions in the area."[45] The resident nevertheless praised the general work of the Catholic missionaries in the area, who took care to learn local languages, did not use intermediaries, and sought no worldly advantages, "all entirely to the opposite of the Protestant direction."[46] A *Memorie* from 1913 deplored the slow advances of Christianity in relation to Islam on Flores, since "a Christianized population creates closer support for our power."[47]

In the eyes of these observers, the Portuguese heritage appears to work in two ways. It forms the basis for further Christianization, which is considered advantageous for colonial penetration and thus land use. Also, the chiefs in East Flores are deemed to be more "developed and civilized" than their peers in other parts of the Timor Residency.[48] However, the power structure with a Catholic raja at the apex is deemed to have little legitimacy and is an obstacle to reaching out to the local districts and villages. With a notion common in Orientalist tradition, traditional rulership is depicted as oppressive and detached from functional governance. As pointed out by Robert Barnes, this is nevertheless a misleading view; the rulers were always believed to possess spiritual strength and authority vested by their ancestors. They received products from the land as tribute from the *kakang*-ships with irregular intervals but had no taxation rights. The Dutch policy that people and lands be surveyed and taxed regularly therefore engendered dissatisfaction and altered the balance from Portuguese times.[49]

Dutch Missionary Investigations

This condescending idea of local authority is also partly gainsaid by a category of writers who had the opportunity to work in Flores, and who were sometimes opposed to the official colonial policy. These were the Catholic missionaries who were active after about 1860. Not much had been published about the former Portuguese possessions by the early twentieth century. There were, however, two short works by the missionary F. C. Heynen (1876), in addition to a number of articles.

Heynen's accounts are especially valuable since they were rather early and conveyed another perspective than those of colonial officials. He notes the importance of ancestral myths in the perception of the settlement structure. In the beginning a brother-sister pair, Liahura and Watewele, arrive from Selayar Island and settle by the volcanic Mount Ilimandiri. They subsequently go separate ways: Liahura goes to the western side of Ilimandiri, marries an autochthonous woman, and sires ten children, of whom one becomes the raja over eight settlements. Meanwhile, Watewele stays close to the seashore, where she meets Pategolo, a fugitive prince from Wewiku, on Timor (which allies with Wehali, the centre of the Timorese political-ritual order[50]). The pair begets five sons, including the ancestor of the rajas of Larantuka. The formation of the settlement pattern is then outlined, with a core of territories under *hoofd-kapalas* (principal headmen) and a number of remote vassals who contribute with certain tributes and auxiliaries.[51] All this is understood to be pre-Christian history.

The account underscores the close relation between authority and land: The order of land division is laid down by the ancestors, who play a fundamental role in East Florenese religion and the local world view. However, Heynen also presents us with myths of the coming of the Portuguese, both for Larantuka and the Sikka kingdom further to the west. In both cases the stories involve culture heroes, local aristocrats who are educated and baptized by the Portuguese, return to their native lands, and bring about the Catholicization of the East Florenese aristocracy.[52] In these oral stories, the Portuguese are basically portrayed in a positive light, as an ordering force. Moreover, among all the Orientalist stereotypes, Heynen does not see the Catholic kingship as actually despotic:

> From olden times the Larantuka kingdom, if one considers the low level of development and the strangeness of its components, seems to have been rather well ordered. Supreme power rests with the raja, who formerly had the rights over life and death; his powers were however tempered by that of the principal kapalas who, being hereditary like him, held far from small power and influence in their negorijen [settlements] and were councillors of the crown by birth.[53]

The Colonial Official as Anthropologist: Looking for Luso-Legacies

While precious little was published about Flores societies, a body of information about the recent acquisitions was piling up in the colonial archives in the form of reports, letters, and statistics, enabling serious historical analysis.[54] There were particular *Memories* about Flores and its various *onderafdelingen*. Unlike our Kupang residents, the writers based in Flores often displayed great interest in the *adat* and traditional past. The dearth of preserved indigenous writings makes their contributions important in spite of their inevitable bias as colonial officials. In part, this is inherent in the genre: Questions of agricultural practice, division of land, statistics for the districts and villages, and religious customs of importance are often found in excessive detail in the particular *Memories* of the Dutch East Indies, since these matters were important for taxation and projects of development. In the Netherlands at the time, there was a lively scholarly discussion on whether the colonial state should appropriate "wastelands" belonging to native communities for ostensibly useful purposes.[55] While the lands in East Flores were largely preserved for indigenous use, the new colonial taxation system was deeply resented and led to serious uprisings in 1913–14, highlighting the necessity of knowledge production.[56] As Assistant Resident G. A. Bosselaar wrote in 1932, "For a correct governance, a solid knowledge of the structure of the indigenous society is the first requirement; this is true in general, but particularly for a land that is still young from a governing point of view, where indigenous governance must still be organized and systematized."[57]

The official A. J. L. Couvreur provided a long report on the Larantuka kingdom in 1907 that remains valuable to this day in spite of its condescending ideas about local authority.[58] Couvreur devoted much space to the mytho-historical and genealogical aspects of the polity. Similarly, C. J. Seegeler's *Nota van Toelichting* (1931) includes a detailed mytho-historical account that is partly different from Heynen's older account and emphasizes other names. Special attention is paid to the first raja of Larantuka, Sirah Demon, who is a true culture hero: Supported by supernatural occurrences, he bonds a number of places in East Flores and the Solor Islands, introduces pre-Christian religious practices, gathers the hitherto scattered populations in real villages, divides them in four *suku* (clans), decrees a fourfold division of village chiefs, and places *kakang* over the various dependencies.[59] Compared to the missionaries, these officials strangely tone down the stories of the Portuguese and the integration of Luso-culture in local governance, and Couvreur repeats the idea that the raja in Larantuka was superfluous and that the kingdom did not even exist "in our sense," but was merely a collection of isles and villages.[60]

The most remarkable contribution is, perhaps, the *Memorie van Overgave* by J. J. M. F. Symons. Apart from the usual details of local economics and population data, he includes a series of appendices on customary rules and the history of the Sikka kingdom, all written in Malay by local informers. The history is anonymous but was clearly authored by Dominicus Pareira Kondi, a raja official who also co-wrote an extended history that has been published and translated in recent times.[61]

It provides a detailed account of the double indigenous-Portuguese origins of the Sikka political order where ten pages out of thirty-six are devoted to the coming of the Portuguese and Catholicism, how the first Christian ruler, Dom Alesu, visited and thus bonded a large number of places in Flores, and how relations were cemented by the bestowal of ivory tusks.[62] As such, it is an interesting case of colonial officialdom co-opting an indigenous counterpart. While this undoubtedly conveys the voices of the colonized, it must be stressed that the choice of the Malay texts is still within the colonial archive's logic of inclusion and omission.[63]

C. J. Seegeler provides a relatively informed idea of ethnographic particularities in the Larantuka territory.[64] It is interesting to note that the author has almost nothing to say about the Portuguese past when surveying ethnohistory, religious ideas, and settlement structure. Indirectly, however, he provides important clues:

> Possession of the land lies in the hands of the *suku* [clans]. Thus the *kottang*, *keleng*, *hurit* and *maring* [chiefly titles] are also, apart from *suku* headmen, *Tuan Tanah* [lord of the land] over the lands of their own *suku*. This applies to the entire territory of Larantuka. The *Tuan Tanah*s are the persons who direct the placement of new gardens and know how the *suku* land is divided up. Where the gardening forms *Etang* and *Netak* occur, the *Tuan Tanah* still has a very large significance. Where the land is practically speaking divided up everywhere, and one works the lands every year, which the forefathers have already worked (*Horowura*, *Tanah Boleng*), the significance and also prestige of the *Tuan Tanah* has declined.[65]

We see here a strongly clan-based society where land is a collective property, similar to many places in Southeast Asia. The ordering notion of quadripartition is, moreover, common in eastern Indonesian societies,[66] and implies a system of authority that is both heavily decentralized and built on strong structural principles. The author concludes that there were originally not even true hamlets. Only later on some were moved to the seashore, and "good and regular" *kampongs* emerged due to Dutch influence. The author furthermore expands on the religious customs. Most people still practise ancestral beliefs at the time of writing, and society is knit together by the *korke* or *rumah pemali*, ritual houses that are present in the various settlements. A *korke* has four wooden pillars who are named after the four clan leaders *kottang, keleng, hurit*, and *maring*. The stronger this structure stood, according to the author, the less successful were the Catholic missionaries in their efforts.

Now, however, there has also been a central *korke* in Larantuka town that reproduces the fourfold symbolism of the pillars. Here, *kottang* is the raja himself, *keleng* is the second raja, while *hurit* and *maring* are prominent lineages in the *kampong* Balela. The setting is entirely non-Christian: Inside the *korke* is a large drum and seven gongs used for war dances, while outside are numbers of sacred stones, *nubanara*. At the time of writing (1931) this central *korke* is in decay, but previously it had been used with the participation by the Larantukan political elite.[67]

Such are the main points of Seegeler's *Nota van Toelichting*. Historical sources clearly point out a long line of Catholicized leaders since the sixteenth century. In other words, local institutions of land use were reproduced on a central level that involved participation by Christian leaders without any known commotion, apparently for hundreds of years. As F. C. Heynen wrote in 1876, "From old, religion in the small Larantuka kingdom was woven together with the character of the state. They both pervaded each other; and in such degree that some peculiar conditions and especially a dignity that should have disappeared with the introduction of Christianity, can only find its explanation in the mutual relation between the state and the original religion. We allude to the dignity of the *Tuan Tanah*."[68] While Heynen seems to regard this as an aberration, it may equally well be seen as functional; Christian and pre-Christian power structures coexisted pragmatically, as the *Tuan Tanah* allocated agricultural land. This is similar to the well-known features of syncretism that may be found in many parts of Southeast Asia, testifying to vibrant local traditions that provided meaning to people and were often, as in Larantuka, tied to land use. Territory was divided into garden land and forest land and understood as sacred space.[69] Perhaps the guardianship of this land, which, apart from a host of spirits and ancestors, also included a supreme being called Lera Wulan, facilitated accommodation with Catholicism.[70]

Concluding Remarks

Of what actually happened when Portuguese seafarers began to settle in the Lamaholot and Sikka worlds and intermarry with the locals, we know strangely little, for the early modern Portuguese and Dutch sources did not tell us much about day-to-day practices. While later traditions depict the introduction of Luso-culture as a set of particular incidents and personal initiatives taking place several generations previously, it was obviously a long and less-than-linear process that began very early. What does appear in the seventeenth- and eighteenth-century sources is a pattern of insecurity and low-level warfare. Raiding between villages were common in the Lamaholot area, often but not always following the ritual Paji-Demon division, and the overlapping division in Dutch and Portuguese spheres of influence. Wouter Schouten, who followed a Dutch expedition in 1660, noted that the small settlements by the Larantuka Strait had pretty fields and gardens but were surrounded by rough palisades for security.[71] In such a volatile world, protection by a well-organized and well-armed force was badly needed, and the Europeans or Eurasians could provide this. Indeed, Lamaholot tradition associates the coming of the Catholic immigrants with the defeat of the Paji adversaries and compensation for military feats via land—again underlining that a colonial situation may not merely be due to European agency.[72] The readiness by some groups to convert should be seen against this background. Black Portuguese groups settled strategically in the coastal places Larantuka-Lewonama, Pantai Besar, Lawerang, Konga, and Wureh (on Adonara),[73] respected for their proficiency in firearms and knit together by their religion. For the Florense they stood out through cultural specifics such as language (Malay and Portuguese), fishing techniques (nets), and craftsmanship (iron smithery), and were known as *kebelen* (people of importance).[74] Similar to Timor, the leading families probably maintained themselves through contributions from the surrounding *kampongs* without interfering in the role of the *Tuan Tanah* in the management of arable land among their *suku*.[75] While they might have been hard masters, we do not find the intense anti-Portuguese resentment present in nearby Timor.[76] Rather, the locals incorporated the Portuguese into their own origin stories, where indigenous interlocutors became culture heroes (João Resi Ona in Larantuka, Dom Alesu in Sikka)—somewhat unusual in Southeast Asian traditions, where Europeans are seldom seen in positive terms.[77] It is possible to see this as a case of "self-colonization" where powerful symbols from outside were accepted as superior and integrated in the Sikka and Lamaholot flow of life. Similar to more well-known cases of self-colonization, such as in Siam and Japan, this seems to have preserved pre-European socio-political relations to a

Image 5.1. Lusophone land legacies epitomized: The last raja of Sikka, Thomas da Silva, in a golden Portuguese morion helmet, with his consort Dua Eba Sadipung and an elephant tusk, the ritual item used to bind the centre to the villages and custodians of the land.

Source: Tropenmuseum, Amsterdam.

large degree. The Catholicized society leaders successfully integrated Christian kingship with a pre-Christian ritual quadripartition, which in turn replicated the local quadripartition with *suku* leaders who allocated agricultural land. Land was taxed through irregular contributions during the Portuguese period, and the

Dutch effort to impose regular taxes immediately met with bitter resistance. On the other hand, lands rights as such remained largely in place, and commercial crops had limited impact during the Dutch era.[78]

This hybrid system evoked mixed feelings among the Dutch colonialists and clerics who began to interfere in East Florenese life after 1859. While perceiving the Larantukan Catholics as distinct from the supposed "savagery" of the pagan Flores populations, the early colonial reporters were skeptical of the position of the raja and distrusted the Catholic missionaries. The latter, conversely, held prejudiced but partly appreciative opinions about the Luso-legacy and pioneered the exploration of the ethnohistory of the region. Educated Dutch twentieth-century officials with personal ethnographic interests paid limited attention to continuities with the Portuguese era—a sort of colonial hybridity that might have complicated rather than facilitated their efforts to manage and transform East Florenese society. However, they probed deeply into questions of governance and land rights, and indirectly highlighted a resilient external-indigenous duality that had evolved during several hundred years.

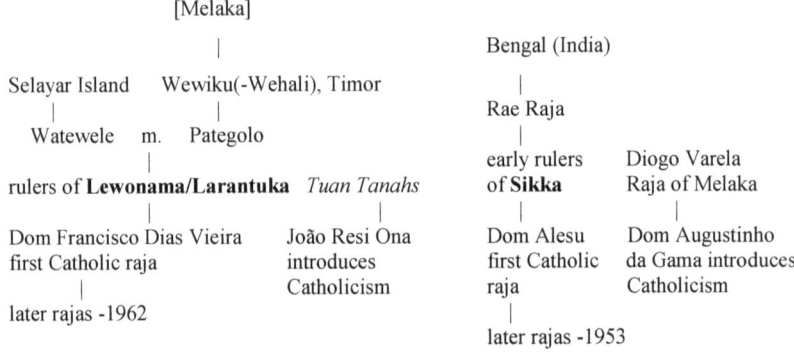

Figure 5.1. Main mytho-historical elements of the emergence of Larantuka and Sikka

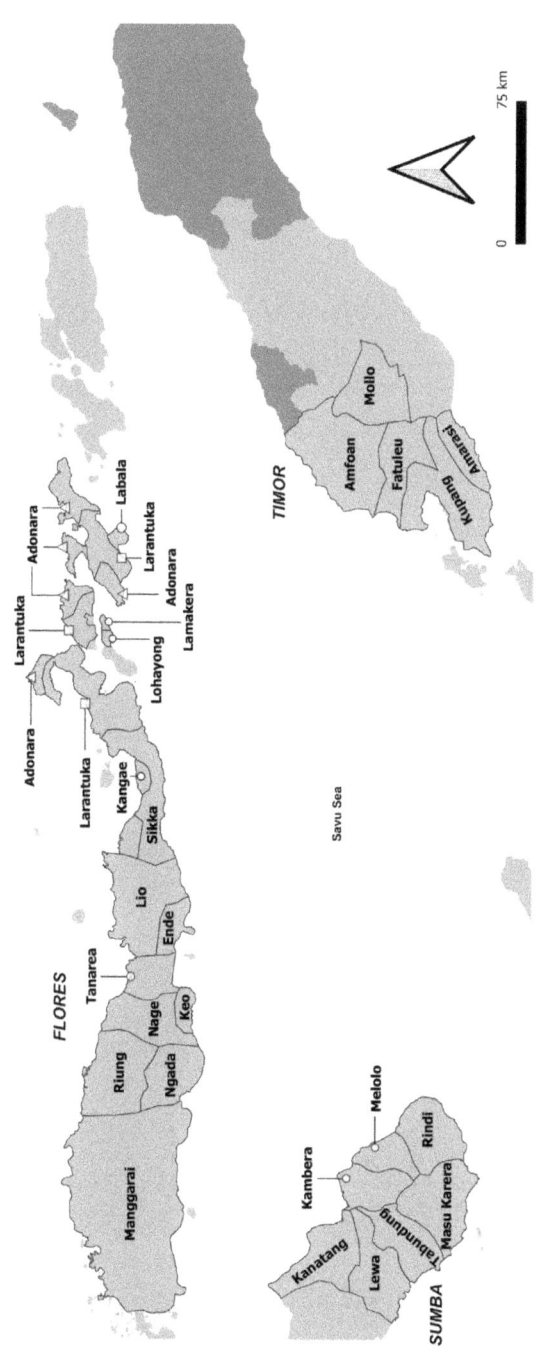

Map 5.1.
Flores in the late colonial period.
Source: Ivan Taniputera, Kerajaan-kerajaan Nusantara pascakeruntuhan Majapahit. Hikayat dan sejarahnya (C.V. Gloria Group, 2013). Cartography: Rui Pinto.

NOTES TO CHAPTER 5

1. Robert H. Barnes, *Excursions into Eastern Indonesia: Essays on History and Social Life* (Yale University, 2013), 98.
2. Up to around 1930 the area was divided into two Catholic *landschappen* (territories, petty kingdoms) called Sikka and Larantuka, and six Muslim ones: Lohayong, Lamakera, Lamahala, Adonara, Trong, and Labala. The Muslim *landschappen* belonged to the Dutch sphere of interest after 1613, while the Catholic Sikka and Larantuka came under Dutch suzerainty in 1859. The population of the subdivision (*onderafdeeling*) Oost Flores en Solor Eilanden in the late colonial period (1930) was 131,301 souls. See National Archives, The Hague, Collection Koninklijk Instituut voor de Tropen (hereafter NA, KIT) 1296, C. J. Seegeler, Memorie van Overgave van den aftredend Controleur van Oost-Flores en Soloreilanden, 1932, 4.
3. Karel E. M. Bongenaar, *De ontwikkeling van het zelfbesturend landschap in Nederlandsch-Indië* (Walburg Pers, 2006), 108; I. Ketut Ardhana, *Nusa Tenggara nach Einrichtung der Kolonialherrschaft 1915 bis 1950* (Universität Passau, 2000), 103.
4. For the history of Larantuka, see the articles in Barnes, *Excursions*; for Sikka, E. Douglas Lewis, *The Stranger-Kings of Sikka* (KITLV Press, 2010). The two polities were governed by rajas until 1953 (Sikka) and 1962 (Larantuka). Ivan Taniputera, *Kerajaan-kerajaan, Nusantara pascakeruntuhan Majapahit: Hikayat dan sejarahnya* (C. V. Gloria Group, 2013), 1292, 1311.
5. There are fifty-three *Memories* about the Timor Islands in the National Archives, The Hague, of which eleven are about Flores, but only four specifically about East Flores.
6. Cees Fasseur, *De indologen: Ambtenaren voor de Oost 1825–1950* (Bert Bakker, 1993).
7. Nicholas Thomas, *Colonialism's Culture: Anthropology, Travel and Government* (Polity Press, 1994), 7.
8. Bernard S. Cohn, *An Anthropologist Among the Historians and Other Essays* (Oxford University Press, 1987), 50–2.
9. Ann Stoler, "Colonial Archives and the Arts of Governance: On the Content in the Form," in *Refiguring the Archive*, ed. Carlyn Hamilton, Verne Harris, Michèle Pickover, Graeme Reid, Jane Taylor, and Razia Saleh (Kluwer Academic Publishers), 92.
10. See Barnes, *Excursions* (a collection of Robert Barnes's articles about Flores and the Solor Islands); Lewis, *The Stranger-Kings*; Stefan Dietrich, *Kolonialismus und Mission auf Flores (ca. 1900–1942)* (Klaus Renner Verlag, 1989). See also Stefan Dietrich, *Kota Rénya, "Die Stadt der Königin"; Religion, Identität, und Wandel in einer ostindonesischen Kleinstadt* (Habilitationsschrift, Universität München, 1997).
11. Dietrich, *Kolonialismus*, 12–14.
12. Arend de Roever, *De jacht op sandelhout: De VOC en de tweedeling van Timor in de zeventiende eeuw* (Walburg Pers, 2002), 63.
13. Malyn Newitt, *A History of Portuguese Overseas Expansion, 1400–1668* (Routledge, 2005), 254–7.
14. W. P. Coolhaas, ed., *Generale missiven van Gouverneurs-Generaal en Raden aan Heren XVII der Verenigde Oost-Indische Compagnie*, vol. 2 (M. Nijhoff, 1964), 374.
15. Frederik Constanijn Heynen, "Het Christendom op het eiland Flores in Nederlandsch-Indië," *Studiën op Godsdienstig, Wetenschappelijk en Letterkundig Gebied* 8, no. 8 (1876): 17; Benno Biermann, "Die alte Dominikanermission auf den Solorinseln," *Zeitschrift für Missionswissenschaft* 14 (1924): 15, 34. Lewonama was adjacent to the later Portuguese settlement Larantuka. The list of royal names does not accord with later genealogical tradition. See, briefly, Hans Hägerdal, *Lords of the Land, Lords of the Sea; Conflict and Adaptation in Early Colonial Timor, 1600–1800* (KITLV Press, 2012), 174–5, 422; Dietrich, *Kota Rénya, "Die Stadt."* The same goes for the rulers of Sikka, where the traditional pedigrees differ from rajas found in European pre-1800 sources. Lewis, *The Stranger-Kings*, 72; E. F. Kleian "Eene voetreis over het oostelijk deel van het eiland Flores," *Tijdschrift voor Indische Taal-, Land- en Volkenkunde* 34 (1891): 514–22.
16. A point also made in a sixteenth-century Maluku context by Victor Lieberman, *Strange Parallels: Southeast Asia in Global Context, c. 800–1830*, vol. 2 (Cambridge University Press, 2009), 853.
17. Manuel Teixeira, *Macau e sua diocese: A diocese de Malaca*, vol. 4 (Tip. do Orfanato Salesiano, 1957), 447. Translations from Dutch and Portuguese texts in this chapter are my own.
18. Artur Teodoro de Matos, *Timor Português 1515-1769: Contribução para a sua história* (Faculdade de Letras da Universidade de Lisboa, 1974), 216–18.
19. Ende was used as a name for the entirety of Flores in some texts.
20. Should be Ilimandiri at the rear of Larantuka. The name Serbite is otherwise associated with Adonara. Barnes, *Excursions*, 79.

21 Artur Teodoro de Matos, *Timor no passado: Fontes para a sua história (Séculos xvii e xviii)* (Universidade Católica Portuguesa, 2015), 35–6.
22 W. P. Coolhaas, *Generale missiven van Gouverneurs-Generaal en Raden aan Heren XVII der Verenigde Oost-Indische Compagnie*, vol. 4 (M. Nijhoff, 1970), 273–4.
23 National Archives, The Hague, Collection Verenigde Oostindische Compagnie (hereafter NA, VOC) 1531, Dagregister, sub 28 October 1692.
24 Hägerdal, *Lords*, 311.
25 NA, VOC 1556, Willem Moerman, Dagregister, 5 October 1693.
26 Jan Sihar Aritonang and Karel Steenbrink, *A History of Christianity in Indonesia* (Brill, 2008), 92–3.
27 NA, VOC 3215, Letter, Francisco Hornay to Alexander Cornabé, 24 May 1767; Affonso de Castro, *As possessões Portuguezas na Oceania* (Imprensa Nacional, 1867), 111, 258.
28 Arsip Nasional Republik Indonesia, Collection K.43 Timor (hereafter ANRI Timor) 140, Report, Emanuel Francis, 1832, f. 110.
29 ANRI Timor 140, Report, Emanuel Francis, 1832, f. 170.
30 ANRI Timor 45, J. C. R Steinmetz, Inlichtende Nota, 1849, in Besluit, 15 April 1850, No. 13.
31 Sartono Kartodirdjo, *Ikhtisar keadaan politik Hindia-Belanda tahun 1839-1848* (ANRI, 1973), 422–4.
32 Alice Viola Kortlang, "Presença histórica 'portuguesa' em Larantuka (séculos XVI e XVII) e suas implicações na contemporaneidade" (PhD diss., Universidade Nova de Lisboa, 2013), 229–31.
33 Sandra Modh, "The Lamaholot of East Flores" (PhD diss., Oxford University, 2012), 117.
34 Kortlang, "Presença histórica," 290.
35 NA, VOC 3215, Letter, Dom Gaspar Dias Vieira to Francisco Hornay, 15 April 1767.
36 Omitting certain disputes: Matos, *Timor portugues*, 229, 434; NA, VOC 3215, Letter, Dom Gaspar Dias Vieira to Francisco Hornay, 15 April 1767.
37 National Archives, The Hague, Ministerie van Kolonien, *Memories van Overgave* (hereafter NA, MMK) 336. Memorie van Overgave van den afgetreden Resident van Timor en Onderhoorigheden H. C. Humme, 1876, n.p.
38 NA, MMK 336. Memorie van Overgave van den afgetreden Resident van Timor en Onderhoorigheden H. C. Humme, 1876, n.p.
39 Aritonang and Steenbrink, *A History*, 230.
40 NA, MMK 337, Memorie van Overgave van den aftredenden Resident van Timor en Onderhoorigheden Ch.M.G.M.M. Ecoma Verstege, 1878, n.p.
41 NA, MMK 338, Nota bij de aftreding van den Resident van Timor J. G. F. Riedel, 1880, n.p.
42 Barnes, *Excursions*, 126–43.
43 NA, MMK 339, J. F. A. de Rooy, Memorie omtrent het toestand van het Gewest Timor en Onderhoorigheden, 1908, p. 13–15.
44 NA, MMK 339, J. F. A. de Rooy, Memorie omtrent het toestand van het Gewest Timor en Onderhoorigheden, 1908, p. 15.
45 NA, MMK 339, J. F. A. de Rooy, Memorie omtrent het toestand van het Gewest Timor en Onderhoorigheden, 1908, p. 16.
46 NA, MMK 339, J. F. A. de Rooy, Memorie omtrent het toestand van het Gewest Timor en Onderhoorigheden, 1908, p. 20.
47 NA, MMK 340, C. H. van Rietschoten, Memorie omtrent den toestand van het gewest Timor en Onderhoorigheden, 1913, p. 36.
48 NA, MMK 340, C. H. van Rietschoten, Memorie omtrent den toestand van het gewest Timor en Onderhoorigheden, 1913, p. 38.
49 Barnes, *Excursions*, 186–7.
50 For this centrality, see H. G. Schulte Nordholt, *The Political System of the Atoni of Timor* (M. Nijhoff, 1971), and Tom Therik, *Wehali—The Female Land: Traditions of a Timorese Ritual Centre* (Pandanus Books, 2004).
51 Frederik Constantijn Heynen, "Het rijk Larantoeka op het eiland Flores in Nederlandsch-Indië," *Studiën op Godsdienstig, Wetenschappelijk en Letterkundig Gebied* 8, no. 6 (1876): 70-2, 79.
52 Heynen, "Het Christendom," 3–9, 74–85.
53 Heynen, "Het rijk Larantoeka," 75.
54 Barnes, *Excursions*; Lewis, *The Stranger-Kings*.

55 George François Elbert Gonggrijp, *Geïllustreerde encyclopaedie van Nederlandsch-Indie* (Leidsche Uitgeversmaatschappij, 1934), 133–4.
56 Ardhana, *Nusa Tenggara*, 171–2.
57 NA, KIT 1295, G. A. Bosselaar, Memorie van Overgave van den aftredend Assistent Resident van Flores, 1932, p. 65.
58 NA, A. J. L. Couvreur, Beschrijving van het rijk Larantoeka, 1907. Coll. C. C. F. LeRoux, No. 7.
59 NA, KIT 1296, C. J. Seegeler, Nota van Toelichting betreffende het zelfbesturende landschap Larantoeka, 1931, p. 74–8.
60 Cf. Barnes, *Excursions*, 183.
61 Lewis, *The Stranger-Kings*, 10; E. Douglas Lewis and Oscar Pareira Mandalangi, *Hikayat Kerajaan Sikka* (Penerbit Ledalero, 2008). Unfortunately, there is nothing comparable for Larantuka, though many notes were gathered in the 1950s, in Coll. M. J. H. Wertenbroek, H 1343, Koninjlijk Instituut voor Taal-, Land- en Volkenkunde (KITLV) Archive/UB Leiden.
62 NA, KIT 1301, J. J. M. F. Symons. Memorie van Overgave van de onderafdeeling Oost Flores en Soloreilanden en Maoemere, 1935; Leonard Yuzon Andaya, "The Social Value of Elephant Tusks and Bronze Drums Among Certain Societies in Eastern Indonesia," *Bijdragen tot de Taal-, Land- en Volkenkunde* 172 (2016): 66–89.
63 Stoler, "Colonial Archives."
64 NA, KIT 1296, C. J. Seegeler, Nota van Toelichting betreffende het zelfbesturende landschap Larantoeka, 1931.
65 NA, KIT 1296, C. J. Seegeler, Nota van Toelichting betreffende het zelfbesturende landschap Larantoeka, 1931, p. 65.
66 Schulte Nordholt, *The Political System*.
67 Seegeler, Nota.
68 Heynen, "Het rijk Larantoeka," 80.
69 Modh, Lamaholot, 18.
70 Cf. Hubert Jacobs, *The Jesuit Makasar Documents (1615–1682)* (Jesuit Historical Institute, 1988), 248.
71 KITLV Archive, H 1341: 2, M. Wertenbroek, De geschiedenis van Flores, p. 67.
72 Kortlang, "Presença histórica," 232.
73 NA, KIT 1298, C. J. Seegeler, Nota van Toelichting betreffende het zelfbesturend landschap Larantoeka, 1931, p. 28.
74 Kortlang, "Presença histórica," 232.
75 Cf. Matos, *Timor Portugues*, 216–17.
76 For some cases of local resistance against Catholic rulers in Dutch times, see, however, Ardhana, *Nusa Tenggara*, 103–5.
77 Anthony Reid, "Early Southeast Asian Categorizations of Europeans," in *Implicit Understandings: Observing, Reporting, and Reflecting on the Encounters Between Europeans and Other Peoples in the Early Modern Era*, ed. Stuart B. Schwartz (Cambridge University Press, 1994), 268–94.
78 Dietrich, *Kolonialismus*, 152.

6

Land Access in a Slave Society: The Case of Maranhão Province, Northern Brazil

Matthias Röhrig Assunção

Introduction

Ownership of land and the control over coerced labour have often been seen as mutually exclusive. According to Domar, free access to land could not exist in a society that combined a landed property class with free labour.¹ But, in a slave society based on coerced labour, nothing would prevent access to land being "free." In this sense, many historians have commented on the "ample availability" of land in colonial Brazil, without questioning the concrete forms that land appropriation took. On the other hand, many authors have also emphasized the almost exclusive predominance of large landholdings in Brazil. Alberto Passos Guimarães, for example, entitled his classic study *Four Centuries of Latifundia*, implying total control of land access by the landed elite.² This perspective did not leave any room for independent producers or peasants. Sérgio Buarque de Holanda had already set the tone when he asserted in his seminal study that, "with very few exceptions, the very word 'village,' in its most common sense, as well as the word 'peasant,' indicating a man rooted to his place of origin through countless generations, do not correspond in the New World to any reality."³ The crucial point to emphasize here is that slaves never constituted the only labour force in the Portuguese colonies in the Americas, and neither did they in imperial Brazil. To what extent, then, was "free" access to "available" land really possible? Research in the case of Southeast Brazil has shown that the reality of appropriation was much more complex. The case of the northern province of

Maranhão also suggests a messier picture, where subsistence agriculture and communal ownership or possession competed with cotton and rice plantations relying primarily on enslaved labour and other forms of agrarian enterprise.

The aim of this chapter is to analyze land access in Maranhão—ownership as well as de facto possession and use—during the first half of the nineteenth century, or from the end of the colonial period and its *sesmaria* system (1822) to the aftermath of the new land legislation of 1850.[4] In other words, I will try to disentangle the process through which land use and land ownership were re-codified in the post-colonial (and to a large extent neo-colonial) framework of the Brazilian Empire, and question their relation to plantation slavery and other forms of labour. Moreover, the various forms of land possession to be found at that time document the existence of a peasantry that developed in the interstices of the plantation economy. This social group and the various forms of land access peasants established endured long after the collapse of the cotton export sector and the abolition of slavery in 1888, until late twentieth-century modernization reframed the land question anew in the region.

The agrarian history of Maranhão displays a significant number of features and practices that can be subsumed under the very broad category of common land use. As Alfredo Wagner wrote,

> The diverse forms of common land use are a frequently ignored aspect of Brazil's agrarian structure. Analytically, they describe situations in which the control of basic resources is not exercised freely and individually by a group of small domestic producers directly or through one of its members. Such control is carried out through specific norms established in addition to the existing legal code and incorporated, by consensus, in the intricacies of social relations formed between different family groups, who make up a social unit. They may express not only stable access to land, as in former colonial areas, but they also reveal relatively transitory forms intrinsic to regions of recent occupation.[5]

In order to analyze these various forms of land use, it is necessary to first get a better understanding of the formal rules of land appropriation, which provided the framework and boundaries for other more informal means to develop in its interstices.

The Consolidation of Private Land Ownership in Brazilian Legislation: From Colonial *Sesmarias* to the 1850 Land Law

Sesmarias were originally an institution created in Portugal in response to the agrarian crisis that followed the *Reconquista* in the fourteenth century. To reactivate farming, town and city councils distributed unproductive land for cultivation. In colonial Brazil, in contrast, *sesmarias* were used to encourage the development of export agriculture and animal husbandry. The Portuguese king initially entitled the aristocratic "donatary captains" to distribute *sesmarias*, or land grants, to predominantly white male settlers in their captaincies (colonial provinces), and they were only allowed to reserve about 20 per cent of the land for their own use.[6] This function was later taken over by the governors, administrators nominated by the Crown. In theory, the subjects applying for a *sesmaria* had to make a convincing case that they were settlers able to set up some form of agricultural enterprise. A small, but significant number of *sesmarias* were also granted to monastic orders such as the Jesuits or to the Indigenous inhabitants of mission villages. The *sesmaria* could hence be part of a strategy to consolidate territorial control and to recompensate Indigenous groups for accepting colonial domination, which implied detribalization and Catholic conversion.

The *Ordenações do Reino* provided that the *sesmeiros* had to cultivate the granted land within five years, a period that could be extended by the king. Once this requirement was met, and assuming the *sesmaria* was not claimed by others, the land became the property of the *sesmeiro* and his heirs. The *sesmaria* concession thus represented a right of use that could be transformed into a property title. However, even when complying with the requirements of the law, the property was still limited by a series of restrictions. The *sesmeiro* had to take care of the "royal woods" in his concession and make them available to the Portuguese Navy for the construction of vessels. If a river flowed through his *sesmaria*, he needed to provide a boat for the use of passers-by and reserve a riverbank for public use. He also had to grant free access to bridges and mines and take responsibility for the maintenance of public roads that ran through his *sesmaria*. He furthermore had to reserve an area for the foundation of villages and sometimes for common pastures (*logradouros*).

The size of granted *sesmarias* was usually of 1, 2, or 3 *léguas* by 1 *légua* (1 *légua* = 6.6 kilometres). In other words, *sesmeiros* were granted huge areas of thousands of hectares of land, but we have to remember that *sesmarias* were also granted in areas that had not yet been colonized, and which eventually escaped Portuguese effective control. A further complication after 1795 was that *sesmarias* had to be "confirmed" by the Crown, another bureaucratic process that only some *sesmeiros* could or wanted to go through.[7] Where *sesmeiros* managed to get physical control of the granted land and were able to invest in the development of their estates, they became part of the tiny class of powerful landowners who also were prominent in local affairs.[8] As *homens bons*, they could sit in town councils or serve as officers in the militia, while also allowing landless poor to settle on parts of their land in exchange for rent or personal services, thus creating a class of rural dependants.

The landowners' power was enhanced with independence, in 1822, when they were allowed to vote for their representatives in the new parliament (Cortes) and mobilize their dependants with voting rights to also do so. At the same time the new independent state decided to no longer grant *sesmarias*. This was largely to meet the demands of a growing number of owners of estates (*fazendas*) that had occupied public land known as *terra devoluta* without formal *sesmaria* grant. The colonial *sesmaria* legislation was to be replaced by a new law, which, for a variety of reasons, was only adopted in 1850, in precisely the same year the transatlantic slave trade to Brazil was definitively abolished (slavery itself was only abolished in 1888). If informal occupation of land had already been common in the colonial period (sometimes, but not always, followed by *sesmaria* grants), this became the rule after 1822. New land on the agrarian frontier could only be occupied informally, as no other legal mechanism existed. These *posseiros*, as informal occupants of land are called in Brazil, were of different social origins and occupied anything from a small plot to vast latifundia. Almost thirty years later the distinction between lawful *sesmaria* and informal possession was even less congruent with the opposition between big landowners and small *posseiros*. There now existed an important group of elite planters and cattle ranchers who possessed vast amounts of land without formal property title based on a *sesmaria* grant or a legitimate proof of purchase. This explains, in part, the heated debates that preceded the passage of the 1850 Land Law. The powerful group of wealthy *posseiros* wanted their rights recognized and managed to ensure that lands that had been "peacefully occupied" ("posse mansa and pacífica"), not being claimed by others, could be registered as well.

Hence in 1850 the gap was closed, and subsequently public land had to be acquired by purchase—at least in theory; in practice occupation of *terras devolutas* continued as before. In that respect the land law of 1850 certainly was a failure. Yet the law became an important reference for future land conflicts, which in many ways superseded the colonial *sesmarias*.[9]

Private Landownership in Eastern Maranhão: A Case Study

The 1850 legislation was followed by a decree in 1854 stipulating that all landowners had to register their property in a special book, in possession of the local parish priest, until June 1857, a deadline later extended to December 1858. Given the conflicts over the text of the law, and its interpretation, there was resistance in some quarters to registering. Some landowners feared that registration could be used against them, especially in cases of previous land conflicts. It also meant that the declarations made were not very uniform. Some landowners provided relatively precise information about the location, size, and origin of their properties, while others only registered their claims but omitted many details. This may also be due to the fact that the registration tax to be paid was calculated according to the length of the declaration (2 reais per letter). Attitudes certainly varied enormously across the different provinces. Márcia Motta, comparing lists of planters in the 1858 *Almanaque Laemmert* with land registers of parishes from a coffee-producing area from Rio de Janeiro Province, concluded that, in this territory of frequent land conflicts, as many as 40 per cent of these landowners may not have registered.[10] Warren Dean calculated that in the municipality of Rio Claro, in São Paulo, 150 smallholders failed to register their land, compared to 450 who did.[11] I am not able to provide a comparable figure for the Maranhão register, although these registers do reveal that many small landowners and *posseiros* did not make a declaration, as we see below.

Admittedly the 1854–8 land registers are incomplete, and the data are not very coherent, yet they still provide, I would argue, fundamental clues about the structure of land ownership as well as the process of land appropriation. They also quickly became an important basis for future land claims and for settling land conflicts. When I first consulted them in Maranhão, in the 1980s, they were kept not in the state archives (Arquivo Público do Estado do Maranhão) but in an institution called COTERMA (later ITERMA), which was created to register, administer, and eventually redistribute public land in the state.[12] At that time, they were still controversial, some people basing their land claims on them, while others dismissed them as inauthentic, even seeking actively to destroy them.

Given my interest in the eastern part of Maranhão, which was the main theatre of the Balaiada rebellion, I chose to work with the registers of the twenty parishes that were part of the four judicial districts (*comarcas*) of that area (see map 6.1).[13] However, less than a dozen of these twenty had survived, and only nine of the books were in a state that one could decipher them. The register of these nine parishes thus forms the basis of my data set, treated with SPSS.

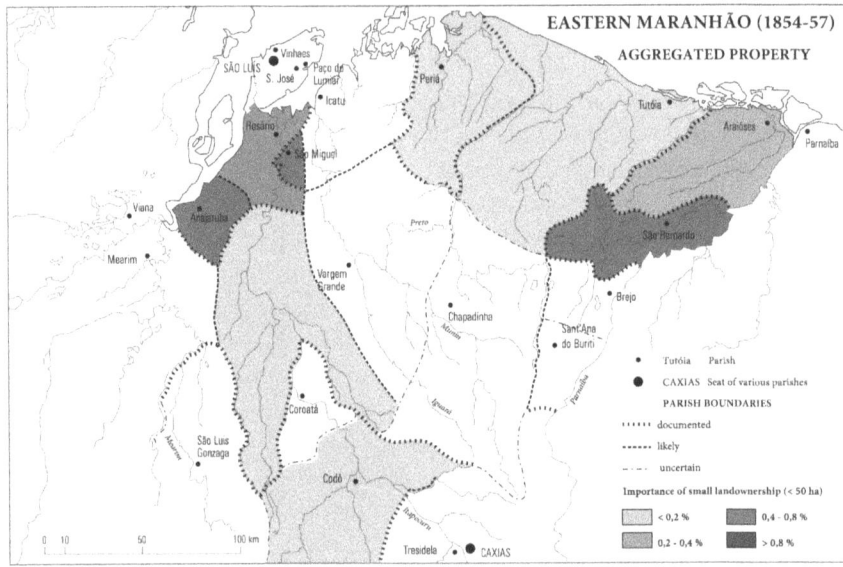

Map 6.1. Eastern Maranhão—parishes and the importance of small ownership

Right from the beginning a methodological problem needed to be solved. A number of declarations were signed by more than one person. Some declarations mentioned various pieces of land. And some owners made various declarations in the same parish, or even in other parishes. Thus, the number of cases in the data set varies according to what constitutes the unit of comparison: properties, owners or groups of owners, in one or all parishes (table 6.1).

The first observation one can make from these registers is that the 1850 law was applied to a reality that only in part conformed to the categories defined by it, and which presupposed private and individual property. Almost 24 per cent of the 3,106 declarations (counting properties/owners) informed that their land was "undivided" (indivisa) or possessed "in common." Another relevant figure is that 19 per cent, almost a fifth of all owners, were women, against 75 per cent male owners, with the rest constituted by various forms of collective or corporate propriety (table 6.2). Fully 38 per cent of owners declared they had inherited their land, against 23 per cent who indicated they had purchased it, with 37 per cent not providing any information about the origins of their property—maybe for good reasons!

Table 6.1. Number of declarations, properties, and landowners in nine parishes of Eastern Maranhão, 1854–57

Parish	Declarations	Properties	Properties/ owners	Owners in each parish	In all 9 parishes
1 São Miguel	91[a]	101	118	76	-
2 Rosário	201[b]	217	254	203	-
3 Itapecuru-mirim	234	344	401	220	-
4 Anajatuba	81	162	180	87	-
5 Codó	274[c]	517	584	259	-
6 São Bernardo	364	640	643	260	-
7 Araióses	281	423	445	198	-
8 Tutóia	280	284	285	109	-
9 Periá	106	190	196	90	-
Total	1.732	2.878	3.106	1.502	1.360

a) A declaration from 10.08.1859 was included.
b) A declaration from 10.06.1858 was included.
c) Two declarations were illegible and were not included.

Table 6.2. Gender of landowners and forms of property in nine Maranhão parishes, 1854–57

	Number	%
a) Individual ownership:		
Women	598	19
Men	2.320	75
b) Collective property	164	5
c) Corporate property:		
Parish	1	0
Regular clergy	5	0
Town council	7	0
Firm	11	0
Total Cases (Property/Owners)	3.106	100%

To measure the concentration of property, I divided owners into four groups (<50 hectares [ha], 50–250 ha, 250–1,000 ha, >1,000 ha) according to the size of (a) single plots and (b) aggregated slots per owner. The register reveals that concentration varies quite substantially from parish to parish. There are two main reasons for this. Because the soils underneath the Amazonian tropical rainforest are generally very poor, plantation agriculture in Maranhão went through a relatively short cycle from opening up the land, expansion, and boom to exhaustion of soils and reconversion to subsistence agriculture and pastures. At the same time, Portuguese and then Brazilian inheritance laws allowed for the systematic subdivision of land among inheritors, resulting in the dividing up of big properties.[14] This is clear from the figures of the parishes of the Itapecuru Valley. In Codó, the newest parish the farthest up the river, big landowners represent 63 per cent of the declarants, and only 1 per cent owned less than 50 ha. In contrast, Rosário, the eldest parish near the estuary, big landowners represent only 21 per cent of declarants, while small owners make up 18 per cent. In the former Indian mission village of São Miguel, small landowners represent 28 per cent. The parish of Itapecuru-Mirim, situated in between, also displays an intermediate pattern of property (figure 6.1). In the Parnaiba Valley (figure 6.2) the situation is slightly different, as here plantation agriculture was not that dominant. At the time of the register there were some very big estates (in part successors of the former Jesuit estates on the coast, the Jesuit order having been expelled in 1759) and a much more significant number of medium-sized properties (between 50 and 250 ha; see tables 6.3 and 6.4, as well as map 6.1).

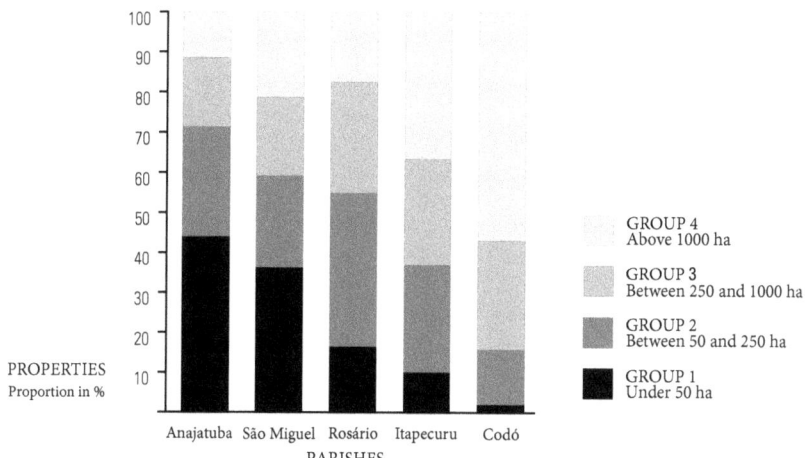

Figure 6.1. Properties according to size in Itapecuru parishes, 1854–7

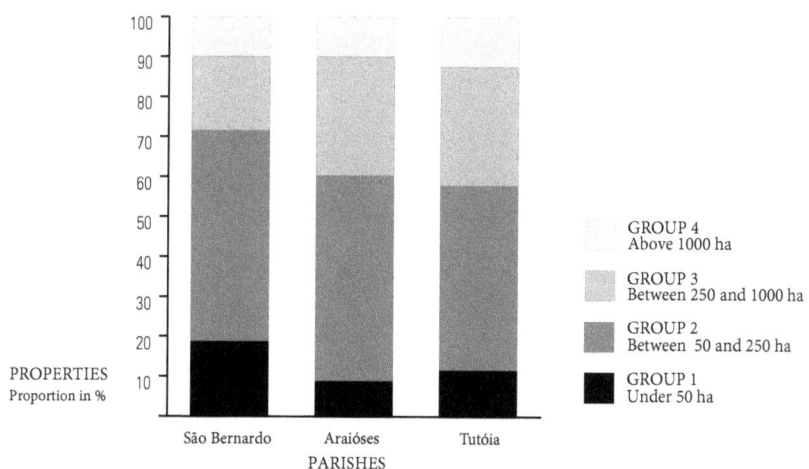

Figure 6.2. Properties according to size in Parnaiba parishes, 1854–7

6 | Land Access in a Slave Society

Table 6.3: Property Size in nine parishes of Maranhao, 1854–57

Group	Size	Properties	% of known cases conhecidos	% of cases
1	Under 50 ha	145	13	
2	Between 50 and 250 ha	267	24	
3	Between 250 and 1.000 ha	330	29	
4	Over 1.000 ha	386	34	
	Total	1.128	100	
	No indication	1.750		
	Total of cases	2.878		100

Table 6.4: Property Size in nine parishes of Maranhao, 1854–57 (with extrapolated depth)*

Group	Size	Properties	% of known cases conhecidos	% of cases
1	Under 50 ha	184	12	
2	Between 50 and 250 ha	372	25	
3	Between 250 and 1.000 ha	427	29	
4	Over 1.000 ha	500	34	
	Total	1.483	100	
	No indication	1.395		
	Total of cases	2.878		100

* Includes declarations that only indicated one dimension of the property (*frente*), but omitted the depth (*fundos*), because of the *sesmaria* standard of 1 *légua*, which is hence taken here as a standard value.

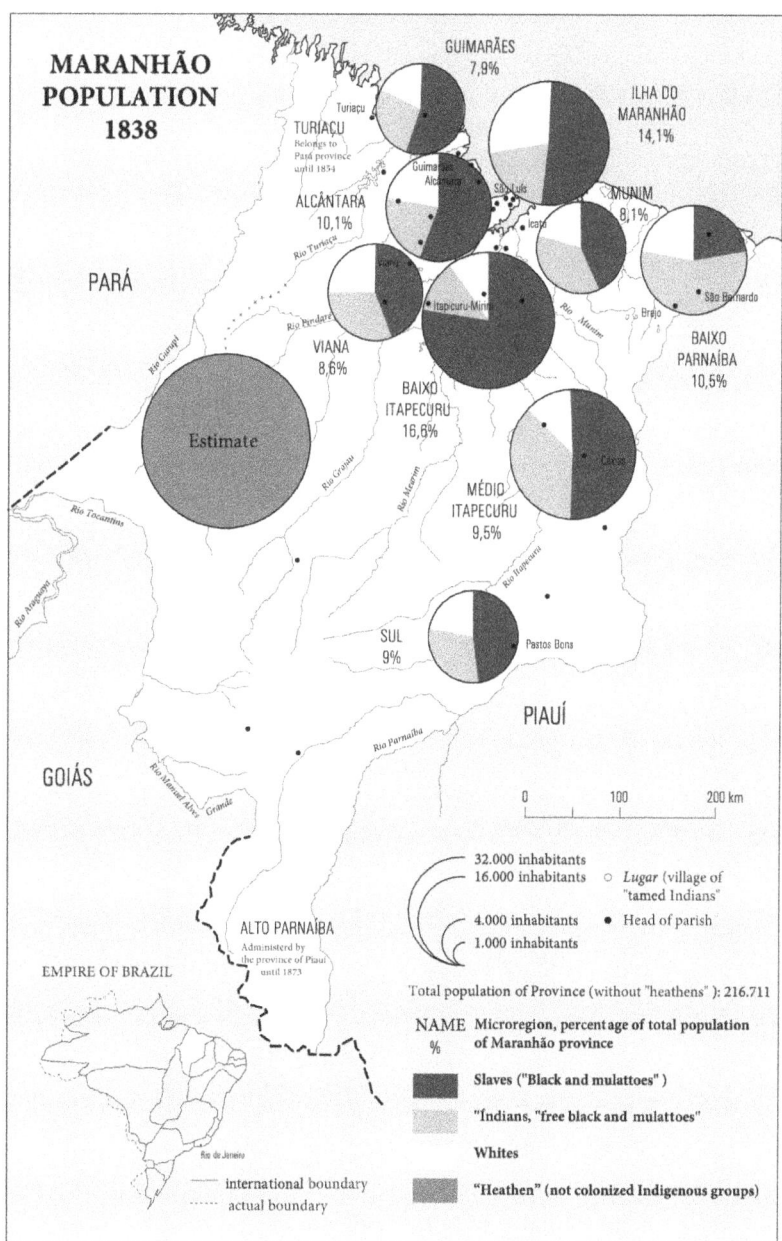

Map 6.2. Population of Maranhão, by microregion (1838)

These statistics need of course to be contextualized and complemented with other data (for instance population), but I believe they show the logic and the particular dynamic of land appropriation in a plantation economy. It needs to be pointed out that the trend toward subdivision among inheritors, women included, coexisted with a trend toward concentration, as some wealthy owners tried to bundle properties by acquiring various bits of land in a parish or neighbouring parish. The reorientation toward subsistence agriculture or of non-export foodstuffs like manioc is documented by the data on agricultural production by micro-region. The contrast between the intensive plantation economy of Itapecuru Valley and the more mixed economy on the coast and in Paraiba Valley is confirmed by the population statistics. The 1838 figures display a greater proportion of enslaved people in the lower Itapecuru Valley and a greater proportion of the free non-white population in the lower Paraiba Valley (map 6.2).

Formal landownership, however, offers only one perspective on land access; it needs to be complemented and contrasted with the real appropriation of land on the ground. This is already clear from the register. Owners were supposed to declare the names of their immediate neighbours, but in many cases these *confrontantes* did not make a declaration themselves. It is striking, for example, that many landowners claim their land was contiguous with that of "the Indians [*índios*] of São Miguel." The latter, however, did not make a register of the former Indian *sesmaria* granted collectively to the inhabitants of the mission village.[15] Similarly, a number of freed or poor people of colour are only cited as neighbours but did not make a declaration on their own:

—"Camilo, freed black";

—"Cecília, free brown woman";

—"Doroteia, free black woman";

—"João Francisco Mendes da Silva and other inheritors and freed people";

—"Land of the freed people of the deceased Maria Rita Gomes Belfort"[16]

By not submitting a declaration to the parish priest, these people—freed people—were opening the gates to subsequent usurpation of their land.[17] At this stage it is not possible to quantify how many were left out by these rule changes, but I suspect quite a significant number.

Informal and Collective Access to Land

Land access through informal or even illegal forms of appropriation (the situations known in Brazil as *posse*), as well as through rent and leases, constituted the basis of peasant production all over Brazil since the colonial era. In Maranhão more specifically, peasant production was based on a variety of forms of land access, from informal *posse* (informal appropriation) to the use of collective property of corporations and townships (*municípios*). Two distinctions need to be made here. The first is between the judicial form and the concrete practice, because the same legal form could contain distinct modes of land use. The systems of common land use, rediscovered by social scientists as typical forms of peasant production in the 1980s, were based on a broad range of different formal ownership situations. Secondly, it is useful to separate direct and indirect access to land. The former refers to situations where peasants have obtained at some point in history a kind of legal recognition, such as collective property title, which may be challenged later on as they do not possess the means to legalize that property or maintain its register during changes to the legal framework of land legislation. The latter refers to situations where peasants use land that they recognize as belonging to others. Even if in practice that distinction may not always be entirely clear (for example, when peasants use land they recognize as belonging to a saint), it will help my exposition here and hopefully clarify the various situations.

POSSEIROS BIG AND SMALL

Even though it was not part of the Portuguese Crown's plans, land access without a formal *sesmaria* title was a frequent practice during the colonial period. It was a rather precarious appropriation, because a new *sesmaria* grant could attribute the same land to another person, which eventually resulted in a number of conflicts. However, possession was the only possibility for land access for settlers without the means to pay the costs of registering and confirming a *sesmaria*. It was certainly the most frequent form of appropriation on the agrarian frontier. Many squatters also occupied the interstices between *sesmaria* grants. The Crown, perfectly aware of these practices, tried to avoid concessions of land already occupied by other settlers in this regard, especially toward the end of the colonial period. Several authors have argued that this meant a legal recognition of possession.[18] But the golden age of informal land appropriation or *posse* certainly were the years between 1822 and 1850, when there was no legal barrier to the appropriation of unclaimed land. As the 1850 Land Law offered the possibility of legalizing "peaceful and gentle" possessions, many squatters registered their lands, the first step to becoming full owners. Even though the peaceful *posse* was legal, only one proprietor in the nine parishes of the 1850 land register in Maranhão openly declared such an appropriation, which I believe shows that even big landowners preferred to play it safe, by not indicating the origins of their property claim.

The opposite process also occurred: A property of *sesmarial* origin could be transformed into an insecure possession, if the formal legalization had not been followed up, as had already happened in the case of unmeasured and unconfirmed *sesmarias* during colonial times. In other words, the distinction between ownership and possession is not a simple one in this transitional phase in the nineteenth century, because the boundaries between the two were imprecise and subject to change and redefinitions. The informal appropriation (*posse*) of planters as well as peasants were most common on the agrarian frontier. In the early nineteenth century, a substantial part of the province in fact still escaped control of the neo-colonial state and provided the territorial basis for a number of Indigenous groups. This fringe territory has been highlighted by Otávio Velho as the space where peasants could thrive, if only momentarily.[19] In the case of Maranhão, a respectable number of runaway slaves formed communities beyond the frontier to set up their subsistence agriculture or even gold mining.

COLLECTIVE LAND I: *TERRA DE ÍNDIO*

Undivided plantation lands were the result of the fragmentation of initially individual ownership, where local and "traditional" arrangements replaced the absence of formal boundaries for individual plots. The collective landownership examined in this section, in contrast, was collective right from the start, and legally enshrined.

Historically the first type of collective ownership were the Indian *sesmarias*. The term "Indian" needs to be contextualized here. During the late colonial period the Portuguese Crown distinguished several stages of acculturation. Indigenous peoples were classified as Indians, or "heathens" (*gentio*), and considered barbarians. Once they had submitted to colonial rule and settlement they were called "tamed Indians" (*índios domésticos*). Finally—at the end of a "civilizing process" lasting several generations—the descendants of the Native Brazilians could now be considered "civilized," and were called *caboclos* in many parts of Brazil, especially in the Amazon. It was in this intermediate stage between barbarism and civilization that, in the eyes of the Crown, the allocation of land to the "tamed" Indians as a collective was justified to help in their transition to the desired state of civilization. For this reason, the concession was always accompanied by a series of requirements, and lands were preferably granted to communities, controlled by missionaries. The decline of the mission villages, especially after the expulsion of the Jesuits in 1759, was often accompanied by the usurpation of their lands by third parties.[20] Yet in some cases the surviving descendants of Indigenous people secured the land of the former Indian *sesmaria*, or parts of it. São Miguel, on the Itapecuru River just above Rosário, is an example of this. The usurpation of most of the colonial Indian *sesmarias* was already well under way after independence, and in the 1980s community leaders complained about a renewed effort by *grileiros* (land grabbers or deed falsifiers) to expel them from their collective land. At the time, the remaining land of the community was still reallocated periodically to each family, as is the case in other collectively owned land in Maranhão.

COLLECTIVE LAND II: *TERRAS DE PRETO*

One of the most prevalent forms of communal land use in modern-day Maranhão are the lands known until recently as *terras de preto* (Black people's lands). Depending on the definition, this category could include a hundred, or even hundreds, of different situations in the state.[21] Due both to the requirements of the 1988 constitution, which only recognizes communal land ownership rights of "remnants of *quilombo* communities that are occupying the land," as well as to the dynamics of the new social movement that aims to protect *terras de preto* from land grabbers, the term *quilombo* was re-semanticized by activists in the 1990s to denominate these lands.[22] Also influenced by the debate on slave resistance and the consecutive expansion of that category to cover a much broader range of actions, including non-violent measures, *quilombo* has now come to designate a number of situations in which a Black community defends its rights to a territory, way of life, and values against broader Brazilian society, which had so far denied them. As a result, all currently existing *terras de preto* can be considered *quilombos* in the modern sense, even if, historically, they cannot be directly traced to territories occupied by groups of fugitive slaves. In fact, most *terras de preto* in Maranhão resulted from the breakup of plantations and the occupation of part of the land by former slaves after nationwide abolition in 1888.[23] Even the first communities to join the struggle to legalize their land with the state, such as Frechal and Jamary, originated from a similar process.[24]

However, there were several cases in which, long before abolition, land was collectively adjudicated to groups of freed slaves by private owners. Even if these cases are now a minority among the currently existing *terras de preto*, they are important for two reasons. First, they show the loopholes in the slave system and that the enslaved made use of them. In that sense they provided an important exception to Tania Murray Li's racialized state/land concepts on landowners' "worthiness."[25]

Furthermore, they introduced a practice that became widespread after abolition. I believe that this pre-emancipation experience was important in terms of creating precedents—models that were more easily adopted in Maranhão for that reason; and could explain why, more than in other states, planters in Maranhão agreed to allow former slaves to settle on their land in exchange for goods or services.

To this day, in eastern Maranhão, there are at least three situations involving *terras de preto* that date back to the early nineteenth century. The oldest is probably Bonsucesso, a village now located in the municipality of Mata Roma. A genealogy painstakingly recollected by the elder Simão, in 1982, traced his ancestry back over eight generations. According to the community's oral history, Brigadier Feliciano Henrique Franco established a plantation with twelve enslaved families in that part of the Rio Preto Valley. Following the brigadier's death in Europe, his son, Anacleto Henrique Franco, is believed to have gone to Maranhão to liquidate and close down the estate. Given that his father had been in debt to merchants in Parnaíba and São Luís, he offered the slaves land and liberty in exchange for the repayment of debts worth 30,000 milréis, to be paid off in a maximum period of twelve years. The enslaved managed to repay the debt in ten, "working day and night," and thereby gained the land and their freedom.[26] I have not been able to find the original donation document, but Brigadier Anacleto Henrique Franco (here, the oral history seems to have confused the father's name with that of the son) also appears in other sources. He was a colonel in the regiment that led the failed expedition against the Axuí *quilombo* in 1794. A sudden voyage to Portugal was due to the fact that, accused of stealing within his regiment, he was sent under arrest to Lisbon, where he managed to convince the judges of his innocence, returning to Maranhão with the rank of brigadier.[27] Through further investigation, Joaquim Shiraishi located, if not the original document, at least the transcript of the brigadier's will in the records of the adverse possession claim filed by the freed people's descendants in the 1950s. According to the transcript, the area was acquired through a donation to the enslaved ancestors of the community, made by order of a last will and testament in the town of Icatu, which transferred the area on condition that they pay off their debts and manumission in ten years.[28]

There are many similarities between this case and the origins of the Rampa community in the municipality of Vargem Grande. According to their oral history, the Portuguese priest Antônio Fernandes Pereira owned a plantation in Pirapemas, on the banks of the Itapecuru River. When Brazil became independent, he decided that leaving the province was the prudent thing to do, so he gave his slaves land and their freedom on condition that they paid him one-third of the income from the donated land for the rest of his life. The donation letter shows that the priest was concerned about organizing the life of the community and avoiding future problems, such as members from the community selling individual plots to outsiders.

In the case of Rampa, the land was in a remote area in the rainforest, a *centro*, and not one of the main parcels of land of the priest's plantation. However, it was densely forested, with a spring that "never dried up," thereby sparking envy in outsiders and making it—like Bonsucesso—the focus of fierce struggles in the twentieth century. Finally, it should be noted that in both cases, the donation was a business transaction, and was not made "free and clear," out of the goodness of the heart of a philanthropic slaveowner. Indeed, the 30,000 milréis the slaves of Bonsucesso are said to have raised to pay the brigadier's debts were worth more, at the time, than the purchase price of the twelve or fourteen enslaved families and the land of Bonsucesso together.

The *terras de preto* in Saco das Almas are a very different case, because the donation was made to reward services rendered outside the master-slave relationship. According to oral history, the military commander of the *comarca* de Brejo, Severino de Carvalho, learned of an imminent attack on the town during the Balaiada. The rebels had even threatened to make Severino's daughters dance naked before his soldiers.[29] In desperation, Severino turned to an elderly Black man, Timóteo, for help. Timóteo mobilized his large family and set up an ambush, managing to fight off the feared attack. As a reward, he is said to have been granted ownership of the land and the rank of captain. The oral history does not say whether, by then, Timóteo was a slave or freedman. Severino de Carvalho was an infamous military commander during the end of the colonial era, who was appointed chief of police of the whole area in 1838. Hated by the poor of the lower Parnaíba micro-region, he and his family were subjected to various attacks from the Balaio rebels during the 1838–41 civil war, and his mother was killed.

In the case of Almas, we do not know if the "donation" was accompanied, at the time, by legal registration. It may not have been, because, according to Januária Patrício, squatters began encroaching on Timóteo's land long before abolition.

The case of Almas helps us see that the relationship between the slaveholding latifundio and peasant lands was more complex than at first appears. If an alliance with a powerful individual made it possible for Black freed people to gain access to land, a change in the local political leadership could pose a threat to their recently acquired ownership. In other words, the real situation of land ownership depended on title deeds and power relations between social actors at the local level, particularly in a period of transition, such as the middle of the nineteenth century, when the 1850 Land Law was attempting to re-establish the boundaries between full ownership, with all the rights it entailed, and what was considered merely *posse* or squatting. We can thus identify several ways through which present-day Black communities historically gained access to land: through services, sharecropping, military service, as well as concubinage.[30]

Indirect Access to Land

THE "PEASANT BREACH"

The issue of food supply was addressed in a variety of ways in plantation societies in the Americas: The planter could either purchase foodstuffs for enslaved workers or have them cultivate fields on his own estate. A third option was to allocate to slaves individual plots so they could feed themselves. In the case of Maranhão, there is evidence for all three of these options.

Robert Hesketh, the British consul in São Luís in the 1830s, mentions provision grounds of the enslaved, which according to him was common only on the large plantations.

Other contemporary sources, such as F. Brandão Jr., son of a planter from the Itapecuru Valley, even consider that this concession to slaves of plots they were allowed to work on Sundays and holidays was the overall rule.[31]

Brandão, despite his social origins, was an advocate of gradual emancipation and did not tend to paint the lives of the enslaved in particularly rosy colours. It is therefore difficult to get a precise idea of the importance of what historians have called, following Lepkowski's work on Haiti, the "peasant breach" in the slave system.[32]

The oral memory of the descendants of slaves in Maranhão also mentions provision grounds on plantations, cultivated by the captives under the surveillance of the overseer (*feitor*). In many cases the enslaved managed to keep these provision grounds after emancipation, often in exchange for their labour. This is in fact by far the most common situation regarding the origins of land access of hundreds of Black communities in the northern part of the state. Due to the modernization waves of the last decades (e.g., the Carajás mining project) the land they occupied for generations has been under threat, if not already lost, a process facilitated by the lack of formal property titles.

RENTING COMMUNAL LAND

Although *sesmaria* legislation stipulated that each town should dispose of communal land to finance their expenses, in practice that depended very much on the historical moment *vilas* were created, as well as how much the town council looked after its property. Not all towns in Maranhão owned significant amounts of land, but a number of them did own plots ranging in size from hundreds to a couple of thousands of hectares. For example, Itapecuru-Mirim, founded in 1818, owned over 2,200 ha, and Codó received 174 ha on its creation, in 1833. Both were grants from rich landowners in all likelihood happy with the creation or "emancipation" of their respective town. Much more significant, though, were the communal lands in Icatu and Tutóia, on the coast. Here poor soils seem to have made the Crown inclined to give away bigger areas. Tutóia, a former Indigenous mission village, was granted the *sesmaria* of the extinct mission on its creation, in 1760, of 26,000 ha.[33]

Icatu, the third-oldest town in the captaincy, was given more than 25,000 ha. The majority of its free poor population were tenants (*foreiros*) of the lands belonging to the municipality. There were 355 registered *foreiros* in 1825. With their families they certainly amounted to more than a thousand people, while the parish counted, in 1821, only 7,265 inhabitants in total, including slaves.

A third type of this kind of land access existed in Maranhão: church lands (usually belonging to a monastic order) rented out to families of peasants. During times of slavery, the Carmelite order in Rosário rented out most of their lands even though tenants (*foreiros*) were not always paying their rent. Some of these situations have endured in the eastern part of Maranhão, where they are known as *terras de santo*. Finally, there are indications that some private owners also rented out their land in the nineteenth century. I have not found enough sources documenting this to be able to assess its importance. Contrary to the *foreiros*, this group, called *agregados*, were pressed into a relationship of personal dependency, had to hand over a substantial part of their harvest to the owner, and on top of that put their labour at his service. This relationship became very important in the interior of Maranhão and other provinces after the abolition of slavery.[34]

USING COMMONS

In addition to the lands granted at their foundation, the town councils also gained control over the *realengos* in 1833, assigned to them by the imperial government during the liberal Regency (1831–40). The *realengos* were defined as the land strip of fifteen *braças* (thirty-three metres) from the seashore, at the highest tide, in a straight line inland. The revenues from the leases of the *realengos* were also to feed the coffers of the municipalities located by the sea.

In Maranhão, due to the enormous difference in sea level between low tide and high tide, these fifteen *braças* could cover great stretches of land. At low tide, these *realengos* thus extended for hundreds of metres in width. They included extensive mangroves on land regularly flooded by the tide or andiroba trees that grew on higher ground, flooded only occasionally, both of which were of great economic importance. The mangroves supplied the population with timber and represented hunting and fishing grounds. Andiroba was used to make soap and oil, the latter used both as medicine and for lighting. The harvesting and processing of andiroba was, along with fishing, the main activity of what town councillors called the "poverty" (*pobreza*) in the borough (*termo*) of Icatu. The cutting of andiroba trees was prohibited by the council during the colonial period, and free access to the forests was guaranteed as a customary right: "The Munim [River valley] abounds in these trees [*andirobeiras*], whose forests belong to the people."[35]

In the 1830s the andiroba forests were the theatre of a multi-layered conflict. Neighbouring landowners started to push their property claims toward the shore and tried to prevent the "poverty" from accessing the *realengos*. I believe this was not convenient for the merchants who bought the oil and soap from the latter, so it was reported to the governor of the province. The provincial government in return wanted the municipal council to rent them out to generate income. Therefore, the council decided to levy a "modest" amount. Unsurprisingly this led to conflict with the andiroba gatherers, who defended their ancestral rights to free use.[36]

The andiroba was only a relatively minor sector of the provincial domestic economy, whose production involved hundreds of families in a limited area. Yet this conflict announced bigger struggles over the appropriation of resources some actors considered to be held in common: rivers, lakes, and even forests. The appropriation of the coconuts of the native *babaçu* palm, for instance, which was the most common secondary vegetation on the soils of the former rainforest, became a source of permanent tension in the latter half of the twentieth century, when owners tried to prevent poor peasants from collecting them on their land, or land they considered theirs.

Conclusion

The interaction of Portuguese legal frameworks, local circumstances, and struggles over resources resulted in the agrarian structure of Maranhão—characterized, since colonial times, by great inequality of access to land. The colonial rationale aimed to create a class of wealthy landowners dominating colonial subjects not only through forced labour, but also by controlling access to land. Contra-colonial agents, however, managed to carve out spaces in the interstices of the plantation system in unoccupied areas beyond the agrarian frontier, such as inaccessible riverheads in the then dense rainforest or territories not yet colonized. Peasants also made use of resources in plain sight of colonial authorities, sometimes backed up by existing Portuguese legal traditions. The latter had found their way into colonial legislation to facilitate strategical alliances of the Portuguese Crown with Indigenous peoples, or to favour the demographic occupation in order to stabilize the colonial project in its early stages. These legal traditions consisted of communal land granted to "pacified" Indian communities or to tenants on municipal land (*foreiros*). The continuous subdivision among inheritors also led to establishment of *minifundia*, or territories that were communally owned (*terra indivisa*). Yet the informality of many of these occupations led to instable and precarious land access for Maranhão peasants or *caboclos*, jeopardized further as almost none of them managed to register their land according to the 1850 law. This resulted in systematic usurpation of peasant land ever since.

The 1988 constitution at least recognized the rights of "traditional people" and of the descendants of *quilombos*, which had for such a long time been excluded from Brazil's legislation and ignored by public policies. The developments in the agrarian sector in the last thirty years have shown how many communities living on "traditionally occupied land" were able to capitalize on these modest policy changes. Their activism and capacity to mobilize other, especially state actors, helped them react against growing encroachments by *grileiros* (land grabbers) or agrobusiness and advance their cause toward formal recognition of their rights.

Hence the interest in examining the formation of these "traditional" land uses and appropriations back in time to illuminate our understanding of peasant mobilization then and now. Back in the 1830s, even though there were quite a number of sporadic land conflicts, some of which have been mentioned here, land was not the common denominator able to mobilize the different subaltern groups of a slave society. There were just too many different situations of land access that prevented an objective common interest.

NOTES TO CHAPTER 6

1. Evsey Domar, "The Causes of Slavery and Serfdom: A Hypothesis," *Journal of Economic History* 30, no. 1 (1970): 18–32.
2. Alberto Passos Guimarães, *Quatro séculos de latifúndio*, 3rd ed. (Paz e Terra, 1963).
3. Sérgio Buarque de Holanda, *Raízes do Brasil*, 17th ed. (José Olympio, 1984 [1st ed., 1936]), 56. Author's translation.
4. Material informing this chapter, including maps, tables, and a more extensive bibliography, can be found in Matthias Röhrig Assunção, *De caboclos a Bem-te-vis: Formação do campesinato no Maranhão, 1800-1850* (Annablume, 2018), chaps. 2–4. For an English translation, see Matthias Röhrig Assunção, *Peasant Rebellion in a Slave Society: The Balaiada in Maranhão, Brazil, 1800-1850* (Routledge, 2024).
5. Alfredo Wagner Berno de Almeida, *Traditionally Occupied Lands in Brazil* (PGSCA-UFAM, 2011), 123.
6. Manuel Diegues Júnior, "Land Tenure and Use in the Brazilian Plantation System," in *Plantation Systems of the New World: Papers and Discussion Summaries of the Seminar Held in San Juan, Puerto Rico* (Pan-American Union, 1959), 14; José da Costa Porto, *Estudo sôbre o sistema sesmaria* (Imprensa Universitária, Universidade Federal do Pernambuco, 1965), 26–7; Jacob Gorender, *O escravismo colonial* (Ática, 1978), 364–8.
7. Research by Carmen Alveal has shown that only a small number of *sesmarias* were confirmed by Lisbon between 1521 and 1777. See Alveal, *Senhorios coloniais: Direitos e chicanas forenses na formação da propriedade na América portuguesa* (Ed. Proprietas, 2022), 311.
8. There is not yet reliable data on the total number of *sesmeiros* in the territory that constituted Maranhão in 1822.
9. For a more detailed discussion of the land law of 1850, see Warren Dean, "Latifundia and Land Policy in Nineteenth-Century Brazil," *Hispanic American Historical Review* 51, no. 4 (1971): 606–25; José Murilo de Carvalho, "Modernização frustrada: A política de terras no Império," *Revista Brasileira de História* 1 (1981): 39–57; Emília Viotti da Costa, *Da Monarquia à República: Momentos decisivos*, 3rd ed. (Brasiliense, 1985), 131–61; Lígia Osorio Silva, *Terras devolutas e latifundio: Efeitos da lei de 1850* (Editora da UNICAMP, 1996); Márcia Maria Menendes Motta, *Nas fronteiras do poder: Conflito e direito à terra no Brasil do século XIX*, 2nd ed. (EdUFF, 2008).
10. Motta, *Nas fronteiras*, 176–7.
11. Dean, "Latifundia," 621.
12. See "Sobre o ITERMA," Govern do Maranhão, accessed 25 April 2021, http://www.iterma.ma.gov.br/iterma-institucional/.
13. Administrative divisions in nineteenth-century Brazil were organized according to three separate, although connected, sectors of the imperial state. In political terms, the empire consisted of provinces, which were divided into the *termos* (territories) of towns and cities, which in turn were divided into districts (*distritos*). In judicial terms, each Court of Appeal was responsible for a number of judicial unities (*comarcas*) presided by professional judges (*juizes de fora*). The *comarcas* in turn were subdivided in districts under the responsibility of a justice of the peace, later substituted by police chiefs and ordinary judges. In ecclesiastical terms, the empire consisted of archdioceses and dioceses, which in turn were divided into parishes. Political and judicial divisions usually (but not always) overlapped and were also—given that Catholicism was the official religion—congruent with ecclesiastical divisions.
14. Alida C. Metcalf, "Fathers and Sons: The Politics of Inheritance in a Colonial Brazilian Township," *Hispanic American Historical Review* 66, no. 3 (1986): 455–84.
15. In the 1980s, the descendants of the mission still owned collectively a slot of land, but according to their testimony, the size of it had diminished substantially since the nineteenth century.
16. See 1854–7 land registries of São Miguel (nos. 44, 62); Rosário (nos. 3, 4, 33, 38, 39); Itapecuru-Mirim (no. 208), Public Archive of the State of Maranhão, São Luís.
17. It is important to remember that a small but significant number of enslaved people succeeded through various ways in obtaining freedom throughout the three and a half centuries of slavery in Brazil. Since freed people had much higher reproduction and survival rates, the free population of colour in Brazil started to outnumber enslaved people during the nineteenth century. Final abolition of slavery in 1888 therefore only freed a relatively small percentage of the total population.
18. Motta, *Nas fronteiras*, 123–5.
19. Otávio Guilherme Velho, *Capitalismo autoritário e campesinato (Um estudo comparativo a partir da fronteira em movimento)* (Difel, 1976).

20 For example, in the case of the former villages of Vinhaes on the island of São Luís, or Barbados on the Itapecuru River. See *Relatório do Presidente da Província do Maranhão, Eduardo Olímpio Machado* (I. J. Ferreira, 1855), 29–30.

21 Projeto Vida de Negro, *Terras de preto: Quebrando o mito do isolamento, Levantamento preliminar da situação atual das chamadas Terras de preto localizadas no Estado do Maranhão* (Sociedade Maranhense de Defesa dos Direitos Humanos, 1989).

22 Alfredo Wagner Berno de Almeida, "Quilombos: Tema e problema," in *Jamary dos Pretos: Terra de mocambeiros*, ed. Projeto Vida de Negro (Sociedade Maranhense de Defesa dos Direitos Humanos, Centro de Cultura Negra do Maranhão, Associação Rural de Moradores do Quilombo Jamary dos Pretos, 1998), 13–25.

23 Alfredo Wagner Berno de Almeida, "Terras de Preto, Terras de Santo, Terras de Índio—Uso comum e conflito," *Cadernos do NAEA* 10 (1989): 172.

24 For the Jamary case, see Luis Antonio Câmara Pedrosa, "Petição de regularização das terras," in Projeto Vida de Negro, *Jamary dos Pretos*, 91; for Frechal, see Projeto Vida de Negro, *Frechal, Terra de Preto: Quilombo reconhecido como reserva extrativista* (Sociedade Maranhense de Defesa dos Direitos Humanos, Centro de Cultura Negra do Maranhão, Associação de Moradores do Quilombo Frechal, 1996), 125.

25 See foreword to this volume.

26 For more details, see the testimony of Simião and others in Matthias Röhrig Assunção, *A Guerra dos Bem-te-vis: A Balaiada na memória oral*, 2nd ed. (EdUFMA, 2008 [1st ed 1988]) 132–7. Also see Benedito Souza Filho, "Bom Sucesso: Terra de Preto, Terra de Santo, Terra Comum" (MA thesis, Universidade Federal do Pará, 1998).

27 "Poranduba Maranhense ou Relação histórica da Província do Maranhão . . . (1820)," *Revista do Instituto Histórico e Geográfico Brasileiro* 54, no. 83 (1891): 117.

28 Joaquim Shirashi Neto, "Prática de pesquisa judiciária para identificação das denominadas Terras de preto nos cartórios do Maranhão" (MA thesis, Universidade Federal do Maranhão, 1998), 11.

29 See the testimony of Januária Patrício in Assunção, *A Guerra dos Bem-te-vis*, 122. For another version of the same episode, see Celecina de Maria Veras Salas, "Os descendentes de Timóteo: Lutas camponesas e interferência do Estado numa terra de preto em conflito, no Baixo Parnaíba, Maranhão," in *Cadernos de Práticas de Pesquisa* (São Luís: UFMA, 1998), 14–15.

30 For more details, see Assunção, *A Guerra dos Bem-te-vis*, 113–25.

31 F. A. Brandão Junior, *A escravatura no Brasil precedida d'um artigo sobre a agricultura e colonisação no Maranhão* (H. Thiry-Vern Buggenhondt, 1865), 42.

32 Tadeusz Lepkowski, *Haiti*, 2 vols. (Casa de las Américas, 1968).

33 For more details and references regarding communal land, see Assunção, *De caboclos*, 140–4.

34 According to the diary of a *fazendeiro* from the lower Parnaíba, the aggregates could only sell their surplus to the owner. This diary is from the beginning of the century (it was written between 1918 and 1932), and the author was born in 1877. See Lena Castello Branco, *Arraial e Coronel: Dois estudos de história social* (Cultrix, 1979).

35 "Poranduba," 143.

36 For more details and references, see Assunção, *De caboclos*, 157–8, 172–3.

7

The Impact of Portuguese Development Thought and Practice on Land Relations in the Late Portuguese Colonial Period

Susanna Barnes

Introduction

Development policies and practices have a profound influence on the dynamics of land relations. In the late colonial period, the Portuguese Empire, much like other European colonial powers, pivoted away from justifications for intervention grounded in the moralizing discourse of a "civilizing mission" to embrace principles of modernization and economic development.[1] Between 1953 and 1974, the Portuguese "Estado Novo" regime (1933–74) implemented a series of development plans known as *planos do fomento*.[2] These plans aimed to organize resources from both metropolitan and overseas regions to stimulate economic growth and promote "integrated development" across the entire Portuguese "nation."[3] As the language of colonial welfare shifted to that of modernization and development, interventions in support of the plans were increasingly expected to draw on scientific knowledge and methods obtained "on the ground." Jeronimo and Pinto aptly describe this era as characterized by "repressive developmentalism," a term encapsulating a combination of "enhanced coercive strategies for governance, carefully planned development initiatives encompassing political, economic, and socio-cultural change, and the deliberate engineering of social-cultural differentiation."[4]

While the development plans implemented across the Portuguese territories shared a common ideological framework and macroeconomic vision, the actual planning and execution were intended to be determined at the local level. In the case of Timor, the development plans were increasingly driven by administrators and governors with prior experience in Portuguese Africa, and directed by scientists and technocrats who brought with them new ideas of "development" and "progress" firmly grounded in modernist discourses. Key elements of the plans in Timor included significant investments in agricultural development, particularly in the cultivation of coffee and rice. One notable aspect of these interventions was the concerted effort to restrict upland, shifting cultivation practices and establish new agricultural areas, especially in the fertile lowlands of the southern coast and the alluvial plains along the northern coast, for the cultivation of irrigated rice.

To date, there has been relatively little written about how "development" was understood, interpreted, and implemented by diverse actors in the late colonial period in Portuguese Timor. Nevertheless, the effects of these policies and plans have had an irreversible impact on relations to land and notions of "property" in Timor-Leste.[5] This work situates the land relations in Timor-Leste within their broader historical, moral, and ideological context. The chapter focuses on the fertile alluvial plain of the Nunura River in the Maliana sub-district, serving as a case study to investigate how planned agricultural development interventions shaped land access and utilization during this period and how they continue to influence claim-making practices in contemporary Timor-Leste. Through this exploration, I aim to shed light on the enduring legacy of Portuguese colonial development and its intricate interplay with land and property in the nation's history.

Estado Novo and Postwar Developmentalism

In the aftermath of World War II, as a new global order emerged and anti-colonial movements gained momentum, the Portuguese government faced mounting pressure to decolonize and recognize the right to self-determination for colonized peoples. In an attempt to evade criticism, the "Estado Novo" government revised the constitution, replacing the term "colonies" with "overseas provinces" and "empire" with "Portuguese overseas." This "semantic decolonization"[6] effectively made the metropole and the former colonies a single political and economic entity. To support integration and uphold the idea of Portuguese exceptionalism, new policies and institutions were created. Constitutional revisions and related legislation such as the Overseas Organic Law (1953) enabled the (re)legitimization of Portuguese sovereignty through the expansion of colonial bureaucracy, scientific methods of governance, and the implementation of models of planned economic development and social and cultural modernization.[7]

If, prior to the 1940s, the relationship between the metropole and overseas possessions was marked by extraction and the civilizing mission of church and state, by the late 1940s there was a significant shift in this discourse, as the language changed to suit the demands of new developmentalism.[8] In the post–World War II era, the concept of "development" emerged as both a set of practices and an ideology that structured relationships between "industrialized, affluent nations and poor, emerging nations."[9] Portugal's colonial welfare vision readily absorbed the idea of "underdevelopment" as a problem that could be solved by technology.[10]

Between 1953 and 1975, the Portuguese government developed a series of *planos do fomento* (development plans) aimed at integrating metropolitan and overseas resources to stimulate economic growth and promote "integrated development" from "Minho to Timor" (as famously declared by Salazar). Under the leadership of the Minister for the Colonies, Marcello Caetano, colonial development referred to "the economic policy of the empire, concerned with production, commerce, industry, credit, transport, and communications."[11] And more explicitly, *fomento* was to be understood as "modernization and should require technical expertise."[12]

Modelled on similar development interventions by France, Britain, and Belgium, funds for the development plans were provided from the metropole to the now provinces in the form of interest-free, repayable loans, reimbursable depending on the resources of each territory.[13] From 1953 to 1979, four plans were elaborated. The first plan ran from 1953 to 1958, the second from 1959 to 1964, and a "mid-term" two-year plan, between 1965 and 1967, preceded the third plan, implemented from 1968 to 1973. A fourth and final plan, never implemented in Portuguese Timor, was elaborated for the period 1974 to 1979. Although these plans were homogenous, throughout the metropole and provinces, in terms of conception, policy, and macroeconomics, specific planning and programming was to be based on localized needs assessments.[14]

Scientific expertise and scientific institutions became critical to evaluating "underdevelopment" and elaborating specific technological interventions. Between 1946 and 1971, the Junta de Investigações Científicas das Colónias / Junta de Investigações Científicas do Ultramar (JIC/JIU) underwent a period of exceptional growth. During this period, "61 new entities were created, of which two were Institutes of Scientific Research, one in Luanda, Angola, and the other in Lourenço Marques, Mozambique, along with five commissions, 16 centers, 26 missions, 11 brigades and one museum (the Museum of Overseas Ethnology, based in Lisbon)."[15] Of these, the Mission for Overseas Agronomic Studies, created in 1960, was of particular significance for Portuguese Timor.[16]

Castelo has argued that the expansion of JIC/JIU during this period is indicative of a shift away from exploitative relations between Portugal and its territories to one of investment in the economic development of places and people through public and private investments.[17] This shift was largely in response to growing international criticism, especially in relation to policies of native labour, the system of dual citizenship, and the lack of investment in education and health services for native populations.[18] In 1961 and 1962 forced labour was outlawed, in 1961 the *indigenato* regime of dual citizenship was abolished, and there was a gradual extension of education and health care. The concept of "Lusotropicalism," which held that Portugal was a multicultural, multiracial, and pluri-continental nation, emerged as a dominant discourse.[19] Yet, legislative and policy change at the "national' level did not necessarily translate into increased equality and freedoms for colonized peoples.[20]

The Five-Year Plans and "Repressive Development" in Portuguese Timor

In many ways Portuguese Timor was an outlier in the greater vision for a pluri-continental nation. Unlike other Portuguese colonies, such as Angola and Mozambique, which had large numbers of European settlers, Timor had a small population of Portuguese colonists who mainly worked in the administration and commerce. The Portuguese did not encourage large-scale settlement in Timor, and there was no significant agricultural or mining industry to support a large Portuguese settler population. Even to this day, few Portuguese consider Timor to have been a "settler colony."[21] Yet, despite its high maintenance costs and low returns, Portuguese Timor was presented as "a model of Portuguese colonization" well into the 1950s. The development of the city of Dili and surrounding townships, the building of the airport and Baucau, plantations, roads, ports, and missions were all presented as evidence of Portugal's commitment to the "civilizing project."[22] As the attitudes and language of the civilizing mission changed, however, the lack of settlement was considered, by some, the greatest obstacle to "development." For example, as Jose Alberty Correia, the governor of Portuguese Timor, pronounced in 1965, "It is no use in having technical advances and big material improvements that the people cannot understand and take advantage of."[23]

The overall assessment of the impact of the plans on the economic development of Portuguese Timor tends to be universally negative.[24] Despite the discourse of "raising the standard of living" and "providing better job opportunities," the first development plan was largely focused on reconstruction in the aftermath of World War II.[25] Budgets for infrastructure and communications continued to outstrip investments in agriculture, and other health and social programs, in the second, mid-term, and third development plans. While there were modest improvements in public education and health care, agricultural production declined in various areas and infrastructure development, the most highly resourced sector, remained limited. Famously, between 1968 and 1970, thirty-three kilometres of road were constructed—an average of eleven kilometres per year.[26] Several authors have pointed to the lack of human and technical resources, weak administrative structures, and poor design and funding models as reasons behind the failure of the development plans.[27] But perhaps it was lack of attention and consideration of the Timorese themselves that had the greatest impact. Commenting on the first development plan, the poet and agronomist (and later ethnographer) Ruy Cinatti lamented the lack of attention to local circumstances and Indigenous Timorese knowledge and practices. He lambasted the administration for its heavy-handed interventions implemented "by the paddle-board," and the focus on cash crops and livestock over diversification and forestation.[28]

Reis notes, however, that the mid-term and third development plans did seek to address the lack of baseline knowledge of the territory.[29] The Brigades for Agronomic Research in Timor first appeared in 1959 but were later integrated into the Mission for Overseas Agronomic Research (Missão de Estudos Agronómicos do Ultramar, or MEAU). Between 1960 and 1975, some 150 scientific publications on a variety of agriculture-related topics appeared.[30] Emerging from this scientific knowledge was the idea that rice and coffee were key to Timor's "development". Under the leadership of Helder Lains e Silva, an ambitious plan to reduce maize production, strengthen coffee cultivation, and aggressively promote the growing of rice was devised.[31]

Lains e Silva and the MEAU's promotion of rice in particular was influenced by broader global and regional agricultural development trends in the 1960s, which emphasized research and development of key staple crops. This focus coincided with the establishment of the International Rice Research Institute in the Philippines in 1962, further accentuating the elevation of rice as a critical crop. While rice was already grown in Timor, the predominant cultivation was upland dry rice, rather than wet rice (irrigated/*sawah*), with maize serving as the primary staple. The implementation of irrigated rice cultivation programs therefore required not only the development and introduction of new and improved seeds and agricultural techniques but also substantial social and demographic change. Previously, "underutilized" or "uncultivated" land in lowland areas, in particular flood plains, on the northern and southern coasts were identified as areas of potential irrigated rice cultivation and agricultural extension programs that drew on scientific methods, and trials were henceforth established. Irrigation developments opened up the possibility of cultivating high-yielding rice varieties in a number of locations, including, as will be explored in the forthcoming case study, Maliana. It is estimated that during the 1960s, approximately seven thousand hectares of land devoted to rice cultivation was established in Timor, a transformation that not only expanded irrigated rice production but also involved a significant reconfiguration of the rural landscape, livelihoods, and land relations.[32]

Scientifically based, technical solutions to the province's development "problems" required the implementation of repertoires of colonial social control and coercion not dissimilar to schemes of resettlement described in the chapters by deGrassi, Adalima, and Direito in this volume. After World War II, the Portuguese colonial government had already begun ordering local populations to move away from forested and upland areas closer to the main roads. These demands were not well-received as people were reluctant to leave their upland gardens and ancestral lands.[33] While technical reports and scientific papers on the efforts to promote rice cultivation in Portuguese Timor do not include information about how populations were encouraged to take part in the process of establishing new areas of rice cultivation, as we shall see in the following case study, it is likely that people had little choice in the matter. For example, the provincial government, via largely Portuguese and mestizo military commanders and *chefe do posto*, continued to commandeer "voluntary" labour well into the 1960s. Individuals unable to pay their tax were forced to provide manual labour as auxiliaries on plantations, building projects, and roadworks, or as *ordenanaça* (ordinaries) working as domestic staff for civil servants and local rulers.[34] Additional labour was also provided by prisoners through various "Agricultural Correction Centres" re-established after World War II and operating until at least 1960.[35]

Moreover, it is likely that local administrators and Indigenous leaders involved in these schemes were offered incentives by way of land and access to services such as education and health care for their active help in relocating the population.[36] For example, in the late 1960s, Metzner observed how "development" had led to the inequitable allocation of land to "peasants," "seasonal labourers," and "elites" in Uato-Lari, on the southeastern coast.[37] The first category was allocated one or two hectares of land to each household for cultivation. The second, at first seasonally and then more permanently, were labourers drawn from upland villages in Quelicai. The third was a small elite class of local leaders capable of extracting labour from the local population who held up to one hundred hectares of irrigated rice land.[38] As Shepherd and McWilliam argue, rather than a path to emancipation, "development tended to consolidate the power and comparative wealth of the Indigenous *liurai* and clan chiefs, whose dominance over subordinate, often displaced and landless, Indigenous households had emerged over the course of a century of Portuguese intervention into local agricultural production."[39]

Although rice cultivation schemes on the Uato-Lari plain gained acceptance as harvests yielded results, the social and political impacts of the scheme had enduring negative effects. Technical advisers of the MEAU and elements of the provincial government at best ignored, and at worst took advantage of long-standing political tensions between local communities to develop irrigated rice-paddy production. To this day, the valuable coastal plains of Uato-Lari are the subject of land disputes. Collectively, these cases have come to represent shifting power relations between Makassae-speaking villages of Makadiki and Matahoe and the majority-Naueti population of Vessoru/Uaitame, Afaloicai, and Babulo, which is linked to respective historical alliances with FRETILIN (Frente Revolucionária de Timor-Leste Independente) and APODETI (the pro-Indonesian Associação Popular Democratica Timorense). However, these cases are not consistently divided along ethnic and political lines, nor is the actual composition of the village populations involved as homogeneous as this analysis might suggest. The risk of oversimplistic analysis is that it serves to obscure the root causes of the conflict and the way the Portuguese colonial administration ordered the development of the Uato-Lari coastal plain for rice cultivation, as well as the real or perceived use of the rice fields as a tool by the Portuguese colonial authorities to "punish" their enemies and by the Indonesian authorities to reward their allies.[40]

In the case study that follows I take a closer look at the implementation of irrigated rice development programs in Maliana. I draw on interviews conducted between 2006 and 2008 in the sub-district to explore how the implementation of rice development under the auspices the five-year development plans and MEAU technical expertise impacted practices relating to land and notions of "property." First, I describe local histories of land use, allocation, and apportionment prior to the implementation of the development plans. Then, I examine how development interventions unfolded across the sub-district and the how this shaped land access and use during this period. Finally, I consider the implications of development interventions on contemporary claims to land.

Map 7.1.
Map of Maliana
Source: Eigenes Werk unter Verwendung von File:Administrative map of the Bobonaro District of East Timor.png von Maximilian Dörrbecker. Cartography: Rui Pinto.

The Impact of Rice Development on Land Relations in Maliana

Today, the sub-district of Maliana has a total population of 28,908 and comprises seven administrative villages.[41] While the people of the villages of Saburai, Tapo/Memo, Holsa, and Odomau are predominantly Bunak-speakers, the villagers of Ritabou, Raifun, and Lahomea are mainly speakers of Kemak. Generations of proximity and engagement mean that there are many bilingual individuals and families, and in Maliana town in particular there are numerous ethnically mixed families where Tetum is spoken as the lingua franca. In the immediate aftermath of World War II, the then *posto* of Maliana was comprised of 3 *reinu*, 6 *sucos*, and 21 hamlets.[42] The vast majority of settlements were located in the upland areas to the east and south of the Nunura flood plain.

The dominant form of agriculture in Portuguese Timor at the time was "bush fallowing."[43] This included two modalities identified by Metzner, *lere rai* and *fila rai*. *Lere rai* interspersed crop rotation with fallow periods of varying lengths; it was used in forested areas where loose soil required no tillage and preferably areas with scrub and low trees, and which did not require the felling of large trees. *Fila rai*, on the other hand, was labour-intensive soil-tillage technique that required turning over the soil with rudimentary hardwood tools called *ai-suak*. *Fila rai* was understood to have come about due to population pressure leading to reduced availability of land suitable for *lere rai* shifting cultivation.[44] Meztner recorded that, "While Timorese peasants unanimously agreed that *fila rai* fields usually yield far higher results than *lere* fields, the labour input of the former is tremendous."[45] He added that evidence of *fila rai* in an area, because of the labour required, was likely to be an indicator of population pressure.[46] During the late 1950s and early 1960s populations were relocated from upland villages to the newly established Maliana town and specific sites on the expansive Nunura flood plain that were targeted for planned development interventions, in particular the cultivation of new irrigated rice varieties.

Interlocutors from Maliana suggested that prior to the implementation of "development" initiatives in the area there were two ways to gain access to land. The first was based on ancestral histories of land settlement and use, where access to land was determined by house membership. Ancestral houses (*uma lisan*) are a fundamental unit of social organization in Timor-Leste. Houses are comprised of living house members and their ancestors. Each house traces its origins genealogically or through histories of migration and settlement to an ancestral founder. House land generally includes areas of land believed to have been first cleared, burned, and cultivated by distinct house-based groups, as well as land belonging to other houses related through marriage.⁴⁷ The second is involves the clearing of "new" or "unused" areas of land. If land was "new," never previously farmed, and did not fall within the territory, authority, or claim of another house-based group, then access and use was determined through the enactment of necessary rituals required to appease the spirits of the land (*rai nain*). If the land was "unused" but fell within the territory, authority, or claim of another house-based group, then access and use had to be negotiated with the relevant landholding group.

For example, interlocutors from Uat, now part of the village of Ritabou, acknowledge that the land on the Nunura flood plain fell under the jurisdiction of ancestral houses from the areas of Saburai to the west and Kailako to the east. In Uat oral histories, members of the houses of Duas Mali and Lua Laben first ventured into the lowlands:

> Balik ulu
>
> Sesa be ka, dudu ma loa
>
> Sama teho, napa gh'e nu
>
> (Open the path by throwing the spear
>
> Spread out, open and broaden
>
> Tread and trample [the eucalypt] underfoot)⁴⁸

Members of these houses claim they were granted access to some land on the Nunura plain by the landholding houses of Atxu and Atxu Plaza, and in exchange were expected to pay tribute. Described in Uat narratives as an offering of palm wine and part of the harvest, this tribute is commonly referred to throughout Timor-Leste as *rai te'en*, the "waste" of the land (*kakata te'e, sura ra'a* in Kemak ritual language).⁴⁹

> Tere bale, lape bale
>
> Datxu bale, prio bale
>
> Dia Duas Mali, Lua Laben
>
> Mara de'ena, m'ghen dia luro
>
> Imi hodi tate, imi hodi toi

(We ask you, we give to you this land

This is the garden, this is the palm wine

Duas Mali, Lua Laben

Use it, the end is ripe, the head is yellow

When we come, give us part of the cob, pour us some of the wine)[50]

Beginning in the mid- to late 1950s, several interlocutors from different villages described how the local population started to graze animals and later cultivate crops on the plain. In the adjacent sub-district of Manapa, home to the landholding houses of Atxu and Atxu Plaza, corn and some "dry rice" was already being cultivated at this time. Coconut plantations existed in and around present-day Maliana town, but these are likely to have been planted at an earlier time.[51]

During fieldwork it was common for people from the predominantly Kemak-speaking villages of Raifun, Odomau, Lahomea, and Ritabou to say that their fathers or grandfathers came to the plains "hodi karau luhan," to build animal enclosures, or "halo to'os" (Tetum), which refers both to the cultivation of permanent gardens as well as shifting plots. During this time, my interlocutors suggested that people built makeshift structures in their fields or enclosures but continued to live in their upland settlements. Some asserted that this movement of people was spontaneous as land became scarcer in the uplands due to population pressure.[52] Others suggested that, already in the 1950s, they were part of planned interventions of the Portuguese administration. Although the MEAU was actively promoting the development of rice farming, coconut cultivation, and cattle breeding at the time, most interventions occurred in the eastern parts of the province.[53]

It was not until the mid-1960s that people recalled the systematic "opening up" of areas of land on the Nunura flood plain for rice cultivation. According to the mid-term development plan (1965–7), during this time "agricultural camps" (*campos agrícolas*) providing agricultural extension services were established in Hale-Cou and Mau-Coli.[54] Under the orders of the local administrator (*administrador do posto*), local rulers (*liurai*), village (*chefe do suco*), and hamlet chiefs (*chefe da povoação*) were recruited to organize the population to work on schemes aimed at "developing" the Nunura plain for agriculture. This process of "development" involved villages not only from the *posto* of Maliana but also Bobonaro and Kailako. For example, interlocutors from Hauba (Bobonaro) described how in 1965, or when "katuas liurai sei ukun" (when the *liurai* ruled), they came down to the lowlands around the area of Hale Cou, where they established rice fields.[55] Similarly, people from Marobo also came to work on the plains. In 1967 they were involved in establishing irrigated rice paddies in an area of land called Mau-Mali.[56]

The implementation of development schemes on the Nunura flood plain occurred at the command of the Portuguese authorities, and certain groups also explicitly acknowledge the involvement of the colonial Agricultural Department.[57] A number of local village heads and members of the sub-district administration considered that, during the immediate post–World War II period, the vast majority of the land on the Nunura plain was uncultivated, or forested land that had never been cultivated or had long been abandoned. Consequently, they deemed this land to be property of the state at the time.[58] It seems likely that under the direction of the colonial administration, then, plots of land were simply allocated to village and hamlet heads, who organized their communities into work groups. The language used to describe this allocation of land included words such as "placed" (*koloka*), "ordered" (*haruka*), and "allocated" (*fahe rai ba*).[59] Some civil servants during the Portuguese period claimed that the authorities actually "measured out plots," suggesting the formal apportionment of land.[60] However, when discussing how access to land was negotiated at the time most villagers I spoke to emphasized the role played by local *liurai*, their *chefe suco*, or *chefe da povoação* in land allocation. Some claimed that these local authorities negotiated access to land directly with local landholding groups on behalf of the community. For example, a representative of the group of people from Marobo who worked on the irrigation scheme in Mau-Mali claimed that the negotiated access with the landholding groups of Atxu and Atxu Plaza "according to custom" (Indonesian: *secara adat*). Others involved in clearing new plots of land considered the thick eucalypt forest (*ai bubur laran*) to be *rai lulik* (Tetum, meaning sacred land) because it was old-growth forest that had not been farmed.

Echoing Metzner's observations on the Uato-Lari plain on the southern coast, a common perception among my interlocutors was that "development" on the Nunura plain benefited some groups more than others. Accusations of "favouritism" were levelled at certain individuals and groups, in particular certain hereditary chiefs (*liurai*) and those deemed "close to the administration."[61] At the time, "assimilated" and mestizo Timorese, the sons and daughters of certain *liurai* and *chefe do suco*, or civil servants were given preferential access to education, housing, and in some cases were free from the burden of head tax.[62] These categories of people were often deemed to have been given preferential treatment in terms of size and quality of land parcels. One interlocutor stated that, in the 1960s, civil servants were the first to be allocated plots of land by the administration "as a top-up, because their wages weren't sufficient" (*tamba vencimento la to'o*). Representatives of the community of Manapa, Kailako, suggested that their land was handed over to the *liurai* and three *chefe do suco* of Marobo because they were close to the "colonialists." In a dispute that occurred in 1967 or 1968, the *administrador do posto* was reported to have said that the people of Marobo "deserved" the land because they were more hard-working.[63] A common criticism was that the descendants of former *liurai* and some *chefe do suco* responsible for organizing village and hamlet work groups to open up the land were now making claims to land cleared under their orders.

There is a striking contrast between the neutral language of the development plans and technical reports of the MEAU and the complex social, political, and economic environment in which they unfolded. Metzner lamented in the late 1960s that there was little reliable information regarding day-to-day activities from the districts or sub-districts,[64] and more archival work and investigation into other Portuguese and Timorese sources (e.g., military and civilian personnel stationed in the *concelho* of Bobonaro or *posto* of Maliana) is required to reconstruct the details of the implementation of development plans on the Nunura plain. However, there are some things that we do know. Today there are numerous land disputes that have their origins in how "development" schemes, including irrigated rice cultivation, in Maliana were rolled out. Some are grounded in the politics of punishment and reward meted out by the Portuguese authorities that shaped how individuals and groups gained access to land. A number of disputes have become entrenched at a communal level between hamlets or villages over areas of irrigated paddy first established in the late 1960s. Often these disputes are inseparable from political tensions arising from Portuguese strategies of *divide et impera*, and which were later projected onto political parties during Timor-Leste's brief and tragic "decolonization" process and persisted through the Indonesian occupation.[65] Others are directly related to how the land was physically "opened" and cultivated in work groups, making individual claims "to own, access, or trade" land difficult to ascertain.[66]

A case in point is the village (*suco*) of Ritabou. During the late Portuguese period the village comprised four hamlets: Uat, Ritabou, Dai Tete, and Meganutu. In the late 1950s and early 1960s, the population of these hamlets was mobilized by their *chefe suco* and *chefe povoação* to work on schemes initiated by the colonial authorities in order to "develop" the Nunura plain for agriculture. Although this presumably occurred under the auspices of the colonial Agricultural Department, few informants describe working on these fields in terms of taking part in a state initiative. Most informants referred exclusively to the role played by their *chefe suco* or *chefe povoação* in "opening up" the land. Some informants claimed that the local authorities negotiated access to land directly with local landholding groups (see above) on behalf of the community at the time. Others consider the vast majority of the land in and around present-day Maliana town was, during the post–World War II period, uncultivated, or forested land, which had never been used or had long been abandoned. Consequently, this land was deemed property of the state by the Portuguese administration, and it seems likely that local authorities, under the direction of the colonial administration, simply identified areas of land and allocated plots to the members of the work groups.

The process of "breaking in" land is critical to customary claims to land based on precedence in Timor-Leste.[67] In narratives of origin, this process is often represented as involving a human or blood sacrifice to the non-human entities that enliven the land, creating a bond of reciprocity between original settlers and the land.[68] Informants' claims to land based on these grounded practices aimed at "opening the land" in Maliana were reinforced by reference to a blood sacrifice made by one of the workers from Uat. Informants from Uat claim that work groups involved in first clearing an area of land called Ai-Kiar came from the hamlets of Uat, Meganutu, and Dai Tete. They had to work hard to clear the land, which they described as thick eucalypt forest (Tetum: *ai bubur laran*). Those involved in clearing the land considered this forest to be sacred land (Tetum: *rai lulik*) because it was old-growth forest that had not previously been farmed. It was prohibited to eat river shrimp in the waterways of the Nunura plain that ran through the land they were clearing, However, one of their group disregarded the prohibition and subsequently died. His death was conceptualized as a "blood sacrifice" to the "keepers of the forest," the non-human entities that enliven the land (*rai nain*) and originally inhabited the area. Maintaining these claims based on customary principles of land access and use requires effort and work; it also requires the support of, or at the very least a lack of opposition from, politico-legal authorities and institutions.

Lack of clarity around who "owns" the land today sometimes manifests itself in the "enrolment"[69] or mobilization of what Li refers to as "inscription devices"[70] that serve to actively (re)shape (or reassemble) what land means and represents at any given time. These include mobilizing histories of grounded practices such as those described above or material representations including tax receipts, land surveys, notices published in the Portuguese-era *Boletim de Timor*, or even physical objects connecting people to the land. For example, in one land dispute documented in Maliana dating back to the Portuguese period, one of the parties to the conflict appeared before the Directorate of Land and Property in possession of a Portuguese-era hoe as proof that their family had been involved in Portuguese-era agricultural schemes. Yet, items such as these are insufficient in themselves to establish legal rights to land. Officials from the Directorate of Land and Property stated that, to their knowledge, only two land titles were ever issued in the *posto* of Maliana during the late Portuguese period. Two individuals were granted *alvará de aforamento "com motivo da criação do animais."* Both were reported to be local businessmen, who, if they were able to obtain title for their animal enclosure, could apply for loans at the bank—so there was an incentive for them to do so.

There are several reasons why many individuals and groups failed to register or obtain title to land at the time of opening the Nunura plain to agriculture in the late colonial period. First, it is possible that neither those involved in the planning and programming of the development interventions in Portuguese Timor, nor the local authorities responsible for enacting the plans, anticipated that land farmed under these schemes was anything but state land. Second, many of those actively involved in farming the land were likely unaware of changes in the legislation that could have provided a basis for land title. For example, the concept of "indigeneity," or *indigenato*, that distinguished *indígenas* (natives) from *civilizados* (Portuguese citizens), as well as the intermediate category of *asimilados*, was abolished in 1961–2, triggering changes to land-related legislation in the province of Timor. Legislative Diploma 865 on the Complementary Regulation of the Occupation and Concession of Land in the Timor Province, which came into effect in 1965, refers to Indigenous peoples as "residents" (*vizinhos de regedorias*); it also provided protections for customary land rights and permitted the delimitation of communal property "used and ruled" according to customary practice.[71] Even if people were aware of the law at the time, they would not have qualified under the ten-year occupancy rule.[72] And finally, even if individuals or groups had wished to register their land, the process was likely inaccessible to the majority of the population of Maliana, who did not necessarily have the education (the ability to read or write in Portuguese) or resources (the ability to pay for legal expenses and taxation).[73]

Ultimately, however, in the process of developing land for irrigated rice cultivation during colonial rule, the colonial authorities did not prioritize addressing potential land-ownership disputes. Their focus was primarily on the economic benefits of expanding rice cultivation, and they often overlooked or disregarded the complex issue of land claims that could arise as a consequence. This oversight reflected a broader pattern whereby colonial administrations prioritized economic development, which often had significant social and cultural implications for the Indigenous populations affected.

Conclusion

In this chapter, I have sought to draw attention to the lingering impacts of late-colonial developmentalism on land claims in Timor-Leste. It is crucial to emphasize that contemporary land tenure systems are not solely shaped by land legislation and policy; they are profoundly influenced by development policy and projects, as well as their implementation. While land laws and regulations provide a legal framework for land ownership and use, the practical application of these policies, particularly through development initiatives, plays a pivotal role in determining how land is accessed, allocated, and managed. Development policies and projects, whether initiated by governments, international organizations, or other stakeholders, often bring about significant changes in land relations. These interventions can include agricultural projects, infrastructure development, urbanization efforts, and more. The way these projects are conceived, planned, and executed can have profound and lasting effects on local communities and their land tenure systems. The historical legacy of late-colonial developmentalism in Timor-Leste continues to influence land claims and disputes to this day. The idea of "economic development" supported by increased public investments, and technical solutions based on scientific knowledge envisaged and enshrined in the five-year development plans and the work of institutions such as the Mission for Overseas Agronomic Research, have left a lasting impact on how land is perceived, accessed, and contested by local populations. In drawing on local recollections and histories of the time, I have sought to highlight how development interventions affected local experiences and meanings of land access and use. Rather than being submissive and passive recipients of "development," my interlocutors demonstrated how people engage with the experiences and challenges of "development" to give meaning to the changes in relations with the land and others. My intention with this exploratory essay has been to recognize that any development intervention is part of a history of interventions that have been proposed and implemented at the local level, and to emphasize that these interventions have shaped and will continue to shape local relations to the land and concepts of land use and access. It is imperative to recognize that the intricate interplay between land legislation and development policy is what shapes the contemporary landscape of land tenure systems. Land laws provide the legal framework, but the implementation of development projects defines the practical realities on the ground. To fully comprehend and address land-related challenges in any region, we must consider both the legal and the practical aspects of land governance, recognizing that the latter often has a more direct and immediate impact on the lives of local communities.

NOTES TO CHAPTER 7

1. Cláudia Castelo, "Developing 'Portuguese Africa' in Late Colonialism: Confronting Discourses," in *Developing Africa: Concepts and Practices in Twentieth-century Colonialism*, ed. Joseph M. Hodge, Gerald Hödl, and Martina Kopf (Manchester University Press, 2014), 63–87.
2. The final plan due to be implemented for the period between 1974 and 1979 was cut short by the Carnation Revolution and the end of the Salazar regime in April 1974. In Timor-Leste, accelerated decolonization and a power vacuum left by the Portuguese created a situation of political unrest and violence. On 28 November 1975, the Frente Revolucionária de Timor-Leste Independente unilaterally declared independence in the face of increasing threats of invasion from Indonesia. Independence was short-lived, and the Indonesian military launched a massive invasion operation on 7 December 1975. Timor-Leste was brutally occupied by Indonesia until 1999.
3. For an overview of the plans, see Luís Manuel Moreira da Silva Reis, "Timor-Leste, 1953–1975: O desenvolvimento agrícola na última fase da colonização portuguesa" (master's thesis, Universidade Tecnica de Lisboa, 2000).
4. Miguel Bandeira Jerónimo and António Costa Pinto, "A Modernizing Empire? Politics, Culture, and Economy in Portuguese Late Colonialism," in *The Ends of European Colonial Empires: Cases and Comparisons*, ed. Miguel Bandeira Jerónimo and António Costa Pinto (Palgrave Macmillan, 2015), 51–80.
5. Daniel Fitzpatrick, Andrew McWilliam, and Susana Barnes, *Property and Social Resilience in Times of Conflict: Land, Custom and Law in East Timor* (Routledge, 2016).
6. Jerónimo and Pinto, "A Modernizing Empire?," 56.
7. Jerónimo and Pinto, 51, 56, 59; Cláudia Castelo, "Scientific Research and Portuguese Colonial Policy: Developments and Articulations, 1936–1974," *História, Ciências, Saúde-Manguinhos* 19 (2012): 391–408.
8. Christopher J. Shepherd, *Development and Environmental Politics Unmasked: Authority, Participation and Equity in East Timor* (Routledge, 2013), 86.
9. Frederick Cooper and Randall Packard, "The History and Politics of Development Knowledge," in *Anthropology of Development and Globalization: From Classical Political Economy to Contemporary Neoliberalism*, ed. Marc Edelman and Angelique Haugerud (Blackwell, 2005), 126.
10. Shepherd, *Development and Environmental Politics Unmasked*, 84.
11. Castelo, "Developing 'Portuguese Africa' in Late Colonialism," 67.
12. Castelo, 67.
13. Reis, "Timor-Leste, 1953–1975."
14. Castelo, "Developing 'Portuguese Africa' in Late Colonialism"; Reis, "Timor-Leste, 1953–1975."
15. Castelo, "Scientific Research and Portuguese Colonial Policy," 6.
16. Shepherd, *Development and Environmental Politics Unmasked*, 93.
17. Castelo, "Scientific Research and Portuguese Colonial Policy," 6.
18. Jerónimo and Pinto, "A Modernizing Empire?"
19. Cláudia Castelo, "Prefácio à presente edição," in Gilberto Freyre, *Um brasileiro em terras portuguesas: Introdução a uma possível lusotropicologia acompanhada de conferências e discursos proferidos em Portugal e em terras lusitanas e ex-lusitanas da Ásia, da África e do Atlântico* (É realizações, 2010).
20. For example, in the eyes of the Estado Novo, "development" increasingly required either assimilation or white settlement. See Castelo, "Prefácio à presente edição." See also chapters by Adalima and Direito in this volume.
21. Marisa Gonçalves, personal communication, 2021.
22. See reference to Dr. Mario Moreira Braga's speech "Timor: A Model of Protuguese Colonization" in Shepherd, *Development and Environmental Politics Unmasked*, 86.
23. Tillman Durdin, "Portugal Pours Money Into Development of Timor," *New York Times*, 13 December 1965.
24. By the 1970s, 80 per cent of the population of Portuguese Timor remained illiterate, the vast majority of the population experienced intermittent hunger, and taxes were high and often had to be paid through labour. Under these circumstances, resentment toward the colonial administration and its allies expressed itself in passive and active resistance. See James Dunn, *Timor: A People Betrayed* (John Wiley and Sons, 1983); Geoffrey C. Gunn, *Timor Loro Sae: 500 Years* (Livros do Oriente, 1999); Estêvão Cabral, "Timor-Leste 1974–1975: Decolonisation, a Nation-in-Waiting and an Adult Literacy Campaign," *International Journal of the Sociology of Language*, no. 259 (2019): 39–61, https://doi.org/10.1515/ijsl-2019-2038.

25 Reis, "Timor-Leste, 1953–1975," 39.
26 Guerra 1970 cited in Reis, "Timor-Leste, 1953–1975."
27 Gunn, *Timor Loro Sae*; Reis, "Timor-Leste, 1953–1975"; L. Thomaz, "O programa económico de Timor," *Revista Militar* 26, no. 8 (1974): 1–10.
28 Cinatti in Peter Stilwell, "Um plano do fomento agrário para Timor (1958)—texto inédito de Ruy Cinatti," *Povos e Culturas*, no. 7 (2001): 117–32.
29 Reis, "Timor-Leste, 1953–1975."
30 Shepherd, *Development and Environmental Politics Unmasked*, 91–3.
31 For an interesting discussion of the geopolitical dimensions of rice promotion in Portuguese Timor, see Shepherd, *Development and Environmental Politics Unmasked*.
32 Shepherd, 95.
33 Fitzpatrick et al., *Property and Social Resilience in Times of Conflict*, 165.
34 Susanna Barnes, "Customary Renewal and the Pursuit of Power and Prosperity in Post-Occupation East Timor: A Case-Study from Babulo, Uato-Lari" (PhD diss., Monash University, 2017); William G. Clarence-Smith, "Planters and Smallholders in Portuguese Timor in the Nineteenth and Twentieth Centuries," *Indonesia Circle* 20, no. 57 (1992): 15–30; Douglas Kammen, "Metaphors of Slavery in East Timor," *Portuguese Literary and Cultural Studies*, nos. 17–18 (2010): 257–79; Christopher J. Shepherd and Andrew McWilliam, "Cultivating Plantations and Subjects in East Timor: A Genealogy," *Bijdragen tot de taal-, land-en volkenkunde / Journal of the Humanities and Social Sciences of Southeast Asia* 169, nos. 2–3 (2013): 326–61.
35 Jill Joliffe, *East Timor: Nationalism and Colonialism* (University of Queensland Press, 1978).
36 Fitzpatrick et al., *Property and Social Resilience in Times of Conflict*, 256–60.
37 Joachim K. Metzner, *Man and Environment in Eastern Timor* (Australian National University, 1977).
38 Fitzpatrick et al., *Property and Social Resilience in Times of Conflict*; Metzner, *Man and Environment in Eastern Timor*; Shepherd and McWilliam, "Cultivating Plantations and Subjects in East Timor."
39 Shepherd and McWilliam, "Cultivating Plantations and Subjects in East Timor," 341.
40 Fitzpatrick et al., *Property and Social Resilience in Times of Conflict*, 256–7.
41 *2015 Timor-Leste Population and Housing Census* (Direcção Nacional de Estatística, 2016).
42 Kevin Sherlock, *East Timor*: Liurais *and* chefes de suco: *Indigenous authorities in 1952* (Kevin Sherlock, 1983).
43 Metzner, *Man and Environment in Eastern Timor*, 117.
44 Metzner.
45 Metzner, 121.
46 Metzner, 121.
47 Fitzpatrick et al., *Property and Social Resilience in Times of Conflict*, 177–205.
48 Abel Pereira, personal communication, 2007.
49 As a performative act, these ritual words serve to legitimize the claims of members of the houses of Duas Mali and Lua Laben to access and use land on the Nunura plain. They reflect a customary understanding of land as part of the cycle of life, and the reciprocal relations that exist between the living and the world of the ancestors. Access here is conceived of as the "ability to benefit" from land. Access to resources is gained and maintained through people and institutions that control the land, but it does not imply any possession.
50 Abel Pereira, personal communication, 2007.
51 This resonates with the testimonies of several civil servants who asserted that the area around present-day Maliana town on the fringes of the plain were, during the 1950s and early 1960s, coconut plantations.
52 Exact figures for *posto* Maliana are required but there was a considerable rise in overall population in the postwar period from 442,378 in 1950 to 517,079 in 1960 and 555,723 in 1965. By 1968, the population had increased to 591,000. Gunn, *Timor Loro Sae*.
53 Reis, "Timor-Leste, 1953–1975."
54 By the end of the 1960s, the Hale-Cou project covered 90 hectares of land and 85 farmers, while Mau-Mali covered 152 hectares of land and involved 123 farmers. See Reis, "Timor-Leste, 1953–1975," 180
55 A. S., catechist. According to Sherlock, in 1952 the *liurai* of Hauba was Bau Mau. The *chefe suku* of Manapa said his name was Manuel Barros. Sherlock, *East Timor*.
56 Some suggested that they were "paid" by the Portuguese Agricultural Department to do this.

57 Interlocutors tended to use the term "Agricola" to describe colonial agricultural officials and extension workers, including those associated with the MEAU.
58 Bernardo Ribeiro de Almeida, *A Sociolegal Analysis of Formal Land Tenure Systems: Learning from the Political, Legal and Institutional Struggles of Timor-Leste* (Routledge, 2022), 62.
59 For some interlocutors there was definitely an element of coercion involved. For example, references were made to the *administrador do posto* (Vitor Sana) declaring that the Timorese were "lazy" (*baruk tein*) and should be put to work.
60 The Indonesian phrase *sukat rai* is used to describe how individual land plots were surveyed during the occupation under the auspices of various land registration programs. See Fitzpatrick et al., *Property and Social Resilience in Times of Conflict*.
61 This was particularly true in relation to those who had supported the Portuguese during the war. As elsewhere in in Portuguese Timor in the immediate aftermath of World War II, the Portuguese authorities went about rewarding those who had steadfastly supported them during the war and punishing those accused of collaborating with the Japanese. See Gunn Geoffrey, "Timor Loro Sae."
62 Gunn Geoffrey, "Timor Loro Sae."
63 Interestingly, one of the main protagonists from Marobo recounted that the then *liurai* of Maliana had provoked the people of Marobo to work hard by announcing that they (the people of Marobo) "would never be able to bring water to these fields and that they would have to piss in the channels."
64 Metzner, *Man and Environment in Eastern Timor*, xxviii.
65 See Fitzpatrick et al., *Property and Social Resilience in Times of Conflict*.
66 Fitzpatrick et al., 192–204 and 50–6.
67 Fitzpatrick et al..
68 Barnes, "Customary Renewal and the Pursuit of Power and Prosperity in Post-Occupation East Timor."
69 Nicholas Blomley, "Performing Property: Making the World," *Canadian Journal of Law & Jurisprudence* 26, no. 1 (2013): 39.
70 Tania Murray Li, "Practices of Assemblage and Community Forest Management," *Economy and Society* 36, no. 2 (2007): 289.
71 de Almeida, *A Sociolegal Analysis of Formal Land Tenure Systems*, 61–2.
72 de Almeida writes that, "According to Du Plessis and Leckie the Portuguese authorities issued 2,709 formal rights." See de Almeida, *A Sociolegal Analysis of Formal Land Tenure Systems*, 62. Da Cruz reported a total of 2,843, with more than half referring to land in the Dili district. See Daniel Fitzpatrick, *Land Claims in East Timor* (Asia Pacific Press, 2002), 148.
73 David Graeber, *The Utopia of Rules: On Technology, Stupidity, and the Secret Joys of Bureaucracy* (Melville House, 2015).

8

The Remaking of Territories and Political Institutions: Community Land Delimitation in Northern Mozambique

Elisio Jossias

Introduction

In August 2012, I arrived in Cóbuè, a subdivision of the Lake District in Mozambique's Niassa Province, to begin my PhD fieldwork. The country's 1997 Land Law allowed for the registration of community tenure rights through a land delimitation process that involved geo-referencing the boundaries of areas used by community groups. During the first stage of this process in Cóbuè, six *régulos*,[1] or kin-based chiefs, were identified and their land delimited. During the second stage, sub-chiefs of each *régulo*, who held the position of village headmen, or *nduna*, were identified and their territories classified as community land. However, by early 2013, the subdivision was experiencing a critical moment in local power relations involving political institutions. In 2001, the state formally recognized community authorities in Cóbuè, ranking them according to territorial criteria established in Decree 15/2000.[2] Chiefs or *régulos* were at the top of the hierarchy, followed by other political institutions created after Mozambican independence, such as *secretários de aldeias e dos bairros*. Sub-chiefs, called *nduna*, were ranked lower. A power struggle emerged when Nduna Minofo wrote a letter to the head of the administrative post of Cóbuè requesting his promotion to the position of *régulo*.[3]

To understand why Nduna Minofo's request for promotion to the position of *régulo* caused tension among local political institutions, it is necessary to delve into the delimitation process. During this process, Régulo Mataka emerged as the most powerful of the six *régulos* in the Cóbuè region. He controlled approximately 40,000 hectares of land and five distinct sub-chiefs, including Nduna Minofo. Additionally, the administrative post of Cóbuè was located in one of Régulo Mataka's territories, which also overlapped with Nduna Minofo's territory. Moreover, Régulo Mataka's position of authority was strengthened by the presence of the Manda Wilderness Community Trust, which was located in his territory and was under the control of another one of his sub-chiefs. The size and scope of Régulo Mataka's territory was established during the colonial period, when kin-based institutions were incorporated into the local government administration, and people were subject to the rule of customary chiefs who governed communal territories on behalf of the colonial government.

While many scholars and practitioners argue that the community lands approach is contributing to improving tenure security for communities and reducing inter-community conflicts in many countries located in sub-Saharan Africa, others emphasize the embedded nature of the customary land tenure systems.[4] In this chapter, I adopt a critical view of community land titling by analyzing the land delimitation process as a means of remaking territories and social boundaries.[5] My argument is that the emphasis on a "community-based" approach to land governance, territorial organization, and development projects has resulted in potential conflicts and disputes among chiefs who are claiming control over political territories and their visibility in the political sphere. In these circumstances, the process of land delimitation in Cóbuè went beyond the mere formalization of customary land or communal property rights, as outlined in the 1997 Land Law. Instead, communal tenure delimitation became intertwined with the historical power struggles and social hierarchies among traditional chiefs vying for control over their respective territories. Viewed in the context of this transitional moment, it's crucial to rethink the concept of ownership, possession, and the revival of the system that perpetuates unequal power dynamics among political authorities in relation to land.

This chapter aims to contribute to the ongoing debates surrounding territoriality and the historical significance of land in Africa. Building on the work of scholars who challenge the conventional view of traditional (customary) land rights as being protected by a coherent, homogenous, and stable set of rules and beliefs, I argue that access to land has been marked by past and present inequalities, differentiation, and conflicts.[6] Furthermore, the emergence of territorial hierarchies and competition among local chiefs after community land

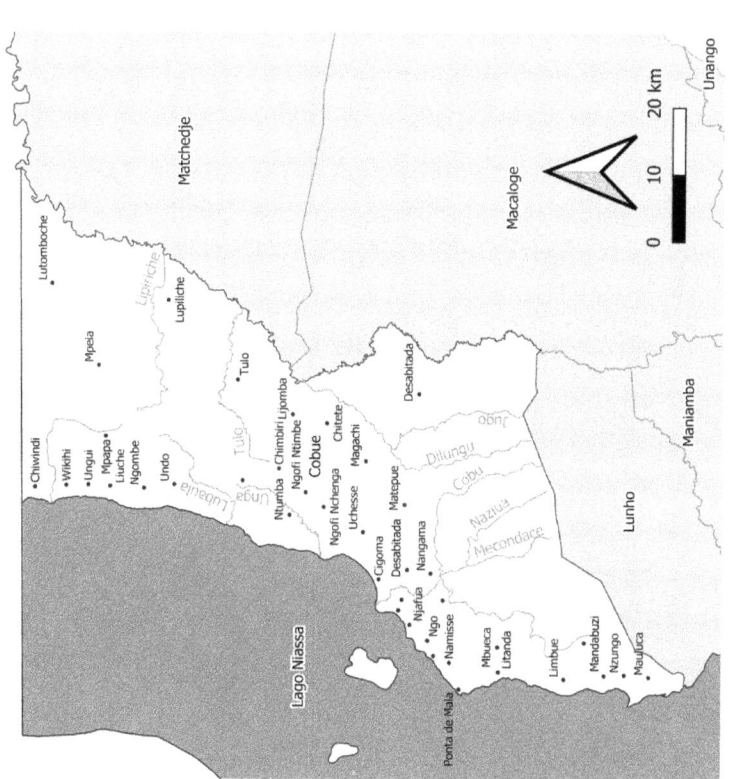

Map 8.1. Administrative post of Côbuè

Cartography: Rui Pinto.

delimitation in the Cóbuè region underscores the complex nature of land governance in Africa.

The Historical Context of Community Land Delimitation in Mozambique

Mozambique has been actively involved in reforming its land tenure policy and legislation for the past three decades. Following the land policy reform in the 1990s, two noteworthy conditions emerged. Firstly, the country's constitution stipulates that all land belongs to the state. Secondly, Mozambique has been ensuring the right to land possession and use by implementing community land delimitation and streamlining the process of granting land use titles.[7] Community land delimitation is a process of formalizing land rights at the community level, as established in the 1997 Land Law. It involves geo-referencing the boundaries of the territories occupied by communities.[8]

The land law of 1997 formally defines community lands as those belonging to a community that has the right to use land based on customary rules. Additionally, the law defines the "local community" as a group of individuals or families residing in the same territory and sharing common interests.[9] This definition encompasses fallow land, inhabited areas, cultivated areas, forests, sites of cultural significance, pastures, and water sources, thus making community lands a territorial dimension. As a result, community lands are intended to be used by community members to meet the present and future livelihood needs of generations.[10]

The definition of community, and principles for delimiting community land, raises questions about the role of traditional chiefs in land governance in Africa.[11] In Mozambique, *régulos* (kin-based political institutions) were institutionalized to serve as intermediaries between the colonial administration and local communities. However, after Mozambique gained independence in 1975, this institution was abolished.[12] After the end of the war in 1992, the same ruling party that had abolished traditional chiefs reintroduced them as "community authorities" (Decree 15/2000), partially using the same principles adopted during the colonial period as intermediaries between local government officials and communities.[13] By adopting the broader concept of "community authorities," the Mozambican government was able to integrate the former *regulado* institution while maintaining the political and administrative institutions created after independence, such as *secretários*. However, the recognition process of these authorities "has activated long-standing power disputes in rural Mozambique."[14]

In 1997, while traditional chiefs were in the process of negotiating their political legitimacy, the land law granted significant authority to "local communities" over land issues, including natural resource management, conflict resolution, titling, and defining the limits of their occupied land.[15] However, this presents a sensitive issue as it involves the legitimacy of traditional authorities in various political processes such as community consultation and decision making concerning land occupation, particularly in situations of private investment.

The significant change in the land law led to the notion of "occupation" (by "good faith") becoming a crucial aspect for local communities in terms of their legitimacy and rights to use the land delimited as a community. But the practical process of having the community recognize their own land is more complex than the methodology adopted in the law, as outlined in the Technical Annex to the Land Law (1997). Despite the delimitation of community land in the field, questions remain about whether "customary norms and practices" can effectively ensure equitable access to land for community members. For instance, in a critical analysis of the land delimitation model in Mozambique, Paul de Wit and Simon Norfolk raised concerns that customary practices are too vague to guarantee land access for community members, and that current legislation does not provide mechanisms for individuals and families to remove their land from customary jurisdiction.[16] Krantz similarly highlights weaknesses in Mozambique's land law, particularly the lack of specification on how the community should be represented in decision-making processes involving outside investors, as observed in his work in Niassa Province.[17] The work of Kaarhus and Dondeyne also problematizes the role of traditional chiefs in decisions about land use and conflict resolution.[18]

Proponents of customary norms and practices in Mozambique argued that formal state laws are impractical to apply in rural societies, leading to a distinction between rural areas, where customary norms and practices apply, and urban contexts and private explorations (which are also rural), subject to the civil laws of the state.[19] This is similar to the example from Indonesia mentioned by Tania Murray Li (in her foreword to this volume), where efforts to strengthen the legal rights of rural communities did not challenge the model that treated community land rights and uses as inferior.

Over the course of the twenty-year term of the land law, the delimitation of community land has entailed identifying territorial limits and delimiting areas based on the history as well as economic, social, and cultural interests of communities. While community delimitation began in 2000, it was only fast-tracked around 2006 through the Mozambique Community Land Initiative. Today, numerous non-governmental organizations (NGOs) are involved in the delimitation process throughout the country, supported by various funding schemes. The process now includes formalizing individual land rights within the community.[20]

The government's national Terra Segura program, launched in 2015, is evidence of this change, as it aims to title five million individual parcels and delimit four thousand communities over a five-year period. In 2019, the program received a grant of US$100 million from the World Bank.

Community Land Delimitation in Cóbuè

The formal land delimitation process, as established in the Technical Annex to the Land Law (1997), includes a participatory rapid diagnosis and a land delimitation matrix. This methodology involves developing a historical chronology of the community, focusing on the community's foundation and forms of land use through separate consultations with men, women, and youth. The land delimitation matrix portrays traditional chiefs as the leaders of their respective communities and, thus, as landowners.

The initiative to map the communities and their lands in Cóbuè began in 1995, two years prior to the approval of the land law and three years prior to the formalization of the delimitation process. This was prompted by the arrival of private investors with the Manda Wilderness Community Trust, which involved the development of a luxury tourist lodge and community park. The project was formally launched in 1999, following two years of consultation with local chiefs, *régulos*, and their sub-chiefs (*nduna*), who represent approximately sixteen villages.

The process was followed by an analysis of the community leadership structures, which was assisted by an NGO called Niassa Union of Peasant Cooperatives and Associations.[21] In 2005, the Swedish Co-Operative Centre funded the Manda Wilderness project to set up a community conservation area,[22] as well as a community-based association named Umoji to manage it. A year later, the boundaries of the community's areas were delimited, covering 250,000 hectares across the six territories of the *régulos*. The Manda Wilderness Community Conservation Area (the community park) was demarcated with 120,000 hectares, and the process was assisted by six officials from the Niassa Provincial Directorate of Agriculture (Provincial Geographic and Cadastre Services).

During a six-day period in August and September 2006, these officials organized several meetings with chiefs and other selected people in the region. In the Mataka community, for example, fifty-one people, primarily men—although women and young people were also involved—participated in the process of drawing participatory maps. Following the process, eleven people were interviewed to write the Mataka community's storyline. In 2007, a land title certificate was issued in the name of the six *régulos*. The US-based Ford Foundation

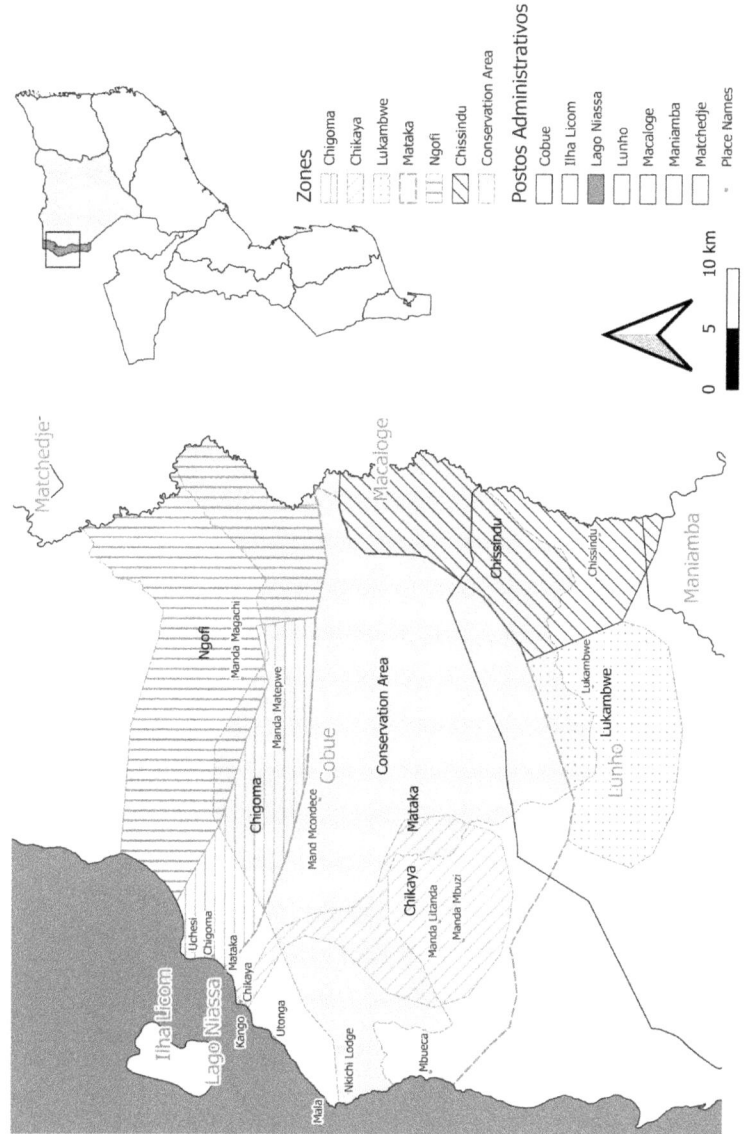

Map 8.2. Community delimited lands, representing the territories of *régulos*
Cartography: Rui Pinto.

mobilized further funding in the same year to develop a management plan for the community conservation area.

The significant role of kin-based institutions in land governance is evident from the extensive "community consultancy" and "community participation" processes carried out by the government, private sector, and NGOs under the 1997 Land Law.

Reclaiming Chieftaincy, Remaking Territories

> Back in history, it is said that our ancestors came here in search for land to settle. They all came as part of the same family and there was no exact division of chiefdoms. When they arrived in this territory, they divided the land equally. The chiefs were born out of their capacity to deal with conflicts and solve problems. This was the origin of the chiefdoms; the village headman emerged and the first-comers in the territory belong to the same lineage. The ancestors are the ones who secured this lineage. (Conversation with Mzama, Cóbuè, April 2015)

As mentioned in the introduction, a letter was sent to the head of the administrative post of Cóbuè by Nduna Minofo,[23] in which he requested to be promoted to the position of chief (*régulo*) and renounce his current status as a sub-chief of Chief Mataka. I present the content of the letter, and I analyze it as a pivotal historical moment in the process of defining territory and hierarchizing traditional chiefs.[24] I transcribed part of the letter that specifically refers to the request:

> 1. The "Minofo" family is historically a ramification of the Régulo M'nchekeni, from the Chiuanga region. He separated with the M'nchekeni, having travelled within the Lake Nyassa area, where he met the Ngoni and Yao ethnic groups certainly in the Chissindo and M'nyandica areas. Then established on the banks of the N'singe River, later descended to the Coast of Niassa Lake, having definitely settled in the small valley of the Khango[25] River. . . .

> 2. The reasons for the split between Minofo Kawawa and M'nchekeni were not well-known at the time, but he always ensured that he would leave his descendants before death in a place with fertile land, where they could farm and fish freely for generations to come. . . .

3. It is worth remembering that it was during the tenure of "Minofo Kawawa" that the Portuguese set up the headquarters of the Cóbuè Administrative Post in the village of Khango before it passed into the villages of "Ngofi" and Chigoma. . . .

4. Minofo Kawawa gave land to the Portuguese, without harming or jeopardizing their population's access to agricultural production. Later, he received several missionaries, including the Catholics who officially founded the Catholic Mission of the Holy Angels in October 1950, with education at the College of St. Michael—Cóbuè. . . .

5. It should be noted that Minofo [Kawawa] had good relations with all local government bodies and structures in his area of jurisdiction, but always defended the population against the interests of foreign domination including all incompatible actions imposed by the Portuguese.

6. However, after the split with the M'nchekeni, Minofo became independent and stated the establishment of his traditional power and structures, based in inherent procedures, under the reign of "Minofo Kawawa," who was replaced by the following chiefs: Bokosi Minofo, Davide Minofo, Wildeny Minofo, and currently Miguel Chembezi, being the "Minofo V."

7. In this context, bringing together the whole Minofo family, we respectfully praise the commitment of the current Nduna Minofo, and on the other hand due to the economic and population growth and development in our area, we want categorically to reassure you that it is time that we ask the Government for our proposal to raise Nduna Minofo to the position of Régulo.

8. As always, the area of jurisdiction of the Minofo has the ndunas: Khuni, Zaiti, and Matucuano, and an nduna that will be appointed later in its replacement at Khango Headquarters. (Letter from Minofo V. requesting his appointment to become a *régulo*)

The letter sent to the *chefe do posto administrativo* (the state's representative at the administrative post level) and the subsequent meeting to discuss it reveal that the state is not a separate entity in the contest for legitimacy between kin-based political institutions, but rather is entwined in the complex historical experience with the state in Mozambique since the arrival of missionaries and Portuguese administration. This experience has led to overlapping claims to political authority and territorial oversight, which were exacerbated by the colonial engagements in the region.

In the late nineteenth century, the University Mission for Central Africa (UMCA) arrived at the shore of Lake Malawi, and their presence had a significant impact on the consolidation of settlements and the power and hierarchies of traditional chiefs.[26] For example, the main building of the Anglican church was located in the Régulo Chiteji village of Povoação de Chigoma, while smaller versions of the building were found in the *nduna* villages, reflecting a hierarchical conception of chiefs and their territories.[27]

The Portuguese administration, which arrived in northern Mozambique by the end of the nineteenth century, had a decisive impact on the chieftaincies and their territories. Portugal had to compete with Great Britain and Germany for territories during the scramble for Africa. In Cóbuè, due to the UMCA missionaries' first arrival, the Portuguese colonial administration avoided Régulo Chiteji and recognized Régulo Mataka as the principal chief. This dispute continued, and the Portuguese administration split Régulo Chiteji's territories in two: one located in current-day Mozambique, and another on Likoma Island, in the British-administered territory of what is now known as Malawi.

Chiefs utilized the arrival of missionaries and Portuguese colonization in two distinct ways: firstly, to reaffirm their position and legitimacy in the hierarchy of chieftaincy, and secondly, to advocate for their recognition in local and land governance. The way Nduna Minofo's territorial history is presented in the letter follows a similar pattern to that of the Nyanja settlement along the Niassa Lake.[28] The narration emphasizes the complexity of territorial dynamics, which places the first-comer's narrative as a unifying element in a long-term historical process, as noted by Lentz.[29]

In present times, the historical experiences of spatial relations and temporalities with missionaries and Portuguese colonial administration have been incorporated into disputes over political legitimacy. These dimensions bring up a complex history of the first arrival narratives, which is a central aspect in power relations between chiefs and their claims to decide questions of land use and territorial control. For example, the first two paragraphs of the letter underline the need to assert the primacy of land occupation by establishing Nduna Minofo's status as a first-comer in the territory. This perspective considers territory as a political space and implies that the space itself is the basis for establishing the political hierarchy.[30] Between paragraphs 3 and 5, the letter reinforces the idea of Minofo's primacy in the territory. In this case, the hierarchies of chiefs and corresponding territories emphasize and reveal the historicity of territorialization experiences by showing the arrival of British missionaries at the UMCA as the moment of the college's foundation on Likoma Island. Then, the arrival of Portuguese officials represents the beginning of the colonial occupation. We can see this example at the beginning of paragraph 4, as follows: "Minofo Kawawa gave land to the Portuguese without harming or jeopardizing their population's access to agricultural production." The same reference is found in the last part of paragraph 5, where it is stressed that Minofo "always defended the population against the interests of foreign domination, including all incompatible actions imposed by the Portuguese."

During the meeting, Chief Chiteji's intervention reflected the recurrent use of the history of missionaries and Portuguese arrival to negotiate the legitimacy of kin-based political institutions and (re)affirm the hierarchies of chiefs. He expressed disappointment at the circulation of information accusing him of selling the islands of Likoma and Chizumulo to the British during the colonial era. To emphasize his position, he referred to the former Chief Chiteji's offering to the missionaries.

The Mataka territories present a complex situation with the involvement of five sub-chiefs (*nduna*), which has led to recent reconfigurations in history and hierarchy among the chiefs. On the one hand, political-administrative reforms demand the identification of one chief to represent all community leaders in dealings with state representatives and NGOs. On the other hand, the existence of multiple community authorities with the same formal rank leads to overlapping types of authority over territories and a resulting conflict over land control. For instance, the administrative headquarters of Cóbuè is located in Khango, a territory of Nduna Minofo, who represents traditional leaders. However, Khango also has a *secretário da localidade* who represents political institutions created after independence and is also a community authority in Khango.

These narratives reveal that the status of land ownership can be divided among the descendants of the founders of the territory, as highlighted in the excerpt from the conversation with Mzama with which I started this section. This living experience with territories grants all inhabitants of a particular territory some piece of land on which they can claim certain rights, leading to a form of inclusive rights. Therefore, the history of the founder of a territory is crucial to legitimizing the territory as part of the constitution of the people who inhabit it and claim ownership over it. In the following section, I delve into the relationship between chiefs and the hierarchy of territories, which serves as a narrative to legitimize claims to land.

Hierarchy of Chiefs as a Hierarchy of Territories

The Nduna Minofo's letter requesting to become a régulo was the subject of discussion on two occasions: first at the administrative post consultative council in Cóbuè[31] held in September 2013, and second at a meeting in October 2013 at the village of Régulo Mataka (Comunidade de Mataka). During both meetings, the hierarchy of chiefs and sub-chiefs was the main point of debate, highlighting the importance of understanding the composite process and experiences involved in the hierarchical system, which is the focus of this section.

In the 1990s, political reforms in Mozambique introduced local councils as a decentralization mechanism. Members of these councils are chosen from community committees, community authorities, and representatives of economic, social, and cultural interests. The Cóbuè consultative council was led by the chief of the administrative post, with assistance from the representative (*primeiro secretário*) of the ruling party, FRELIMO (Frente de Libertação de Moçambique). The presence of the ruling party representative reflects the continuity of the former socialist regime, where FRELIMO was the only political organization. However, disputes between administrative institutions created after independence, such as the *secretários*, and kin-based political institutions present a significant challenge in the decentralization process in Mozambique.

The administrative post consultative council decided that the request of Nduna Minofo to become a *régulo* must be discussed by his superior, who was himself a *régulo*. This is because, in terms of community authority, members of the communities elect and rank their leaders. Additionally, it was stated that Minofo, as *nduna*, must have the permission of his superior to become a *régulo*. During the meeting in Mataka village in October 2013, Chiefs Chiteji, Mtaya, and Mapunda were invited, along with five village secretaries, six *ndunas*, a representative of the head of the administrative post, a representative of FRELIMO, and five members of the Mataka *mfumu* council.

As mentioned above, the hierarchical system of chiefs in Cóbuè is complex and has roots in the colonial period. The Portuguese colonial administration established their administrative headquarters in Khango, which became the territory of Chief Mataka in the early twentieth century. This led to Mataka becoming the main chief in the region. In 1905, Cóbuè became a military post, and from 1918–19 territorial divisions were based on the number of huts and the importance of kin-based political institutions, which in turn became the basis for villages. The area of each administrative division, called *conselho*, covered about ten thousand huts. The proximity of the headquarters was a significant criterion in the appointment of the most important chief.

In recent times, the chief of the administrative post appointed Chief Mtaya, of the territory of Chicaia, as the representative of Cóbuè in the district council. Mtaya has been a constant representative of the chiefs in the district consultative council, speaking on behalf of the Cóbuè District. However, the hierarchy of chiefs is not a universally agreed matter in Cóbuè. According to historical accounts of the territories, Chief Chiteji belongs to the list of founding chiefs in the area.[32] This is supported by various sources, including the missionaries who located the main church building in Chigoma, which is Chief Chiteji's village. The missionaries' account portrays Chiteji as belonging to the west-south group along Niassa Lake, having first settled in Chilowelo, near Makanjila, then in Messumba, which includes a passage through Likoma, before settling indefinitely in Chigoma.[33]

In the previous section, it was mentioned that the historical account of the region suggests that most chiefs in the area originated from the South and migrated northward. However, in the delimitation process, Chief Mataka's origin was traced back to the East, which is recognized as the territory of the Yao people.[34] In this he differs from the majority of other chiefs in the region. Chief Mataka is unique in that he is recognized as being of Yao origin and became Nyanja due to his settlement in the lake region.

> The Mataka community, led by Régulo Mataka, comes from Muembe, land of Yao people. In their arrival in Muembe, the Mataka people comprised a very large family. For this reason, they decided to split up and they spread out looking for better sites and places for dwelling. One of the Mataka family's members had travelled through Calanga and Macusi region before his arrival in the lake region, where he founded the Mataka territory. The Mataka family had arrived in the lake region before the Ngoni war, the so-called "territorial occupation war." Since the foundation of the Mataka community, has succeeded nine chiefs, the current chief included. The Mataka community was involved in a tribal war against the Ngoni, who had been trying to enslave the Mataka population. But the Mataka had succeeded in this war. . . . Around 1920, the Portuguese arrived in the community. In their arrival, they offered salt, clothing, soap, and other products, but in return came the oppression, the Machila, coercive high tax collection, both for men and women. In that period people who didn't pay tax had been taken for forced labour, for example in the opening of roads. In 1962, the Liberation Front of Mozambique (FRELIMO) started mobilizing

meetings to engage people in the fighting for independence against the Portuguese. In the same year, the first FRELIMO members were registered in the community and their membership cards were handed over.[35]

The officials involved in the delimitation process have described the history of the region in three parts, in line with the Mozambican ideal of nation building: pre-colonization, colonization, and the fight for independence led by FRELIMO. However, the first part of the narration also highlights the origins and conflicts of the people currently inhabiting the lake region. This is an important aspect of the debate on land ownership and control in Cóbuè.

During fieldwork I met Chief Mataka, who told me a territorial history of Mataka and also mentioned his relationship with seven sub-chiefs, the villages' headmen, as follows:

> Zumani and Machila are part of the history of Mataka [the founder of the title]. The remaining *ndunas* were not part of the Mataka, they were *ndunas* of Chief Mtaya. Because of conflicts between this chief and his sub-chiefs both decided to disengage. That's when they came to ask Mataka to become their chief and he accepted. He then called a meeting with all existing *ndunas* at the time and Minofo [the founder] was appointed as the first *nduna* of the Mataka, just for living in the administrative headquarters. The one who was the first *nduna*, Zumani, became the second *nduna*, Bwanali become the third *nduna*, and then followed Khuni and Matukwanu. (Conversation with Mfumu Mataka, Cóbuè, September 2012)

This statement presents Chief Mataka's perspective on the hierarchy of his *nduna* and the process through which Nduna Minofo was incorporated into that hierarchy. It highlights that the power relations among *nduna*, similar to those among chiefs, are subject to debate. Nduna Zumani, who is under the authority of Mataka, reacted to Nduna Minofo's claim of being the first in the hierarchy of sub-chiefs under Mataka.[36] Zumani stated that he was present during the definition of boundaries between Mozambique and Tanzania, when the dispute between Portugal and Britain for territories was ongoing. He also played a role in defining the southern boundary of Régulo Mataka's territory in the Ngoo region, thereby contrasting the status claimed by Minofo.

> Minofo says he is Mataka's first *nduna* and has a lot of population, but I do not agree with him. The present recognize the Zumani as

the main symbol of the Mataka and not the Minofo. Zumani went to Ngoo to recognize Manyika, Lupilichi to recognize Tama Tama and Tanzania in marking the border between Mozambique and Tanzania. Zumani was called and no one can say that this is not true! By the time Mataka himself had reached these lands, Zumani had already been here for a long time, and yet Zumani cannot claim the status of *régulo*. Minofo has no history like Zumani, nor is another here with the same history. The fact that Minofo is [dwelling] at Cóbuè headquarters does not mean that he has under his control many people, and, consequently, he must become a *régulo*! We have a purpose, which is to attract more people to settle at Khango headquarters so we can claim our territory as a district. We don't need you to become a *régulo*. In any case, if you want to become a *régulo* you should not deal with matters aggressively and you need to know how to apply. (Nduna Zumani, during the meeting at which Minofo's letter was discussed)

After Nduna Minofo's request to become a *régulo* became known throughout Cóbuè, he was ridiculed by other *ndunas* and *régulos* who were close to Mataka. This mockery continued during a meeting held at Régulo Mataka's house, where several *ndunas*, who were under Chief Mataka's leadership, denounced Minofo as "ambitious," prone to "intrigue," and "without character." They claimed that he was unfit to exercise the position of *régulo*, and even accused him of plotting to kill Chief Mataka. The contrasting example was Nduna Zamani, who had a historical connection to the territorial boundaries between Mozambique and Tanzania and was seen as integrated into the region's history.

In response, Nduna Minofo argued that his ancestors (*makholo*) had asked Mataka for a place to dwell (*malo*), and now that he had grown up and gotten married, it was time for him to have his own household (*muji*). Among the Nyanja people, when a man comes of age and gets married, he has to build his own household. Minofo's use of the word *muji*, translated as "family" in the letter, emphasized the principle of independence that defines social units and linked it to territories, stating that the birth of a new social unit or family (household) represented a separation from the central nucleus ruled by a headman.

The tensions between equal recognition of territorial histories and inequalities in land control and power were brought to light through the contradictions and confrontations of various narratives during moments of co-presence among traditional chiefs. These controversies were also informed by historical experiences of colonization and the post-colonial state, and were often used to hierarchize traditional chiefs and define territory. In the next section, I will explore how the first-comers' narrative and persuasion were used in territorial disputes.[37] The validation code of arrival and the historicist dimension of territoriality define this status, and were used to confront hierarchies and statutes among kin-based political institutions, as well as to determine who was the first arrival to the territory and their respective status, and who arrived afterward.

Negotiating the First-Comer Narrative as a Remaking of the Community

Anthropological literature that examines historical territorial narratives in many African contexts has highlighted moments of crisis, such as succession conflicts, wars, witchcraft accusations, and famines associated with the fission, dispersion, and formation of new social units.[38]

The case of Cóbuè illustrates how historical narratives are a continuous process of remaking the territory and the sense of community. In Cóbuè, everyone acknowledges their descent from ancestors who settled in the region and thus belongs to the territory, which reminds us that the "cultural politics of belonging is a key dimension of authority and decision-making mechanism over land in Africa."[39] However, they also recognize that hierarchies were established as a result of historical experiences with missionaries, colonial administration, and the post-colonial state. In fact, post-colonial African states continued colonial-era policies, laws, and practices, and had recognized, in some places, the authority of chiefs or different kinds of traditional authorities over customary land as a way to extend their power and control over land and territories.[40]

The letter from Nduna Minofo and the ensuing discussion showed that the kin-based authorities were interested in ensuring equal recognition from state officials in land control, rather than in the separation of territories and chiefs.

When Nduna Minofo suggested incorporating the sub-chiefs who belonged to Chief Mataka into *his* future chieftaincy, he challenged Chief Mataka's authority. This is because the principles of authority in Cóbuè are based on two factors: being a first-comer and corresponding histories of arrival, as well as paying respect to hierarchies.

Below, I present a dialogue between chiefs and sub-chiefs during the meeting that took place at Mfumu Mataka's house in September 2013, where it was decided to decline the request of Nduna Minofo. The dialogue highlights the strength of the evaluation of his character traits and the principles of authority based on two factors: (1) histories of arrival, and (2) respect toward superiors. The letters *A, B, C, D,* and *E* identify the different interventions:

A. Then the time has come to clarify this matter. Nduna Minofo is said to have come to Mfumu Mataka to say goodbye. It seems that in the past he requested from Mfumu Mataka a place to live. Where did he live before? I stop here! Thanks!

B. I want to start there, where they say that Nduna Minofo came to Mfumu Mataka to ask for a place to live. Where did he come from? When did he arrive here [a reference to Cóbuè region], where Nduna Minofo was coming from?

C. Nduna Minofo, I would like to know how many were you when you arrived here [again, in Cóbuè region]. Mr. Mtaya [a chief] was already there, he had always been chief for a long time. He was *mfumu* and Minofo was his *nduna*, but they had disagreements.

D. I see Minofo being frequently called to the administration, and going without informing his mfumu. Mr. Minofo no longer gets along with your Mfumu Mataka, is that true? You left Mtaya to ask Mataka for a place to live and now you don't understand each other? *This is called trampling the rules and has been so for a long time* [emphasis added].

E. Who is superior between *mfumu* and *nduna*? The superior is *mfumu*! To the government, who is *nduna*? That depends on *mfumu*. Now, what are we discussing here? *There is a lack of consideration here* [emphasis added]. Historically *nduna* cannot be superior to a *mfumu*. In the Portuguese language, it is called *chefe de povoação* [head of the village group]. However, *nduna* cannot rise straight to the top of the government structure; there must be the head of the group to update the government on issues related to the population.

(Meeting at Mfumu Mataka's house, September 2013)

The desire of Minofo to become a *régulo* was the main point of contention between him and his peers, including Chief Mataka. The meeting I described above served as a moment of alignment in the ongoing historical process, as demonstrated by these debates. The emphasis on respect is more evident in interventions D and E, but the first three interventions also emphasize the importance of being a first-comer, specifically the moment of arrival in the territory.

Nduna Minofo lost support from his allies due to the evaluation made by the other *régulos* and *nduna*, which found that his claims lacked legitimacy. This lack of legitimacy was not about the accuracy of Minofo's narrative but about the infringement of hierarchical relations. As a result, Minofo could not persuade all kin-based authorities and some members of the community. Ultimately, it was decided that Minofo had violated the code and language of the chieftaincy relationship, including the principles of arrival and respect.

In my research, I encountered two versions of Minofo's territorial narrative. The first was mentioned in his letter, and the second was told to me by people who identified themselves as under the authority of Régulo Mataka. According to this version, Nduna Minofo originally belonged to Mtaya chieftaincy when he arrived in the territory. The Portuguese colonial administration then allocated Minofo to Chief Mataka because of the latter's location at the chosen headquarters of Cóbuè territory (Concelho de Cóbuè). This version suggests that the Portuguese administration played a role in the emergence of hierarchies between chiefs.

Conclusion

The 1997 Land Law reintroduced the distinction between rural and urban contexts and adopted customary land systems while introducing the delimitation of community land as a way to secure and register community land rights.[41] This community-based tenure system was seen as a way to prevent external threats and conflicts between investors and rural communities and thus promote development.[42] However, despite the flexible approach to customary tenure systems proposed by the 1997 law, the colonial view that *régulos* (kin-based political institutions) are landowners in rural communities, and that individuals access land as members of these political entities, still persists in the process of community land delimitation.

Viewed as a new and positive approach to land governance, land delimitation is remapping the territories of kin-based political institutions created during the colonial period. Different from the past, the present approach has forced the rights and obligations based on relationships between people to coincide with the community represented by the kin-based political institution.

In a different way, when chiefs narrate territorial history, they enable a more contextual understanding of the complexity of experiences with the territory by underlining the changes in chieftaincy and settlement in the region in different temporalities. Additionally, first-comers' narratives, presented in different versions at different times, unsettle the idea of community land as a homogeneous entity, which means that conflict and tension are related to the historical process of territorial constitution. So, the historical narrative used to validate the legitimacy of chiefs and territories is uncertain and also contested, meaning that they don't enjoy uncontested authority over the land. This example from Cóbuè shows that land delimitation goes beyond the confirmation of one's ownership of customary land. It is, in fact, a process of creating value attached to the land and its resources. This is the case in community land delimitation, which tends to transform land use practices into notions of possession and rights. Related to this, the main disputes or conflicts registered after the delimitation process involve not the land itself but the territory, in the sense that the main debate was about the definition of the status of those who have control over territories and their respective legitimacy.

To conclude, I would like to highlight two important points. Firstly, it is crucial not to reduce customary tenure systems to just the community or the political entity. This reductionist view is a result of the colonial conception of territory and rights to the land of the people who inhabit it. Secondly, property relations, landholding, and land use are all subject to endless negotiation processes, which are shaped by people's lived experiences in the territories.

When the communities in Cóbuè were mapped based on assumptions of internal coherence and homogenization related to one chief, it became clear that the notion of land, territory, and political institutions in rural Africa must be contextualized as historical and dynamic processes. This integration of colonial language and experience shows that customary land systems and land governance and transfers are marked by conflicts.[43] All in all, changes introduced by legislation and land governance demonstrate their potential to produce tensions on the criteria that define access to land as well as territorial claims. As registered in many parts of Africa, even when clarifying rights is an urgent matter, it reveals the importance of recognizing customary tenure systems as socially and politically embedded, as well as contested.[44]

The delimitation process involved not only the formalization of customary land or communal property rights, as stipulated in the 1997 Land Law; it also incorporated a historical contestation of hierarchies and statutes among traditional chiefs, and debates over control of the corresponding territories. As a moment of transition, it was crucial to reshape the notion of ownership and possession and to address the re-emergence of the system that produced inequalities between political authorities over land.

NOTES TO CHAPTER 8

This chapter is based in part on my dissertation, "'O primeiro a chegar é o dono da terra': Pertença e posse da terra na região do lago Niassa" (2016). Institute of Social Science, University of Lisbon, 2016).

1. *Régulos* were part of the framework of a native administration system, and they worked as native intermediaries who interfaced with the Portuguese. Euclides Gonçalves, "Local Powers and Decentralisation: Recognition of Community Leaders in Mocumbi, Southern Mozambique," *Journal of Contemporary African Studies* 24, no. 1 (2006): 31.
2. The formal recognition of traditional leaders is part of administrative reforms started in the early 1990s (Decree 15/2000).
3. Nduna Minofo is a second-rank community authority (*autoridade comunitária de 2° escalão*), as established by Law 8/2003 of 3 December and regulated by the Decree 11/2005 of 10 July.
4. L. Krantz, "Applying a Community Based Approach to Tenure Formalization: A Case Study from Northern Mozambique," Working Papers in Human Geography (Goteborg University, 2018); Simon Norfolk, Julian Quan, and Dan Mullins, "Options for Securing Tenure and Documenting Land Rights in Mozambique: A Land Policy and Practice Paper" (Natural Resources Institute, University of Greenwich, 2020); Liz Alden Wily, "The Law and Land Grabbing: Friend or Foe?," *Law and Development Review* 7, no. 2 (2014): 207–42.
5. Cf. Ward Anseeuw and Chris Alden, eds., *The Struggle Over Land in Africa: Conflicts, Politics and Change* (HSRC Press, 2010); Ben Cousins, "Characterising 'Communal' Tenure: Nested Systems and Flexible Boundaries," in *Land, Power and Custom: Controversies Generated by South Africa's Communal Land Rights Act*, ed. Annika Claassens and Ben Cousins (UCT Press, 2008), 109–37; Carola Lentz, "Is Land Inalienable? Historical and Current Debates on Land Transfers in Northern Ghana," *Africa: The Journal of the International African Institute* 53, no. 1 (2010): 56–80.
6. Jean-Pierre Chauveau and Paul Richard, "West African Insurgencies in Agrarian Perspective: Côte d'Ivoire and Sierra Leone Compared," *Journal of Agrarian Change* 8, no. 4 (2008): 515–52; Carola Lentz, "First-Comers and Late-Comers: Indigenous Theories of Land Ownership in the West African Savannah," in *Land and the Politics of Belonging in West Africa* (Brill, 2006), 35–56; Pauline E. Peters, "Challenges in Land Tenure and Land Reform in Africa: Anthropological Contributions," *World Development* 37, no. 8 (2009): 1317–25.
7. Paul de De Wit and Simon Norfolk, *Reconhecer Direitos sobre os Recursos Naturais em Moçambique* (Maputo, 2010); Krantz, "Applying a Community Based Approach to Tenure Formalization."
8. Mário Monteiro and Alexandre Oliveira Tavares, "What Is the Influence of the Planning Framework on the Land Use Change Trajectories? Photointerpretation Analysis in the 1958–2011 Period for a Medium/Small Sized City," *Sustainability* 7, no. 9 (2015): 11727–55.
9. Art. 1, 1997 Land Law.
10. De Wit and Norfolk, *Reconhecer Direitos sobre os Recursos Naturais em Moçambique*, 26.
11. Paul Bohannan, "'Land,' 'Tenure' and Land Tenure," reprinted from *African Agrarian Systems*, ed. Daniel Biebuvck (Oxford University Press, 1973), online via US Agency for International Development, accessed 12 January 2025, https://pdf.usaid.gov/pdf_docs/pnabi322.pdf; Cousins, "Characterising 'Communal' Tenure"; Carola Lentz, *Land, Mobility and Belonging in West Africa* (Indiana University Press, 2013); Peters, "Challenges in Land Tenure and Land Reform in Africa"; Johan Potier, "Customary Land Tenure' in Sub-Saharan Africa Today: Meanings and Contexts," in *From the Ground Up: Land Rights, Conflict and Peace in Sub-Saharan Africa*, ed. Chris Higgins and Jenny Clover (Institute for Security Studies, 2005), 55–76.
12. Gonçalves, "Local Powers and Decentralisation," 65.
13. Cf. Gonçalves, "Local Powers and Decentralisation"; Harry G. West, "'This Neighbor Is Not My Uncle!': Changing Relations of Power and Authority on the Mueda Plateau," *Journal of Southern African Studies* 24, no. 1 (1998): 141–60.
14. Gonçalves, "Local Powers and Decentralisation."
15. Christopher Tanner, "Implementing Mozambique Law in Practice," in *The Struggle Over Land in Africa: Conflicts, Politics and Changes*, ed. Ward Anseeuw and Chris Alden (HSRC Press, 2010), 85; West, "'This Neighbor Is Not My Uncle!,'" 160.
16. De Wit and Norfolk, *Reconhecer Direitos sobre os Recursos Naturais em Moçambique*, 27.
17. Krantz, "Applying a Community Based Approach to Tenure Formalization."
18. Randi Kaarhus and Stefaan Dondeyne, "Formalising land Rights Based on Customary Tenure: Community Delimitation and Women's Access to Land in Central Mozambique," *Journal of Modern African Studies* 53, no. 2 (2015): 193–216.

19 Cf. José Negrão, *Repensando a terra e as modas do desenvolvimento rural* (Texto Editores, 2008).
20 Norfolk, Quan, and Mullins, "Options for Securing Tenure and Documenting Land Rights in Mozambique."
21 "A Glimpse of the Peasant and Small Farmer," La Via Campesina, 17 December 2008, https://viacampesina.org/en/2008/12/a-glimpse-of-the-peasant-and-small-farmer/.
22 The "local community" is defined as a "group of people or families living in the same territory and [who] share common interests" (art. 1, 1997 Land Law).
23 Ranked second in the community authority structure.
24 Cf. Lentz, "First-Comers and Late-Comers"; John C. McCall, "Rethinking Ancestors in Africa," *Africa* 54, no. 2 (1995): 256–70; William Murphy and Carolina H. Bledsoe, "The Importance of Being First: Kinship and Territory of a Kpelle Chiefdom (Liberia)," in *The African Frontier: The Reproduction of Traditional African Societies*, ed. Igor Kopytoff (Indiana University Press, 1987), 123–47.
25 Khango is a settlement of Sub-Chief Minofo and a location of Cóbuè headquarters.
26 Cf. Arianna Huhn, "Sustenance and Sociality: Footways in a Mozambican Town" (PhD diss., Boston University, 2013).
27 In the account of missionary William Johnson, Chiteji is part of the west-south group along Niassa Lake, having first settled in Chilowelo near Makanjila, then in Messumba, before settling indefinitely in Chigoma. William Percival Johnson, *Nyasa the Great Water: Being a Description of the Lake and the Life of the People* (UMCA, 1922), 96–7.
28 Huhn, "Sustenance and Sociality"; Johnson, *Nyasa the Great Water*; Assahel J. Mazula, "História dos Nianjas," *Revista de Cultura Missionária* 19 (1962): 154–67.
29 Lentz, "Land, Mobility And Belonging in West Africa," 18.
30 Marilyn Strathern, "Land: Intangible or Tangible Property?," *In Land Rights*, ed. Timothy Chesters (Oxford University Press, 2009), 13–38.
31 Administrative post consultative councils were established by Law 8/2003 of 3 December, and regulated by Decree 11/2005, 10 July.
32 Huhn, "Sustenance and Sociality."
33 Ambali quoted in Huhn, "Sustenance and Sociality," 43–4; Johnson, *Nyasa the Great Water*, 96–7
34 Huhn, "Sustenance and Sociality."
35 Union of Cooperatives and Associations, *Delimitação da comunidade de Mataka, distrito do Lago Cóbuè* (Lichinga, 2006).
36 Meaning the ancestor or founder of the territory.
37 McCall, "Rethinking Ancestors in Africa."
38 Lentz, "First-Comers and Late-Comers"; McCall, "Rethinking Ancestors in Africa"; Murphy and Bledsoe, "The Importance of Being First."
39 Blair Rutherford, "Land Governance and Land Deals in Africa: Opportunities and Challenges in Advancing Community Rights," *Journal of Sustainable Development Law and Policy* 8, no. 1 (2017): 235–58.
40 Rutherford, "Land Governance and Land Deals in Africa"; Catharine Boone, "Land Tenure Regimes and State Structure in Rural Africa: Implications for the Forms of Resistance to Large-Scale Land Acquisitions by Outsiders," *Journal of Contemporary African Studies* 33, no. 2 (2015): 171–90; Horman Chitonge, "'We Owned the Land Before the State Was Established': The State, Traditional Authorities, and Land Policy in Africa," in *African Land Reform Under Economic Liberalisation: States, Chiefs, and Rural Communities*, ed. Shinichi Takeuchi (Springer, 2022), 41–64.
41 João Carrilho and Simon Norfolk, "Beyond Building the Cadastre: Proposed Next Steps for Mozambique in Participatory Land Governance and Decentralized Land Rights Administration," paper presented at the Annual World Bank Conference on Land and Poverty, Washington, DC, 8–11 April 2013; Kaarhus and Dondeyne, "Formalising Land Rights Based on Customary Tenure"; Krantz, "Applying a Community Based Approach to Tenure Formalization"; Tanner, "Implementing Mozambique Law in Practice."
42 Monteiro and Tavares, "What Is the Influence of the Planning Framework on the Land Use Change Trajectories?"
43 Cf. Lentz, "First-Comers and Late-Comers."
44 Anseeuw and Alden, *The Struggle Over Land in Africa*; Cousins, "Characterising 'Communal' Tenure."

PART III
Economic Imperatives and Global Articulations

9

The Trajectory of the Plantation System in Mozambique: The Case of Madal in Micaúne

José Laimone Adalima

Introduction

How local long-term changes in land relations have affected different actors and interests is a topic under-researched in Mozambique. A relevant example is provided by the plantation systems developed in northern Mozambique by international private companies, which alienated land from the local people to produce a variety of cash crops under a plantation regime. Of special interest here is an enclave economy based on a coconut plantation established by the French-owned Société du Madal in Zambézia Province around 1900. While Madal primarily engaged in copra production, its business activities diversified over time.[1] In this chapter, I rely on ethnographic research, complemented by interviews and life histories, to chronicle the continued existence of the colonial plantation system in Mozambique.

The Madal case combines labour and land relations and provides an entry point to understanding social relations of production, power dynamics, and processes of accumulation and dispossession across the twentieth and twenty-first centuries. Following Lloyd Best and Kari Levitt and Cooper, I use the concept of plantation economy to describe an economy based on a monoculture produced in a regime of plantations as an integral part of industrial capitalism, where peripheries of western Europe are the suppliers of labour and producers of raw materials and agricultural produce.[2]

The chapter is concerned with coconut and its centrality in the economy, and for that reason I adopt the concept of "coconut economy" as used by Mathew for Kerala; similarly, coconut has been central to the economy of Micaúne since the 1880s.[3]

From a historical perspective, I delve into the connection between land tenure and the livelihoods of the inhabitants of the administrative post of Micaúne District in Chinde, Zambézia Province. A fundamental premise for this analysis is that understanding the historical basis for the livelihoods of the people in Micaúne is inseparable from the history of Madal. It reveals how Madal evolved, adapting to the changing landscape of the country. It functioned as a "total institution," serving as the major employer, a primary supplier of goods, a chief purchaser of coconut from the family sector, and the principal landholder in the region. Bertelsen locates Madal not only as a colonial actor in a narrow economic sense, but also as an important player within the colonial political field as the company was an integral part of Portuguese colonial rule and strategy in Mozambique.[4]

To build contextual understanding of Micaúne's economy, the next section describes the political and economic development of the plantation system in central Mozambique since the 1880s. This is followed by the description and analysis of the trajectory of the coconut economy to highlight continuities over time. The final section focuses on the legacy of the plantation system and how it continues to shape land governance to date.

The *Prazos* of Zambézia

Before the arrival of the Portuguese, historians note that Arab merchants were involved in extensive long-distance trade in Mozambique's coastal areas and the hinterland domain of the Mwenemutapa Empire. Their primary aim was the trade of cloth and beads for valuable commodities like gold and probably ivory. In stark contrast, the Portuguese conquerors who arrived in the sixteenth century and the first half of the seventeenth pursued a multi-faceted agenda. Their objectives encompassed the occupation of the Mwenemutapa's gold and silver mines, the displacement of the Arabs through military conquest, and the religious assimilation of the African people.[5] To achieve these goals, the Portuguese Crown established the *"prazos* of the Crown," a chain of territories along the Zambezi River valley, spanning from Quelimane on the coast to Zumbo, situated on the western border adjoining Mashonaland (present-day Zimbabwe).[6]

The *prazos* of the seventeenth to nineteenth centuries primarily functioned as land grants to people of Portuguese origin across three generations, with a requirement for or preference toward succession through the female line. These *prazos* consisted of *prazo* holders and their families, along with African settlers, enslaved individuals, and livestock.⁷ The *prazos* primarily engaged in trade, building upon pre-existing routes and networks that were in place before the Portuguese arrival.⁸ As time progressed, particularly from the 1880s onward, *prazo* holders were authorized to govern the regions under their control. This granted them the ability to facilitate the growth of agricultural production, trade, and the collection of taxes, all of which could then be directed toward the Portuguese treasury.⁹

The Crown maintained ownership rights while granting usage rights in exchange for a leasing fee in gold starting in 1633.¹⁰ However, the *prazo* system, in many instances, did not significantly alter the production relationships of the local inhabitants, who continued with subsistence farming as before and were allowed access to a hectare per hut.¹¹

According to Negrão, *prazos* were categorized based on their geographic location, specifically the ones in the Zambezi Delta, those situated north of the Zambezi River, and those within the territory of the Mwenemutapa Empire.¹² The first category possessed ample land but didn't immediately pique the interest of adventurers due to the absence of gold and ivory resources; the second category was located in a region governed by the Marave Empire and produced cotton and ivory, which were sources of income overlooked by the Portuguese; and the last category fell under the control of the Mwenemutapa Empire and yielded precious metals, which was the primary incentive for Portuguese presence in the area.

The "*prazos* of the Crown" in the Mwenemutapa Empire territory gained significance following the treaties signed with Mwenemutapa in 1607 and 1629, acknowledging Portuguese Crown ownership of extensive territories in exchange for military assistance.¹³

As noted by Zonta, the replacement of the indigenous chiefs by the *prazo* holders at the helm of the African political structures occurred without significant disruptions to the social cohesion of the local communities. The inhabitants of the region gradually perceived the *prazo* holders as the legitimate successors or delegates of their former chiefs.¹⁴ These *prazo* holders initiated the collection of taxes on agricultural output from peasant lands. Importantly, akin to the precedent set by the traditional chiefs, the *prazo* holders never asserted ownership rights over the land, as it remained under communal ownership according to indigenous law.

Because the administration of the colonies was centralized under the authority of the Ministry of Marine and Overseas Affairs in Lisbon, Portugal faced significant challenges in maintaining effective law enforcement in its overseas territories. Moreover, conflicts between the metropolitan political elite and the

Map 9.1.
Map of the
prazos in the
Zambezi Delta

Source: José Negrão,
"One Hundred Years
of African Rural
Family Economy:
The Zambezi Delta
in Retrospective
Analysis" (PhD
diss., University
of Lund, 1995), 54.
Cartography: Rui
Pinto

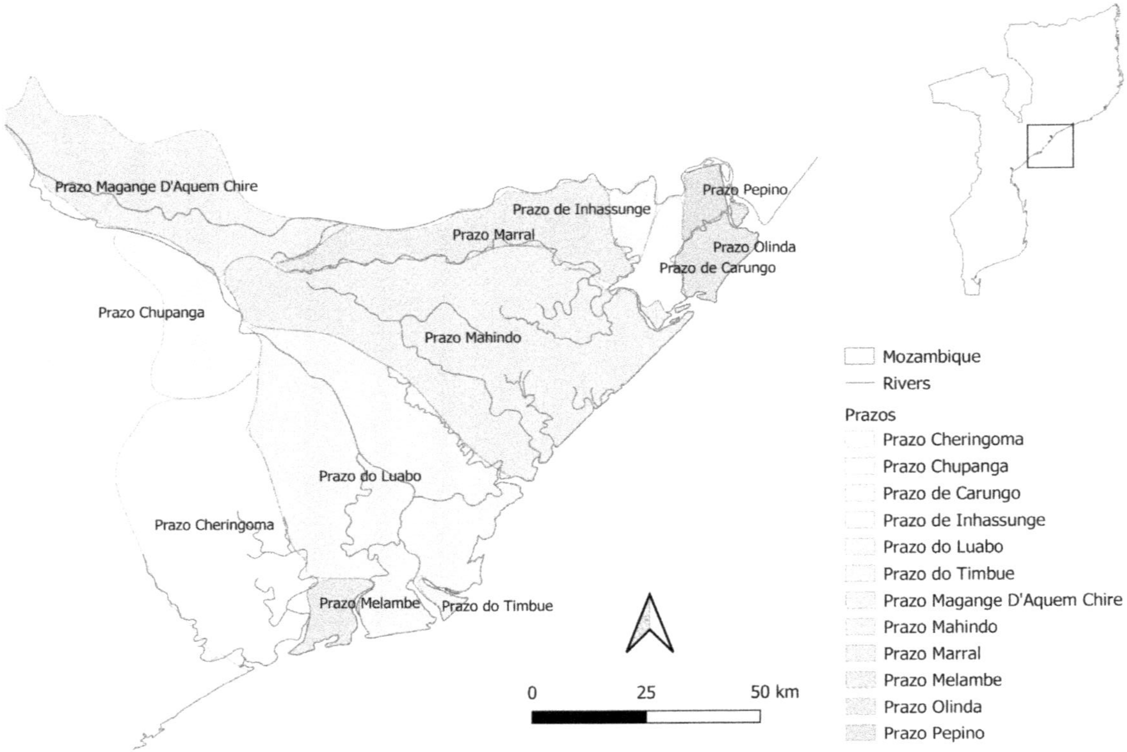

administrative personnel stationed in the colonies further complicated the governance of Mozambique.[15]

This situation ultimately benefited the colonial companies, as the supervision of their compliance with various regulations, especially labour laws, was often insufficient or lacking. This lack of oversight frequently resulted in disputes and labour shortages.[16]

The display of impunity by *prazo* companies in Zambézia during the first two decades of the twentieth century raised significant concerns among government officials. Complaints regarding the operations of these *prazo* holders were rife. They were accused of active involvement in the recruitment and provision of labour, all while generating substantial profits in flagrant disregard of prevailing legislation. Some officials went as far as to suggest the *prazo* system should be abolished, primarily because *prazo* holders were blatantly flouting the terms of their contracts and actively resisting government oversight of their activities.[17]

In the 1880s, a significant transformation occurred due to Portugal's inability to modernize the *prazo* system as well as the mounting pressure from other colonial powers, particularly following the Berlin Conference of 1884–5. This pressure was aimed at compelling Portugal to demonstrate its effective control over the territories for which it claimed historical rights.

In the case of Zambézia, Portugal's presence was primarily limited to Quelimane, which it had occupied in 1870,[18] and a small coconut plantation in Micaúne owned by the Correia and Carvalho company.[19] In response to this situation, the Portuguese state initiated land reforms in 1871. The primary objective of these reforms was to establish a land tenure system that would facilitate private Portuguese investment in agriculture. This would be achieved through a judicious allocation of land concessions on the *prazos*, thus marking a shift in the administration and utilization of these lands.

In 1873, several investments were approved, one of which came from João Correia, a nephew of Isidoro Correia, a well-known Zambezian slave trader. Correia, together with Carlos Nandim Carvalho, rented the Prazo Mahindo in Micaúne and co-founded the Correia and Carvalho firm. This enterprise initially entered the copra business in 1877 with a modest plantation of 70,000 palm trees. In 1883, the company made a significant decision to heavily invest in coconut production, resulting in an annual output of 130 tons by the turn of the century.[20] Overall, the strategy aimed at boosting private Portuguese investment in agriculture proved to be ineffective. Consequently, Portugal ended up leasing approximately two-thirds of Mozambique to foreign companies, primarily of British, French, German, and Swiss origin.[21] The above-mentioned foreign entities established two major chartered companies, the Mozambique Company and the Nyassa/Niassa Company,[22] alongside a leasing company known as the Zambézia Company.[23]

Following this, new labour and land laws were approved, and designed to align with the preferences of foreign investors. These changes altered the pre-existing production relationships and significantly curtailed the autonomy previously enjoyed by Africans in the various *prazos*. As a consequence, all Africans were turned into a reservoir of cheap labour, and work became obligatory, encompassing various forms of forced labour.[24]

The Zambézia Company, established in 1892, obtained leasing rights from the Portuguese government under the decree of September 24, 1892. This granted it a ten-year mandate to manage the Crown *prazos* located north of the Zambezi River, extending to the west of the Luenha and Mazoi Rivers, encompassing an expansive area of 100,000 square kilometers.[25] With ownership stakes in the Zambézia Company, the Portuguese government strategically chose to sublease a portion of the company's territory. This initiative led to the establishment of several enterprises, including Maganja Aquém Chire (founded in 1894), Boror (established in 1898), Société du Madal (formed in 1903), Companhia Agricola de Lugela (established in 1906), and Sena Sugar Estates (founded in 1920). These companies primarily specialized in cultivating various crops such as sisal, copra, sugar, tea, rice, and cotton within the region.[26]

This marked the inception of the plantation system in Mozambique. According to Serra,[27] plantations extended across four distinct regions, with the coconut area being the most significant, situated between the mouths of the Zambezi and Raragra Rivers. The sisal area encompassed the banks of the Licungo River, while the sugar cane area stretched along the Zambezi River, covering Luabo and Mopeia. The fourth area extended to the regions bordering the Shire River.

In this chapter, my attention is directed toward the coconut plantations owned by Madal, which will be further elaborated on in the following section. Subsequently, the ensuing section will delve into the dynamics of these coconut plantations as envisioned by Madal.

Madal's Plantations and the Coconut Economy of Micaúne in Colonial Mozambique

Micaúne, previously known as Prazo Mahindo, was an *aringa* (a brick-built stronghold) situated on the coast, covering a vast surface of 700,000 acres, equivalent to 280,000 hectares.[28] This fortress featured four bastions, serving as a defence against the indigenous populations who were far from submissive during that period.[29] It was categorized as a first-class *prazo*, and was owned by several *prazo* holders from 1630 before it was leased to Madal in 1904.[30]

There is a lack of consensus regarding the identification of the people inhabiting the Prazo Mahindo area. According to Zonta, the inhabitants of this region are known as the Podzo. They primarily engaged in agriculture, cultivating crops such as maize, sorghum, millet, sweet potatoes, rice, beans, cassava, and peanuts.[31] Land ownership rights were granted to those who had some trees, including palm trees and citrus. During the oilseed production boom in Zambézia between the late 1860s and the 1880s, the Podzo played a significant role in the production of sesame and peanuts.[32] Isaacman contends that the Podzo should be considered part of the e-Chuabo ethnic group rather than an independent ethnic group.[33] On the other hand, Rita-Ferreira categorizes them as one of the peripheral minorities within the ci-Sena.[34]

This disparity could be indicative of the fusion of diverse elements from e-Chuabo and ci-Sena, as well as the influences of Islam and Christianity in shaping the local culture. Currently, the individuals I have spoken to do not identify themselves as either Podzo or ci-Sena but rather as the Mahindo, signifying those who communicate in the Mahindo language. In fact, in contemporary official records, "Mahindo" refers to the community residing in Micaúne.

While the local population had a certain familiarity with coconuts, their production remained comparatively limited in contrast to the 1900s. During that period, companies like Madal initiated palm plantations, taking advantage of forced labour legislation and land expropriations. The pivotal moment in copra production occurred during the 1880s when a surge in oilseed production in Zambézia was catalyzed by the soaring demand from Europe, stemming from the repercussions of the Crimean War (1853–6). This conflict disrupted the trade of fatty oils from the Russian Far East and eastern Europe, prompting an increased reliance on copra.

In 1853, France and Portugal entered into an agreement that granted complete freedom of commerce and navigation between the two nations. This agreement also permitted French ships to export a wide range of goods from Portuguese territories.[35] As a result of this accord, French enterprises started to play an ever-growing role in the copra production and export industry in Mozambique.

In Micaúne, the establishment and growth of the coconut economy received its most significant impetus through the efforts of the French-owned Madal company, which was founded in 1903. A year later, they expanded their operations by renting Prazo Mahindo and commencing the establishment of additional coconut plantations, achieved through the clearing of forests and the strategic

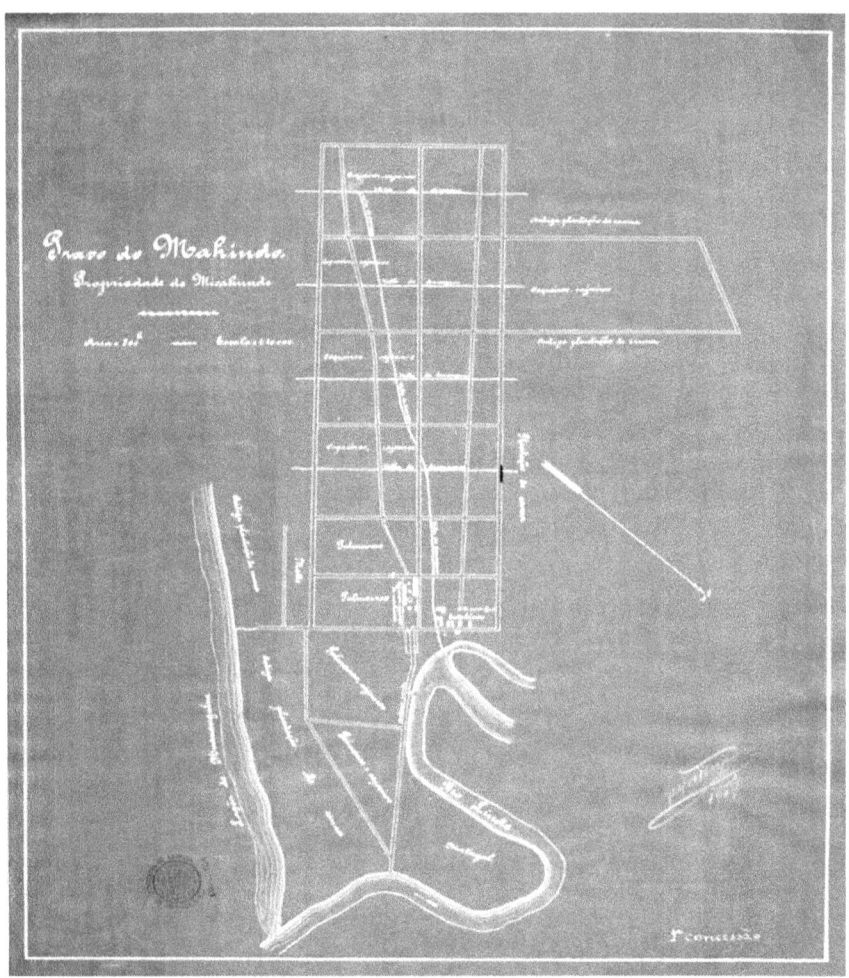

Map 9.2. Map of Prazo Mahindo
Source: Sociedade de Geografia de Lisboa.

planting of trees.[36] Madal significantly expanded its palm tree holdings within the designated third section of Micaúne by leasing additional land and consolidating ownership in neighbouring Prazo Mahindo areas.[37]

By 1908, they had successfully cultivated palm trees across 544 hectares of land.[38] Over the years, their efforts bore fruit, and by 1920, the number of palm trees in Madal's possession had grown to an impressive total of over 225,000, with more than half of them bearing fruit.[39]

Brandão asserted that Madal played a pivotal role in establishing the production infrastructure, which encompassed the construction of housing for managers, roadways, and a network of stations that served as the focal points for copra production. Typically, these stations featured a central house, auxiliary facilities, and worker accommodations arranged in a spacious quadrangle, with plantations encircling them.[40] Furthermore, Madal devised an innovative management model that emphasized the supervision and control of plantations from multiple stations, facilitating the conversion of coconuts into copra. Following this transformation, copra was transported via boats from Micaúne to the port of Quelimane, where the company maintained its warehouses.

This meant that Madal had a tight grip on the entire coconut production chain, exercising control over incentives within it. My informants noted that palm trees were ubiquitous across the landscape, with little land remaining untouched by these trees. These observations align with Negrão's research, which indicated that "on average, there were around 100 palm trees per hectare but in some cases, one could find between 120 and 160 palm trees."[41] Consequently, through Madal's influence, the coconut industry became the linchpin of all activities in Micaúne. In essence, the entire society revolved around this cash crop, leaving limited room for pursuits beyond it.

The local economy relied on two key factors: the availability of cheap labour and the outsourcing of production from the residents to remain competitive in the global market. These two income streams, to varying extents, sustained the livelihoods of the residents for over a century. Consequently, a mutually dependent and symbiotic relationship between Madal and the residents flourished. In a short period, Madal emerged as the primary employer in Micaúne, predominantly hiring men as seasonal labourers on its plantations. Simultaneously, residents could sell coconuts from their palm trees to the company. In a sense, as my informants emphasized, the coconut economy was considered reliable, offering a steady and dependable source of income. However, the coconut-based economy posed significant challenges for many informants.

Endurance of the Colonial Plantation Regime After Independence

The predictability of the coconut-based economy persisted even after Mozambique gained its independence in 1975, despite the government's rhetoric of radical change from the colonial state. The post-colonial government maintained the colonial economic structure, characterized by significant land concentration and investments in areas such as plantations and state farms, rather than prioritizing the redistribution of land to family producers.

Inspired by Tanzania's Ujamaa, Algeria's communal villages and the relative success of production in the liberated zones in Mozambique during the colonial war, FRELIMO[42] embarked on an ambitious mission to establish people's democratic power by advocating for a society free of the exploitation of "man by man," in line with Marxist-Leninist principles. With a state-controlled economy, agriculture took centre stage in shaping its economic policies. However, the tumultuous violence that accompanied the transition of power from Portugal to FRELIMO upon independence led to widespread fear, insecurity, and political chaos.

As a result, many owners of both large and small businesses, as well as managers and officials who had uncertainties about their future, hastily abandoned their properties, residences, and other assets, including land. Following Mozambique's independence in 1975, these properties were subsequently nationalized and repurposed into state-owned farms and enterprises.[43]

The investors who felt aggrieved by the newly established government lent their support to the formation of the rebel group RENAMO[44] when it emerged in 1976, initiating a conflict against the nascent government. This conflict eventually concluded with a peace accord signed in Rome in 1992. This situation highlights a connection between affected businesses and RENAMO's discontentment with FRELIMO's Marxist policies.

The inclusion of provisions in the 1975 new constitution recognizing private property and permitting foreign investors to engage in activities, as long as such activities were in alignment with the constitution's stipulations,[45] gave rise to a persistent source of tension within the post-colonial state's political landscape. This tension emerged because the government persisted in implementing its Marxist policies,[46] while at the same time certain plantation companies, like Madal, were able to persist in their operations. Having survived nationalization, Madal continued to have a monopoly on the commercialization of copra in the country, given that its rival company, Boror,[47] was nationalized at the end of the 1970s.[48]

Madal retained possession of the land it had acquired during the colonial era, without any state farms or collective villages being established in Micaúne. Moreover, for many decades, the copra production process remained unchanged. Production methods remained rudimentary and labour-intensive, with workers receiving meagre wages, often falling below the minimum wage established by the Mozambican government.[49] As per Mr. Abudo, a former Madal employee in Micaúne during the 1980s, there were no discernible improvements in working conditions.

According to his account, the company's remuneration scale was structured as follows: Specialized workers received 10.00 meticais per day, equivalent to US$0.40 (at an exchange rate of US$1.00 for 23.88763 meticais),[50] while non-specialized workers, including coconut pickers and loaders, received 7.50 meticais per day, equivalent to US$0.30. Each worker was expected to complete a daily quota of 1,000 coconuts. Mechanics and carpenters earned relatively more, around 20.00 meticais per day, equivalent to US$0.80. It's worth noting that the majority of the physically demanding tasks were performed by men due to the perceived greater physical strength required. Women, on the other hand, were primarily engaged in domestic responsibilities such as caring for children, cooking, fetching water, and subsistence farming.[51]

In the 1980s, just as in the colonial period, the company actively encouraged children to collaborate with their fathers to acquire the skills of their trade. Mr. Ricardo fondly reminisced about Madal's profound influence on his life, stating,

> As a child, I would accompany my father to Madal every single day. I eagerly supported him in his tasks, and through this hands-on experience, I mastered the intricacies of his work. While Madal did not provide me with a regular wage, when my father faced physical limitations that hindered his work, the company recognized my ability to step in and take his place. This marked the beginning of my journey as a Madal employee. Furthermore, within my extended family, many other members, at various points in their lives, also embraced roles within the Madal workforce. It seemed like almost everyone in my family had their own Madal story to tell.

During his lifetime, Mr. Ricardo served as a blacksmith at Madal until his retirement in 1985. He took over the position from his father, who tragically lost his life in 1992 after being captured by RENAMO soldiers in the district of Mocuba, situated approximately two hundred kilometres away.[52]

During the armed conflict, Madal's operations, including those in Micaúne, were partially impacted. Nevertheless, the company managed to maintain profitability, even when the international market copra price dropped from US$750 to US$140 in 1985–6. As per register number 2025, dated 23 January 1985, the company reported profits of 14,940,908 meticais, equivalent to US$6,254,671 in 1983. From 1983 to 1986, Madal exported 18,819 metric tons of copra, generating revenues of US$6,830,000. This accounted for more than 60 per cent of Mozambique's copra exports during that period. Additionally, Madal contributed to the domestic industry by producing another 8,961,134 kilograms of copra.[53]

The country's shift toward a market economy, initiated by the structural adjustment program in 1987, re-emphasized the significance of private property, mirroring a historical trend from the colonial era. Madal seemingly emerged as a beneficiary of the privatization process, capitalizing on its connections with the political elite.[54] Leveraging these connections, the company acquired multiple state enterprises and engaged in collaborative ventures with the government.[55]

In Micaúne, apart from Madal, which retained land from the colonial period, new private landholders have been acquiring land through the privatization process that commenced in 1987. During this period, the government granted approximately 39,962 hectares of new land concessions in Micaúne. Of these, 19,428 hectares were allocated to Madal, while the remaining land was distributed among three other companies: Companhia de Sena (formerly known as the Sena Sugar Estate), with 102.59 hectares, Sociedade Micaúne Eco-Turismo, with 9,400 hectares, and Pro-Hunter Safari, with 9,600 hectares. Additionally, 1,431.20 hectares were allocated to six individuals and the Quelimane Diocese.

Madal also appeared to have capitalized on the post-conflict period following 1992, drawing in seasonal labour, especially from individuals displaced by the war who resettled in Micaúne. During this time, Madal seized the opportunity to boost its production by taking advantage of the surplus labour force. According to a Madal representative in Micaúne, the company had approximately seven thousand employees in Micaúne by 1992, indicating a significant upturn in the coconut industry.

During this period, a new generation of coconut traders emerged in the region, primarily consisting of Mozambicans based in Micaúne. They acted as intermediaries between Madal and local household coconut producers. Over approximately a decade, these traders purchased coconuts from local families at reduced prices and then included a profit margin when selling to Madal and other companies. Additionally, they were actively engaged in the production of coconut oil, which they marketed in Quelimane, the provincial capital.

In the year when the new land law (Law 19/97 of 1 October) was approved, Madal acquired three plantations previously owned by Boror. As the 2000s unfolded, Madal solidified its position as the foremost private landowner in Mozambique, overseeing the employment of approximately five hundred workers at its Micaúne plantation.[56] The emergence and rapid spreading of coconut lethal yellowing disease (CLYD) in the late 1990s had a profound and transformative impact on the local economy. As Rønning reported, "CLYD was observed for the first time in Madal's coconut plantation in Micaúne in March of 1998 and it was rapidly spreading through the palms of the local people bordering the company's plantations."[57]

The disease continued to proliferate, eventually reaching a critical point in 2004, necessitating the removal of palm trees belonging to both residents and Madal. This, unfortunately, resulted in a substantial loss of income and employment opportunities, engendering a climate of uncertainty and exacerbating food insecurity in the region. One might have anticipated Madal leaving the area once the coconut industry declined. However, to the contrary, the company has persisted to the present day, retaining ownership of the land where the plantations once thrived.

They have diversified land use since the onset and subsequent upsurge of CLYD, patiently awaiting recovery from the disease while actively participating in the cultivation of cash crops such as sesame, engaging in game farming, and promoting tourism.

During my fieldwork in 2012, it was observed that approximately 118,199 out of the 200,000 hectares encompassing Micaúne were under private control, with Madal alone occupying 42,424 hectares. The remaining land was held in a shared capacity, with both state and communal ownership, including areas like deserts, mangroves, and rivers. In most cases, these land concessions, including Madal's, complied with the legal requirement to pay an annual levy for land occupation.

Nonetheless, the persistence of the company has engendered ongoing tensions with residents who urgently require land for their livelihoods. In 2020, I reached out to one of my sources to gather updates on the latest developments in Micaúne. According to my contact, Madal continued to maintain significant control over the local territory.

The absence of government intervention in this matter may imply the continued prioritization of plantation-style agricultural production in Mozambique. Subsequent sections will illustrate how the historical plantation system endures, influencing contemporary land governance. This is especially evident as (agri) business enclaves adopt operational models reminiscent of those employed by colonial enterprises, such as Madal.

The Legacy of Plantations in Contemporary Mozambique

While Law 1/86 of 16 April, an amendment to the original post-colonial Land Law 6/79 of 3 July 1979, did acknowledge the existence of two distinct systems of land use rights—formal and customary—it notably established a framework for issuing land use rights for a renewable period of fifty years. This provision aimed at incentivizing significant foreign investments, as local communities maintained unrestricted land use rights. To comprehensively assess the nation's land utilization and lay the groundwork for future land policies and legislation, the government established a research initiative in the early 1990s. This endeavour was carried out under the auspices of the then "Ad Hoc" Land Commission, with substantial support from the University of Wisconsin Land Tenure Center and the United States Agency for International Development (USAID).[58] It is noteworthy that this occurred in tandem with the privatization of state-owned assets that was initiated in 1989. Between 1989 and 1997, the government embarked on an extensive program to divest state-owned assets. As part of this initiative, the government granted fifty-year renewable concessions for thousands of acres of agricultural land, undertook a significant restructuring of approximately 740 enterprises, and facilitated the establishment of 120 new privately owned enterprises.[59]

A specific cohort of individuals closely associated with the FRELIMO party and state leadership played a crucial role in shaping the Mozambican business elite during the transition from socialism to a multi-party system in the late 1980s. Given the limited capital available to the majority of Mozambicans, the political elite actively pursued partnerships with foreign investors from a variety of nations, including Portugal, South Africa, the United States, Great Britain, Holland, Denmark, Norway, Cyprus, Zimbabwe, Swaziland, Mauritius, India, and China.[60] These elite figures amassed wealth as "silent partners"[61] and were instrumental in driving the push for the privatization of former colonial concessions and plantations, as they aspired to profit from the sale of the land obtained through these privatization efforts.[62]

This pattern of economic transformation was not unique to Mozambique. Russian oligarchs, for example, exhibited similar characteristics. In both cases, the transition from socialism to capitalism led to individuals with close ties to the ruling political regime gaining preferential access to privatized state assets, enabling them to establish substantial businesses.[63]

The influential figures within successive governments have consistently advocated for extensive plantation agriculture and forestry, ultimately leading to the privatization of land. During the deliberations that preceded the enactment of the 1997 Land Law, the concept of privatization was actively promoted not only by the World Bank and the United States but also by the Mozambican elites who eagerly pursued land concessions to profit from potential sales.[64] The pretext put forth by proponents of privatization was the necessity of using land as collateral to access credit, but in reality, the underlying motive was to acquire substantial land holdings for speculative purposes.[65]

Civil society organizations and local communities have vehemently opposed this through a series of actions, notably the land campaign established in 1996. This campaign comprised around two hundred non-governmental organizations, both national and foreign, as well as churches, associations, co-operatives, and other entities representing civil society and academics. Together, they collaborated to disseminate information, primarily aimed at rural families.⁶⁶

Similarly, in response to the tactics employed by proponents of land privatization, peasant organizations were quick to oppose them and successfully made their case.⁶⁷ For instance, the Rural Association for Mutual Support, a rural residents' association founded in 1996, organized a public demonstration against the privatization of land, using the slogan "no to land privatization." This demonstration garnered support from a broad spectrum of participants, including peasants, political parties, and even FRELIMO, just a week before the new land bill was presented to the country's parliament. ⁶⁸

Amid the heated opposition to land privatization, the 1997 Land Law was enacted, followed by its rural area regulations in 1998, notably devoid of any provisions for privatization.

The most significant aspect of the land reforms was the state's formal acknowledgement of rights acquired through customary law and the introduction of incentives to encourage private interests to invest in land for a renewable period of fifty years. According to Law 19/97, local communities possess the authority to establish DUATs (*Direito de uso e aproveitamento de terra*, or state-granted land rights) for themselves, which represents a permanent and legally recognized entitlement to land use. Furthermore, within a given community, both men and women have the opportunity to request individual land rights once the community demarcates its respective land areas.⁶⁹ Moreover, the law allows for the inheritance of land use rights, with no gender-based distinctions. Oral testimonies regarding land rights are also legally recognized and valid.⁷⁰

Remarkably, this legislation received global recognition, with organizations such as the World Bank and United Kingdom's Department for International Development applauding its protection of peasant rights and its skillful management of collective and community land tenure.⁷¹ This accomplishment can be seen as a victory for families and small-scale landholders who tenaciously opposed land privatization efforts, though it did not mark the conclusion of the struggle against land privatization.

The government's stance on the land issue remained ambiguous. Policy documents and strategies convey one set of intentions, while the actual situation on the ground appears to lean toward granting extensive land concessions to both foreign and domestic investors. As pointed out by Hanlon, "there remains a division within the government . . . [over] whether the priority should be given to large-scale or small-scale investments."⁷²

In 1996, shortly before the implementation of the land law (Law 19/97), the government launched a fifty-year commercial agricultural joint venture known as Mozagrius. This endeavour entailed the allocation of a significant land parcel in Niassa Province to South African farmers. However, this ambitious undertaking encountered several hurdles and ultimately faltered within a few years. These challenges included insufficient infrastructure, financial difficulties, and conflicts with community leaders and the local population.

Just one year after the new land law was approved, the government gave its nod to the National Programme for Agricultural Development (PROAGRI I) in 1998, with a substantial budget of US$202 million. This pioneering endeavour received support from a collaborative donor fund, showcasing the steadfast dedication of development partners to advancing large-scale farming initiatives.[73]

Three years after the approval of PROAGRI I, the issue of land privatization once again came to the fore. This time, it was championed by Hélder Muteia, who was then serving as the minister of agriculture and rural development. It appeared that he had garnered support from influential entities such as the World Bank and USAID. However, despite these efforts, resolute opposition to land privatization was evident during FRELIMO's Eighth Congress in June 2002, as well as within the government. Both FRELIMO and the government reaffirmed the constitutional principle of state land ownership.[74]

This stance has been consistently reiterated in subsequent FRELIMO congresses to this day, despite the government's ongoing efforts to attract substantial foreign investments. However, the unresolved contradictions within FRELIMO, specifically between small-scale and large-scale agriculture, including plantations, persisted.

A clear example of this situation emerged in 2005 when the land once held by the unsuccessful Mozagrius project was transferred to the Malonda Foundation.[75] This foundation operated as a joint venture between the Swedish government and the local population, aiming to utilize the land for the common good.[76] Nevertheless, the Malonda Foundation soon faced challenges as it grappled with disputes from local communities, necessitating substantial alterations in its leadership and operations.[77] In the same year, the government approved PROAGRI II (2006–10), which aimed to transition subsistence farming into commercial agriculture and bolster current production levels.[78]

Foreign investments in large-scale agriculture have shown a consistent and remarkable surge since 2002. This upward trajectory can primarily be attributed to the perceived abundance of expansive, under-exploited arable land in Mozambique, totalling an impressive thirty-six million hectares.[79] This perception has become a significant driving force behind the government's active promotion of large-scale concessions, including plantation development. Between 2004 and 2010 Mozambique granted concessions to foreign companies of close to one million hectares, around 73 per cent for forest and 13 per cent for agrofuels and sugar.[80] In 2008, the Ministry of Agriculture initiated an agrarian zoning project to gain a comprehensive overview of available land within the country and identify additional areas suitable for substantial foreign investment in agriculture.

The findings of this initial study revealed the existence of 7 million hectares of land that could support large-scale agricultural endeavours, accounting for 19.4 per cent of the total arable land. Among this land, 3.7 million hectares were deemed suitable for large-scale agricultural activities, including agrofuel production, while the remaining 3.2 million hectares were allocated for various other purposes, such as forestry and grazing. However, the cabinet expressed reservations about the level of detail in the initial zoning report and subsequently decided to commission a follow-up study conducted by an external consultant. This second zoning study was slated for completion by 2012.[81]

One year following the implementation of the agrarian zoning initiative, additional substantial land concessions were allocated to various entities. Portucel, a Portuguese paper company, secured one such concession, while two Nordic groups, the Malonda Foundation and the Global Solidarity Forest Fund, which includes Nordic churches and a significant Dutch teachers' pension fund,[82] were also granted concessions. In addition, Chikweti received a concession for an expansive area spanning 30,000 hectares.[83]

In December 2009, the Mozambican government through its cabinet granted 10,000 hectares of an area in Gurué to a Portuguese company, QUIFEL, to sow soybean and sunflower for biodiesel. It should be noted that of the total area granted to QUIFEL, 490 hectares were already occupied by 244 local people for more than ten years, and according to the law, they were entitled to rights over that land. Nevertheless, the people were expelled by the government in December 2010.[84]

Gonçalves has highlighted that the prioritization of substantial land investments, including plantation projects, in Mozambique has received renewed impetus in recent years, thanks to the emergence of policies and programs for agricultural development across Africa, collectively referred to as agricultural growth corridors.[85] The Mozambican government has identified six specific corridors within the country for these developments—namely, Nacala, Maputo, Limpopo, Beira, the Zambezi Valley, and Pemba-Lichinga.

The investments mentioned above undeniably demonstrate a significant emphasis on industrial tree plantations, with multiple northern governments participating through various channels, including pension funds.[86] This sustains the continuation of plantation projects, despite extensive research indicating that such endeavours often result in more negative than positive consequences. For instance, Kosenius and colleagues conducted a comprehensive study that highlights several advantages associated with plantations. However, their research also underscores potential drawbacks, such as reduced water availability, limited job creation prospects, and conflicts with local communities.[87] In the specific case of Mozambique, the available evidence overwhelmingly points toward unfavourable outcomes stemming from plantation initiatives, with negative repercussions outweighing the positive ones.[88]

I did fieldwork in 2016 and 2017 in Zambézia and Nampula provinces, two important sites of the Nacala corridor. I observed an increasing tension between the plantation companies and the local people concerning access to both land and water resources. My observations resonate with those of Kosenius and colleagues as well as Almeida and Delgado's assessment of plantations' negative effects on land use changes affecting local livelihood possibilities.

Conclusion

The establishment of a plantation system in Mozambique was a direct consequence of the Portuguese authorities' attempt to administer their country's overseas territories amid the pressure from other colonial powers' expansion projects. Portugal's leasing of the territory to colonial companies was an attempt to respond to two basic problems: first, to ensure an effective occupation of Mozambique, which had been pursued since the fifteenth century, and second, to promote the economic development of Mozambique through the exploitation of human and natural resources. A plantation system encompassed both the above-mentioned problems, resulting in a focus on plantations as the model of land governance.

I argue that Madal epitomizes the Mozambican plantation system and the long-lasting coconut economy is a result of two interconnected factors. First, colonial capitalism consolidated an existing principle of wealth in people and things through several policies and legislation. Second, local customary law was adapted to the colonial law, leading to the coconut economy becoming embedded in society. There was a balance between the control of people (labour) by Madal and of things (palm trees and land) by both Madal and the local people. This pattern of social reproduction is similar to that of other colonial economies where companies paid low wages to keep labour working while households were obliged to carry a large burden. Being a company established more than a hundred years ago, Madal continued to manage plantations until recently, when an ecological crisis in the form of CLYD struck, killing the palm trees belonging to both the residents and Madal. This led to uncertainty and contributed to food insecurity in the area. The failure of the post-independence government to transform land relations in Mozambique attests to the strong structural nature of the economy inherited from the colonial period.

Isaacman and colleagues, Hanlon, and Bowen have shown that there is not much difference between World Bank–approved investments and colonial plantations in terms of the tactics used to dispossess local people, expand corporate control, use local labour, and promote monoculture.[89]

Structural adjustment programs and later the intensification of the scramble for Africa as a result of multiple crises (e.g., fuel, food, finance) have added further incentives for large-scale land deals, in spite of the criticisms related to negative impacts for the people who rely on the land to derive their livelihoods. The plantation system in Mozambique has been confronted historically with the challenge of striking a balance between cash and food crop production. It is well-documented how the tension between the two has led to hunger and death.[90]

Current contract farming arrangements between large-scale investors and residents mirror the colonial project (see, for instance, the prominence of Madal in copra production and export) and will lead to people's alienation from their ancestral land.

Despite the problems associated with large-scale foreign investment in land, the Mozambican government continues to support it. This strong reliance on large-scale investments (plantations for that matter) that provide little benefit for the country has led some analysts to label the current Mozambican economy as an "extractive economy," one that generates but does not accumulate wealth socially (at the dimension of the economy as a whole).[91]

This chapter has highlighted the policy contradictions on land and the role the political elite plays in pushing for a model of large-scale investments that benefit (a few) investors amid the tension between forestry and cash crop plantation investments.

NOTES TO CHAPTER 9

1. Madal was involved in the production of latex used for producing rubber around the 1910s; the company was also involved in other agricultural enterprises and the Electro-Mechanical Company in the 1950s; and, in recent times, the company was involved in navigation services, mining prospection, cereals marketing, game reserves, distribution of food and related products, communication and information services, and fisheries and marine assemblages. Elsa Reiersen, "Scandinavians in Colonial Trading Companies and Capital-Intensive Networks: The Case of Christian Thams," in *Navigating Colonial Orders: Norwegian Entrepreneurship in Africa and Oceania*, ed. Kirsten Alsaker Kjerland and Bjørn Enge Bertelsen (Berghahn Books, 2014), 267–90; Sérgio Chichava, "Vieux Mozambique: L'identité politique de la Zambézie" (PhD diss., Université Montesquieu Bordeaux 4, 2007); Nelson Edwards, Matt Tokar, and Jim Maxwell, *Agribusiness Development in Sub-Saharan Africa: Optimal Strategies and Structures: Final Report*, Technical Paper 83 (Office of Sustainable Development Bureau for Africa, US Agency for International Development, December 1997), https://pdf.usaid.gov/pdf_docs/PNACB834.pdf; Olívia Da Silva Mavie, "Bolsa de valores de Moçambique: a emissão das obrigações do grupo Madal, SARL" (Trabalho de fim de curso de licenciatura, Universidade Eduardo Mondlane, 2001); M. Anne Pitcher, "Sobreviver à transição: O legado das antigas empresas coloniais em Moçambique," *Análise Social* 38, no. 168 (2003): 793–820.
2. Lloyd Best and Kari Levitt, *Externally Propelled Growth in the Caribbean: Selected Essays* (McGill University, 1967); F. Cooper, *Plantation Slavery on the East Coast of Africa* (Yale University Press, 1977).
3. Ajoy Mathew, "Coconut Economy of Kerala," *Social Scientist* 14, no. 7 (1986): 59–70, https://doi.org/10.2307/3517251.
4. Bjørn E. Bertelsen, "Colonialism in Norwegian and Portuguese: Madal in Mozambique, 1904–1930," in *Navigating Colonial Orders: Norwegian Entrepreneurship in Africa and Oceania*, ed. Kirsten A. Kjerland and Bjørn E. Bertelsen (Berghahn Books, 2014), 291–320.
5. José Negrão, "One Hundred Years of African Rural Family Economy: The Zambezi Delta in Retrospective Analysis" (PhD diss., University of Lund, 1995), 101–2.
6. C. Serra, *História de Moçambique, Volume I* (Livraria Universitária, 2000).
7. Negrão, "One hundred Years of African Rural Family Economy."
8. Nina Renee Bowen, "Traders and Livelihood Strategies in Post-Conflict Zambezia Province, Mozambique" (PhD diss., London School of Economics, 2000).
9. José Negrão, *Cem anos de economia da família rural africana: O delta do Zambeze em análise*, 2nd ed. (Promédia, 2001), 12.
10. Allen Isaacman, *Mozambique, the Africanisation of a European Institution: The Zambezi Prazos 1705-1902* (University of Wisconsin Press, 1972); José Capela, "Conflitos Sociais na Zambézia, 1878–1892: A Transição do Senhorio para a Plantação," *Africana Studia 1* (1999): 143–73; Eugénia Rodrigues, "Portugueses e africanos nos Rios de Sena. Os Prazos da Coroa nos Séculos XVII e XVIII" (PhD diss.,Universidade Nova de Lisboa, 2002); Serra, *História*.
11. Negrão, *Cem anos*.
12. Negrão, "One Hundred," 103.
13. Negrão, 101–2.
14. Diego Zonta, "Moçambique e o Comércio Internacional das Oleaginosas (1855 c.–1890 c.)" (master's thesis, Universidade de Lisboa, 2011).
15. James Duffy, *Portuguese Africa* (Harvard University Press, 1959).
16. António Rita-Ferreira, "O Movimento Migratório de Trabalhadores entre Moçambique e a África do Sul," *Junta de Investigação do Ultramar*, 1963.
17. Filipe C. Carvalho, "Distrito de Quelimane: Relatório do Governador 1912–1913" (Imprensa Nacional, 1914).
18. Allen Isaacman and Barbara Isaacman, "Os Prazeiros Como Trans-raianos: Um Estudo Sobre Transformação Social e Cultural," *Arquivo: Boletim do Arquivo Histórico de Moçambique* 10 (1991): 5–48; Serra, *História*.
19. Leroy Vail and Landeg White, *Capitalism and Colonialism in Mozambique: A Study of Quelimane District* (Heinemann, 1980), 107.
20. Vail and White, *Capitalism*, 120.
21. While maintaining control over the remaining regions, which included the southern areas situated south of the Save River, encompassing Inhambane, Gaza, and Maputo Districts. These regions had already become part of a service-driven economy that primarily exported labour to the South African mines.

Furthermore, they were connected to a complex transport system that linked South African railways and ports to the Port of Maputo. Bowen, "Traders."

22 The Mozambique Company was founded in February 1888 and occupied the then Manica and Sofala Districts in an area of approximately 140,000 square kilometres. The Niassa Company was established in September 1891 and occupied the Niassa and Cabo Delgado District in an area of approximately 200,000 square kilometres. Leroy Vail, "Mozambique's Chartered Companies: The Rule of the Feeble," *Journal of African History* 17, no. 3 (1976): 389–416; Vail and White, *Capitalism*; Negrão, "One Hundred."

23 Vail and White, *Capitalism*; Serra, *História*; Bowen, "Traders."

24 According to the legislation, there were four categories of labour—namely, correctional, obligatory, contract and voluntary. Although, in theory, the four types described above indicate a clear separation of labour categories, in reality, the conditions under which all the Africans worked could be considered forced labour. Marvin Harris, "Portugal's African 'Wards': A First-Hand Report on Labour and Education in Mozambique," *Africa Today* 5, no. 6 (November–December 1958): 3–36; Allen Isaacman, "Coercion, Paternalism and Labour Process: The Mozambican Cotton Regime 1938-1961," *Journal of Southern African Studies* 18, no. 3 (1992): 487–526; Esmeralda Simões Martinez, "O Trabalho Forçado na Legislação Colonial Portuguesa: O caso de Moçambique (1899-1926)" (master's dissertation, Universidade de Lisboa, 2008).

25 Vail and White, *Capitalism*; Negrão, "One Hundred."

26 Isaacman, "Coercion"; Judith F. Head, "State, Capital and Migrant Labour in Zambézia, Mozambique: A Study of the Labour Force of Sena Sugar Estates Limited" (PhD diss., University of Durham, 1980); Serra, "Capitalismo."

27 Serra, "Capitalismo," 44.

28 Capela, "Conflitos."

29 Francisco Gavicho de Lacerda, "A Júlia do Carungo," in *Figuras e episódios da Zambézia* (Livraria Rodrigues, 1944), 143–8, http://macua.blogs.com/files/a-julia-do-carungo.pdf.

30 Rodrigues, "Portugueses"; Negrão, "One Hundred."

31 Zonta, "Moçambique."

32 According to my informants from Micaúne, coconut production and trade have been a continuous tradition passed down through generations, predating the establishment of plantation companies.

33 Allen Isaacman, "The Tradition of Resistance in Mozambique," *Africa Today* 22, no. 3 (1975): 37–50.

34 António Rita-Ferreira, *Fixação Portuguesa e Hhistória Pré-colonial de Moçambique* (Instituto de Investigação Científica Tropical, Junta de Investigações Científicas do Ultramar, 1983).

35 Arlindo Chilundo, "Quando Começou o Comércio de Oleaginosas em Moçambique? Levantamento Estatístico da Produção e Exportação do Período 1850 e 1875," *Cadernos de História* 7 (1998): 107–23, quoted in Negrão, "One Hundred," 44.

36 João Rodrigues Sequeira, "Palmares da Zambézia: A Sociétè du Madal (Fearnley. Bobone and Cie) Moçambique," *Moçambique Documentário Trimestral* 38 (Abril-Junho 1944): 61–71; Vail and White, *Capitalism*; Negrão, "One Hundred"; Negrão, *Cem Anos*.

37 César Brandão, "Baptismo em Moçambique: Uma Nota a Rufar," *Magazine*, 27 April 2008, http://brando-magazine.blogspot.com/2008/08/baptismo-em-moambique-uma-nota-rufar.htm.

38 Negrão, "One Hundred," 62.

39 Great Britain Naval Intelligence Division, *A Manual of Portuguese East Africa* (H. M. Stationary, 1920), 166, http://audio11-bu.archive.org/stream/cu31924028621286#page/n3/mode/2up.

40 Brandão, "Baptismo."

41 Negrão, *Cem Anos*, 84–5.

42 FRELIMO (Frente de Libertação de Moçambique) was established in 1962 as a merger of three nationalist movements—the Mozambique African National Union, the National African Union of Independent Mozambique, and the Democratic National Union of Mozambique—to fight against Portuguese colonialism in Mozambique. The movement waged a war against the Portuguese Army in 1964, which culminated with the signing of the Lusaka Accord in 1974 and the declaration of independence by FRELIMO in 1975.

43 Pitcher, "Sobreviver."

44 The creation of RENAMO (Resistência Nacional Moçambicana) was allegedly attributed to Portuguese settlers and business people based either in Rhodesia or South Africa who had lost or were on the way to losing their investments in Mozambique due to the new government's policies as well as to mercenaries, Black and white secret police agents, and former African members of the elite special forces of the Portuguese colonial army who had fled to Rhodesia after Mozambican independence. To this initial

group was added the ex-FRELIMO guerrillas who had been expelled for corruption or had left because of unfulfilled personal ambitions. William Minter, "An Unfinished Journey," in *No Easy Victories: African Liberation and American Activists Over a Half Century, 1950–2000*, ed. William Minter, Gail Hovey, and Charles Cobb Jr. (Africa World Press, 2007), 4, http://www.noeasyvictories.org/select/chap1_lead.php.

45 1975 Constitution, arts. 12, 13, and 14.

46 It is estimated that between 1977 and 1983, approximately 90 per cent of the total state agricultural investment was allocated to state-run farms, with only 2 per cent going to co-operatives, and negligible resources were directed toward household production. Marc Wuyts and Bridget O'Laughlin, "A Questão Agrária em Moçambique," *Estudos Moçambicanos* 3, no. 3 (1981): 9–32.

47 During the colonial and post-colonial periods, both Boror and Madal, which were French-owned companies, established themselves as the primary copra producers in the country. Adolphe Linder, *Os Suíços em Moçambique* (Arquivo Histórico de Moçambique, 2001).

48 The nationalization of Boror was based on the accusation of its owners by the government of depleting the company's capital, sabotaging equipment, destroying documents, and neglecting to pay employees, while the company's managers were accused of smuggling copra out of the country. M. Anne Pitcher, *Transforming Mozambique: The Politics of Privatisation, 1975–2000* (Cambridge University Press, 2002).

49 Morten Rønning, *Development or Exploitation? Grupo Madal in Mozambique* (NorWatch, 2000).

50 The exchange rate is taken from Conversão no Passado, accessed 21 January 2025, https://fxtop.com/pt/conversao-no-passado.php.

51 This illustrates the pervasive promotion of gendered discriminatory policies and practices by colonial companies.

52 During the 1980s, the conflict in Mozambique had escalated to a critical stage, with RENAMO gaining control over substantial parts of the country. This period was marked by the tragic loss of civilian lives, significant damage to economic infrastructure, and a massive displacement of people. According to Hanlon, "From a mid-1980s population of 13–15 million, one million people died (seven per cent of the population) and five million were displaced or made refugees in neighbouring countries (one-third of the population)." Joseph Hanlon, "Killing the Goose that Laid the Golden Eggs," *Moçambique On-line*, September 21, 2001, http://www.mol.co.mz/noticias/metical/2001/en010921.html.

53 Madal, *Relatório de actividades* (1987).

54 For instance, one former minister of the FRELIMO socialist government became a manager of Madal at the beginning of the 1990s. Hanlon, "Killing."

55 Pitcher, "Sobreviver."

56 Rønning, *Development*.

57 Rønning, 10.

58 Joseph Hanlon, "Renewed Land Debate and the 'Cargo Cult' in Mozambique," *Journal of Southern African Studies* 30, no. 3 (2004): 603–25; Joseph Hanlon, *Understanding Land Investment Deals in Africa: Country Report: Mozambique* (Oakland Institute, 2011).

59 Ministry of Planning and Finance, *Privatisation in Mozambique: On the Home Stretch in 1997* (Technical Unit for Enterprise Restructuring, 1997).

60 Merle L. Bowen, "Beyond Reform: Adjustment and Political Power in Contemporary Mozambique," *Journal of Modern African Studies* 30, no 2 (1992): 255–79; M. Anne Pitcher, "Recreating Colonialism or Reconstructing the State? Privatisation and Politics in Mozambique," *Journal of Southern African Studies* 22, no. 1 (1996): 49–74; Ministry of Planning and Finance, *Privatisation*; Edward Lahiff, *The Politics of Land Reform in Southern Africa: Sustainable Livelihoods in Southern Africa*, Research Paper 19 (Institute of Development Studies, 2003).

61 Bowen, "Beyond"; Pitcher "Recreating"; Joseph Hanlon, "Mozambique: 'The War Ended 17 Years Ago, But We Are Still Poor,'" *Conflict, Security & Development* 10, no. 1 (2010): 77–102.

62 Joseph Hanlon, *The Land Debate in Mozambique: Will Foreign Investors, the Urban Elite, Advanced Peasants or Family Farmers Drive Rural Development?* (Oxfam GB, Regional Management Centre for Southern Africa, 2002).

63 Sergei Guriev and Andrei Rachinsky, "The Role of Oligarchs in Russian Capitalism," *Journal of Economic Perspectives* 19, no. 1 (2005): 131–50.

64 Hanlon, "Renewed," 11.

65 José Negrão, "Land in Africa: An Indispensable Element Towards Increasing the Wealth of the Poor," *Universidade de Coimbra: Oficina do Centro de Estudos Sociais* 179 (2002): 1–21; Lahiff, *The Politics*.

66 The campaign centred on the recognition of land possession rights without requiring a land title. It advocated for the state's obligation to consult with rural dwellers before transferring land use and benefit rights to others, aimed at preventing land conflicts. Additionally, it proposed a system of land taxation based on the area's size for commercial purposes and limited recognition of customary rights within constitutional principles, with a focus on defending women's land rights. In essence, the goal was to ensure that every individual was well-informed about their rights and the procedures outlined in the new law. As a result, this movement came to be known as the "Land Campaign," symbolizing the moment when the rural population regained control over their contributions to a national legislative act. José Negrão, "The Mozambican Land Campaign in Mozambique, 1997–1999," paper presented at the Associative Movement of Mozambique, Maputo, December 1999, http://www.caledonia.org.uk/land/mozambiq.htm; José Negrão, "The Mozambican Land Campaign, 1997–1999" (paper presented at the Conference on the Associative Movement of Mozambique, Maputo, December 1999), http://www.caledonia.org.uk/land/mozambiq.htm; Negrão, "Land in Africa."
67 Hanlon, "Renewed."
68 Nazneen Kanji, Carla Braga, and Winnie Mitullah, *Promoting Land Rights in Africa: How Do NGOs Make a Difference?* (International Institute for Environment and Development, 2002).
69 Law 19/97, art. 13, no. 5.
70 Law 19/97, art. 15.
71 Hanlon, "Renewed"; Tanner, "Law-Making," 49.
72 Hanlon, *Understanding*, 3.
73 MINAG (Ministério da Agricultura), *Plano Estratégico para o Desenvolvimento do Sector Agrário (PEDSA) 2011–2010* (MINAG, 2011).
74 Joseph Hanlon, "Resposta às comunidades, doadores e investidores: Terra move-se para topo da agenda política," *Boletim Sobre o Processo Político em Moçambique* 48, no. 1 (2011): 31.
75 Hanlon, "Resposta."
76 The Malonda Foundation managed a substantial land area, encompassing over 75,591 hectares independently and an additional 210,000 hectares in partnership with *Florestas de Niassa*, a company owned by Rift Valley. Rift Valley, registered in Mauritius but based in Zimbabwe, had been controlling Madal since 2005 and owned 80 per cent of Florestas de Niassa, while Malonda held a 20 per cent stake.
77 Hanlon, "Resposta."
78 "Segunda fase do PROAGRI vai custar 270 milhões de USD," *Notícias* (Maputo),10 June 2004.
79 The total land area of Mozambique is 80 million hectares, of which 15 million hectares are protected areas and 10 million hectares are municipalities and roads. Of the remaining 55 million hectares, only 36 million are potentially arable land. Hanlon, "Resposta."
80 Hanlon.
81 Hanlon, *Understanding*, 14.
82 Hanlon, 2.
83 According to Hanlon, more than 10 per cent of Chikweti is owned by Mozambican stakeholders, including entities like the Anglican Diocese of Niassa (approximately 9 per cent), the Malonda Foundation, Eduardo Mondlane University, and individual Mozambicans. Hanlon, *Understanding*, 31.
84 Hanlon, *Understanding*.
85 Euclides Gonçalves, "Agricultural Corridors as 'Demonstration Fields': Infrastructure, Fairs and Associations Along the Beira and Nacala Corridors of Mozambique," *Journal of Eastern African Studies* 14, no. 2 (2020): 454–74.
86 Hanlon, *Understanding*, 2.
87 Anna-Kaisa Kosenius, Matleena Kniivilä, Maja Pitiot, and Paula Horne, "Location of Forest Plantations in Mozambique: Gains and Losses in Water, Firewood and Land Availability," *Land Use Policy* 88 (2019): 104–75, https://doi.org/10.1016/j.landusepol.2019.104175.
88 Kosenius et al., "Location of Forest"; Leonor Serzedelo de Almeida and Christopher Delgado, *The Plantation Forestry Sector in Mozambique: Community Involvement and Jobs* (World Bank Group, 2019).
89 Allen Isaacman et al., "'Cotton Is the Mother of Poverty': Peasant Resistance to Forced Cotton Production in Mozambique, 1938–1961," *International Journal of African Historical Studies* 13, no. 4 (1980): 581–615; Joseph Hanlon, *Mozambique: Who Calls the Shots?* (Indiana University Press, 1991); Bowen, "Beyond."
90 For instance, see Isaacman et al., "'Cotton.'"
91 Carlos N. Castel-Branco, *Economia Extractiva e Desafios de Industrialização em Moçambique* (IESE, 2010); Hanlon, *Understanding*.

10

Land Governance as a Source of Legal Opportunities in Struggles Around Large-Scale Land Acquisitions in Mozambique

Laura Gerken

Introduction

External control and land use in Mozambique has taken multiple forms from colonial times until today. In the context of the food, financial, and energy crises, specifically since 2008, large-scale land acquisitions (LSLA)[1] became a globally increasing phenomenon as investors tried to find solutions to bypass these challenges. The rush for land targets mainly areas in the Global South,[2] particularly in sub-Saharan Africa. On the one hand, such investments promise economic growth and development for the target countries. On the other, the rural population living in the areas covered by these investments often lacks strong protection of its used land, mainly because 90 per cent of the total land area in sub-Saharan Africa is governed through customary systems.[3]

In the same period, the governance of land increased on several levels. Transnationally and regionally, many rights and regulations particularly focus on land issues. But also documents about development, human rights, and environmental issues increasingly recognized the crucial role of land for rural livelihoods and well-being. Similarly, several countries adopted more detailed approaches to address land issues in their legislation. In the context of increasing LSLA and the protection of land tenure, Mozambique provides a puzzling frame. While it already strengthened customary rights in its land law of 1997, it was still one of the main targets of LSLA in Africa since the beginning of the rush for land.[4] Moreover, large-scale investments in land provoked resistance or conflicts addressing social and environmental impacts in most, if not all, cases.

Drawing on social movement literature about legal opportunity structures, I compare the Luso-historical trajectory and analyze the social mobilization around two examples of LSLA in Mozambique to discuss the following question: How is land governance a source of legal opportunities for social movements in struggles around LSLA? To this end, the chapter starts with an overview of the characteristics of LSLA. This is followed by a section about the trajectory of the Mozambican land legislation. The approach of legal opportunity structures is then depicted. Based on data gathered during fieldwork in Mozambique, I will present the cases of the Wanbao project and the ProSavana program and provide insights into the Luso-history of the project sites. This is followed by a reflection on the use of rights and regulations as reference points in the social mobilization in both. Finally, a concluding discussion contrasts the findings.

The Rise of Large-Scale Land Acquisitions

Since the mid-2000s, academics, non-governmental organizations (NGOs), and the media have paid increasing attention to LSLA. Particularly after a report of the NGO Grain describing a "rush into farmland," different actors have problematized this phenomenon.[5] LSLA is characterized by a sharp increase of investments in land on a global scale and, consequently, more competition for land. Target areas of these investments are often located in sub-Saharan Africa, Asia, Latin America, and to a lesser extent in Oceania and eastern Europe.[6] Countries of the Global South, especially, were the main targets in the early stages of LSLA. In many of these countries, land use is regulated through customary rights.

Acquisitions, taking, and loss of land happened throughout history, especially during colonialism, and LSLA shares some similarities with those processes. As in the first decade of the 1900s, global economic commodity crises triggered the rush for land in Africa.[7] In Mozambique, large-scale production on plantations of colonial companies dates back to the same period. As in colonial large-scale production—for instance, in the case of Madal[8]—current large-scale projects are closely related to the setting up and expansion of infrastructure. Moreover, in both circumstances, the rationale behind agricultural modernization is the substitution of the peasantry with larger production patterns.[9] Also, foreign investors were often involved in Mozambican large-scale production during colonial times, and they remain so today.[10]

Yet, LSLA still has some specific characteristics that mark it as a new development. As Potts notes when comparing LSLA with the colonial past in southern

Africa, land is offered by sovereign states and not within a colonial system.[11] Payments for the current transfer of land are made, though to different extents. Also, the economic interest behind the large-scale production differs insofar as colonial production was mainly incentivized for intensification, while LSLA focuses more on exports. Lastly, she stresses the differing cultural component. While colonial large-scale production was implicated in questions of tradition, settlement, and identity, current investments do not address these aspects.[12] The communities in the vicinity of such projects are not forced labourers, as happened in colonial large-scale production,[13] nor are they regarded as hindrances of modernization, but may become part of the project and may profit from it.[14] Another difference is the Mozambican legal context—namely, the requirement to consult potentially affected communities before starting a project.[15]

Besides these (dis)continuities with colonial large-scale investments in Mozambique, the phenomenon of LSLA cannot be regarded independently from the context of globally rising LSLA and its peculiarities since the mid-2000s: States voluntarily transfer the land to investors and promote large-scale projects to support economic growth.[16] The stakeholders involved are not necessarily governments or governmental corporations but cover a wide variety of transnationally linked actors, foreign direct investments, or development projects in North-South and South-South relations.[17] The overall development, size, and velocity points, following Sassen, "to a break in a long-term trend that might indicate a larger structural transformation in an old practice."[18] Such land investments are characterized by the transfer of land (use) rights of large areas of more than two hundred hectares of land,[19] and for long periods ranging between thirty to ninety-nine years, either in the form of leases or sales.[20] The complex interrelations of investors are one reason for the opacity of LSLA deals, many of which are undertaken without sufficient information about large-scale land projects.[21]

The Trajectory of Mozambican Land Regulation

Mozambique provides an especially interesting frame through which to study large-scale land projects and land rights. First, it has been one of the main targets of LSLA in Africa since the beginning of this phenomenon, in terms of both the number and size of investments, in accordance with land use prices and the political will needed to attract investments that would yield the promised benefits of LSLA.[22] Second, at the same time, several of these projects provoked resistance that ranged from *everyday forms of resistance*, including sabotage from the local population, to large-scale transnational networking and campaigns of social movements. Third, the Mozambican land law is often described in the literature as "one of the most progressive land laws in Africa" because it is a formalization of the customary land right.²³ The current land law, the Lei de Terras, dates back to 1997 and follows the legacy of the independent constitution in which land use rights are granted, yet land cannot be possessed by anybody other than the state. In the following, I summarize the development of land governance in Mozambique, depicting customary, colonial, post-colonial, and post-independence land regulation up to today's debate about the revision of the land policy and land law.

The customary law is not uniform throughout the whole country, but what can be said in a general way is that land is traditionally passed through inheritance.²⁴ Until the eighteenth century, the Portuguese colonizers, whose presence dates back to the landing of Vasco da Gama in 1498, had little interest in the interior and only opened provisioning stations along the coastline. In the late seventeenth and early eighteenth centuries, they introduced the *prazo* system, in which Portuguese settlers, the *prazeiros*, governed the land and the people on it in a feudal-like system.²⁵ This was still focused on the coasts until what is today Mozambique was annexed to Portugal at the Berlin Conference of 1884–5. Thereupon, the Portuguese established provincial governors in the 1890s and early 1900s and restructured, often while downsizing, existing chiefdoms and maintained control by involving the chiefs.²⁶ This system ignored differences between the North and the South of the country, as traditionally in the North, local elders, rather than chieftaincies, were the ruling institution. The social organization was thus oriented along southern Mozambican traditions and artificially imposed on the northern parts of the country.²⁷

In the same period, the Portuguese introduced three big companies, the Niassa Company, the Zambezia Company, and the Mozambique Company, to produce cash crops in the central and northern parts of the country. The economic model in southern Mozambique was based on labour migration to South African mines, which created cash revenues for the area.²⁸ In 1901, a land law allocated all land not privately owned into state ownership, resulting in land loss and displacement of the African population, as traditional land tenure was disregarded. While Africans were able to claim use rights for land utilized for more than twenty years, it was only granted if nobody else showed interest in it, leaving Africans at a legal disadvantage.²⁹ In his book of 1969, Mondlane concludes that the Portuguese land rights did not change much after that.³⁰

After the Portuguese abandonment of colonial farms in 1975, all land was nationalized in the Republic of Mozambique's first constitution. These areas turned into state farms and communal fields, where Mozambicans were expected to work.³¹ Consequently, after independence, land use was characterized by collectivized farms, villagization, and state farms. The collectivized farms date back to the armed struggle of the 1960s. For the villagization, more than 20 per cent of the population were resettled after 1975 (see Aharon deGrassi's chapter in this volume for more on this process). As for the state farms, the villagization program led to land use conflicts, were costly, and negatively affected agricultural production.[32]

The first post-independence land law dates to 1979, four years after independence. It puts a focus on the family sector, including households and communities. As in the 1975 constitution of the republic, land is owned by the state and cannot be possessed.[33] Instead, individuals or communities can get the right to use and benefit from land (Direito de Uso e Aproveitamento da Terra, or DUAT).[34]

Due to the difficulties in the collectivized production, the FRELIMO[35] party's Fourth Congress in 1983 changed the economic development strategy, reorganized the state farms, and shifted the focus from large-scale to rather small-scale production support.[36] Accordingly, the private sector gained more attention as FRELIMO opened it with a structural adjustment program, following donor support for economic recovery, structural rehabilitation, demobilization, and other measures.[37] This unlocked the opportunity for private investors to occupy and invest in land, such as abandoned co-operative and state farms.[38]

With the revision of the land right in 1995, a more liberalized land policy was introduced, which enabled further investments to support economic development after consulting communities.[39] These changes laid the legal ground for the land law of 1997. The land policy resulted from a debate between a large variety of actors, including officials, civil society organizations, international organizations, peasants, and others. Between interests for liberalization and aims to support customary rights, the resulting law builds on traditional land distribution and use.[40] As mentioned before, land was also owned by the colonial state or its companies during Portuguese rule. However, under independence, the rationale is the state's socialist ideology, as the state that owns the land is constituted by its own people.

According to the current land law, if nationals, individually and collectively, use land for more than ten years and have a witness for that, they have a DUAT. It does not matter whether this is officially registered or noted; the right is in place as soon as these conditions are fulfilled.[41] It can, however, be additionally registered at public registration services. The existence of land use rights even in the absence of documentation allowed this practice to persist without a comprehensive cadastral system. DUATs may be revoked for the sake of public interest.[42] The above-mentioned opportunity of the African population to claim land if they used it for more than twenty years in the early twentieth century was imbalanced and unequal. Still, the mechanism behind granting the land (i.e., the base for land claims) is very much alike.

Those interested in claiming land that was not used before by an individual or a community must first consult the community living in the area to ensure that the land is available and not already used. If land is then granted to nationals for family farming or habitation, the DUAT does not expire and can be passed through inheritance.[43] If the interest in the land is economic in nature, communities in the area must be consulted at least twice—first to inform them about the intended project, and second to discuss (dis)agreement and compensation.[44] Investors must provide a project plan and get a provisional DUAT once an agreement with the community is made. After two years for foreigners and five years for nationals, the project's progress is evaluated and, if found to be in accordance with the project plan, the use right is renewed to a fifty-year DUAT.[45]

In 2017, President Filipe Nyusi announced the revision of the land policy. The ensuing debate has taken place, especially since 2020, alongside public hearings involving different actors, including civil society organizations. While this process aims to respond to current socio-economic developments in the country, the land is supposed to remain in state ownership. In sum, some mechanisms of land assessment and the ownership of land by the government resemble colonial land regulation. What is different is that the current Mozambican land right includes and supports customary rights, and civil society organizations are involved in past and ongoing debates addressing land.[46]

Rights and Regulations as Legal Opportunities

As just described, civil society organizations push for and are involved in creating and elaborating legal instruments dealing with land governance. Activists may use these rights and regulations in campaigns and various efforts at social mobilization to support claims. Building on social movement literature, I argue that such legal instruments offer opportunity structures for social mobilization around land. More specifically, if activists regard rights or regulations as useful in their work, they become *legal opportunity structures*. Actors must perceive opportunities as such, as they are not objectively given but actively created by agents.[47]

Legal opportunity structures encompass norms, guidelines, legislation, access to courts, and judicial receptivity, thus the legal context in which social mobilization unfolds. Focusing in this contribution on land rights, activists may refer strategically to such to embed their claims and increase their legitimacy.[48] Also, if such legal instruments are violated, they may point at this, call for their improvement, or hold actors accountable. To be clear, the repeated reference to legal instruments that have been violated may open up this legal opportunity.[49] In the following, I will show how multi-level rights and regulations as legal opportunities unfold in two cases of mobilization around LSLA. While the national legal framework is the first reference point for claims in both cases, other domestic laws and cross-border legal instruments likewise constitute important benchmarks when addressing the lack of information about projects or social and environmental (anticipated) impacts.

Data and Methods

The data for the comparative case study is a result of fieldwork conducted from March to June 2019 in Mozambique, where I researched two examples of resistance to large-scale projects: the Wanbao rice farm in Gaza Province and the ProSavana program in the country's North. In a most-similar case design, both projects share certain general aspects, such as an agricultural purpose, experiencing resistance, involving several civil society actors, and social mobilization beginning in 2012 (see table 10.1). Beyond these similarities, the cases differ in many general conditions. In the case of Wanbao, the social mobilization began once the project started, while ProSavana experienced resistance in its planning phase. Lastly, both varied substantially in terms of size. The Wanbao project area, never fully exploited, covers 20,000 hectares, while ProSavana was planned on up to 14.5 million hectares.[50]

Luso-historically, due to the ambiguities of the ProSavana project plan, descriptions about the area can only be made in broad terms,[51] in contrast to more specific details about the history of the Wanbao project area. In the latter, rice production dates back to colonial times, when intensification through an irrigation scheme increased the agricultural output, but this stopped when the Portuguese abandoned the country in 1975.[52] In the three provinces included in the ProSavana project plans, broadly speaking, either colonial companies or other colonial plantations schemes were active. Nampula, the province addressed to the largest extent by ProSavana, produced especially cotton, which was sometimes successful but other times not.[53]

After independence, large parts of Mozambique underwent restructuring to villagization, state farms, and co-operative farms, as was the case with the Wanbao area and parts of the ProSavana project area.[54] The infrastructure makes both areas attractive for large-scale agricultural production; in the case of Wanbao, the irrigation scheme, and in the case of ProSavana, the railway. Both were constructed in the colonial period and have been rehabilitated and extended since the 2000s.[55]

Table 10.1. Comparison of Wanbao and ProSavana

	Wanbao	ProSavana
Investor	Chinese Private Company	Governments of Mozambique, Japan, Brazil
Location & Size	Gaza Province	Nacala Corridor
	20,000 hectares (originally planned)	14.5 million hectares (disputed, not officially confirmed)
Purpose	Agricultural development project;	Agricultural development project;
	Large-scale plantations	Large-scale plantations
Luso-History	Rice plantations set up in 1950s	Partly managed by colonial companies between 1890s and 1930s.
		plantations for different cash crops, as in Nampula around 1950s
Infrastructural Special Features	Drainage and irrigation Scheme	Railway with connection to ports
Beginning	Followed smaller Chinese project of 2005	Basic framework signed in 2009
Public Information	2012 with project implementation	2011 in planning phase
Involved Actors in Mobilization	Alliance of local groups, national* NGOs, and individuals	Alliance of local, national* and international NGOs, and individuals (Mozambique, Brazil, Japan)
Activities (Selected)	Occupation, Demonstrations, Petitions, (Open) Letters	Demonstrations, Petitions, Open Letters, Lawsuit
Situation until 2020	Project Area Reduced	Project Paused, Adjustment since 2015, Abandoned in 2020

*embedded in transnational networks.
Source: Compiled by author.

While Wanbao is located in the country's South, ProSavana was planned for the North, two areas that differ demographically and politically. Historically, large colonial companies were only set up north of the Save River. Many labourers from southern Mozambique migrated to South African mines and supported the local economy back home through remittances.[56]

Methodologically, this depiction and discussion of the historical background are based on a secondary literature review. Further, I studied the mechanisms that enable social mobilization to unfold in situations of LSLA. My assumption is that information about project plans and intentions are vague, as this is characteristic of such projects, and that the increasing governance of land offers opportunity structures to activists. The data derive from thirty-four semi-structured expert interviews with a broad variety of actors, such as activists, researchers, officials, business experts, and a small number of peasants. Interview transcripts were analyzed with a structuring content analysis after Mayring.[57] Additionally, campaign documents serve as complementary sources for the analysis. Regarding limitations, it is essential to mention the lack of clarity in several regards as relates to LSLA. For instance, publications about project size, people living in the project area, and related issues are often contradictory.[58] Also, the limited access to officials from different levels as interviewees results in a lack of broader governmental perspectives on the cases.

The Case of Wanbao

The Wanbao project is a privately owned rice plantation in the area around the city of Xai-Xai, the capital of Gaza Province. Ganho distinguished four historical phases of irrigated agricultural production in the area: "from colonial capitalism (1950s–1975) to Socialist/planned economy (1975–1983), and transition to market economy (1983–2000) to the current (2000–present) market economy."[59]

White immigration to Mozambique only gathered pace after World War II, and large irrigation schemes, as well as grants and loans, attracted Portuguese settlers.[60] As happened in the Lower Limpopo Valley, where the Portuguese introduced a drainage and irrigation scheme for flood controls,[61] the Regadio do Baixo Limpopo (RBL) enabled rice and other cash crop production. With as many as half of the male workers from that area migrating to South African mines, mainly female forced labourers worked at the production sites.[62] The area of the RBL extended from 400 hectares in 1952 to 11,300 hectares by 1967. As a consequence, agricultural production intensified.[63]

After independence in 1975, a mass out-migration of white settlers, who controlled most sectors of the colonial economy, caused an economic crisis. In the Lower Limpopo Valley, specifically, it caused the disintegration of colonial commercial agriculture, as it resulted in the abandonment of the coordination and maintenance of the irrigations scheme.[64] From 1975 to 1983, besides communal villages and co-operatives in the area, FRELIMO created the Unidade de Produção do Baixo Limpopo (UPBL). This large state farm sector took over the former Portuguese agricultural land in the context of the national agricultural development plan after independence.[65] In 1977, a severe flood decreased the productivity in the area, and damaged homes and livestock as well as the drainage and irrigations system.[66] Another agency, the Lower Limpopo Irrigation System, has managed water and water infrastructure since 1978.[67]

After FRELIMO's Fourth Congress, which reformed the collectivized agricultural production, regional coordination structures, called Unidade de Direcção Agricola (UDA), were created. The UDA of Xai-Xai was set up in 1985. It divided the UPBL into six smaller state farms. At the same time, some abandoned land from unsuccessful co-operatives and state farmland was allocated to private medium-scale farmers and peasants.[68]

After 1992, with the end of the civil war, rehabilitation of the irrigation system was planned but delayed until the early 2000s. For a decade, production at the RBL stopped, due to further destruction of infrastructure by another large flood in 2000 and further labour migration to South Africa. With the financial support of the African Development Bank, a rehabilitation project targeting parts of the former infrastructure and the reorganization of agricultural production started in 2003.[69] RBL is now organized into twelve blocks, used by different groups, including smallholder groups, medium-scale farmers, and a Chinese and a Portuguese company. Still, RBL is publicly owned and covered around 12,000 hectares in 2013.[70]

In 2005, the Chinese Hubei Province and the Mozambican Gaza Province signed an agreement for a co-operative project to test different varieties of rice and implement production on 300 hectares. In 2008, this program started similar testing on a smaller scale, but this ended in 2012.[71] That year, a private Chinese investor took over and founded Wanbao Africa Agriculture Development Limited, intended as a development program. It aims to improve local rice production through technology transfer and the introduction of more fertile varieties. The project was planned on an area of 20,000 hectares and included the setting up of rice processing facilities.[72] It is embedded in a national strategic plan for agricultural development. By 2014, the project was running on 7,000 hectares.[73]

After the flooding of the project area in 2013 and 2015, the Chinese government cancelled a loan due to the flood-prone location. Since then, the financing has remained insecure.[74] Still, the project was running during my fieldwork in 2019, and an interviewee reported that it was active on 8,000 hectares by that time.

Once the private Wanbao project started in 2012, it gained more attention from the local population as civil society organizations raised concerns about displacement and water access.[75] Extending the project area, workers started plowing up family farms and small-scale farms. They destroyed crops ready for harvest, so local producers organized and addressed the district government. Confronted with unresponsiveness on the part of local officials, they went back to their farms and blocked the land to stop further destruction.[76] Wanbao, in turn, did not see itself as responsible for the conflict, as this land was granted to the project in the agreements concluded with the state.[77]

In parallel, civil society organizations of national reach started investigating Wanbao after hearing about the project and the resulting conflict. After some unsuccessful requests at the RBL agency, they finally arranged a meeting, and the land was returned to the farmers within the year.[78] In 2013, Wanbao resumed its work on the same land, which provoked an even larger response from peasants, peasant associations, and provincial and national civil society organizations. Activities included a demonstration that ended with handing over a petition to the provincial governor in 2014, and an open letter to the then–President of the Republic Armando Guebuza, among others.[79] Also, activists continue to use the biannually meeting provincial exchange platform Observatório de Desenvolvimento (Observatory of Development) to raise concerns repeatedly. The network of individuals and organizations involved in the social mobilization continuously exchanges information about the situation.

Rights and regulations on the transnational, domestic, and traditional levels present essential reference points for activists in statements and campaign documents. Activists explained that legal instruments help them to support claims and show that issues raised are not mere sensitivities but are in fact legally grounded. Foremost, the land law and the Constitution of the Republic are central domestic legal tools to address land access, traditional customs, and the importance of rural development, and both place the people at the centre. Further, activists stressed that the right of community consultation, compensation after the transfer of land rights, and the DUAT itself was violated. This is because people were not included in planning processes and the land was granted to the company, even though the DUAT exists through the use of land for ten years. Other domestic laws not directly addressing land issues supported claims and campaign documents, including the environmental law, the decree of resettlement, and others.

Transnational rights and regulations, then, embed concerns legally to further increase the legitimacy of claims: "It gives more weight, more emphases, to show that not only the national right, but also internationally this issue is recognized and defended. So, this gives more weight and more emphasis."[80] Understanding traditional rights as rules within local communities likewise constitutes legal opportunity structures. Peasants living around the Wanbao project area backed their concerns by first explaining their ownership of the land due to inheritance. Still, they added that the domestic land right also supports this claim. The lack of transparency concerning the project especially is thematized in the context of transnational concepts, such as free, prior, and informed consent (FPIC), rooted in the rights of Indigenous peoples. In the same regard, different campaign documents refer to regulations that link land rights and information access in the context of investments, such as the International Labour Organization's ILO Convention 169. In sum, concerns are raised with the support of domestic and transnational legal opportunity structures, entwining social rights, such as community or labour rights, environmental rights, and transparency.

The Case of ProSavana

The Program of Triangular Co-Operation for Developing Agriculture in the Tropical Savannahs of Mozambique (hereafter ProSavana) was a trilateral development project of the governments of Mozambique, Brazil, and Japan. The implementation area was located in parts of the Nacala Corridor, specifically in its eastern sector in the provinces of Niassa, Zambezia, and Nampula, covering nineteen districts.[81] As mentioned above, the information about the intended project size varies hugely, with some sources mentioning 6 million hectares,[82] but many others saying 14.5 million hectares.[83] An interviewee involved in the project planning stated that the latter figure is based on miscommunication.

This uncertainty about the actual extent of the project makes it challenging to trace its history. Following the program's master plan, large parts of the three provinces are included in a ProSavana study. This area (see map 10.1) is also a reference point for many of ProSavana's critics. Following the master plan, of the 19 districts involved, 10 are located in Nampula Province, 7 in Niassa Province, and 2 in Zambezia Province.[84]

Looking at the Luso-history of the project area, the Companhia do Niassa, or the Niassa Company, was established in 1891 to manage today's Niassa and Cabo Delgado Provinces. It had sovereign rights in its territory and could grant sub-concessions. Established to strengthen the Portuguese presence and develop the economy, the company failed to fulfill these purposes.[85] Sub-concessions to foreign investors undermined Portuguese dominance, and ongoing under-financing prevented the desired economic development.[86] In 1928, the company was consequently dissolved.[87] While another colonial company was found in Zambezia Province,[88] the two districts of the province included in the ProSavana project plan were not part of its territory.

The majority of ProSavana's area is in Nampula Province. Due to fertile soils and the production of cash crops, such as sisal, cashews, and especially cotton in the area, the colonial government built an east–west railroad in the province to reach the port of Nacala.[89] Agricultural production at colonial companies, such as the cotton producer Companhia dos Algodões de Moçambique, turned some small-scale farms into production sites around the 1950s.[90] While some of those

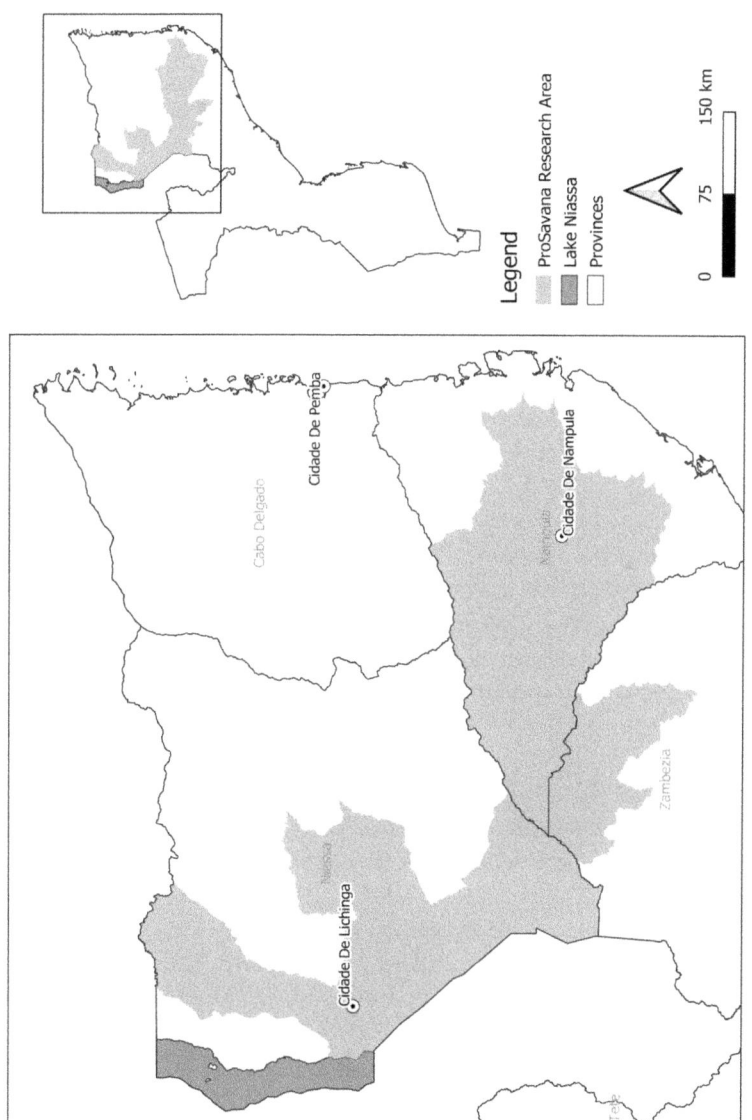

Map 10.1. ProSavana research area in northern and central Mozambique

Source: Gerken based on Ministério da Agricultura e Segurança Alimentar, "Plano director para o desenvolvimento agrário do Corredor de Nacala em Moçambique." Esboço versão 0. Cooperação triangular para o desenvolvimento agrário da savana tropical em Moçambique (2015); Open Street Map. Cartography: Rui Pinto.

10 | Land Governance as a Source of Legal Opportunities   *231*

production patterns prospered in the province, others were unsuccessful. The latter often occurred in areas with poor infrastructure.[91]

Regarding infrastructure, many argue that the existing infrastructure today, especially the railway, made the area of the Nacala Corridor particularly attractive for the ProSavana project. A decree for the construction of the railway was signed in 1912 to connect, as said before, the cotton production of Nampula Province first with the Lumbo port and later with the Nacala port. The first track sections opened in 1924. In the 1970s, it was extended to Malawi.[92] To connect the Moatize coal mines in Tete Province with the port, the railway was further expanded in the 2000s. This project is embedded in the Nacala Agricultural Growth Corridor, part of a national strategic development plan for economic development.[93]

Following the original ProSavana project plan, the area should be used to grow soybeans and maize on plantations. The project Prodecer in the Brazilian Cerrado served as a model and dated back to the 1970s when it was supported by Japanese capital.[94] Brazil's role in the ProSavana project thus was to transfer gained know-how to increase the production in Mozambique, as happened in Prodecer. Politically, then–President of Brazil Luiz Inácio Lula da Silva and his government also promoted South-South co-operation.[95] Japan's input in ProSavana is the capital, but also its experience of agribusiness co-operation with Brazil. Further, the produced crops would be exported to the Japanese market. Mozambique itself was supposed to provide land, labour, and fiscal benefits for the project, and was expected to increase production and economic development.[96]

ProSavana's basic framework was signed in 2009, but the Mozambican public only learned about it in 2011 after an interview with the country's minister of agriculture, José Pacheco, with a Brazilian newspaper.[97] This information travelled via Brazilian activists to those in Mozambique, the two groups already co-operating in other contexts. Followed by further reports in the media and speeches, more insights into the intended project were given. The lack of clear information about ProSavana raised mistrust, and, driven by concerns about land loss and potential social and environmental impacts, civil society actors tried to learn more about it.[98] Using existing networks, activists reached out to already established partners in Brazil and created new linkages with civil society in Japan. In 2012, members of Mozambican peasant organizations were invited by their Brazilian partners to visit the Cerrado. Networks already existed through memberships in umbrella organizations, such as La Via Campesina, and international NGOs that are active in both countries. After the trip, a documentary about the environmental and social impacts of monocultures in the Cerrado was released in Mozambique to inform about the project and mobilize people.[99] Partnering

Japanese NGOs raised concerns at a policy dialogue forum with the Ministry of Foreign Affairs in Japan in the same year.[100]

In 2013, a confidential master plan for the project was leaked, which led to further contestation of the agribusiness-oriented project. Though the three governments involved stressed that the plan was merely preliminary, it triggered further mistrust.[101] Activists intensified their trilateral network, published joint statements and open letters, organized exchange conferences in the three countries, and launched the campaign *Não ao ProSavana* (No to ProSavana).[102] In the following month, the program received less attention because the upcoming elections in Mozambique shifted the public focus. Likewise, in Brazil, attention moved toward the elections in 2014 and the country's political crisis, which led to the impeachment of Dilma Rousseff in 2016. The subsequent interim administration did not revive the Brazilian role in the ProSavana project.[103]

In 2015, a revisited master plan was published; it sought to respond to some of the raised concerns but was still contested as it failed to address all reservations and was often vaguely formulated. Besides that, the Ministry of Agriculture and Food Security invited civil society actors to annual exchange meetings to further revise the program.[104] Though these meetings still took place in the following years, the end of the ProSavana project was announced in 2020.[105]

As in the case of Wanbao, several rights and regulations were invoked in the activism around the project. Likewise, they served the purpose to either support and legally embed claims or point toward the violation of specific legal instruments. However, the latter was used less frequently in the case of ProSavana, which is mainly due to the fact that the two social mobilizations started at different points in time. In the case of Wanbao, the project was already running, while in the case of ProSavana, complaints were raised in its planning phase. Again, rights and regulations were thought to be useful for showing that activists' concerns were not random but enforced through legal documents. Though the whole social mobilization involved the transnational realm, the domestic land law and the Constitution of the Republic were still core reference points for claims, as was mentioned, for instance, in a campaign document ("We encourage the government to scrupulously observe the Land Law and the Article 109, paragraph 3 of the Constitution of the Republic and ensure its implementation"),[106] which talks about the crucial role of land for the wealth and well-being of the Mozambican people.[107]

As in the other case, further domestic laws together provided legal opportunities, especially rights addressing information access and transparency. Transnational rights and regulations again comprised complementary benchmarks and covered the topics of human rights, food security, and information access. These issues are not treated individually, but are instead closely interrelated, as a campaign statement demanding more transparency claims: "1) respect for human rights, 2) improved transparency and accountability, and 3) valid and 'Meaningful Dialogue' based on FPIC."[108] As in the case of Wanbao, domestic and transnational rights and regulations thus constitute legal opportunity structures to embed and legitimize claims or show that existing rules have been violated.

Concluding Discussion

The comparison of the Luso-historical background of the two cases and the resistance they engendered indicated similarities and differences but also pointed to larger (dis)continuities of practices and regulation since colonial times. At the same time, innovative aspects of legal instruments constitute reference points in activism to challenge continuities of agricultural production schemes.

Before diving into the case comparison, it is necessary to frame and stress the extent to which LSLA constitutes a new phase and is not a straight continuation of land concessions. Though foreign investors were already involved in the concessions of colonial companies in Mozambique, the current wave of new investments in farmland is embedded in a global context. Still, as outlined above, Porsani sees a continuation of the production model that aims to substitute smallholder farmers with large-scale production schemes.[109] In the same regard, Li points out that monocultures are still given preference over small-scale farmers in Indonesia,[110] and this chapter showed that the same happened in the two cases studied in Mozambique.

Comparing the trajectory of land use in Wanbao and ProSavana, even if much more concrete in the first and vague in the second, they share some similarities regarding the colonial past. In both cases, the closeness to particular pieces of infrastructure makes the project area highly attractive for cash crop production. Both under Portuguese rule and today, access to an irrigation scheme in Gaza or the railway in the Nacala Corridor promises benefits.

Another trajectory points toward contrasts between the projects themselves. Wanbao is set up in the area of a former colonial plantation. Yet the dimensions of both the colonial production and the Wanbao project are much smaller than the intended ProSavana project. Likewise, the central and northern areas of Mozambique were governed by gigantic colonial companies in the past. This divide thus constitutes another continuity of land use in the different parts of the country. The differences between the country's North and the South are a long-standing issue. Northern customs were ignored during colonial land governance, and southern social structures were imposed on the North. As shown in the area of the Wanbao project, labour migration to South Africa supported the local economy through remittances. And even today, the South of Mozambique is wealthier than the North.

Regarding the legal context in Mozambique, the current land law features some widely praised paragraphs, especially those espousing support of community rights, the closeness of the law to customary land governance, and the requirement to consult potentially affected communities before signing an investment treaty. Still, some continuities from the colonial regime appear in the area of land governance. It is the case that the state owns the land and that use rights might be granted. While the ideologies in the different periods differs strongly, the mechanism for granting land use rights is very similar to that of the past. Also, as mentioned in the beginning of this discussion, concessions to companies are often granted, even without implementing community consultations, or informing local communities at all.[111]

Still, the law protects peasant rights and community rights, making it a useful tool to challenge large-scale projects like Wanbao and ProSavana. In both cases, governance instruments play an essential role in advancing claims as legal opportunity structures, linking social, environmental, and transparency issues. As described above, legal opportunities in the form of rights and regulations can be used in two ways: either to increase the legitimacy of a claim by legally embedding it, or to point toward the violation of a specific rule. About the first, complaints are made in an anticipatory way to bring about compliance with rights and regulations in the future. In the activism around Wanbao and ProSavana, legal opportunities were used in this way. However, I argue that this type was more prevalent in the case of ProSavana, as the project itself has not yet started, so concerns instead addressed potential harmful impacts.

Regarding the second way of using rights and regulations as legal opportunities, claims are made about neglecting a specific right. This occurred in both cases and often thematized a lack of transparency in the projects. Specifically, the land law and its language related to community consultation offered in this context an important benchmark. The activists are agents creating this legal opportunity by repeatedly referring to a law, even if it has been violated. Following my analysis, this type was used in the case of Wanbao due to the fact that the social mobilization only started once the project began—that is, when specific rights had already been violated.

Besides domestic legal instruments, transnational ones also constituted reference points for advancing claims. Domestically, a variety of laws, but foremost the land law and the Constitution of the Republic, with its focus on community rights, proved helpful. In this regard, linkages were created between land use, the inclusion of (potentially) affected communities, and transparency. Likewise, transnationally, a broad range of rights and regulations concerning human rights, transparency, and community inclusion are reference points in documents and claims.

Overall, both cases are alike in that each project saw a lack of transparency that shaped the resistance and social mobilization around it. In such situations, even if information is later shared, the atmosphere is already marked by mistrust about the specific project, as well as the general perception about large-scale investments.

NOTES TO CHAPTER 10

1. The phenomenon is described in different terms, some of which some (e.g., "land grabbing") are normatively loaded. I instead use the more neutral "large-scale land acquisitions."
2. I am aware of the generalization the term "Global South" makes and try to be specific where possible. For a deeper discussion about the use of such terminology, see Nina Schneider, "Between Promise and Skepticism: The Global South and Our Role as Engaged Intellectuals," *Global South* 11, no. 2 (2017): 18–38.
3. Liz Alden Wily, "Enclosure Revisited: Putting the Global Land Rush in Historical Perspective," in *Handbook of Land and Water Grabs in Africa: Foreign Direct Investment and Food and Water Security*, ed. Tony Allan, Martin Keulertz, Suvi Sojamo, and Jeroen Warner (Routledge, 2013), 11–23; Lorenzo Cotula, Sonja Vermeulen, Rebeca Leonard, and James Keeley, *Land Grab or Development Opportunity? Agricultural Investment and International Land Deals in Africa* (International Institute for Environment and Development, 2009); Annelies Zoomers, "Globalisation and the Foreignisation of Space: Seven Processes Driving the Current Global Land Grab," *Journal of Peasant Studies* 37, no. 2 (2010): 429–47.
4. Klaus Deininger et al., *Rising Global Interests in Farmland: Can It Yield Sustainable and Equitable Benefits?* (World Bank, 2011); GRAIN, *Seized! GRAIN Briefing Annex: The 2008 Land Grabbers for Food and Financial Security* (GRAIN, 2008); Kerstin Nolte, Wytske Chamberlain, and Markus Giger, *International Land Deals for Agriculture: Fresh Insights from the Land Matrix: Analytical Report II* (Land Matrix, 2016), 17.
5. Deininger et al., *Rising Global Interests*, xiv, 51f.; GRAIN, *Seized!*, 8.
6. Saturnino M. Borras Jr., Ruth Hall, Ian Scoones, Ben White, and Wendy Wolford, "Towards a Better Understanding of Global Land Grabbing: An Editorial Introduction," *Journal of Peasant Studies* 38, no. 2 (2011): 209–16. The current academic literature increasingly discusses land grabs in northern countries. For an example, see Ramona Bunkus and Insa Theesfeld, "Land Grabbing in Europe? Socio-Cultural Externalities of Large-Scale Land Acquisitions in East Germany," *Land* 7, no. 3 (2018): 1–17.
7. Wendy Wolford, "The Colonial Roots of Agricultural Modernization in Mozambique: The Role of Research from Portugal to ProSavana," *Journal of Peasant Studies* 48, no. 2 (2021): 255.
8. See Adalima, this volume.
9. Juliana Porsani, "Livelihood Implications of Large-Scale Land Concessions in Mozambique: A Case of Family Farmers' Endurance" (PhD diss., Södertörn University, 2020), 69.
10. See Adalima, this volume.
11. Deborah Potts, "Land Alienation under Colonial and White Settler Governments in Southern Africa," in Allan et al., *Handbook*, 24–42.
12. Potts, "Land Alienation," 39.
13. Potts, 38.
14. Porsani, "Livelihood Implications," 69.
15. Porsani, 69.
16. Saskia Sassen, "Land Grabs Today: Feeding the Disassembling of National Territory," *Globalizations* 10, no. 1 (2013): 29.
17. Leah Temper, "From Boomerangs to Minefields and Catapults: Dynamics of Trans-Local Resistance to Land-Grabs," *Journal of Peasant Studies* (2018): 18; Zoomers, "Globalisation."

18   Sassen, "Land Grabs," 26.
19   Following most publications on LSLA and the Land Matrix, a database about large-scale land projects.
20   Cotula et al., "Land Grab," 52f.
21   Lorenzo Cotula and Emma Blackmore, *Understanding Agricultural Investment Chains: Lessons to Improve Governance* (International Institute for Environment and Development, 2014); David Zetland and Jennifer Möller-Gulland, "The Political Economy of Land and Water Grabs," in Allan et al., *Handbook*, 257–72.
22   Deininger et al., "Rising Global Interests"; GRAIN, *Seized!*; Nolte et al., "International Land Deals," 17.
23   Saturnino M. Borras Jr. and Jennifer C. Franco, "Global Land Grabbing and Trajectories of Agrarian Change: A Preliminary Analysis," *Journal of Agrarian Change* 12, no. 1 (2012): 50.
24   Gregory Myers, *Land Tenure Development in Mozambique: Implications for Economic Development* (Land Tenure Center, 1995), 10f.
25   Eduardo Mondlane, *The Struggle for Mozambique*, 2nd ed. (Zed Books, 1983), 23f.
26   Mondlane, *The Struggle*, 28f.
27   Myers, "Land Tenure," 13.
28   See Adalima, this volume.
29   José Laimone Adalima, "Changing Livelihoods in Central Micaune, Central Mozambique: From Coconut to Land" (PhD diss., University of Pretoria, 2016), 44f; Mondlane, *The Struggle*, 30f.
30   Mondlane, *The Struggle for Mozambique*.
31   Bridget O'Laughlin, "Past and Present Options: Land Reform in Mozambique," *Review of African Political Economy* 22, no. 63 (1995): 99–106; Porsani, "Livelihood Implications," 45.
32   Myers, "Land Tenure," v, 6f., 15.
33   Assembleia da República, *Constituição*, art. 8.
34   Myers, "Land Tenure," v.
35   FRELIMO (Frente de Libertação de Moçambique) was the movement that led the armed struggle and transformed in 1977 into a political party. Edalina R. Sanches, *Party Systems in Young Democracies: Varieties of Institutionalization in Sub-Saharan Africa* (Routledge, 2018). It governs Mozambique today.
36   Otto Roesch, "Rural Mozambique Since the Frelimo Party Fourth Congress: The Situation in the Baixo Limpopo," *Review of African Political Economy* 41 (1988): 78.
37   Myers, "Land Tenure," vi, 8.
38   Roesch, "Rural Mozambique," 86.
39   Juan Obarrio, *The Spirit of the Laws in Mozambique* (University of Chicago Press, 2014), 49; República de Moçambique, *Política nacional de terras; Aprova a política agrária* (1996), Resolução No. 10/95.
40   Scott Kloeck-Jenson, *Análise do debate parlamentar e da nova Lei Nacional de Terras para Moçambique* (Land Tenure Centre, 1997), 2; Boaventura Monjane, "Is Nationalisation and State Custodianship of Land a Solution? The Case of Mozambique," *Amandla* 65 (2019): 33; Maria de Conceição de Quadros, *Breve nota sobre a questão de terras em Moçambique* (Maputo, 1999), 3.
41   *Lei de Terras. Lei No 19/97* (1997), arts. 12–14.
42   *Lei de Terras. Lei No 19/97*, art. 18.
43   *Lei de Terras. Lei No 19/97*, arts. 13, 17.
44   Ministério da Agricultura, *Diploma Ministerial No. 158/2011* (2011), art. 1.
45   *Lei de Terras. Lei No 19/97*, arts. 15, 25, 26.
46   Centro de Integridade Pública, *Custos e consequências das dívidas ocultas para Moçambique* (Bergen, 2021).
47   Donatella Della Porta and Sidney G. Tarrow, "Transnational Processes and Social Activism: An Introduction," in *Transnational Protest and Global Activism*, ed. Donatella Della Porta and Sidney Tarrow (Rowman & Littlefield, 2005), 13; Doug McAdam, Sidney Tarrow, and Charles Tilly, *Dynamics of Contention* (Cambridge University Press, 2001), 43.
48   Scott L. Cummings, "Law and Social Movements: An Interdisciplinary Analysis," in *Handbook of Social Movements Across Disciplines*, ed. Conny Roggeband and Bert Klandermans (Springer International, 2017), 260; Gianluca de Fazio, "Legal Opportunity Structure and Social Movement Strategy in Northern Ireland and Southern United States," *International Journal of Comparative Sociology* 53, no. 1 (2012): 3–22.
49   Ellen Ann Andersen, *Out of the Closets and Into the Courts: Legal Opportunity Structure and Gay Rights Litigation*, 4th ed. (University of Michigan Press, 2008), 27; Lisa Vanhala, "Legal Opportunity Structures

and the Paradox of Legal Mobilization by the Environmental Movement in the UK," *Law & Society Review* 46 (2012): 543, 548.

50   The size of the ProSavana project must be treated with caution, as numbers vary largely, as will be discussed in the section about the program.

51   The sheer size of the ProSavana project is the reason why the "Luso-history" row in table 10.1 only mentions examples from the different provinces included in the project outline.

52   Eléusio Filipe and Simon Norfolk, *Understanding Changing Land Issues for the Rural Poor in Mozambique* (International Institute for Environment and Development, 2017), 78; Roesch, "Rural Moçambique," 75.

53   M. Anne Pitcher, "Disruption Without Transformation: Agrarian Relations and Livelihoods in Nampula Province, Mozambique 1975–1995," *Journal of Southern African Studies* 24, no. 1 (1998): 120ff.

54   Roesch, "Rural Moçambique," 76.

55   Phyllis Bussler, "Wachstumskorridore als neue geographische Scale? Das Beispiel des Nacala Korridors in Mosambik," in *Kritische Geographien ländlicher Entwicklung: Globale Transformationen und lokale Herausforderungen*, ed. Michael Mießner and Matthias Naumann (Westfälisches Dampfboot, 2019), 229; Sérgio Chichava et al., "Brazil and China in Mozambican Agriculture: Emerging Insights from the Field," *IDS Bulletin* 44, no. 4 (2013): 107; Ganho, Ana Sofia, "'Friendship' Rice, Business, or 'Land-Grabbing'? The Hubei-Gaza Rice Project in Xai-Xai," *Land Deal Politics Initiative* 32 (2013): 4ff.; Antonio Gomes de Jesus Neto, "Entre trilhos e rodas: Fluidez territorial e os sentidos da circulação de mercadorias em Moçambique" (master's thesis, University of São Paulo, 2016), 20f.; Pitcher, "Disruption," 120; Porsani, "Livelihood Implications," 42f.

56   Porsani, "Livelihood Implications," 42f.; Roesch, "Rural Moçambique," 74.

57   Philipp Mayring and Thomas Fenzl, "Qualitative Inhaltsanalyse," in *Handbuch Methoden der empirischen Sozialforschung*, ed. Nina Baur and Jörg Blasius (Springer VS, 2014), 543–56.

58   See, e.g., Sérgio Chichava, "Chinese Agricultural Investment in Mozambique: The Case of the Wanbao Rice Farm," *SAIS China Africa Research Initiative* (2014): 4.

59   Ganho, "'Friendship,'" 4.

60   Porsani, "Livelihood Implications," 43; Potts, "Land Alienation," 38.

61   While Roesch, "Rural Moçambique," dates the construction of the irrigation scheme to 1930, others suggest that it was only constructed in the 1950s (such as Chichava et al., "Brazil and China," 107; Ganho, "'Friendship,'" 4).

62   Porsani, "Livelihood Implications," 42f.; Roesch, "Rural Moçambique," 74.

63   Ganho, "'Friendship,'" 5.

64   Filipe and Norfolk, "Understanding," 78; Roesch, "Rural Moçambique," 75.

65   Roesch, "Rural Moçambique," 76.

66   Roesch, 76.

67   Ganho, "'Friendship,'" 6.

68   Ganho, 6; Roesch, "Rural Moçambique," 79, 86.

69   Ganho, "'Friendship,'" 6.

70   Chichava et al., "Brazil and China," 107; Ganho, "'Friendship,'" 4ff.

71   Sérgio Chicava, "Chinese Rice Farming in Xai-Xai: A Case of Mozambican Agency?," in *China and Mozambique: From Comrades to Capitalists*, ed. Chris Alden and Sérgio Chichava (Jacanda Media, 2014), 129; Chichava et al., "Brazil and China, 107.

72   Chichava et al., "Brazil and China," 107; Ganho, "'Friendship,'" 10.

73   Chichava, "Chinese Agriculture," 3; Margarida Madureira, "Mega-projectos e transição agrária. O caso do projecto Wanbao (Moçambique)," *CEsA Working Paper* 126 (2014): 1–33.

74   Timothy Wise, *Eating Tomorrow: Agribusiness, Family Farmers, and the Battle for the Future of Food* (New Press, 2019), 80.

75   Chichava et al., "Brazil and China," 108.

76   Justiça Ambiental, "No Regadio do Baixo Limpopo" (Maputo, 2016), 15f.; Wise, *Eating*, 72ff.

77   Chuanhong, Li Xiaoyun, Qi Gubo, and Wang Yanlei, "Interpreting China-Africa Agricultural Encounters: Rhetoric and Reality in a Large-Scale Rice Project in Mozambique," *CBAA Working Paper* 126 (2015): 12.

78   Justiça Ambiental, "No Regadio," 16.

79   Chichava, "Chinese Agriculture," 4; Justiça Ambiental, "No Regadio, 16; "Petição 1" (2014).

80   Activist K., interview, 6 June 2019.

81 João Mosca and Natacha Bruna, "ProSavana: Discursos, prácticas e realidades," *Observador Rural* 31 (2015): 2, 11.
82 E.g., Patrícia Campos Mello, "Moçambique oferece terra à soja brasileira," *Folha de São Paulo*, 14 August 2011.
83 E.g., a court sentence about the project talks about 14.5 million hectares.
84 Ministério da Agricultura e Segurança Alimentar, "Plano Director para o desenvolvimento agrário do Corredor de Nacala em Moçambique" (Esboço Versão 0. Cooperação triangular para o desenvolvimento agrário da savana tropical em Moçambique, 2015), 1–2.
85 Leroy Vail, "Mozambique's Chartered Companies: The Rule of the Feeble," *Journal of African History* 17, no. 3 (1976): 393f.
86 Vail, "Mozambique's," 393ff.
87 Vail, 415.
88 See also Adalima, this volume.
89 Pitcher, "Disruption," 118.
90 Pitcher, 120.
91 Pitcher, 123.
92 Gomes de Jesus Neto, "Entre trilhos," 20f.
93 Bussler, "Wachstumskorridore," 229.
94 Mosca and Bruna, "ProSavana," 12; Tomás Selemane, "A economia política do Corredor de Nacala: Consolidação do padrão de economia extrovertida em Moçambique," *Observador Rural* 56 (2017): 10; Wise, *Eating*, 49.
95 Mosca and Bruna, "ProSavana," 9; Wise, *Eating*, 53.
96 Pedrito Carlos Chiposse Cabrão, "A (emergente) sociedade civil: Um olhar sobre o papel das suas organizações nas políticas de inclusão social e de desenvolvimento sustentável: O caso de Moçambique (1990–2015)" (PhD diss., Universidade do Porto, 2016), 266; Mosca and Bruna, "ProSavana," 9.
97 Campos Mello, "Moçambique."
98 Mosca and Bruna, "ProSavana," 12.
99 Alex Shankland, Euclides Gonçalves, and Arilson Favareto, "Social Movements, Agrarian Change and the Contestation of ProSavana in Mozambique and Brazil," *CBAA Working Paper* 137 (2016): 21; Wise, *Eating*, 55.
100 Sayaka Funada-Classen, "The Rise and Fall of ProSavana: From Triangular Cooperation to Bilateral Cooperation in Counter-Resistance," *Observador Rural* 82 (2019): 14.
101 Shankland et al., "Social Movements," 16ff.; Wise, *Eating*, 55.
102 Shankland et al., "Social Movements," 23; Wise, *Eating*, 56.
103 Shankland et al., "Social Movements," 23.
104 Mosca and Bruna, "ProSavana," 2; Selemane, "A economia," 10f.; Shankland et al., "Social Movements," 19.
105 "Governo anuncia o fim do ProSavana," *Diario Economico*, 28 July 2020, https://www.diarioeconomico.co.mz/2020/07/28/negocios/agronegocios/governo-anuncia-o-fim-do-prosavana/.
106 Não ao ProSavana, "No to ProSavana Campaign: Peoples' Declaration," Farmlandgrab.org, 25 October 2017, https://www.farmlandgrab.org/post/27603-no-to-prosavana-campaign-peoples-declaration.
107 Assembleia da República, *Constituição*.
108 Não ao ProSavana, "Joint Statement and Open Questions on ProSavana by the Civil Society of Mozambique, Brazil and Japan in Response to Newly Leaked Government Documents," Não ao ProSavana, 27 August 2016, https://www.ngo-jvc.com/jp/projects/advocacy-statement/data/prosavana-joint-statement.pdf.
109 Porsani, "Livelihood Implications."
110 Li, this volume.
111 As also described by Li's example, this volume.

11

Colonial Concessions: The Antinomies of Land Policy in Portuguese Timor

Douglas Kammen and Laura S. Meitzner Yoder

Introduction

Land concessions granted to state-owned enterprises or to private companies are one of the most significant and enduring colonial legacies in the Global South. Claiming and designating vast tracts of land facilitated expansive sugar cultivation in the Americas, jute plantations in South Asia, and the Cultivation System in the Netherlands East Indies, to name some (in)famous instances. The outcomes, including indigenous land dispossession and labour exploitation, are well-known, but less noticed is how the idea of land concessions emerged in tandem with changes in colonial governance and the diffusion of emerging international norms regarding land. This is particularly true in the case of smaller and less profitable colonies. In this chapter, we excavate the lineages of successive systems of land control in Portuguese Timor. These competing systems remain readily perceptible and jostle for recognition in modern Timor-Leste as it seeks to reconcile the legacies of these paradigms while building its own laws and policies.

Recent scholarship on Timor-Leste has emphasized the appearance of large land concessions, including both those owned by the state and those granted to private corporations, under the long and brutal governorship of Celestino da Silva (1895–1908). Shepherd and McWilliam, for example, draw a direct connection between the pacification campaigns waged by Governor Silva at the start of his tenure and the emergence of plantations in Portuguese Timor.[1] Similarly, Fitzpatrick draws attention to "new land concession regulations instituted in

1901" in the colony.² The seizure of indigenous land and new accompanying coercion of labour had a brutal impact on the population, not only where plantations were established but also in non-plantation regions where labour was recruited. But the origins of Portuguese land policy and the designation of land concessions are by no means specific to a particular governor. Critical antecedents to the emergence of large-scale land concessions in Portuguese Timor include empire-wide legislation passed in the middle of the nineteenth century to promote settler colonialism, especially in Angola and Mozambique; land seizure as punishment of recalcitrant local rulers; and the pernicious myth of the "lazy native" and reformatory power of (forced) labour.

Colonial land policy in Portuguese Timor did not emerge *de novo* around the turn to the twentieth century. Rather, the broad conception of land and specific policies intended to promote a plantation economy were responding to an older regime of Portuguese rule that included a very different understanding of local power and land rights. Beginning in the early eighteenth century, the Portuguese sought to impose a system of "vassalage" modelled on medieval Iberian practices. By the nineteenth century, Portuguese officials not only described Timor as being "feudal,"³ but indigenous Timorese rulers (*liurai*) increasingly came to enjoy a fusion of political and economic power. Crucially, the backing provided by Portuguese governors to loyal *liurai* strengthened these rulers at the expense of lesser aristocrats and agents of what had once been the corresponding "spiritual realm" within indigenous polities. We refer to this model of vassalage and land relations as the "feudal-paternalistic" land model. During the second half of the nineteenth century, however, legislation passed in Lisbon, the security concerns of governors in Portuguese Timor, and ideas borrowed from the Netherlands Indies paved the way for the dispossession of indigenous land by the colonial state. Out of this emerged a new model based on private ownership of land (though always through the intermediary of state recognition) and market relations.

This chapter explores the transition from the old feudal-paternalistic model to the new in four stages. The first section provides a bird's-eye view of the origins and dynamics of the feudal-paternalistic model up to the mid-nineteenth century. The second section examines colonial encroachment on indigenous land through new legal notion of "wastelands" and the establishment of the first experimental state plantations. The third section examines the connection between colonial retribution against troublesome indigenous rulers and land dispossession. The fourth section considers the emergence of the new model of private property and market relations, though we emphasize a critical distinction between the early version of this model under Governor Silva and its full expression following Portugal's transition from monarchy to republican rule.

The Portuguese Feudal-Paternalistic Model and Land in Timor

While the Portuguese presence in Timor dates to the early sixteenth century, it was not until three centuries later that land emerged as a specific concern for colonial representatives. In 1769, Governor Teles de Meneses moved the base of Portuguese operations eastward to Dili and summoned dozens of local rulers (termed *rei/regulo*) to the new capital—then just an encampment dependent on the goodwill of the local ruler of Motael—to pledge vassalage to the king of Portugal, and thereby recognize Portuguese suzerainty and loyalty to the governor himself.[4] This practice, which the Portuguese had first applied in Timor in the late seventeenth century and intensified after the first Portuguese governor was resident in 1702, was to have crucial consequences with direct relevance to land policy. In the nineteenth century, the imposition of vassal relations was intended to achieve two primary aims—ensuring security and delivering annual "tribute" (*finta*) from the vassal kingdoms to the Portuguese governors.[5] Unstated in the written terms of vassalage was a third element: that the *rei/regulo* (and at times female *rainha*) was the "lord of the land," a translation of the indigenous term *liurai* (*liu* meaning "more"/"greater than"/"above" and *rai* meaning "land"), which Hägerdal translates as "surpassing the earth."[6] In short, the terms of vassalage agreed to in 1769 and thereafter were tacit acknowledgement by Portuguese officials of the near-absolute authority of local rulers over their domains, including the population and all land within it.[7] For the purposes of exposition, we call this the feudal-paternalistic model.

The feudal-paternalistic model on which Portuguese suzerainty in Timor rested was reaffirmed in 1811 when Bernardo José Maria da Silveira e Lorena (the Count of Sarzedas), then serving in the colonial administration in Goa, wrote a survey of the religious, civil, administrative, military, and political affairs of Timor. He highlighted the contribution of tribute (*finta*) to the colonial treasury (in 1727 and 1770) but made no mention of land ownership or policy. Four years later, with the end of the Napoleonic Wars, the secretary to the Portuguese governor in Dili compiled a new list of the fifty-five vassal kingdoms and their rulers.[8] The aim, as in 1769–70, was to collect tribute from the vassal kingdoms. What the exercise revealed was that vassal relations with many of the kingdoms had lapsed; what it exposed was the precarious basis of state revenue. The feudal-paternalistic model was based on annual deliveries, not dispossessing the indigenous population of their land or directly overseeing agricultural or forestry production. That does not mean that Portuguese officials had no interest in agriculture.[9] The problem, in the eyes of officials, was that the indigenous population was ill-suited to producing a surplus beyond their own subsistence needs. For this reason, officials discussed the possibility of importing agriculturalists from China to supply Dili and the other Portuguese outposts along the northern littoral with produce.[10] But with the flight of the monarchy to Brazil in 1807 and ensuing decade of struggle between Rio de Janeiro and Lisbon, little attention was paid to the most distant outpost of the empire in the East, and nothing came of these proposals.

The first inkling of a turning point in Portuguese policy regarding land came in the 1850s, but it would take a decade to mature into an actual policy. Arriving in Dili in 1851, Governor Lopes de Lima recognized the precarity of the Portuguese presence in Timor, limited to Dili and a few other settlements on the northern coast. The administrative apparatus was miniscule, its reach limited, and the revenue collected insufficient to cover operating costs. Lopes de Lima's solution lay in establishing a private company, in which all Chinese merchants were required to invest, and regularizing the border with Dutch territory. His vision rested on collecting customs revenue from imports and exports, not a fundamental alteration of the feudal-paternalistic model. These initiatives bore no immediate fruit—the private company quickly collapsed and the border agreement was not completed until 1859—but Lopes de Lima had pioneered the construction of a functioning state. Six years later, newly arrived Governor Luis Augusto de Almeida Macedo was to take the next, fateful step when he travelled to Batavia, the capital of the Netherlands Indies, to observe first-hand Dutch colonial policies and practices.[11] In the two decades since its inception in 1830, the *Culturrstelsel* (Cultivation System) in Java had generated enormous profits. In lieu of a tax on land, the system required peasants to set aside a fifth of their land for cash crops (indigo, coffee, tea, etc.) to be delivered to the colonial state. In the words of historian Onghokham, "the colonial government made the village the basis of its system. The village, as the lowest political and administrative unit, was declared to own all the land [communally]," and hence was collectively responsible for meeting the quota of deliverable crops.[12]

It was not Macedo but his successor who would act on the Dutch model. Affonso de Castro was elected as the representative for Timor in the Portuguese parliament from 1854 to 1858, so had several years to acquaint himself with colonial policy and the state of affairs in Timor. It was on this basis that he was appointed to succeed Macedo as governor in the distant colony, a post he took up in 1859. Castro's first major initiative was promulgation of a thirty-point reform of the administration in 1860, the core of which was the creation of eleven districts.[13] The first twenty points of Castro's code were essentially a set of instructions to the new district commanders to maintain order, while the last three points concerned collection of the annual *finta*. Castro explicitly instructed the district commanders not to interfere in the internal matters of the kingdoms.[14] This was, in other words, a continuation of the feudal-paternalistic model. Castro's innovation, following the Cultivation System in Java (about which he would have learned both from parliamentary discussion in Lisbon about colonial affairs and Macedo's correspondence with Lisbon), was to overlay the forced planting and delivery of coffee on top of the existing feudal-paternalistic system already in place, to which local rulers were accustomed (though not always enthusiastic partners).[15] Just as the Dutch had declared all land to be communally owned by the village, Castro's system implicitly acknowledged that the jural authority of the *rei/regulo* extended to land. Castro, Katharine Davidson writes, "made the assumption that the people accepted the *liurai* and *datus* as owners of land, and for those elites who acknowledged the supreme authority of the King of Portugal, he assumed their subjects must accept that traditional dues due to the *liurai*, such as tribute and services, were equally due to the [Portuguese] state."[16] While official statistics on the number of coffee trees, harvested coffee, and exports indicate that the new system led to an increase in production over the next two decades, it is not at all clear this was a result of state policy. Rather, there is good reason to think the Timorese cultivators (at times in tandem with ethnic Chinese) independently recognized the market value of coffee and were responsible for these increases.

Between the promulgation of Castro's code in 1860 and the end of his term in 1863, the colonial state set quotas for the planting of coffee trees in many of the upland kingdoms where conditions were suitable.[17] The new system of commands, reinvigoration of terms of vassalage, and orders to plant coffee trees were met with stiff opposition, with rebellions breaking out to the east (Laclo) and west (Ulmera) of Dili in 1861, in Laga in 1863, and a mutiny within the colonial army in 1864.[18] There is nothing surprising about indigenous resistance to the extension of colonial power: Timor had been wracked by "rebellion" and inter-kingdom fighting throughout much of the eighteenth century. Instead, what is remarkable is the temporal relationship between Castro's initiative and his model in Java. By 1860, the Cultivation System in Java was coming under increasing criticism and eventual dismantlement for being exploitative and wreaking havoc on Javanese welfare.[19] Portuguese uptake lagged behind its regional model, coming into use just as the Dutch transitioned to another system for economic extraction.

Colonial Encroachment

The feudal-paternalistic model (which, for comparative purposes, we might also think of as indirect rule) had a fundamental weakness: personalization. The bond was based on pledges made by individual indigenous rulers to a specific governor;

a change in either could weaken the bond, or draw it into question altogether. So, each newly appointed governor felt a need to renew the terms of vassalage with as many of the *rei/regulos* as possible. Nevertheless, terms of vassalage and *finta* payment remained the core of Portuguese colonial rule throughout the second half of the nineteenth century. But creeping changes were taking place in the Portuguese understanding and attitude toward land in the late 1860s and '70s. Fuelled by a combination of empire-wide legislation and practical considerations, the legal concept of "wasteland" (*baldios*, which could also be understood as empty or unused land; see chapter by Bernardo Almeida in this volume) provided governors of Portuguese Timor a way around the restrictions imposed by the feudal-paternalistic model, thus enabling encroachment on indigenous land.

The nineteenth century saw passage of successive new legislation in the Portuguese metropole governing land classification in the colonial territories. The major impetus for this was the loss of Brazil in 1822. With this, Portuguese officials redirected their focus to Angola, and by extension Mozambique and Portuguese Guinea. The new legislation aimed to facilitate land alienation and land grants to Portuguese colonists. Of particular importance was passage of the law of 21 August 1856, which established guidelines for alienating state-owned "wastelands" (*baldios pertencentes ao Estado*) in the colonial territories.[20] This was a legal innovation that sought to resolve two long-standing antinomies in single stroke. The first of these was that while the overseas colonies "belonged to" the Crown (and later the state), the Portuguese practice of indirect rule through terms of vassalage acknowledged indigenous rulers as owners of the land. The second issue stemmed from Portuguese perceptions that indigenous agricultural practices were inefficient.[21] Land not being put to what colonial officials thought was optimal use was easily deemed "wasteland." Finally, this law recognized two different mechanisms for the allocation of "wastelands": sale (*contrato de compra e venda*) and emphyteusis, which is functionally akin to long-term use rights (*aforamento* or *emprazamento*).[22]

The first known efforts to establish state-owned plantations in Timor were undertaken by Castro's successors. In 1864, newly arrived Governor José Maria Pereira de Machado proposed extending the decree of 1861 to the province of Timor, but there is no evidence that he acted on this.[23] His successor, Governor Francisco Teixeira da Silva (served 1866–9), first created state plantations. In a study of coffee cultivation in Timor, the Portuguese agronomist Helder Lains e Silva noted that in 1868, Governor Teixeira established an experimental state plantation worked by soldiers who were unsuited to military duty in the kingdom of Lacluta, Viqueque District, on the southern coast.[24] In fact, Lains e Silva's source was not quite correct: A report in the colonial gazette in 1868 notes two new state plantations, in Carahil/Caimauc and in Lacluta.[25] The report also notes that the governor, continuing the policy of his predecessor, was providing a great many coffee seedlings to the kingdoms of Laclo, in Manatuto District, and Laga, in Baucau District.[26] (Further promotion of land concessions as a means to develop coffee as well as sugar plantations in Timor followed in 1875 and in the early 1880s.)[27]

This raises two critical questions: Why did Governor Teixeira da Silva select Caimauc and Lacluta to establish the first state-owned plantations in 1868? And on what basis did he obtain land within recognized vassal kingdoms? The location of the two experimental state plantations could not have been more different. Carahil (which was renamed Remexio in 1900) is an upland valley located a mere twenty kilometres south of Dili, while Lacluta is located in the remote northwestern corner of Viqueque District, perhaps a week's travel from Dili in the 1860s.[28] By all appearances, both Caimauc and Lacluta were on good terms with the Portuguese administration, and in the case of Lacluta, the Catholic mission.[29] The most likely explanation for why these two locations were chosen is not simply that they were upland areas suited to coffee cultivation, but that district military commanders charged with promoting coffee cultivation offered the rulers of Caimauc and Lacluta forgiveness of arrears in the annual tribute in return for land.[30] In both cases, given what is known about the estimated population at the time and later, as well as terrain that is most suitable for coffee, it is likely that the land that was ceded to or taken by the state for the experimental plantations was sparsely populated or even uninhabited. In short, there may not have been any need to appeal to the 1856 law on "wastelands."

But that does not mean that the concept of wastelands or the laws that empowered colonial regimes to dispossess the indigenous population are not relevant to Portuguese Timor. Instead, the primary influence simply may not have come from the metropole, but rather from neighbouring colonies. Two years after Governor Teixeira da Silva's pioneering plantations were established, the government of the Netherlands East Indies passed a new agrarian law (*Agrarische Wet*, 1870). This contained provisions that pulled in opposite directions: It prohibited "the sale or permanent transfer of land from natives to Europeans and Chinese,"[31] but also included a provision on *domein verklaring* (statement of domain) according to which "all land not held under proven ownership shall be deemed the domain of the state." The second of these provisions effectively superseded the implicit rights conferred under indirect rule. In other words, an indirect ruler remained responsible for maintaining order and meting out justice according to local "uses and customs," but the new agrarian law enabled the Netherlands Indies government to claim unused or empty land. This was of particular use in the Outer Islands (i.e., beyond Java), where geologists had identified deposits of minerals, coal, and other valuable natural resources. Just as Governor Affonso de Castro had looked to the Cultivation System in Java as a model for his 1860s effort to promote coffee cultivation, Portuguese governors in the 1870s must have known about the latest Dutch legal mechanism that provided a way to encroach on indigenous land.[32]

From the 1870s onward, the colonial gazette included increasing numbers of notices about border disputes among indigenous kingdoms. Even when these disputes did not involve outright violence or require the governor to deploy troops, they attracted greater scrutiny from the state, and hence greater knowledge of rural, and especially upland, regions of the colony. As attractive sites for coffee cultivation became better known, governors and their staff could draw on the precedent set by the 1856 law and the immediate example of Dutch practices to dispossess kingdoms of land seen to be unoccupied or just not put to maximal economic use. Increasing state encroachment on land represented a gradual erosion of the terms of vassalage and model of indirect rule, but this did not alter the fact that the ruling model was drawn from medieval Portugal and applied to Timor through the nineteenth century. In the 1870s and '80s, governors continued to summon the indigenous *rei/regulo* to Dili to sign terms of vassalage, and the district commanders continued to estimate the number of *almas* (souls), which formed the basis for the administration's assessment of the annual tribute. Actual collection of the tribute was another matter, of course.

Retribution and the Origins of the New Land Model

What prompted the shift from the old feudal-paternalistic model, in which indigenous authority over and ownership of land was protected, to a new regime in which the state dispossessed the indigenous population of land and made it available to outsiders as land "concessions"? Scholarship on colonial land policy in Portuguese Timor usually jumps directly from Governor Castro's initiatives in the early 1860s straight to Governor Silva's brutal military campaigns and land seizure starting in 1895.[33] In fact, there are four possible sources of the emergence of the new land regime and the introduction of land concessions in Portuguese Timor in the late nineteenth century: (a) application of or changes in Portuguese law pertaining to overseas possessions; (b) foreign affairs and models; (c) purely practical considerations; and (d) the personal interests of the governors. All of these played a role in the period between the late 1870s and the end of the century, but we must unpack the order in which they were applied, the types of land in question, and the logic that this entailed.

The origins of direct Portuguese involvement in the question of land qua land lie neither in application of the 1856 law nor in an intentional plan to acquire land, but instead in retribution for disobedience to the colonial state. The first clearly documented instance of this emerged after an extended dispute between the kingdoms of Laleia and Vemasse, which in 1879 resulted in the governor ordering military operations to punish the "rebel" ruler of Laleia, Manoel dos Remedios. Although Remedios evaded capture, Governor Hugo da Lacerdo declared his intention to "distribute the constituent parts of the rebel kingdom so that it will remain only in memory.... Because we have not yet captured the ex-*regulo* ... we must set an example to those ... who might be susceptible to identical errors."[34] Although unstated, the decision to redistribute land to neighbouring polities reflected the official assessment of the land itself. Eight years later, when Governor Maia sent a military force to punish the kingdom of Maubara, which was the richest coffee-growing region in all of Portuguese Timor, a new twist was added to the punishment. In his report about the rebellion, Governor Maia wrote, "But the best of all that happened was the possession of the lands of Babequinia, that I took over immediately as Lands of the King [*Terras de El-Rei*]. These are not only the best plantations in Maubara, producing a profit of 500 piculs of coffee, or 2,000 arrobas, with possibilities of even more; but we can extend our dominion to the interior, whereas up to now we have only occupied the littoral."[35] The difference between the lands of Laleia in 1879 and those in Maubara in 1887 was that the latter were not only suited to coffee cultivation but were already producing a valuable crop.

While the governors of Timor were engaging in futile attempts to assert their authority over a territory that was only partially mapped in the 1880s, two legal developments on the international stage were to play a critical role in shaping future colonial land policy in Portuguese Timor. The first of these was the Berlin Conference of 1884–5, organized by German Chancellor Otto van Bismarck. Best known for setting off the scramble for Africa, the critical principle enshrined by the conference participants was that recognition of colonial claims would be based on demonstrating "effective occupation."[36] As Portuguese authority was essentially limited to the northern coast of Timor, this new principle provided impetus for the Dili-based authorities to demonstrate their "occupation" of all districts. Colonial administrations sought to demonstrate that their claims were based on actual presence; and an actual presence necessitated demonstrating order. Anything that disrupted order, in turn, could be used to justify the seizure of land. A second legal influence may have come from the Torrens title system, first introduced through the Real Property Act of 1858 in South Australia, for land titling.[37] The core principle informing this was that registration of land was the basis for a title, rather than title (or tracing ownership back in time through a series of documents or other claims) being the basis for registration. Although actual land deeds would not be introduced in Portuguese Timor until the early twentieth century,[38] the principles of the Torrens system in a colonial context where "natives" did not have deeds provided legal cover for dispossession of land.

Developments in international law help to contextualize the wider atmosphere in which a new land regime was emerging in Portuguese Timor, but they have little explanatory power on their own. The first uses of the term "concession" in Portuguese Timor may stem from the example set by business practices elsewhere in the world: requests for the right to prospect for minerals. By the 1890s, a number of investors submitted requests to the colonial government in Dili for the right to prospect for minerals. In 1890, a Portuguese citizen resident in Hong Kong was granted rights to prospect for oil in the kingdoms of Laclubar and Funar, in the highlands of Manatuto District,[39] and a Chinese resident of Singapore wrote to the administration in Dili requesting a permit to prospect for minerals.[40] Two years later, another investor was granted rights to mine for gold in the kingdoms of Bibicusso and Turiscai.[41] Other requests followed, including for oil in Viqueque, eventually leading to the granting of mining concessions. In understanding the origins and application of land concessions, it is essential to recognize that requests made by mineral prospectors, who knew that a formal concession would be necessary, foreshadowed the granting of large-scale concessions for coffee and other plantations in Portuguese Timor.

Yet, as was the case in 1887, it was what the colonial regime termed "rebellion" that provided justification for the emergence of a new land regime based on alienating indigenous land and granting concessions. And, again, it was Maubara that set the new ball rolling. In 1893, Governor Cypriano Forjaz personally led a military force to quash troubles that had arisen, according to his information, because an alliance between the local ruling family and the ethnic Chinese had sent an emissary to Dutch territory to request the Dutch flag and seek a return to Dutch overlordship. Governor Forjaz and his troops laid waste to the kingdom. This time, rather than directly seize land, the governor removed the old ruling family and installed a compliant new ruler, who would facilitate Portuguese access to land and labour. Governor Forjaz also issued a fateful order banning the indigenous population from travelling between kingdoms in the northwestern part of the territory without a permit.[42]

This was the backdrop to the arrival of a new governor, the cavalry officer and staunch monarchist Celestino da Silva, in 1894, who ruled until 1908. In one of his first reports, he wrote, "All the kingdoms of the west were in revolt ... and so were the twelve *reinos* of the central west and seven of the southern *reinos*. . . .

Only three hours from the city [of Dili], Manomera was in rebellion and in Mothael eight jurisdictions were disobedient."[43] This was a gross exaggeration, but a useful one. Over the next several years, Governor Silva launched a series of brutal pacification campaigns, first in the western districts, and later in the east. These campaigns, Katharine Davidson writes, provided Governor Silva with "a nucleus of controllable land and labour in the form of deserted territories and prisoners-of-war."[44] The widespread seizure of land, however, was in direct violation of Lisbon's decree of 27 September 1894 (the so-called *Decreto-travão*, or "break decree"), that specified that land alienation in the colonies could no longer be made directly by the colonial or metropolitan government, but had to be submitted to parliament for authorization. The objective, with the African colonies clearly in mind, was to curb the growing influence of foreign capital in Portuguese territories.[45]

The combination of land directly seized during the pacification campaigns and the intimidation of *rei/regulo* or their replacement with pliable figures provided the foundation for Governor Silva's plan to turn the tide on Portuguese Timor's long-standing fiscal deficit. The centrepiece of this initiative was the establishment of agricultural societies. The first of these, Sociedade Agrícola Pátria e Trabalho (SAPT), was established in 1897, and over the next decade four other major companies were established: the private Companha de Timor, with seven plantations in the kingdom of Ermera; Empreza Preservença, which was owned by Silva's family and started with a large cocoa plantation in the kingdom of Deribate; Empreza Agricola de Timor, which started with a 2,000-hectare plantation in Deribate; and Empreza Comercial Agricola de Timor, with coffee plantations in the devastated kingdom of Maubara and neighbouring Mahubo.[46]

The second prong in Governor Silva's approach was to promote coffee cultivation in as many parts of the colony as possible. To this end, he founded a "Plantation School" in Remexio, on the site of Governor Teixeira da Silva's 1868 experimental coffee plantation, to teach agricultural extension workers "who would go around the island to train the natives."[47] The third prong of his strategy combined purely economic with implicitly political motives: granting tracts of prime land to Portuguese officials and military officers as reward for their service (and often personal loyalty to the governor). Unfortunately, the colonial gazette is not fully available for the critical years 1897–9, so it is not known if the earliest of these land grants were publicized or the legal basis on which they were made. But both the seizure and distribution of indigenous land required proper authorization from the Portuguese parliament. For this reason, it is likely that many of the land grants made to officials in Governor Silva's service were not publicized. One example will suffice here: In the late 1890s, Governor Silva granted several hundred hectares of land on the upper reaches of Mount Maubara to his son, Julio Celestino de Montalvão e Silva, who, despite being a member of the Portuguese Navy, had been tasked with helping to manage the SAPT plantation in Fatubessi.[48] Such grants were a cost-free and effective way to reward loyalists and to encourage the development of new plantations.

During his first six years in office, Governor Silva neither abolished the old, feudal-paternalistic model nor established a new regime from scratch. His early methods built on his predecessors' practice of punishing rebellious *rei/regulo* by redistributing or seizing land within their kingdoms. But up until the turn of the century, he continued to recognize the indigenous kingdoms and engage them through formal terms of vassalage. Furthermore, his methods were motivated as much by a desire to extend the reach of the state, and hence its effective occupation, to the borders of the colony as they were by a desire to dispossess the indigenous population. And during the early period, there is no evidence that legal niceties ever motivated his actions or were raised to legitimize his actions; he was a cavalry officer interested in furthering the glories of the empire, not a lawyer.

The New Land Model in Full Bloom: Confiscation (Primitive Accumulation)

The new model based on the alienation of indigenous land, open grants or sale of land concessions for agricultural development, a market for land transactions, and registration of those transactions burst onto the scene during the first decade of the twentieth century. This appears to have involved a convergence of influences—metropolitan or specifically overseas law (made with the African colonies in mind), international norms (specifically, the need to demonstrate "effective occupation"), an eye on Dutch practice (including the shift to a liberal model based on market forces and transactions), and practical considerations of power. This developed over two distinct periods—initially in the first decade of the twentieth century, which was the last decade of the monarchy; and later during the first decade of republican rule, after the 1910 revolution. Importantly, while we focus on the blossoming of the new model, note that the older model did not suddenly disappear; it continued to operate in parallel both because economic forces were too weak to sweep it away and because the old model remained useful to the colonial state.

The year 1900 marked the beginning of the great fire sale of indigenous land (and the accompanying loss of sacred sites and cultural heritage) in the central highlands.[49] But the dynamics differed in several critical aspects from those during the first few years of Governor Silva's tenure, and from the picture painted by several authors of a direct link between pacification campaigns and the

Table 11.1. Recipients of major land concessions in 1900

Name	Status/position	Residence	Concession	Location
Amandio Baptista de Souza	?	Lisbon	1,000 ha	Ermera
Conde de Mendia	Portuguese nobility	Lisbon	1,000 ha	
Visconde de Carnaxide	Portuguese nobility	Lisbon	1,000 ha	
Marquês de Fayal	Portuguese nobility	Lisbon	1,000 ha	
José da Silveira Vianna	cavalry officer	Lisbon?	1,000 ha	
Anselmo de Assis e Andrade	famous economist	Lisbon	1,000 ha	
Francisco Mantero	landowner in S. Tomé	Lisbon	1,000 ha	
Augusto de Silva Carvalho	Pres. Medical Society	Lisbon	1,000 ha	
Henrique J. M. de Mendonça	capitalist in Sao Tomé	Lisbon	1,000 ha	
Jacintho Isla M. Santos e Silva	aide to Gov. C. da Silva	Dili	1,000 ha	
D. Francisco Martins	Timorese	Ermera?	1,000 ha	

Source: *Boletim Oficial do Districto Autonomo de Timor*, various issues in 1900

appropriation of land from the indigenous rulers and/or populace within those kingdoms.[50] First, and most remarkably, in 1900 the sequencing was reversed from earlier retributive actions: Massive land tracts were designated as land concessions (*concessão*) in Motael and Ermera *prior to* the start of military operations that year (and with no operations in Motael and only minimal operations in the western and southern fringe of Ermera in the preceding years).[51] Second, the announcements in the colonial gazette specified that the concessions were "in a location of the grantee's own choosing" in the listed kingdom, "or in any other indigenous *reino* of their choosing." The final point concerns the recipients of the 1,000-hectare concessions of "wasteland" (*terreno baldio*), listed in table 11.1.

A group of Lisbon-based men who received land concessions enjoyed close business ties, with one of the founders of the Companhia de Timor, Francisco Mantero, at the centre. In 1896 Mantero and Vianna established Sociedade Agricultura Colonial to run plantations in São Tomé; in 1899, Mantero, Andrade, Carvalho, Mendia, Mendonça, and Vianna established Companhia Portugueza das Minas de Oiro de Manica to prospect in Mozambique; in 1900, Mantero and Conde de Mendia created Companhia Agricola de Cazengo to explore agricultural lands in Angola; and, in 1903, Mantero established Companhia de Cabinda to develop agriculture in Angola.[52] Company board members had broad economic, academic, governance, and military influence in Portugal. Francisco Mantero, for example, "was an expert in the coffee and cocoa businesses. Having lived in Angola, Mozambique, Timor, and S. Tomé, he [helped develop] the farming structures which were central in the territorial organisation of those places."[53] Santos e Silva was a relative of Governor Silva. This was an exercise, overseen by the governor, in the wholesale seizure and privatization of indigenous land. And it was only the beginning.

For the law was not far behind. In early 1901, a Portuguese parliamentary commission presented a new proposal regarding land alienation in the colonies so as to reconcile the conflicting interests of the state and private investors. The ensuing parliamentary discussion of the proposal included debate about the merits and drawbacks of the 1856 legislation that was still in use, with some local modifications, in the colonies. In May, parliament passed the new law of 9 May 1901 on land concessions in the overseas provinces that opened the way for alienation of state-owned wastelands, followed by a Timor-specific implementing regulation.[54] It starts by decreeing that "all the lands that at this time are not private property" are considered state domain and that all state-owned wastelands can be alienated (with certain exceptions made for land adjacent to infrastructure, water, and common lands used by villagers).[55] The amount of wasteland that could be alienated varied from colony to colony: 1,000 hectares in Lourenço Marques, 250 hectares in Cabo Verde and Índia, 25,000 hectares in Guiné and Timor, and 50,000 hectares in Angola and Mozambique. The colonial governors could grant concessions (*aforamento*) of up to one-tenth of these sizes, but these were subject to approval by the metropolitan government. Importantly, all alienation of land had to be preceded by public auction, with announcements posted in the colonial gazette.[56] The new law was a mixed blessing for Governor Silva. While he could no longer grant land at will, the law opened new opportunities, not to mention legal cover. Governor Silva soon added his own twists. In 1905 he issued a decree that "all kingdoms which do not have at least six hundred households will be declared extinct,"[57] thereby facilitating further alienation of land. The next target was labour. A 1906 decree went further, erasing the distinction between natives and *reinóis*, and hence bringing far larger numbers of Timorese into the labour pool.[58]

Between the passage of the new law on wastelands in 1901 and the end of his tenure in 1908, Governor Silva's administration allocated tens of thousands of hectares of land concessions.[59] At least four 1,000-hectare concessions were granted in 1902. The following year, the government granted 11,000 hectares of land to Companhia de Timor. And the numbers continued to rise. In addition to the new agricultural *sociedade*, government officials and military officers also received significant tracts of land, as did private Portuguese citizens and a number of non-Portuguese citizens (including Australians, Germans, and others). Alongside these grants of "wastelands," there was also a boom in private land sales by Timorese, in many cases by *regulo*. At the same time, there were an increasing number of land purchases by ethnic Chinese (both those from families long-established in Timor and new sojourners), particularly in urban areas, in the *posto* (sub-district seats), and in some instances of coffee plantations. What the colonial gazette notices do not reveal is the level of coercion involved in at least some of these sales. But that was by no means the entire story. Governor Silva's 1905 decree also contained a provision that the *regulo* were to be granted the right "to have up to fifty hectares of land cultivated in their kingdoms by their subjects."[60] This is perhaps the clearest, but by no means the only, example of the continuation, and even deepening, of the old feudal-paternalistic model alongside the emergence of the new land regime based on expropriation and the granting of land concessions.

The revolution of 1910, which overthrew the House of Bragança and established the First Portuguese Republic, promised to liberalize the metropole and overseas empire. In doing so, however, this undermined the symbolic foundations on which colonial rule had been erected during the nineteenth century. In Portuguese Timor, these changes, together with the introduction of a territory-wide head tax (*imposto de capitação*) in 1908, undermined the position of the *regulos* in Timor and placed new burdens on the lesser nobility, thereby precipitating a major rebellion in 1911–12. For the purposes of this chapter, it is sufficient to note that the liberalizing impulse included thoroughgoing alternations to colonial land policy.[61] The provisional republican government, Fernando Augusto de Figueiredo writes, "approved new legislation for the concession of wastelands, following increasing pressure towards greater liberalization. The main innovations were that concessions by *aforamento* and property transmissions up to 2,500 hectares were now made under the authority of the provincial government, without the necessity of approval by the metropolitan government."[62] Alongside land law, a great many new labour laws were introduced, essentially prizing the peasantry away from the *regulos* and making their labour available to agricultural companies and private planters.

It was against this backdrop that the colonial administration first came to recognize and grant deeds for indigenous landownership. In 1914 the colonial government issued an edict on the registration of indigenous land,[63] and beginning the following year the colonial gazette published a large table for each district listing Timorese (mostly men, but in a few cases women) who had registered their land, complete with descriptions of the boundaries and the status of neighbouring land (either owned or "wasteland"). Most of these registered plots of land were in the district seat, where ethnic Chinese were rapidly purchasing land, but there are also instances of larger plots of rural land.[64] Based on the names, and in some cases titles, it appears that many of these individuals were members of indigenous ruling families. This suggests that at least part of the aristocratic class realized the opportunities that the new land regime presented. In a sense, this marks the fulfillment of the new land model, based on the right to alienation and an emerging market for legally recognized land transactions.

Conclusion

It would be grossly simplistic to treat the story of late-colonial land policy in Portuguese Timor as the story of the rise of large coffee plantations. As this chapter has argued, it is productive to understand colonial land policy in Portuguese Timor in terms of overlapping, borrowed, and phased transitions that variably prioritized economic interests, governance priorities, and legal elements. The "feudal-paternalistic" land regime, in which non-interference in the internal workings of the kingdoms was recognized (though not always respected), faded with the rise of the new land regime based on outright confiscation and the establishment of private property. This emerging regime was based on the dispossession of indigenous land and the granting of concessions in the beginning of the final decade of the nineteenth century, alongside the emergence of a land sale market in the first decades of the twentieth century. It is crucial to recognize that the new land regime did not displace the old one. Rather, from the start of the twentieth century, both regimes were in operation at the same time.

What were the driving forces behind colonial land policy in Portuguese Timor? This volume seeks to understand common features across the Portuguese overseas empire—laws, models, influences, even personnel. This chapter, however, argues that throughout the nineteenth century, law—even when supportive of colonial aims—was often ignored or treated as an afterthought, and that actual policy and practice in Timor developed more as a result of other factors, often exhibiting in Timor a decades-late uptake of legal and governance mechanisms from elsewhere. These included envy and attempted emulation of Dutch success in Java (Governor Castro in the 1860s), borrowing of international and Dutch legal innovations (state claim to land declared unused, made eligible for alienation), ad hoc measures (redistributing land to other kingdoms, then declaring rebellion land to be Crown property), and international norms regarding mineral prospecting.

Today, the most important legacy of Portuguese rule on land in independent Timor-Leste is not the passage of land law per se, but the continued coexistence of two competing land regimes: The first, with origins during the older feudal-paternalistic model, is often glossed as "customary" and based on *adat/lisan/* communal rights; the second, reflecting a combination of state power and the encouragement of market forces, involves the introduction of a new legal system in which private rights over land are recognized (even if only selectively), and within which the land entanglements around Portuguese, Indonesian, and independent Timor-Leste legal regimes are focused. The tension between these dual systems is still being worked out today.

NOTES TO CHAPTER 11

1. Christopher. J. Shepherd and Andrew McWilliam, "Cultivating Plantations and Subjects in East Timor: A Genealogy," *Bijdragen tot de Taal-, Land- en Volkenkunde* 169 (2013): 326–61.
2. Daniel Fitzpatrick, *Land Claims in East Timor* (Asia Pacific Press, 2002).
3. Affonso de Castro, *As Possessões Portuguezas na Oceania* (Imprensa Nacional, 1867).
4. Geoffrey C. Gunn, *Timor Loro Sae: 500 Years* (Livros do Oriente, 1999).
5. In the nineteenth century these written terms typically included pledges "to fulfill all orders," "to pay the annual tribute," and "to provide auxiliaries in war."
6. Hans Hägerdal, *Lords of the Land, Lords of the Sea: Conflict and Adaptation in Early Colonial Timor, 1600–1800* (KITLV, 2012), 62. Compare the above/below dichotomy in Timor to the Indic-inspired titles taken by rulers in Central Java that place the emphasis on being the "centre": in Surakarta, Sultan Nail of the Cosmos (Pakubuwono), and in Yogyakarta, Sultan Axis of the Cosmos (Hamengkubuwono).
7. Portuguese officials were not particularly interested in the "inner workings" of the kingdoms, and specifically the relationship between the *rei/regulos* and the various members of the lesser aristocratic class (*datos, tumanggãos*, etc.). Positing something akin to absolute rule made indigenous society more legible.
8. "Relação dos Reinos, e Reis, da dependencia do Governo de Timor, com residencia na Fortoleza de Delly," signed by the secretary to the governor, 28 February 1815, in Manoel José Gomes Loureira 1835: 234–5.
9. In fact, at precisely the same time da Silveira e Lorena was compiling his document and the governor in Dili was seeking to renew relations with the indigenous kingdoms, there was a flurry of correspondence about the excellent prospect for agricultural development in Timor.
10. Douglas Kammen and Jonathan Chen, *Cina Timor: Baba, Hakka and Cantonese in the Making of East Timor* (Yale Council on Southeast Asia Studies, 2019), 22.
11. Luis Augusto de Almeida Macedo, hand-written diary for 1857, held in Kroch Library, Rare and Manuscripts Collection, Cornell University. Macedo was not the only foreign observer. In 1858, the Indian-born British planter J. W. B. Money was also in Batavia and the Priangan highlands of western Java, studying the Cultivation System; this resulted in his classic book *Java: Or How to Manage a Colony* (1861).
12. Onghokham, "The Myth of Colonialism in Indonesia: Java and the Rise of Dutch Colonialism," in *The Thugs, the Curtain Thief, and the Sugar Lord*, ed. Onghokham (Metafor Publishing, 2003), 173.
13. In 1866, when the colony was placed under the Province of Macau, the number of districts was reduced to ten.
14. Luna de Oliveira, *Timor na História de Portugal*, vol. 2 (Fundação Oriente, 2004), 58–62.
15. Castro, *As Possessões Portuguezas na Oceania*, 421–37.
16. Katharine Davidson, "The Portuguese Colonization of Timor: The Final Stage, 1850–1912" (PhD diss., University of New South Wales, 1994), 90.
17. According to Shepherd and McWilliam, "Cultivating Plantations and Subjects," 329, this was applied to thirty out of the fifty kingdoms.

18   René Pélissier, *Timor en guerre: Le crocodile et les Portugais (1847-1913)* (Pélissier, 1996), 41-58.
19   Eduard Dowes Dekker's scathing novel *Max Havelaar: The Coffee Auctions of the Dutch Trading Company* was published in 1860, and marked the beginning of the end of the Cultivation System, which the Dutch abandoned in 1870. It is highly unlikely that Castro was aware of the publication of *Max Havelaar* when he introduced his thirty-point code and promotion of state quotas for coffee planting and delivery.
20   The new policy regarding empty lands was first communicated to the Macau Senate in 1862. Maria Luisa Abrantes, Miguel Rui Infante, and José Sintra Martinheira, *Macau e o Oriente no Arquivo Histórico Ultramarino 1833-1911*, vol. 3 (Instituto Cultural de Macau, 1999), 72. It is not known when this was communicated by officials in Macau to their counterparts in Timor.
21   Criticism centred on "primitive" methods such as use of dibble sticks or broadcasting of seeds rather than use of the plow; shifting swidden practices that required leaving land fallow for a certain period of time; low yields; or forest, wetlands, or arid land that were not planted but from which produce, game, and other resources were collected.
22   It is notable that the term "concession" (*concessão*) only appears twice in the extensive 1856 law: in article 29, where a "Decreto de concessão" is needed for a provincial governor to alienate land parcels over five hundred hectares; and in article 57, which discusses the "titulos de concessão" in the demarcation of *sesmarias* (Crown land grants).
23   AHU_ACL_SEMU_DGU_CU_01, Pt42-1910, cited in Abrantes et al., *Macau e o Oriente*, 239.
24   Hélder Lains e Silva, *Timor e a Culture do Café* (Imprensa Portuguesa, 1956), 33, citing Gonçalo Pimenta de Castro, *Timor—Subsídios para a Sua História* (1944).
25   One was in "Carayli" [*sic*: Carahil] under the "king of Caiman" [*sic*: Caimauc, in Motael District], using "invalid soldiers," and with a target of ten thousand coffee trees by the end of the year; a second plantation in "Lachita" [*sic*: Lacluta, in Viqueque District], where similar results were expected (but for which there is no mention of the use of military personnel). *Boletim da Provincia de Macau e Timor* 16, no. 15 (13 April 1868): 74.
26   Das Dores, who served as military commander in Viqueque in 1878, later wrote about Lacluta: "O Governo mandou fazer plantacoes de café neste reino em 1867, nas quaes empregou gente para as cuidar, e gastou uma importante somma, mas os governadores que se seguiram deixaram taes plantacoes ao abandon, de forma gue em 1891 ja esavam reduzidas a mato maninho." Raphael das Dores, *Apontamentos para um Diccionario Chorográphico de Timor* (Imprensa Nacional, 1903), 36.
27   AHU_ACU_SEMU_DGU_005, Cx0044 and AHU_ACL_SEMU_DGU_2R_002, Cx0001, cited in Abrantes et al., *Macau e Timor*, 100, 125-6.
28   While both Laga and Laclo (mentioned above) had been the sites of rebellions in the early 1860s, which meant not only counter-insurgency campaigns but also subsequent Portuguese meddling in the selection of local rulers, neither Carahil/Caimauc nor Lacluta were sites of resistance to colonial rule prior to Governor Teixeira da Silva's tenure. There is no evidence to suggest that Governor Teixeira dispossessed indigenous rulers of part of their kingdoms, perhaps by appealing to the 1856 law on wastelands.
29   In the 1890s, Portuguese officials estimated that 60 per cent of the 1,000 inhabitants of Lacluta were Christian. Bento da Franca, *Macau e os seus Habitants; Relações com Timor* (Imprensa Nacional, 1897), 246-7.
30   In 1866, the kingdoms were 60,000 rupias in arrears (see Castro, *As Possessões Portuguezas na Oceania*), and by 1878, that had risen to 72,000 rupias. But neither Caimauc nor Lacluta were greatly indebted. See Arquivo Historico Macau, AO682, Doc. P. 180, document dated 9 December 1878, signed Manoel Antonio Teixeira, secretary to the governor.
31   C. Fasseur, "Cornerstone and Stumbling Block: Racial Classification and the Late Colonial State in Indonesia," in *The Late Colonial State in Indonesia: Political and Economic Foundations of the Netherlands Indies 1880-1942*, ed. Robert Cribb (KITLV Press, 1994), 88.
32   During the second half of the nineteenth century, there were Portuguese consuls in the cities of Surabaya and Makassar, in the Netherlands East Indies, who corresponded with the governors in Dili.
33   W. G. Clarence-Smith, "Planters and Smallholders in Portuguese Timor in the Nineteenth and Twentieth Centuries," *Indonesia Circle* 57 (March 1992): 15-30; Shepherd and McWilliam, "Cultivating Plantations and Subjects."
34   Davidson, "The Portuguese Colonization of Timor," 157.
35   Quoted in Douglas Kammen, *Three Centuries of Conflict in East Timor* (Rutgers University Press, 2015), 72 (with minor adjustment to the translation). Nowhere in the available documentation does Governor Maia provide a legal basis for the seizure of indigenous land or its redesignation as Crown lands, but the basis may well have been the 1856 law discussed above.
36   In a sense, this is to international law what the concept of "empty land" was to the internal claims in the 1850s: What was "empty" could be (il)legitimately be claimed.

37 The Torrens system became known in Portugal. In 1910, University of Coimbra law professor Ruy Ennes Ulrich included extended commentary on Torrens in his lectures. Ruy Ennes Ulrich, *Economia Colonial: Lições feitas ao curso do 4.º ano jurídico no ano de 1909-1910*, vol. 1 (Imprensa da Universidade, 1910), 470-82, https://web.novalaw.unl.pt/Anexos/Investigacao/1374.pdf.

38 Edict 193 of 1914, *Boletim Oficial do Governo da Província de Timor* 15, no. 31 (1 August 1914): 225-6.

39 *Boletim Official da Governo de Macau e Timor* 38, no. 52 (29 December 1892): 248.

40 Kammen and Chen, *Cina Timor: Baba, Hakka and Cantonese in the Making of East Timor*, 62.

41 *Boletim Oficial do Governo da Provincia de Macau e Timor* 38, no. 52 (29 December 1892): 1.

42 Davidson, "The Portuguese Colonization of Timor," 182. By locking the peasantry to the land, this policy was the logical culmination of the process of fusion and parcellization that had begun in the eighteenth century with the imposition of vassal relations. The combination of political and economic power within nested territorial units lies at the heart of Perry Anderson's classic analysis of the feudal system in Europe. Anderson, *Lineages of the Absolutist State* (Verso, 1979).

43 Quoted in Davidson, "The Portuguese Colonization of Timor," 181 (punctuation altered).

44 Davidson, 218.

45 *Legislação Novíssima* 22 (1894): 683. For Mozambique, this phenomenon is discussed in the chapter by José Adalima in this volume.

46 Pélissier, *Timor en Guerre*.

47 Davidson, "The Portuguese Colonization of Timor," 95.

48 Kammen, *Three Centuries of Conflict in East Timor*, 104.

49 Caveat: The colonial gazette is not fully available for the years 1897-9, so we simply do not know what land grants were made in this period.

50 Shepherd and McWilliam, "Cultivating Plantations and Subjects."

51 In 1900, military operations were conducted in the northern part of Manufahi District and Motael District between 14 July and 15 August. Pélissier, *Timor en Guerre*, 234. Meanwhile, the concession of the first three 1,000-hectare grants in Aileu/Motael together with other 1,000-hectare grants in Ermera was made public through the colonial gazette on July 7! See *Boletim Official do Districto Autonomo de Timor* 1, no. 27 (7 July 1900): 113.

52 See, respectively, *Legislação Novíssima* 24 (1901): 121-5; *Legislação Novíssima* 27 (1901): 178-84; Maria Eugénia Mata, Leonor Fernandes Ferreira, and João Pereira dos Santos, "Success and Failure in Portuguese Colonial Africa: The Case of the Cazengo Agricultural Company (1900-1945)," *Entreprises et histoire* 3, no. 88 (2017): 53-73; and *Legislação Novíssima* 31 (1904): 253-8.

53 Mata, Ferreira, and Santos, "Success and Failure in Portuguese Colonial Africa," 61.

54 Bernardo Ribeiro de Almeida, "Building Land Tenure Systems: The Political, Legal, and Institutional Struggles of Timor-Leste" (PhD diss., Universiteit Leiden, 2020), 58, 301.

55 *Carta de lei de 9 de Maio de 1901 sobre concessões de terrenos no ultramar*, available at https://debates.parlamento.pt/catalogo/mc/cd/01/01/01/015/1901-02-09/15.

56 *Legislação Novíssima* 29 (1901): 69-79.

57 Decree of 13 September 1906, quoted in Davidson, "The Portuguese Colonization of Timor," 103.

58 *Portaria Provincial* no. 30, in *Boletim Official do Districto Autonomo de Timor* 7, no. 13 (31 March 1906): 67-8.

59 Some concessions were provisory and dependent on effective exploitation of the land, so they might have expired without occupation.

60 Davidson, "The Portuguese Colonization of Timor," 102.

61 Almeida, "Building Land Tenure Systems," 60, notes that "Júlio Celestino Montalvão e Silva, son of the Governor Celestino da Silva, claimed that 'the property regime is being perfected along [with] the evolution of the people, starting from the initial uncertainty until the final individualization' (Silva, 1910: 33)."

62 Fernando Augusto de Figueiredo, "Timor: A Presença Portuguesa (1769-1945)" (PhD diss., Universidade do Porto, 2004), 541-2. For full land legislation under the republic, see Afonso Camacho Rodrigues, *Concessões de Terrenos, 1913, Geral e Privativa da Colónia, até 1913*; Afonso Camacho Rodrigues, *Concessões de Terrenos, 1924, Geral e Privativa da Colónia, até 1923*.

63 *Portaria* no. 193 of 27 July 1914, published in the *Boletim Oficial do Governo da Província de Timor*, no. 31 (1 August 1914).

64 Kammen and Chen, *Cina Timor*, 42-6, 61.

Afterword

The Amphibious Colonial Empire

Ricardo Roque

Introduction

This volume is an invitation to look at the resilient forms of colonial land relations. I call them colonial mutants. They do not remain in the past; in fact they are neither simply "past" nor "present." They blend different timelines while undertaking several mutations. They are active and cut across different temporalities. Consider, to begin, a minor and apparently innocuous linguistic colonial mutant—the term "Lusophone." This is now one common way of designating the spaces that once formed the "Portuguese colonial empire," the imperial formation that, over almost five centuries, comprised a vast overseas geography in Asia, Africa, and the Americas—from India to Mozambique, Angola, Brazil, Timor, São Tomé, Guinea-Bissau, and Cabo Verde, and including Portugal itself.[1] Companion to the idea of *lusofonia*, it emphasizes a self-centred Portuguese geography based on constructs of spiritual, affective, and linguistic commonality; in doing so, some critics have noted, the term applied to Portugal and its former colonies perpetuates imperial imaginaries and helps camouflage the violent nature of the empire.[2] The term "Lusophone" insinuates the presence of these legacies in language; it is a discursive mutation that former colonial imaginaries have undertaken over time; and, at the same time, one form of (re)naming the "empire" that allows us to articulate its resilience in the post-imperial present. Yet resilience is also a feature of the imperial past, considering the longevity of the Portuguese colonial empire for almost five centuries. In effect, Portugal's dispersive imperial formation became circumstantially distinctive for one basic chronological aspect: it began earlier and lasted longer than its European counterparts—from an early start in the 1400s to a late termination in 1974–5, when a democratic revolution in Portugal put an end to the fascist Estado Novo regime and prompted decolonization. This characteristic makes the Portuguese overseas empire and its Lusophone avatar suitable observatories for analyzing the complex and pressing issue of colonialism's land legacies, as the editors of this volume propose. Of course, longevity is an effect of complex patterns of historical contingencies, never some epiphenomenon of a fabled national essence. Hence idioms of Portuguese racial and colonial exceptionalism are flawed constructs of nationalist imperial ideology that must be rejected as interpretive lenses through which to consider this issue.[3]

The essays in this volume further expose the uselessness of these ideological idioms, addressing the question of resilience of empire against the grain of both colonial imaginaries and post-imperial nostalgia. For they encourage us to question how, or whether, such an enduring empire might be re-narrated and reassessed around the tangible problems of control, governance, and domination of land and land-based resources. Bypassing the traps of the Lusophone lexicon, the chapters engage in stimulating ways with how human relations to land, and the materiality of land itself, might constitute a lasting imprint of Portugal's overseas colonial power on places as distinct as Angola, Mozambique, or Timor-Leste. To simply call these imprints "legacies," however, Ann Stoler reminds us, hinders an understanding of the varied and complex ways through which imperial formations endure; the simple term "legacy," Stoler criticizes, makes no "distinctions between what holds and what lies dormant,"[4] and as such it leaves unexamined the nuanced ways through which the past is (or is not) reinvested in practice. This volume, however, brings to light especially those legacies that hold and remain active—because they are recurrently, even if intermittently, reactivated and performed. It is adequate perhaps to conceptually differentiate these "active legacies" and call them, as I advanced above, colonial mutants: enduring forms of land relations of colonial origin that live on and mutate actively across a wide spectrum of activities, materials, and institutions. Past, present, and future are not categories that easily apply to these figures that travel in time while metamorphosing their original configurations.

This volume, then, brings together accounts of land relations that are also histories of colonial mutations, and it places these narratives in the long duration of the Portuguese colonial empire. However, the latter is an imperial formation that some do not traditionally consider an empire focused on land. This raises the question of whether the Portuguese Empire, traditionally viewed in Portugal as primarily seaborne for most of its existence, should be reconsidered in terms of land control and domination. In this afterword, I would like to briefly reflect on this issue. I first suggest that the volume's sustained focus on land challenges sea-centric nationalist mythologies and sea/land dualisms ingrained in the history and public memory of Portuguese imperialism. From the outset, land was at the core of the Portuguese imperial ventures through trade; it was never a purely seafaring and ocean-obsessed enterprise.[5] I thus propose the Portuguese Empire would be best approached as a shifting amphibious formation, a dispersive power-driven ensemble that moved on water as much as it moved on land. I then briefly reflect on how Portuguese language and conceptions of "land" might help capture this long-term amphibious element. I consider the relevance of the conceptual pair *terra/sertão* as a way to translate the notion of "land" in Portuguese colonizing cosmovisions. Finally, I call attention to this volume's contribution to the question of temporal comparison as regards the diversity and durability of mutant forms of colonial land relations.

Reassessing Sea-Centric Narratives

The volume's focus on land legacies matters for several reasons. As Tania Murray Li highlights in her foreword, current concerns with land justice following settler dispossession and repossession make projects aimed at historicizing land governance of pressing urgency and relevance today. This holds true most notably in countries where colonial relations to land dominantly fall under the category of settler colonialism, marked by the foreigners' voracious drive to expropriate and possess the land, and by extreme violence and destruction of the native peoples and societies.[6] In the specific context of Portuguese historical imaginaries, however, the volume's focus on land matters for one additional reason. It advances a land-based counternarrative to the seafaring discourse dominant in Portuguese histories and the public imagination.

The sea, not the land, is the quintessential element of the imagination of the Portuguese overseas empire that originated in the Age of Discovery in the sixteenth century. When thinking of so-called Portuguese expansion from the vantage point of the metropole, a set of familiar images come to mind: oceans, caravels, sailing ships, navigators, sailors, seafaring knowledge. This romantic imagery of a virtuous sea—rather than land—venture of the Portuguese Crown was forged from the outset in the 1500s through political discourses, art, and literature.[7] Consider for example Luís de Camões's famous verse in the sixteenth-century epic poem *Os Lusíadas*: "Across never sailed seas." Note Camões did not write, "Across never walked lands." Hence this verse is paradigmatic of the celebratory imagery of Portugal as an essentially maritime nation-empire that lasts until the present day.

Critical projects aimed at historicizing land relations in Lusophone geographies are fundamental to counter a memory excess of sea-centred narratives. Indeed, by placing the problematic of the colonial government of land at the core of a wide comparative understanding we are encouraged not simply to focus on land—we shift focus away from the sea. This shift away from the sea interferes with a pervasive narrative of the foundational and perhaps intrinsic nature of Portuguese colonial empire as being a sea- rather than a land-oriented colonial venture. Sea-centrism is a long-standing feature of a Portuguese national mythology. Any attempt to conceive of Lusophone colonial land legacies, therefore, must first confront a long historiographical tradition and a powerful nationalist mythology concerning Portuguese imperialism as ultimately a maritime colonial venture that is essentially defined by a drive to cross and dominate oceans and water, rather than land and soil.

Violent and intrusive settler practices of grabbing the land are hardly absent from Portuguese colonization. Recent historical scholarship on colonial Angola and Mozambique—including work represented in this volume—makes abundantly clear that a settler dynamic focused on land appropriation, village reordering, and territorial engineering and planning was central in particular to the late colonial and capitalist projects of the colonial state and its chartered companies in several colonies during the nineteenth and twentieth centuries.[8] The complex history of the Portuguese imperial formation cannot be subsumed under the concept of a white settler colonialism. Nevertheless, rarely is the very *identity* of Portugal's colonial empire considered from land-centred perspectives. In effect, although it seems undisputed that land control and settler violence were part of Portugal's *late* imperial venture, there is still some difficulty in placing land issues at the heart of Portugal's *early* modern empire, that is, the time of the so-called Age of Discoveries. This is not to say that historians disregard this dimension altogether. In recent years, as noted below, and as several essays in this volume demonstrate, new scholarship highlights the significance of territorial dynamics of conquest in early modern Portuguese imperialism in Asia and Africa. Yet, that difficulty exists because, I believe, the idea of the Portuguese colonial empire has merged with notions of Portuguese national identity that have long been dependent on historical imageries of an early modern seafaring past.

The wider dissemination and commemoration of this sea-centric national narrative took place during the nineteenth and twentieth centuries. It became a mythology of empire ingrained in the territorial politics of late Portuguese overseas expansionism. After Brazil became independent in 1822, sea-centric narratives of the imperial past accompanied the rise of euphoric and bellicose imperial nationalism during Portugal's nineteenth-century constitutional monarchy; it continued under the short-lived First Republic (1910–26) and, especially, under the hyper-imperial nationalism of the dictatorial regime of the Estado Novo (1926/1933–74). Thus the sea-centric narrative of Portugal's national-imperial past gained momentum when the imperial state was investing in hard-line and settler-type forms of conquest, knowledge, governance, and possession of land, so well-documented and analyzed by chapters in this volume. The myth of oceans and discoveries continued alongside actions of land grabbing. In fact, the two processes—growing mythologization of maritime glories, and growing interest in effective occupation of land—were historically coincidental and can be seen as interdependent. Nineteenth-century sea-centric nationalist myths of self-aggrandisement offered inspiration and symbolic legitimacy to new brutal ways of extending colonial power to inland zones—often the type of lands that, I hypothesize below, can be classified as *sertão*. The aquatic myth of Portugal's golden imperial age, in short, became a model image for a rising Portuguese terrestrial colonialism anxious to replicate on land the imagined glories of an ancient seafaring past. This mythic sea-centrism, however, did not disappear with the end of empire; it became an active legacy, a mutant, and it is constantly relived and re-enacted by the current Portuguese democratic regime. The revived post-imperial nationalism of Portugal's democratic regime after 1974 is no less inclined to commemorate the glories of the early modern seafarers. In effect, in Portugal, decolonization and the rise and consolidation of democracy did little to change sea-centric colonial imaginaries in the public space, as attested by the overload of state-authorized discourses, monuments, and events that continue to reiterate ad nauseam the mythic oceanic identity of Portugal. From the commemorations of Vasco da Gama in 1898 to the Lisbon world exhibition of 1998 (Expo '98), for instance, the "oceans" remain the core mythic element of the commemorative discourse about Portugal's Age of Discovery.[9] Informed public debate and rigorous scholarly analysis and criticism of the oceanic myth of discovery have grown in Portugal in recent years, yet these continue to be opposed by viciously defensive positions.[10]

Historical narratives obsessed with a maritime past thus come with several political effects—including the neglect of inconvenient historical truths and the production of historical silences. "Facts are not created equal," Haitian historian Michel Rolph-Trouillot wrote: "the production of traces is also the production of silences."[11] Occultation and ignorance can be a political effect of an unequal focus on certain facts to the detriment of others—say, on "maritime" versus "terrestrial" facts. In this light, even if unintentionally, histories of the Portuguese Empire that invest repeatedly in the reproduction of traces about the "facts" of oceanic expansion and the achievements of "discovery" might contribute to sideline or even to conceal certain historical realities. They contribute, to begin, as some critics recently observed, to a biased romantic and heroic image of the seas.[12] Self-celebratory sea-centrism hides the fact that the seas were the place for the performance of the horrors of Portuguese imperialism tragically documented by the massive transatlantic trade of enslaved Africans until the 1800s—and, later on, by flows of impoverished Portuguese labour migrants. The so-called sea glories of Portuguese expansion therefore read as sea horrors instead. In addition, I argue, this sea-centric memory excess has resulted in a relative occultation of Portuguese forms of land colonialism. Portuguese nationalism is obsessed with the image of a glorious past maritime empire. This helps to downplay, or even obscure, the forms of inequality and domination of people that were associated with both sea and land violence in Portugal's overseas endeavours since the early modern era. It is thus one of the merits of this volume, in contrast, to make these hidden facts unreservedly visible.

Historicizing an Amphibian Empire

The sea-centric mythology of Portugal and its colonial empire, a true "hagiography of the seas,"[13] is not limited to political discourse and public memory. It resonates in historiography. This is obviously the case among a Portuguese historiography with nationalist overtones proliferating since the late nineteenth century, but this resonance is not limited to nationalist literature. In fact, there is an abundant body of historical work on the so-called Portuguese "expansion" that follows the sea-centric track. To be fair, much of this more recent work is neither hagiographic nor nationalistic; it is critical of Portuguese self-glorifying narratives and of the dark dimensions of maritime voyaging and human mobility. Yet, even historiography critical of nationalist imperial mythology—from Charles R. Boxer to A. J. R. Russell-Wood,[14] to name just two prominent historians of this critical tradition—is structured around the notion of *the* "maritime" or "seaborne" character of Portugal's empire from the 1400s to about 1822.[15] This is an empire defined by oceanic, not terrestrial, identity; an empire that gained traction over waves and water rather than woods and dust. This kind of historiographical sea-centrism prospers through a selective focus on the early modern period as dominantly trade-based and maritime, as if land-bound events and orientations were only to become a meaningful trait of later Portuguese imperial expansionism in the nineteenth century. The ascription of Portuguese imperialism to the "maritime trade" pigeonhole, turned into unquestioned academic common sense, risks analytical reductionism. Historian Patricia Seed provides an example of such tendency to category oversimplification when she states, "The principal object of overseas possession for the Portuguese was not land, as it was for the English, or people, as it was for the Spanish, but trade and commerce."[16]

The concept that Portugal's empire was created without a primary focus on controlling and occupying large swaths of land, as if in essence interested in maritime trade and commercial transactions and virtually uninterested in exerting domination over territories and peoples, needs revision. In Brazil, most obviously, Portuguese expansionism was overtly territorial from the outset.[17] Yet to represent even the early modern empire in Asia as purely maritime and commercial, in its essence ocean-centred and "non-territorial," in opposition to land-bound and conquest-oriented overseas empires (such as the Spanish in the Americas), can be misleading.[18] The Portuguese expansionism in South Asia and the drive to conquer and take territory, to conquer lands and take souls, were often inextricable processes.[19] In his masterly account of the Portuguese Empire in Asia, historian Sanjay Subrahmanyam already questioned that concept.[20] Between 1580 and 1640, before and especially after the union of Portuguese and Spanish Crowns, Portuguese activities in the Indian Ocean revealed both "growing neglect of the maritime vocation" and "growing interest in the land and territorial adventurism" across a wide set of locations in Asia and East Africa.[21] Sea and land became concomitant imperial concerns by the late 1500s, as interest in conquering and grabbing Indigenous soil intensified. British historian A. J. R. Russell-Wood, whose works influentially shaped the concept of Portugal's seaborne imperial identity, acknowledged late in life that he had come to learn "the importance of rejecting a view of the Portuguese Empire exclusively from a maritime angle."[22] In an interview shortly before his death in 2019, the late Portuguese historian António Manuel Hespanha again called attention to this point with his usual wit: "We all know of Portuguese historiography's attraction for the 'gesta marítima' [maritime deeds]. The series of chronicles about the achievements on sea is vaster than those about the history of the Portuguese who set feet on land."[23]

This volume's analytical focus on colonial land relations therefore contributes to destabilizing widely diffused images of the exclusively oceanic identity of the Portuguese Empire as an essentially seaborne undertaking. Recent historiography and several chapters in this volume make clear that there were many concerns revolving around land occupation, conquest, property rights, land access, and land-based exploitation in the early centuries of Portuguese expansionism across a wide range of locations.[24] Land, empire, and power were connected from the outset. Sailors and navigators were always looking forward to sighting land—and to claim and possess it. They performed ceremonies of possession and planted *padrões* to take ownership of land in the name of the king of Portugal. They conquered lands and subdued Indigenous rulers; they negotiated treaties with local landlords to establish outposts and gain rights of taxation, resource extraction, and/or property over land and people, even if they did so through the mediation of Indigenous groups. The right to conquest and the principle of territorial occupation also were inherent to early notions of overseas imperial legitimacy; it was not exclusive to later forms of imperialist occupation. The legal grounds of the Portuguese rulers' early claims to legitimacy of the conquest and possession of overseas lands were certainly complex and varied.[25] It seems early modern Portuguese imperialists nonetheless followed Roman legal notions of sovereignty, Vicente Serrão observes, according to which "the fundamental title of acquisition of property, which could be applied to lands as well as territories, rested on the principle of occupation (*occupatio*)," and they used this principle "to justify territorial occupation, land ownership and sovereignty rights in overseas territories."[26] Indeed, the desire to conquer land, as well as the self-entitlement to appropriate and dispossess Indigenous soil, was rarely absent in many early colonizing projects. A variety of legal forms also came into being overseas with a view to regulate the outsiders' eagerness to take the land. The *prazos* system, for example, instituted first in the Northern Province in India and then in Mozambique in the seventeenth century, and the Portuguese medieval laws of *sesmarias* transplanted to Brazil, here discussed by José Adalima, Matthias Röhrig Assunção, and Carmen Alveal, are emblematic forms of this early colonial intrusiveness in Indigenous land property and rights, the marks of which remain effective today. However, the intrusions of colonial forms of land governance did not operate simply by imposition of external norms, nor did they necessarily imply the erasure of pre-existing local systems. Their emergence, and their mutations, often involved complex modes of interaction, coexistence, adaptation to, and/or incorporation of local forms of land governance—a process eventually exemplified by the Portuguese state's lasting engagement with the Indian *gaunkari* system of land management (also known as "village communities") in Goa since the early modern period.[27]

We may thus speak of an ocean- or sea-centric bias that needs historiographical correction; one that requires balance, for example, through writing land-centred narratives such as those offered in this volume. This is not to say maritime accounts should now simply be discarded and replaced by another, say, land-centric, narrative of Portugal's imperial formation. Instead, it is to the complex coexistence of both aquatic and terrestrial orientations that we need to attend and that we need to examine further. Re-narrating Portuguese imperial history beyond sea-centric imaginaries, in other words, should start with the concept of the structurally amphibian condition of the colonial empire in the long term. There were no doubt differences and mutations between early and late imperial formations, as there were between trade- and settler-oriented colonial ventures. Yet, it is difficult to sustain a simplistic dualistic contrast between an early modern empire of seafarers and a late-modern empire of land-grabbers. The very application of the taxonomy of empires around a strict land/sea dichotomy in fact obscures the manifold ways through which the Portuguese overseas empire simultaneously sought to extract power from and take advantage of both sea and land in different regions. It is thus time to think through the amphibious condition of the Portuguese colonial empire and to examine the transits between aquatic and terrestrial ambient in which colonial power dwelled. It is time to address, finally, how the constancy of focus on land within the amphibious empire changed while also enduring, as this volume proposes, for several centuries.

How Colonizers Think About Land

The chapters in this volume clearly suggest it is worth considering the varied meanings land rights, ownership, and occupation, as well as the notion of "land" itself, could take in a wide range of colonial and post-colonial discourses and practices, over time and in different spaces. Attention to these shifting meanings may also help to grasp the significance of "land" concepts in colonial cosmovisions. Were colonizing practices accompanied by distinctive conceptions of land? What specific or distinctive meanings, if any, did the term "land" acquire within the activities and world views of Portuguese imperialism? How were certain notions of "land" created, shaped, configured as part of imperial and colonial praxis and cosmologies? A satisfactory response to these questions is certainly beyond the scope of this afterword. Yet, I think the pursuit of these answers should consider the complex meanings of the term "land" in the Portuguese language, seen in connection to the history of Portugal's amphibian overseas empire.

The English term "land" is ordinarily translated to Portuguese as *terra*. This literal translation, however, does not cover an important conceptual opposition entailed in colonial conceptions of land from a Portuguese perspective. The Portuguese *terra* alone, I argue, does not fully capture the colonial conceptions of land. Land as colonial concept was an internally complex notion inherent to which were conceptual dualities such as coast versus interior, cultivated versus uncultivated, productive versus unproductive, and wild versus domesticated, for example. In this regard, I think it is especially interesting to historicize and to attend to the differences and changes in the meanings ascribed to the complementary Portuguese terms *terra* and *sertão*.

In Portuguese colonizing visions "land" is at least a double space, a conceptual pair. It encompasses the idea of coastal, cultivated, productive, civilized, and domesticated lands, and the contrasting notion of interior, unproductive, uncultivated, and wild and uncivilized bush hinterlands. "Land" as Portuguese colonial cosmovision should thus perhaps be translated as an ensemble of complementary conceptual opposites, central to which were (importantly though not exclusively) the terms *terra* and *sertão*. My hypothesis is that these connected yet contrasting terms became a significant component of Portuguese colonial imaginaries of lands over the long duration.[28] Of course, this hypothesis must be addressed with caution. This duality of terms certainly does not convey a more complex plethora of Indigenous concepts; it also does not simply exhaust colonial vocabularies, and this volume offers abundant examples of a diversity of Portuguese colonial terms and approaches to land (*prazos, sesmarias, aldeias,* and so forth). Yet, I believe these two terms encapsulate a conceptual contrast of wider significance in colonial land relations; together, they point to a structural, though historically shifting, figure within Portuguese colonial cosmovisions of land that need to be taken into consideration. A brief, necessarily exploratory inspection of how these two terms appear in two historically representative Portuguese-language dictionaries—those compiled by Raphael Bluteau[29] and Cândido de Figueiredo[30]—might help illuminate this point.

Terra, the Coast Opposite the Sea

Father Raphael Bluteau's referential Portuguese dictionary of 1789 begins to address the polysemic term *terra* as the Portuguese name for our planet (Earth) and the term for a generator of plant life ("the heaviest of elements that ordinarily creates vegetables").[31] Bluteau alludes only in passing to an economic dimension, an idea of land as productive factor. Yet, another, perhaps more revealing trace of an earlier colonial relation to land, I believe, is to be found in Bluteau's definition of *terra* as "the coast opposite the sea" ("a costa opondo-se ao mar") as used in the phrase "Quem vai embarcado avista a terra, toma a terra" (The one who is onboard a ship sees the land, takes the land). *Terra* is here construed as the object of gaze and desire of someone who comes from the sea.[32] It stands for that portion of land that existed in relation to the interdependent experiences of navigating the sea *and* possessing the land—*see the land, take the land*. Portuguese rule in many areas was basically confined to the seaside and coast until the nineteenth century—even if constant connections existed with the world of the hinterland. This structure of colonial occupation could lead to seeing control over coastal lands more like a conceptual extension of control over the seas. Thus conceived, Bluteau's notion of *terra*—a contact zone with water as much as point of entry into inner lands—perhaps expressed an early colonial desire to extend the domination of seas to the domination of lands. By the early twentieth century, however, *terra* loses its connotation with seafaring and acquires a more strictly *extractive* meaning as the "soil that produces." The maritime notion of *terra* as land that is touched by the sea seems to fade in favour of a pronounced connotation of this term with a strict physical, agricultural, and economic definition. Thus

Cândido de Figueiredo in 1913 simply defined *terra* as the "soil, on which one walks. The soft part of the soil, that *produces the* vegetables."[33] A colonial extractive and settler-oriented notion of *terra*—a solid part of soil to be walked upon; an object of nature to be exploited as a productive factor—apparently supersedes, or somehow juxtaposes with, the earlier idea of *terra* as land sighted and possessed by seafarers.

This difference in meaning of course begs the question of whether this shift in the meaning of *terra*/land reflects changes in the imperial projects, or mutations within the broader Portuguese colonial cosmovisions of land. In any case, differences notwithstanding, it is significant that both dictionaries suggest the Portuguese term *terra* alone does not fully cover the range of meanings that the idea of "land" could take in Portuguese colonial activity overseas. In reality, a reading of both Bluteau and Figueiredo suggest that in order to convey the *other* part of land beyond the coast—land that is remote, wild, barely populated by humans, uncultivated, uncontrolled, unproductive—a companion term at least is required: the noun *sertão*.

Sertão, the Backlands

The use of the Portuguese term *sertão* is not exclusive to overseas lands. It could sometimes refer to certain rural areas perceived to be wild or ungoverned in Portugal itself. Thus, compared to African, Asian, and American interior lands, certain Portuguese forested areas and interior landscapes could be caught up in colonizing cosmovisions of land as *sertão* that demanded cultivation, control, civilization. Nevertheless, it seems clear the term gained stronger and wider currency in the context of the colonization of overseas possessions from an early date; it eventually became widespread across Portugal's overseas colonies, most noticeably in Brazil, Angola, and Mozambique. There, it became the common term to refer to the alterity of inner spaces opposite to the coastal areas where colonial settlements were first established. Bluteau's definition makes clear the term *terra* did not mean *all* land. It conveyed only a certain part of land—the seafront, the coast. In fact this eighteenth-century notion of *terra* as primarily the seacoast was incomplete without the complementary and contrasting concept of *sertão*. *Sertão*, Bluteau asserted, is "the interior, the heart of lands, it is opposed to the maritime, and to the coast.... *Sertão* is taken by bush [*mato*] far from the coast."[34] The term expressed the alterity of inner lands as regards the coast (*terra*, properly called) and apparently this meaning was preserved more or less intact in subsequent centuries. In fact, in the same vein of Bluteau, Figueiredo in 1913 defined *sertão* as an "uncultured place, distant from settlements [*povoações*] or from cultivated lands. Forest in the interior of a continent or far from the coast."[35]

Hence *sertão* conveyed the idea of an ultimate colonial *other* space, the kind of heterotopian spaces (such as deserts, mountains, or forests) associated with perceived interiority, wilderness, and remoteness, the idea of which both repelled and attracted colonizers.[36]

The significance of *sertão* as a Portuguese-language colonial category applied to *other* land spaces, a driving force to possess, occupy, cultivate, civilize, did not pass without notice to perceptive observers such as French anthropologist Claude Lévi-Strauss. In 1955, Lévi-Strauss referred to the local meaning and importance of this term. In a passage of his *Tristes Tropiques*—the famous memoir of his time in Brazil in the 1930s (Portugal's former colony and an independent country since 1822)—he distinguished the meanings of *mato* and *sertão* while admitting it was insufficient to translate the Portuguese term *sertão* as just *brousse* (a French term meaning "bush") because, he added,

> the word has a slightly different connotation. Mato relates objectively to the bush as an element in the landscape which contrasts with the forest. Sertão, on the other hand, has a subjective significance: landscape, in this case, is considered in relation to human beings, and sertão means "the bush," as opposed to land that is inhabited and cultivated—a region, that is to say, where man has not yet contrived to set up his home. French Colonial slang has an equivalent in the word "bled."[37]

Lévi-Strauss sees *sertão* as the Portuguese term for the type of landscape that stands in a specific "relation to human beings"—or one could say instead in a specific *colonial* relation. In this passage, I believe Lévi-Strauss captures—perhaps inadvertently; he makes no further reference to the local history of the term—the distinctive specificity of the notion of *sertão* in Luso-Brazilian praxis as a colonial mode of relating to Indigenous lands as wild and uncultured entities to be possessed, conquered, occupied, cultivated, civilized by settlers. Lévi-Strauss's description is evocative of the relationship that first the Portuguese settlements, and, after 1822, the Brazilian coastal states, maintained with the otherness of the vast interior backlands of Brazil. These were settler-colonial imaginaries of Brazil as a nation created out of heroic movements of frontier occupation and conquest of the *sertão* epitomized, for instance, in Euclides da Cunha's epic novel *Os Sertões* of 1902. In the Luso-Brazilian colonizer's eyes, Lévi-Strauss suggested, *sertão* were empty and wild lands requiring actions of conquest, settlement, and cultivation by colonial men. This perception entitled settlers to selfishly (dis)possess, occupy, and extract Indigenous land property and resources, by violence if needed. The term *sertão* encompasses a colonial mode of conceiving of, and relating to, land that is by no means exceptional to Portuguese-speaking contexts. The heterotopia of *sertão* is suited to wider comparisons; it features in colonial activities elsewhere. Indeed, Lévi-Strauss notes, *sertão* went by different names in different colonial imaginaries and languages. Hence the French anthropologist ends with a quick note of comparison, proposing a French translation of the Portuguese term *sertão*: the "French colonial slang" word *bled*. The French word *bled*—a derivation from the Arab *balad* (for country, settlement)—originated in the colonization of North Africa, and it was the term used there by French settlers to designate "the interior of lands, the countryside."[38]

Lévi-Strauss's insight also might be extended to Anglophone contexts. A brief reflection about English translations of the term *sertão*—which includes the terms "bush," "backlands," as well as "hinterland" or "outback"—is suggestive of comparable colonial connotations. "Outback," for example, common in Australian settler usage since the 1800s to refer to the "backcountry" and interior regions, pairs well with the land concept of *sertão*, similarly conveying colonial ideals of adventure and possession of wild nature and interior spaces. Moreover, this galaxy of land concepts, colonial in essence, seems to be a perfect companion to that kind of naturalist thought that, in anthropologist Phillippe Descola's views, conceives of "nature" as a purely inanimate ontological domain and as such suitable to colonizing acts of settlement, cultivation, and land extractivism.[39] Of course, those spaces classified as *sertão*, outback, or *bled* in reality did not simply fit the naturalist image of wild and unpeopled nature. Dense forests, arid deserts, or steep mountains in Africa, Brazil, or Australia were and are deeply connected to the long-standing Indigenous human communities who have inhabited and animated these spaces in complex cultural ways. These are colonial land concepts that conveniently erase this obvious fact; they set the stage for predatory activities.

Comparisons Across Time

Concepts of land, just like empire itself, persisted, but also mutated. A valuable and also challenging proposal of this volume is the focus on these mutations in the *longue durée* of the Portuguese Empire as well as *after* the formal end of the empire. They need to be historicised also in relation to the present. This framework involves exploring comparisons and crossings in *space*, a consideration of colonial land legacies in different places that were former colonies of Portugal. But also, I think more importantly and innovatively, it calls for a comparison in *time*. This approach urges us to think beyond rather static historiographical periodizations and consider not only continuity and change but also the cyclical and recursive nature of themes across time and space. This focus on temporal comparisons reminds us that one must not overemphasize the notion of a temporal dichotomy between past and present, as if at some point in time forms of land relations and concepts simply gave way to another. Problematizing the notion of a definite break between past and present land relations and conceptions is precisely the aim of the editors of this volume. The complex forms of land relations that accompanied the Portuguese amphibian imperial formation are also not something that magically disappeared with the end of formal colonial rule. They have an active life in the present. Nor do these forms remain constant. They change. They endure.

Changing meanings and relations to land, and the need to understand them comparatively through time and space, draw our attention to the plurality and durability of colonial forms of relating to land that existed and continue to exist throughout the so-called Lusophone world. It is clear from the chapters presented in this volume that colonial governmentality of land appears under different figures and forms, both in the colonial era and after the end of empire. We are not simply talking about a white settler takeover of Indigenous lands, but a complex layering of forms of land possession and dispossession; where the authority and power to apportion, allocate, alienate, or reclaim and occupy land becomes entangled and enmeshed in relations between colonizers and colonized. The chapters in this volume show well this diversity of forms across time and space. For example, we find that colonial state legal or normative orders sought to regulate ownership, access, and use of land by enforcing norms and practices of external origin. We also find some mutual borrowing: colonizers tentatively imitating local uses, invoking "customary" authority or drawing on "customary" claims to benefit from the land—but also vice versa, as when customary indigenous authorities reuse or repurpose colonial legacies to their own ends.[40] We find the state or the Crown distributing its own sovereignty to others through land concessions.[41] We have squatters and peasantry forming from descendants of slaves whose histories are entwined with the land through layers of colonial engagement.[42] Land dispossession was clearly a strategy of an extractive settler colonialism, but it did not occur without resistance from local populations in the form of displacement,[43] squatting, negotiation, and conflict.[44] Thus we see also Indigenous peoples resisting, opposing, and giving shape to colonial constructs and experiences relating to land. In sum, a plurality of actors intervenes in the making and unmaking of colonial land relations over time. The result is an image of the "colonial" that is not limited to the European who stakes a claim to land—it is an image composed of a more complex ensemble of actors. This means attention should be paid to the manifold ways through which colonial land legacies mutate not simply as the outcome of the actions and plans of the European colonizer—but also, and importantly, as the result of being opposed and/or appropriated and re-signified by a variety of Indigenous actors.

The problem of these interrelations that shape the mutant colonial order of land needs finally to attend to the question of durability. There is, in many cases, a strong sense of institutional continuities between colonial and post-colonial land relations. Although decolonization and independence were followed by a rhetoric of discontinuity and change, ultimately they did not represent a profound transformation or end of colonial land relations, as several of the chapters in this volume attest. For example, in the case of Mozambique, FRELIMO (Frente de Libertação de Moçambique, or Liberation Front of Mozambique) identified agriculture as the base of its economic policy. Land was nationalized and converted into state farms and companies.[45] Yet, at the same time this approach added new layers of state control to the pre-existing colonial chartered companies, which maintained most of their areas of intervention and privileges untouched. In addition, national independent states have continued modes of land governance that are colonial in origin—think of "concessions," "plantations," even the recognition of limited "customary" rights. Similarly, Indigenous peoples and systems have also incorporated traits and mechanisms that one may see as "colonial" in origin as they seek recognition from or benefits in formal land administrative systems, in some cases engaging with them creatively and giving them new meaning on their own terms.[46]

Conclusion

The passage of the long-lasting Portuguese colonial empire left numerous durable marks. But the grand narrative of an early empire, driven by sailors and caravels, no longer holds. The sea-centred mythology of empire is a strong and active "colonial legacy" in its own terms, a colonial mutant itself, which must be countered and balanced by land-centred accounts such as the ones presented in this volume. Yet a straightforward opposition between an early modern seaborne and a late modern land-bound Portuguese overseas imperialism is a misleading analytic, because it obscures the conjunction between the aquatic and terrestrial voracity of Portuguese colonial expansionism. The debate over the Portuguese Empire as "seaborne versus landbound" should thus give way to a heuristic focused on historicizing the amphibious dynamic of Portuguese imperial formations.

Significant colonial durability, this volume reveals, is perceptible in how different colonial-era and post-colonial governments and companies regulate land relations; it is perceptible also in how people actually live with and relate to these former colonial land relations as active legacies, or as I propose to call them, as colonial mutants. Colonial forms of land relations take resilient manifestations in the present order and lives of many African, Asian, and Latin American countries that once were under Portuguese colonial rule. The theme of "legacies" central to this volume evokes this resilience, exploring colonial land relations as temporal crossings and enduring performances. I began this afterword by suggesting this resilience might be approached as a sequence of mutations. The hypothesis is that of the strong mutant character of many of the plural and durable colonial forms of relating to land, of governing land, and of accessing or using land. Taken together, then, the essays in this volume show that historicizing Lusophone land relations based on solid archival and ethnographic research is critical for re-narrating the Portuguese colonial empire beyond sea-centric mythologies, and recovering its amphibious complexities. Furthermore, finally, this volume is an important demonstration that histories of colonialism are deeply entangled with contemporary lives in multiple places. The question of the legacies of colonialism cannot reduce to a matter of "judgmental assessments," and as such be excluded from historical scholarship.[47] This volume bears proof to the contrary: non-judgmental and rigorous historical analysis of colonial legacies is possible—indeed it is necessary. Histories of empire and colonialism often are also histories of the present. More than shedding light on a presumably distant imperialist past, therefore, the fine historical and anthropological essays collected herein make clear that the project of historicizing the mutant lives of colonialism is vital for shedding light on contemporary realities.

NOTES TO AFTERWORD

I am grateful to Susanna Barnes and Laura Yoder for their generous editorial work and for encouraging me to develop my closing remarks to the conference Lusophone Land Legacies held in 2021 for the present essay. I thank the editors Susanna Barnes and Laura Yoder, Bárbara Direito, and the anonymous reviewers for valuable suggestions and critiques that helped to improve this essay. I have translated into English all passages originally in Portuguese. A project grant from FCT, Fundação para a Ciência e Tecnologia, *Indigenous Colonial Archives: Micro-Histories and Comparisons* (PTDC/HAR- HIS/28577/2017), supported my research for this work.

1. The term "Lusophone," used to convey juxtaposition to the former imperial formation, tends to leave out a variety of diasporas contained within and extending beyond the imperial geography. See Cristiana Bastos, "Intersections of Empire, Post-Empire, and Diaspora: De-Imperializing Lusophone Studies," *Journal of Lusophone Studies* 5, no. 2 (2020): 27–54; Pamila Gupta, *Portuguese Decolonization in the Indian Ocean World: History and Ethnography* (Bloomsbury Academic, 2020).

2. There is already a significant critical literature on the traces of colonial imageries in the notions *lusofonia* and related "Luso-" constructs, including the colonial ideology of *Luso-tropicalismo*. See, for example, Cláudia Castelo, *O modo português de estar no mundo: O luso-tropicalismo e a ideologia colonial portuguesa (1933-1961)* (Afrontamento, 1998); Michel Cahen, "Lusitanidade e lusofonia: Considerações conceituais sobre realidades sociais e políticas," *Plural Pluriel: Revue des cultures de langue portugaise* 7 (2010): 3–17; Victor Barros, "A lusofonia como retrato de família numa casa comum," *Revista Angolana de Sociologia* 7 (2011): 83–106.

3. See also Warwick Anderson, Ricardo Roque, and Ricardo Ventura Santos, eds., *Luso-tropicalism and Its Discontents: The Making and Unmaking of Racial Exceptionalism* (Berghahn Books, 2019).

4. Ann Stoler, *Imperial Debris: On Ruins and Ruination* (Duke University Press, 2013), 353.

5. Zoltán Biedermann, *(Dis)Connected empires: Imperial Portugal, Sri Lankan Diplomacy, and the Making of a Habsburg Conquest in Asia* (Oxford University Press, 2018).

6. Patrick Wolfe, "Settler Colonialism and the Elimination of the Native," *Journal of Genocide Research* 8, no. 4 (2006): 288.

7. See Ângela Barreto Xavier and Nuno Senos, *1498* (Tinta-da-China, 2019), 20–54.

8. See Cláudia Castelo, *Passagens para África: O Povoamento de Angola e Moçambique com Naturais da Metrópole (1920–1974)* (Afrontamento, 2007); Tiago Saraiva, *Fascist Pigs: Technoscientific Organisms and the History of Fascism* (MIT Press, 2016), chap. 6; Samuël Coghe, "Reordering Colonial Society: Model Villages and Social Planning of Rural Angola, 1920–45," *Journal of Contemporary History* 52, no. 1 (2016): 16–44; Bárbara Direito, *Terra e colonialismo em Moçambique: A região de Manica e Sofala sob a Companhia de Moçambique, 1892–1942* (Imprensa de Ciências Sociais, 2020).

9. Elisa Lopes da Silva and José Miguel Ferreira, eds., "History of the Commemorations of the 'Portuguese Discoveries,'" special issue, *Práticas da História*, no. 8 (2019).

10. For a critical overview, see Pedro Cardim, "Reassessing the Portuguese Imperial Past: Scholarly Perspective and Civic Engagement," *Journal of Lusophone Studies* 8, no. 1 (2023): 176–205.

11. Michel Rolph-Trouillot, *Silencing the Past: Power and the Production of History* (Beacon Press, 1995), 29.

12. See Cristiana Bastos, "Portuguese in the Cane: The Racialization of Labour in Hawaiian Plantations," in *Changing Societies: Legacies and Challenges: Ambiguous Inclusions: Inside Out, Inside In*, ed. Sofia Aboim, Paulo Granjo, and Alice Ramos (Imprensa de Ciências Sociais, 2018), 65–96, and the papers collected in André Nóvoa, "Introduction: the Sword and the Shovel," *Portuguese Literary and Cultural Studies* 33 (2020): 1–12.

13. Nóvoa, "Introduction," 2.

14. Charles R. Boxer, *The Portuguese Seaborne Empire, 1415–1825* (Hutchinson and Co., 1969); A. J. R. Russell-Wood, *A World on the Move: The Portuguese in Africa, Asia, and America 1415–1808* (Carcanet, 1992).

15. But for updated and sophisticated comparative reassessments of the notion of Portuguese seaborne empire, see Gabriel Paquette, *The European Seaborne Empires: From the Thirty Years' War to the Age of Revolutions* (Yale University Press, 2019); Cátia Antunes, "The Portuguese Maritime Empire: Global Nodes and Transnational Networks," in *Empires of the Sea: Maritime Power Networks in World History*, ed. Rold Strootman, Floris van den Eijnde, and Roy van Wijk (Brill, 2019), 294–311. On maritime historiography of empire and its ideological limits, compare also Jaime Rodrigues, "Vicente d'Almeida Eça e a historiografia marítima em 1898," *Práticas da História* 8 (2019): 139–61, and Ângela Barreto Xavier, "Tendências na historiografia da expansão portuguesa: Reflexões sobre os destinos da história social," *Penélope* 22 (2000): 141–79.

16 Patricia Seed, *Ceremonies of Possession in Europe's Conquest of the New World, 1492-1640* (Cambridge University Press, 1995), 154.
17 For example, Márcia Motta, José Vicente Serrão, Marina Machado, eds., *Em terras lusas: Conflitos e fronteiras no Império Português* (Editora Horizonte, 2013).
18 Building on this dichotomy, for instance, historian Luís F. R. Thomaz influentially defended the early Portuguese expansion in Asia, claiming that it "aspired more to controlling the seas than to the domination of land"; that it was in essence a sea-centred "network" where power in and over land was, at best, of secondary value. Luís F. R. Thomaz, *De Ceuta a Timor* (Difel, 1994), 201, 215-16.
19 A point demonstrated most notably by the works of Zoltán Biedermann (for Sri Lanka) and Ângela Barreto Xavier (for Goa). Ângela Barreto Xavier, *A invenção de Goa: Poder imperial e conversões culturais nos séculos XVI e XVII* (Imprensa de Ciências Sociais, 2008); Biedermann, *(Dis)connected Empires*.
20 Sanjay Subrahmanyam, *The Portuguese Empire in Asia, 1500-1700: A Political and Economic History* (Longman, 1993), 107-143.
21 Subrahmanyam 122, 137.
22 A. J. R. Russell-Wood, quoted in Mafalda Soares da Cunha, "The Historiographical Reception of A. J. R. Russell-Wood's *A World on the Move: The Portuguese in Africa, Asia, and America, 1415-1808*," *E-Journal of Portuguese History* 11, no. 1 (2013): 104.
23 António Manuel Hespanha and André Nóvoa, "Uma entrevista com António Hespanha," *Portuguese Literary and Cultural Studies* 33 (2020): 199. Hespanha added this historiographical emphasis was "very selective." For while it overemphasized the sea voyages, it left out important social history dimensions concerning the ways African slaves or Portuguese subaltern groups, ordinary sailors, fishermen, and other groups lived through the ocean experiences.
24 José Vicente Serrão, Bárbara Direito, Susana Münch Miranda, and Eugénia Rodrigues, eds., *Property Rights, Land and Territory in the European Overseas Empires* (CEHC-IUL, 2014); José Vicente Serrão, M. S. Motta, Susana Munch Miranda, dirs., *e-Dicionário da terra e do território no Império Português* (CEHC-IUL, 2013).
25 Early Portuguese claims to "conquest" of Asia and Africa, for example, seem to have entailed a complex juridical distinction between *jus in re* and *jus ad rem*, between a merely potential and an actually realized right to land acquisition. See Thomaz, *De Ceuta a Timor*, 218.
26 José Vicente Serrão, "Introduction: Property, Land and Territory in the Making of Overseas Empires," in Serrão et al., *Property Rights*, 8-9; cf. Wolfe, "Settler Colonialism," 391. The Roman notion of *nullius* could also be used to claim legitimate control of overseas lands "discovered" or conquered by force of arms. Eduardo dos Santos, *Regimes de terras no ex-ultramar: Evolução da política legislativa até 1945* (Instituto de Ciências Sociais e Políticas, 2004), 16. But see also, on the diversity of Portuguese ways of claiming legitimate land acquisition overseas, Thomaz, *De Ceuta a Timor*, 224-43.
27 See, for instance, Nagendra Rao, "The State, Village Communities and the Brahmanas in Goa (1000-1600 ce)," *Indian Historical Review* 49, no. 1 (2022): 51-68; Rochelle Pinto, "The *Foral* in the History of the Comunidades of Goa," *Journal of World History* 29, no. 2 (2018): 185-212.
28 The contrast revealed in the *terra/sertão* pair is perhaps noticeable under different linguistic guises and, in this regard, it is also worth considering the expression *terra/s firme/s* (dry or steady land/s) and its complementary opposites. In early modern Goa, for instance, this term referred to the coastal regions that stood in relation to the so-called *outra banda* (the other side), a term that conveyed the *terra firme*'s surrounding lands that were untouched by ocean waters. Similarly, in northern Mozambique, *terra firme* conveyed the wide coastal strip of land as opposed to its hinterland, which went by the name of *Macuana*. See José Miguel Ferreira, "As Novas Conquistas: Florestas, agricultura e colonialismo em Goa (c. 1763-1912)," (PhD diss., University of Lisbon), 22-4; Maria Bastião, "Entre a ilha e a terra: Processos de construção do continente fronteiro à Ilha de Moçambique (1763-c. 1802)," (MA thesis, Universidade Nova de Lisboa, 2013).
29 Rafael Bluteau, *Diccionario da lingua portugueza composto pelo padre D. Rafael Bluteau, e accrescentado por Antonio de Moraes Silva*, 2 vols. (Officina de Simão Thaddeo Ferreira, 1789).
30 Cândido de Figueiredo, *Novo dicionário da língua portuguesa* (Lisbon: A. M. Teixeira, 1913).
31 Bluteau, *Diccionario*, 454.
32 It is worth noting the famous early modern Portuguese stone pillars (*padrões*) were often planted on promontories and capes with the purpose of being seen from *sea* rather than from land. They were a sign aimed primarily at those sailing and approaching land/*terra* from the ocean.
33 Figueiredo, *Novo dicionário*, 1940.

34 Bluteau, *Diccionario*, 396. P: "o interior, o coração das terras, opõe-se ao marítimo, e costa . . . o *sertão* toma-se por mato longe da costa."
35 Figueiredo, *Novo dicionário*. P: "Lugar inculto, distante de povoações ou de terrenos cultivados. Floresta, no interior de um continente, ou longe da costa."
36 See Ricardo Roque, "Mountains and Black Races: Anthropology's Heterotopias in Colonial East Timor," *Journal of Pacific History* 47, no. 3 (2012): 263–82.
37 Claude Lévi-Strauss, *Tristes Tropiques* (Librairie Plon, 1955), 183. I cite the English translation: Claude Lévi-Strauss, *Tristes Tropiques*, trans. John Russell (Criterion Books, 1961), 142.
38 I follow here Pierre Varrod, dir., *Le Nouveau Petit Robert: Dictionnaire alphabétique et analogique de la langue française* (Dictionnaires Le Robert, 2001), 259. See also "Définitions de 'bled,'" *La langue francaise*, accessed 24 February 2022, https://www.lalanguefrancaise.com/dictionnaire/definition/bled#3.
39 Philippe Descola, *Par delà nature et culture* (Gallimard, 2005).
40 Jossias; Barnes; Alveal, all this volume.
41 Adalima; Direito, both this volume.
42 Rohrig, this volume.
43 deGrassi, this volume.
44 Kammen; Hagerdahl; Rohrig, all this volume.
45 Direito; Adalima, both this volume.
46 Jossias; Barnes, both this volume. See also Serrão, "Introduction," 10.
47 Serrão, "Introduction," 10.

About the Contributors

DR. JOSÉ LAIMONE ADALIMA earned his doctorate in anthropology from the University of Pretoria in South Africa. He is currently an assistant professor of anthropology at Eduardo Mondlane University in Mozambique. His research focuses on natural resources and livelihoods, land rights, land dynamics and economic transformation, and civil society and democracy.

DR. BERNARDO ALMEIDA is an assistant professor at Leiden University College and the Van Vollenhoven Institute for Law, Governance and Society at the Leiden University Law School. He works as a socio-legal researcher and practitioner in land tenure, law, lawmaking, and development, and is currently researching the nexus between climate change response and land rights.

DR. CARMEN ALVEAL is an associate professor in the Department of History at the Federal University of Rio Grande do Norte, Brazil, and a researcher at CNPq. She received a PhD from Johns Hopkins University in 2007. Her research interests include the history of property rights, rural history, colonial Brazilian history, and the Portuguese Empire. She is also the director of LEHS, the Laboratory of Experimental Social History.

DR. MATTHIAS RÖHRIG ASSUNÇÃO is professor of history at the University of Essex, United Kingdom. His research deals with the history of slavery and post-emancipation society in Brazil, in particular in Maranhão, popular culture, capoeira and the martial arts of the Black Atlantic. He coordinates the Capoeira History website (www.capoeirahistory.com). You can learn more about his work at https://essex.academia.edu/MatthiasRöhrigAssunção.

DR. SUSANNA BARNES received her doctorate in anthropology from Monash University. Her research interests include the anthropology of island Southeast Asia, customary governance and land tenure, intergenerational well-being and healing, colonial and post-colonial history, and international development. She is currently an associate professor of anthropology at the University of Saskatchewan.

DR. AHARON DEGRASSI is an interdisciplinary geographer focusing on the political economy of rural development in Africa. His research examines the agrarian geo-history of Angola, Amílcar Cabral's political ecology, and the colonial contexts of Weberian approaches in African studies. He obtained his PhD at UC Berkeley, held fellowships at Yale and Bayreuth Universities, works with international organizations, and is an assistant professor at College of the Desert.

DR. BÁRBARA DIREITO holds a PhD from the University of Lisbon (2013) and since 2019 has been a research fellow at the Centro Interuniversitário de História das Ciências e da Tecnologia (School of Science and Technology, NOVA University Lisbon, Portugal). She is interested in the history of colonial Mozambique in the twentieth century, in particular in agrarian history, the history of medicine, and environmental history, on which she has published in national and international journals.

DR. LAURA GERKEN is a political sociologist. She pursued her doctorate at the International Max Planck Research School on the Social and Political Constitution of the Economy in cooperation with the University of Duisburg-Essen. Her research interests include social movements, global governance, and rural livelihoods.

DR. HANS HÄGERDAL is a professor of history in the Department of Cultural Studies, Linnaeus University, Sweden. His research areas include colonial diplomacy in Southeast Asia, slavery and the slave trade in the Indian Ocean world, and colonial-Indigenous interaction in eastern Indonesia, in particular the Timor islands and Maluku.

DR. ELISSIO JOSSIAS is an assistant professor of social anthropology at Eduardo Mondlane University (Mozambique) and a guest researcher at the School of Global Studies, University of Gothenburg (Sweden). His research interests include the historicity of land and transformative notions of property and belonging, the impacts of changing land governance systems, and land acquisitions (large-scale national and international investments in land) in northern Mozambique.

DR. DOUGLAS KAMMEN is an associate professor in the Department of Southeast Asian Studies at the National University of Singapore. He is the co-author of *A Tour of Duty: Changing Patterns of Military Politics in Indonesia in the 1990s* (Cornell Southeast Asia Program) and *Cina Timor: Hakka and Cantonese in the Making of East Timor* (Yale Council on Southeast Asia Studies), the author of *Three Centuries of Conflict in East Timor* (Rutgers University Press) and *Independent Timor-Leste: Between Coercion and Consent* (Cambridge University Press), and has written numerous articles and book chapters.

DR. TANIA MURRAY LI is a professor of anthropology at the University of Toronto, Canada. Her field-defining research has been grounded in long-term, comparative analysis of the Indonesian uplands and beyond, spanning research on land and labour, Indigenous rights, development, governance, and environmental advocacy. Her research engages activists and policy-makers, and her recent work on plantations (*Plantation Life: Corporate Occupation in Indonesia's Oil Palm Zone*, with Pujo Semedi) examines the intersection of land governance, the politics of commodity production, and Indigenous livelihoods and well-being in historical and modern contexts.

DR. RICARDO ROQUE is research professor in history at the Institute of Social Sciences of the University of Lisbon, Portugal, where he is the current group leader of the Empires, Colonialism, and Postcolonial Societies research group and teaches in the history and anthropology doctoral programs. His current research includes projects on the history and ethnography of colonial collections and Indigenous archives in the Portuguese Empire.

DR. LAURA S. MEITZNER YODER is professor of environmental studies and John Stott Chair and director of the Human Needs and Global Resources Program, Wheaton College, Illinois, USA. Her work centres on environmental histories and political ecology of Southeast Asia, especially the smallholder farmers and forest dwellers of Oé-Cusse, Timor-Leste, as they relate to state institutions on land and forest governance.

Index

A

abandoned land, 12, 52, 69, 76, 87–88, 93–94, 100, 162, 164, 204, 223, 225–226, 228, 258
administration, 9–10, 14, 24, 26, 31, 37, 46, 50, 66, 68–69, 72, 74, 83, 87, 92–94, 96–97, 101, 154–155, 157, 161–165, 167, 172, 174, 180, 182, 186–188, 190–191, 197, 199, 233, 243–244, 247–250, 254–255
aforamento, 6, 58, 102, 165, 246, 254–255
African farmers, 46–48, 50–57, 61–62, 210
African land access, 41–42, 56–57
aftershock of the empire, 88, 99
Age of Discoveries, 263–265
agrarian relations, 42, 53, 57
agricultural production, 4, 11, 24, 26, 46–47, 61, 69, 81, 138, 155, 157, 179, 181, 197, 207, 223, 225, 227–228, 230, 234
agricultural projects, 15, 166
agricultural societies, sociedade, 61, 202, 206, 251, 253, 255
agriculture, 4–5, 13, 15, 44, 47, 50–52, 54–55, 57, 61–62, 83, 90–91, 110, 114, 128–129, 134, 138, 140, 155, 159, 161, 163, 165, 176, 199, 201, 204, 208, 210–211, 227–228, 230, 232–233, 243, 254, 275
aldeias, 55, 171, 270
alvará indígena, 6, 94, 165
ancestral beliefs, 119
ancestral land, 156, 213
Angola, 1–4, 6, 11, 17–18, 59, 62–72, 74–75, 78–81, 83–86, 153–154, 242, 246, 254, 261–262, 264, 282
authoritarianism, 90

B

BALADI—Federação Nacional dos Baldios, 92,
baldio, baldios, 12, 87–101, 103, 246, 253
Berlin Conference, 5, 199, 222, 249
border disputes, 248
Brazil, 1–4, 10, 12–14, 17–18, 23–24, 28–30, 33–35, 38–39, 68, 83, 127–130, 134, 139–142, 147–148, 226, 230, 232–233, 244, 246, 261, 264, 267–268, 271–273, 281
bureaucratic systems, 10, 26, 36, 91, 130

C

caboclos, 140, 147–148
capitalism, 2–3, 5, 37, 50, 83, 195, 208, 212, 227, 238, 253, 264
Carnation Revolution, 3, 91, 167
Carta de Lei (1901), 5–6, 58, 93
Casa de Ponte, 32, 34–36
cash crops, 4, 42, 62, 155, 195, 207, 222, 226, 230, 244
cassava, 63, 66–67, 83, 201
Catholicism, 6–7, 13, 107, 109–116, 118–122, 124, 126, 129, 148, 179, 247
Chief Mataka, 178, 182–188
chiefs, traditional authorities, 7, 9, 14, 50, 53, 55, 57, 63–64, 68–70, 72–74, 115, 117, 143, 148, 157, 161–162, 171–172, 174–176, 178–189, 191, 196–197, 222
Chimoio, 46–48, 50–51, 53–54, 60–62
citizens, citizenship, 6–7, 15, 75, 154, 165, 255
civilizing mission, 4, 6–7, 151, 153–154
Cóbuè Region, 14, 171–174, 176, 178–189, 191
coconut, 45, 48, 146, 161, 168, 195–196, 199–201, 203, 205–207, 212, 214–215
codification, 7, 13, 60

285

coffee, 73, 76, 83, 85, 103, 113, 131, 152, 155, 244–251, 254–256, 258
collectivism, 6, 13, 89–90, 93, 95, 101, 118, 132–133, 138–141, 148, 157, 204, 209, 211, 223, 244
colonatos, 42, 61–62
colonial officials, 44–45, 50, 108, 116–117, 246
Commission for Internal Colonization, 88, 90–91, 98–99
communal land, 12, 87–89, 92–94, 96, 98–102, 141, 144–145, 147, 149
communal ownership, 6, 12–14, 41, 53, 62, 87–102, 128, 141, 144–145, 147, 163, 165, 172, 189, 197, 204, 207, 222, 227, 244–245, 257
communities, 8–10, 12, 14, 64, 88–90, 92, 95–96, 98, 101–102, 109, 117, 140–141, 144, 147, 157, 162, 166, 172, 174–176, 182, 188–189, 197, 207–210, 212, 221, 223–224, 229, 235, 268, 273
community land delimitation, 14, 171, 174, 176, 188–189
compartes, 92
concessions, *concessão, concessões*, 5–6, 8, 11, 15–17, 41, 44, 47–48, 50, 52–53, 58, 59, 61, 74, 93, 139, 199, 206–209, 211, 230, 234, 241–242, 247–248, 250, 252–256, 258–259, 274–275
confiscation, 16, 252, 256
conflict, 5, 10, 13–14, 23–24, 26–28, 33, 37, 47–48, 52, 130–131, 139, 146–147, 157, 164, 172, 175, 178, 181, 184, 186, 188–189, 197, 201, 204–206, 210, 212, 216–217, 220, 223, 229, 274, 283
copra, 15, 52, 195, 199–201, 203–205, 213, 216
Court of Appeal, 29, 33–34, 39, 96, 148
Crown land grants, 4, 10, 258
customary authorities, customary systems, 7–8, 12, 14, 18, 26, 41, 91, 94, 102, 109, 111, 118, 146, 164–165, 168, 172, 174–175, 186, 188–189, 207, 209, 212, 217, 219–220, 222–224, 235, 257, 274–275, 281
customary land, customary land rights, 7, 14, 94, 165, 172, 186, 188–189, 222, 235
customary law, 41, 209, 212, 222
customary tenure, 8, 18, 188–191

D

de Almeida, João, 68
de Matos, Norton, 69–71, 74, 76, 84
development, 2–4, 9–12, 14–16, 18, 23, 36, 42, 44, 46, 54–55, 58, 62, 68, 75, 81, 90, 96, 114, 116–117, 129–130, 147, 151–157, 159, 161–163, 165–167, 172, 176, 179, 188, 196, 207–212, 219–224, 226–230, 232, 249–250, 252, 257, 281–283
development plans, *planos do fomento*, 151–153, 155, 157, 163, 166
Diniz, João Ferreira, 71–72, 74, 85
displacement, 11, 42, 63, 65–66, 82, 87, 196, 216, 222, 228, 274
dispossession, 5, 8, 11, 15–16, 45, 96, 195, 241–242, 250, 256, 263, 274
Doctrine of Discovery, 3, 18
DUAT (Direito de uso e aproveitamento da terra), 209, 223–224, 229
Duque de Bragança, 74
Dutch/Netherlands (East) Indies, 7, 32, 117, 241–242, 244, 247

E

economic exploitation, 5–6, 8, 10, 88, 93
effective occupation, 15, 212, 249, 252, 265
elites, 8–10, 12, 14, 16, 156, 208, 245
empty land, 247, 258
enclosure, 100, 161, 165
encroachment, 44, 51, 147, 242, 245–246, 248
Estado Novo, 7, 14, 100, 151–152, 167, 261, 264
ethnicity, 86, 111, 113, 157, 159, 178, 201, 245, 250, 255–256
ethnography, 1, 9, 11, 14, 53, 59, 65, 108, 118, 122, 195, 276, 283
extractive practices, 2, 5, 213, 270–271, 274

F

feudal land relations, 3
feudalism, 2–4, 222, 242–246, 248, 252, 255–257, 259
fidalgos, 10, 24–25, 36, 39, 110–111
finta, tribute, 115–116, 160, 243–248, 257
first-comer narratives, 178, 180, 186–188
Flores, 1, 13, 17–18, 107–115, 117–118, 122–124
forced labour, 2–3, 7, 44, 47, 52, 59, 63, 65–66, 82, 146, 154, 183, 200–201, 215, 221, 227
forced relocation, 11, 64
foreign investments, 15, 207, 210

foreiros, 145, 147
formal land tenure system, 6, 12, 92
formalization of customary tenure, 14, 172, 189
FRELIMO (Frente de Libertação de Moçambique), 182–184, 204, 208–210, 215–216, 223, 227–228, 237, 275

G

gender, 11, 63–64, 66–67, 81–83, 133, 209, 216
geography, 1, 47–48, 63–64, 72, 81–83, 86, 110, 261, 263, 277
Goa, 2–3, 6, 18, 84, 243, 268, 278
Guedes de Brito, 29–36, 39
Guinea-Bissau, 3, 261

H

head tax, 7, 70, 72, 162, 255
health, 66, 73–74, 154–156
hierarchies, 10, 14, 16, 52, 172, 180–181, 186, 188–189
hybridity, 12–13, 108–109, 122

I

imperial debris, 2, 11, 16, 37, 87–88, 99
indigenato, 75, 154, 165
indigenous kingdoms, 248, 252, 257
indigenous land, 4, 12, 14–16, 241–242, 246, 248, 250–252, 254–256, 258, 268, 272, 274
Indigenous populations, 4, 6, 10, 24, 73, 85, 109, 165, 200
indigenous rulers, 242, 245–246, 253, 258, 267
indirect rule, 9, 65, 82, 113, 245–248
individual property rights, 41, 44, 50–51, 54, 132
individualization, 6, 90, 98, 259
Indonesia, 94, 114, 118, 157, 162–163, 167, 169, 175, 234, 257, 282–283
infrastructure, 3, 10–11, 44, 47, 63–64, 71, 82, 91, 102, 155, 166, 203, 210, 216, 220, 225, 228, 232, 234, 254
Inhambane, 45–48, 51, 53, 59, 84, 214

J

Java, 5, 109, 244–245, 248, 256–257
Junta de Investigações Científicas das Colónias, later do Ultramar (JIC/JIU), 153–154, 215

K

Kalandula, 74
kin-based political institutions, 174, 179, 181–182, 186, 188
kingship, 114, 116, 121

L

labour, 2–4, 7, 11, 13, 15, 17, 42, 44–48, 50–52, 54, 56–67, 71–73, 75, 82, 85, 107, 127–128, 144–146, 154, 156, 159, 167, 183, 195, 199–201, 203–204, 206, 212–215, 222, 228, 230, 232, 234, 241–242, 250–251, 254–255, 266, 283
land alienation, 46, 213, 246, 251–252, 254, 256
land allocation, 8, 44, 112, 140, 156–157, 162, 199, 210, 246
land appropriation, 3–4, 12, 92, 127–128, 131, 138–140, 146–147, 253, 264, 275
land concessions, 5–6, 8, 11, 15–17, 41, 44, 47–48, 50, 52–53, 74, 93–94, 102, 129, 139–140, 144, 165, 199, 206–209, 211, 230, 234–235, 241–242, 247–248, 250, 252–256, 258–259, 274–275
land conflicts, 130–131, 147, 217
land dispossession, 5, 241–242, 274
land governance, 1–2, 8–9, 12–15, 17, 166, 172, 174, 178, 180, 188–189, 196, 207, 212, 219–220, 222, 224, 227, 234–235, 263, 268, 275, 282–283
land grabbing, 83, 141, 147, 236, 264–265, 267–268
Land Law, 12, 14–16, 41–42, 44, 46, 50–51, 53–54, 58, 59, 88, 94, 96–97, 102–103, 129–130, 139, 144, 166, 171–172, 174–176, 178, 189, 191, 200, 206–210, 219, 221–223, 229, 233, 235, 255, 257
land ownership, 4, 8, 12, 14–15, 23, 35, 96, 128–129, 131, 141, 143, 166, 181, 184, 201, 210, 243, 268, 272
land policy, 1, 5, 8, 10, 13–18, 42, 47–48, 88, 174, 207, 222–224, 241–243, 248–249, 255–256
land possession, 128, 174, 217, 274
land registration, 13, 131, 143, 169, 171, 223, 249–250, 252, 255
land rights, 7–8, 11–13, 15, 17, 23, 26–28, 87–88, 90–96, 98–99, 102, 165, 172, 174–175, 188, 190–191, 209, 217, 221–222, 224, 229–230, 242, 269, 281

Index *287*

land tenure, 5–6, 8, 12, 42, 44, 61, 92–93, 148, 166, 169, 172, 174, 196, 199, 208–209, 219, 222, 281
land title, land titling, 7, 25–26, 41, 50, 54, 165, 172, 176, 217, 249
land use rights, 93, 207, 209, 222–223, 235
landlords, 23, 25, 52, 110, 267
Larantuka, 107, 109–120, 122, 124, 126
large-scale agriculture, 210
large-scale land acquisitions, 191, 219–220, 236
legacy, legacies, 1, 8, 10–11, 13, 16, 19, 23, 62, 64, 81, 87, 96–98, 107–108, 112–113, 117, 121–122, 152, 166, 196, 207, 222, 241, 257, 261–265, 273–277
legal language, 11–12, 87–88, 98
legal opportunities, 219–220, 224–225, 229–230, 233–235, 237
legal status, 7, 11, 89
Lei de Terras, 222, 237
Li, Tania Murray, 2, 8–9, 16–17, 23, 100, 141, 175, 263, 283
liurai, 7, 157, 161–163, 169, 242–243, 245
livelihoods, 53, 56, 74, 81, 91–92, 98–99, 156, 196, 203, 207, 213, 219, 281–283
lusofonia, 261, 277
Lusotropicalism, 154

M

Macau, 2, 109, 257–259
Madal, 15, 195–196, 200–207, 212–217, 220
maize, 15, 45, 47, 51–52, 59, 112, 155, 201, 232
Malacca, 2
Malanje, 63–64, 65, 68–69, 71, 74–77, 79
Manica, 44, 46–48, 50–56, 58, 59–62, 215, 253
maps, mapping, 7, 9, 11, 43–44, 48–49, 63, 65, 68, 75–76, 78–81, 86, 123, 131–132, 134, 137–138, 148, 158, 173, 176–177, 198, 202, 230–231
maritime, 263–268, 270–271, 277
Micaúne, 195–196, 199–207, 215
military, 24, 30–31, 65, 68–69, 73, 82–84, 114, 120, 143–144, 156, 163, 167, 182, 196–197, 243, 246–251, 253–255, 258–259, 283
mineral prospecting, 16, 28, 113, 256
mines, 2–3, 28, 33–34, 39, 46–47, 69, 72, 112, 129, 140, 196–197, 214, 222, 226–227, 232, 250
mining concessions, 250
Missão de Estudos Agronómicos do Ultramar (MEAU) / Mission for Overseas Agronomic Studies, 154–155, 157, 161, 163, 169

missionaries, 13, 58, 111, 113–117, 119, 122, 140, 179–181, 183, 186, 191
modernization, 14, 90, 128, 144, 151, 153, 220–221
Mozambican land law, 221
Mozambique, 1, 3–4, 6–7, 11, 14–15, 17–18, 37, 41–48, 50–53, 55–57, 58, 59, 61–62, 69, 81, 83, 86, 153–154, 171, 174–175, 179–180, 182–185, 195–196, 199–201, 203–208, 210–213, 215–217, 219–222, 225–227, 230–235, 237–238, 242, 246, 253–254, 261–262, 264, 268, 271, 275, 278, 281–282
Mozambique Company, 44, 46–47, 51–53, 55–57, 59, 199, 215, 222
myths, 116, 242, 262, 264–266, 275–276

N

national mythology, 264
nationalization, 91, 93, 98, 204, 216
native land holding, 5
native policy, 42, 58
native reserves, 11, 42, 45–47, 49–50, 53–54, 58–59
Nduna Minofo, 171–172, 178–182, 184–188, 190
Netherlands, the Dutch, 5, 7, 13, 16, 30, 101, 107–109, 111–115, 117, 119–120, 122, 124, 126, 211, 241–242, 244–245, 247–248, 250, 252, 256, 258

O

oil palm, xx, xvi, xxii, 283
overseas law, 252

P

pacification, 9, 241, 251–252
paternalism, 5–6, 11, 42, 56–57, 215, 242–246, 248, 252, 255–257
peasantry, 14, 25, 28, 83, 127–128, 139–140, 143–147, 156, 159, 176, 197, 209, 220, 223, 227–229, 232, 235, 244, 255, 259, 274
physiocracy, 89
plantations, plantation system, 2–3, 5, 9, 13, 14–16, 18, 46, 48, 67, 72, 76–77, 79, 113, 128, 138, 141, 142–144, 146, 154, 156, 161, 168, 195–196, 199, 200–201, 203–204, 206–208, 210–213, 215, 220, 225–227, 232, 234, 241–242, 246–247, 249–253, 255–258, 275, 283
political institutions, 171–172, 174, 179, 181–182, 186, 188–189

Portugal, 2–6, 10, 12, 14–15, 17–18, 23–26, 29–32, 34, 38, 41–42, 45, 57, 58, 61–62, 81, 83, 85–86, 87–94, 97–101, 110, 129, 142, 153–154, 180, 184, 197, 199, 201, 204, 208, 212, 215, 222, 242–243, 245, 248, 254, 259, 261–269, 271–273, 282–283
Portuguese colonial administration, 74, 97, 157, 180, 182, 188
Portuguese colonial legacy, 1, 87, 97, 215, 241, 274–276
Portuguese Crown, 3, 24, 26, 29, 139–140, 147, 196–197, 263
Portuguese empire, 2–3, 5–6, 8, 36–38, 81, 151, 262–263, 265, 267, 273, 275, 278, 281, 283
Portuguese overseas colonies, 88, 92
Portuguese Timor, 1, 5–7, 15, 18, 93–94, 152–154, 156, 159, 165, 167–169, 241–242, 246–251, 255–256
posseiro, posseiros, 25–28, 33, 130–131, 139
post-independence state, 12, 45, 64, 213, 222–223
prazo, prazo system, 3–4, 8, 18, 37, 196–202, 202, 222, 268, 270
private property, 4, 95, 102, 204, 206, 242, 254, 256
privatization, 90, 93, 100, 206, 208–210, 254

Q

quilombo, 13, 30, 38, 141–142, 147

R

race, racial, racialism, 7, 10, 16, 23, 32, 58, 74–75, 86, 109, 262
realengos, 145–146
regedor, 70, 74
régulo, 171–172, 174, 176–180, 182–185, 187–188, 190, 243, 245–246, 248–249, 251–252, 255, 257
rendas, 25, 28, 34–35
resettlement, 11, 42, 68, 73, 83, 156, 229
resilience of empire, 262
retribution, 242, 248–249
Ribeiro, Aquilino, 91
rice, 13–15, 48, 55, 112, 128, 152, 155–157, 159, 161–163, 165, 168, 200–201, 225–228
roads, 10–11, 48, 63–75, 78–85, 114, 129, 154–156, 183, 217
rubber, 214

S

Salazar, António de Oliveira, 7, 73, 90, 153, 167
São Tomé, 18, 253, 261
sea-centrism, sea-centric narrative, 263–266
seafaring, 111, 120, 263–265, 268, 270–271
seigneurs, 24–25, 39
seizure of land, 242, 248–249, 251, 254, 258
senhores de terra, 27–28, 31, 35–36, 39
sertão, 263, 265, 269–273, 278–279
sesmaria, 3, 8, 10, 13, 23–27, 29–39, 128–130, 136, 138–139, 141, 144–145, 148
sesmeiros, 26–30, 33, 35, 37, 129–130, 148
settler colonialism, 242, 263–264, 274, 278
settlers, 3–4, 6, 8–9, 25–27, 33, 35, 41, 44, 46–48, 50–53, 79, 109, 114, 129, 139, 154, 164, 197, 215, 222, 227, 272–273
Sikka, 107, 109, 111–113, 116, 118, 120–122, 124
slave trade, 2, 4–5, 13, 130, 199, 282
slavery, 2, 4–5, 13, 25, 28, 30, 33, 127–128, 130, 140–145, 147–148, 199, 274, 278, 281–282
smallholder agriculture, 11, 33–34, 41–42, 53, 55–57, 58, 83, 100, 131, 228, 234, 283
social differentiation, 11, 52–53, 56, 151, 172
social movements, 141, 220–221, 224, 282
socio-economic, socio-legal issues, 2, 5, 8, 10–14, 56, 87, 224, 281
Southeast Asia, 118–119, 281–283
soy, 15, 211, 232
spectacles, 66, 83
spice trade, 2
state domain, 254
Stoler, Ann, 16, 23, 108, 262
sugar, 2, 26, 46–48, 200, 206, 211, 241, 247

T

taxation, 14, 65–66, 69, 73, 82–85, 112, 115, 117, 165, 167, 183, 197, 217, 267
tea, 200, 244
terra, 3, 25–28, 31, 35–36, 39, 59, 85, 113, 130, 140–143, 145, 147, 176, 209, 222–223, 249, 263, 269–271, 278
terra de índio, 140
terra devoluta, 130
terras de preto, 141–143
terras de santo, 145
territorial histories, 180, 184–185, 188

Timor, Timor-Leste, East Timor, 1, 5-7, 11-14, 15-19, 87-88, 93-99, 102-103, 107, 109-112, 114-116, 120, 122, 124, 152-160, 162-167, 169, 241-251, 253-259, 261-262, 278, 282-283
Torrens title system, 249
traditional chiefs, 14, 172, 174-176, 178, 180, 185-186, 189, 197
twentieth century, 3, 5, 11, 42, 44, 46-47, 64, 68, 90, 97, 109, 114, 116, 122, 128, 143, 146, 182, 199, 223, 242, 250, 252, 256, 258, 264, 270, 282

U

uncultivated land, 89, 93-95, 101, 155, 162, 164, 269, 271
unproductive land, 129
unused land, 12, 88-89, 95, 98, 160, 246-247, 256

V

vassalage, 4, 242-243, 245-246, 248, 252
village concentration, 11, 63-65, 65n5, 67-70, 74-75, 81-82, 85-86
villagization, 10, 55, 57, 64, 66, 73-75, 83, 222-223, 225
violence, 27-29, 32-34, 74, 82, 113, 167, 204, 248, 263-264, 266, 272

W

water, 11, 45, 65-67, 70-72, 75, 82, 169, 174, 191, 205, 212, 228, 236, 254, 263-264, 266, 270, 278
women, labour burden, 11, 64-65, 67, 72
World War II, 7, 62, 68, 75, 81, 108, 152-153, 155-156, 159, 162, 164, 169, 227

Z

Zavala, 46-47, 59

www.ingramcontent.com/pod-product-compliance
Lightning Source LLC
Chambersburg PA
CBHW041439300426
44114CB00026B/2935